CHILD WELFARE
AND
CHILD PROTECTION

CHILD WELFARE
AND
CHILD PROTECTION

David Royse and Austin Griffiths

cognella®
SAN DIEGO

Bassim Hamadeh, CEO and Publisher
Amy Smith, Project Editor
Jess Estrella, Senior Graphic Designer
Stephanie Kohl, Licensing Coordinator
Kim Scott/Bumpy Design, Interior Designer
Natalie Piccotti, Senior Marketing Manager
Kassie Graves, Vice President of Editorial
Jamie Giganti, Director of Academic Publishing

3970 Sorrento Valley Blvd., Ste. 500, San Diego, CA 92121

This book is dedicated to all of the frontline child welfare professionals and their supervisors who are inspired each and every day to do their best to improve the lives of children and families with challenges. Although often unrecognized and silent about the work they do, these selfless individuals are heroes nonetheless. We thank them, too, for their service and willingness to receive and supervise student interns who will be the next generation of child welfare professionals.

BRIEF TABLE OF CONTENTS

TABLE OF CONTENTS

PREFACE

We are excited to make available *Child Welfare and Child Protection* for those who want to learn about working with families to address child maltreatment and prevent its future reoccurrence. What makes this book distinct from the others is our emphasis on practice. That is, the goal of this text is to prepare future child welfare professionals. Along that line, *Child Welfare and Child Protection* discusses the practitioner's roles and tasks in a realistic way—it does not sugarcoat the difficult decisions that have to be made or misguide readers to expect that they will always work with cheerful and compliant families eager to address problems.

Child Welfare and Child Protection uses detailed and practice-informed case vignettes to accurately portray many common problems that the practitioner will encounter, the critical process of assessment, potential implications, and the roles associated with assisting families to become stronger.

In addition to the cases that introduce material or are the focus of attention, our emphasis on practice can also be seen in the *Practice Tips* found in the chapters, as well as in the numerous studies that have been cited supporting research-informed practice. These suggested studies and readings allow students and instructors to go beyond the pages of this text and continue to develop new knowledge. *Questions for Class Discussion* at the end of each chapter allow instructors to encourage students to think critically about the content on a deeper level. Readers are also given opportunities for introspection and self-reflection through *Self-Assessments for Personal Consideration.*

Child protection workers tackle the toughest problems in society, such as mental illness, substance abuse, domestic violence, homelessness, abject poverty, and child abuse and neglect. Knowing this, we have attempted to provide a well-balanced college text that can be used to educate and train child welfare professionals and students at either the undergraduate or graduate level.

In short, *Child Welfare and Child Protection* goes beyond merely presenting information about different types of families and various ways children may be traumatized and provides the reader an opportunity to consider possible actions and responsibilities that they will likely experience in child protection *before* they are in the field. It does *not* superficially cover important topics or go into such exhaustive depth that the reader will lose interest. It is our hope you will find that this book provides timely, essential knowledge needed by those wanting to practice in the field of child protection.

COUNCIL ON SOCIAL WORK EDUCATION (CSWE) 2015 COMPETENCIES

COMPETENCY	CHAPTER 1 History	CHAPTER 2 Child Abuse	CHAPTER 3 Causes of Mistreatment	CHAPTER 4 Investigation	CHAPTER 5 Ongoing Services
1. Demonstrate Ethical and Professional Behavior				✓	✓
2. Engage Diversity and Difference in Practice	✓	✓			✓
3. Advance Human Rights and Social, Economic and Environmental Justice	✓			✓	
4. Engage in Practice-Informed Research and Research-Informed Practice			✓	✓	✓
5. Engage in Policy Practice	✓			✓	
6. Engage with individuals, families, groups, organizations, communities.				✓	✓
7. Assess with individuals, families, groups, organizations, communities		✓		✓	✓
8. Intervene with individuals, families, groups, organizations, communities		✓	✓	✓	✓
9. Evaluate with individuals, families, groups, organizations, communities					✓

COMPETENCY	CHAPTER 6 Permanency	CHAPTER 7 Risk Assessment	CHAPTER 8 Juvenile Court	CHAPTER 9 Special Populations	CHAPTER 10 Foster Care
1. Demonstrate Ethical and Professional Behavior	✓	✓			✓
2. Engage Diversity and Difference in Practice		✓	✓	✓	✓
3. Advance Human Rights and Social, Economic and Environmental Justice	✓	✓	✓	✓	✓
4. Engage in Practice-Informed Research and Research-Informed Practice	✓	✓	✓	✓	✓
5. Engage in Policy Practice	✓		✓		
6. Engage with individuals, families, groups, organizations, communities.				✓	✓
7. Assess with individuals, families, groups, organizations, communities	✓	✓		✓	✓
8. Intervene with individuals, families, groups, organizations, communities	✓			✓	
9. Evaluate with individuals, families, groups, organizations, communities	✓	✓			

COMPETENCY	CHAPTER 11 Working on CPS Team	CHAPTER 12 Self-Care	CHAPTER 13 Future Issues
1. Demonstrate Ethical and Professional Behavior	✓	✓	✓
2. Engage Diversity and Difference in Practice	✓		✓
3. Advance Human Rights and Social, Economic and Environmental Justice	✓		✓
4. Engage in Practice-Informed Research and Research-Informed Practice	✓	✓	✓
5. Engage in Policy Practice			✓
6. Engage with individuals, families, groups, organizations, communities.		✓	✓
7. Assess with individuals, families, groups, organizations, communities	✓	✓	✓
8. Intervene with individuals, families, groups, organizations, communities	✓		✓
9. Evaluate with individuals, families, groups, organizations, communities			✓

CHAPTER 1

HISTORY OF CHILD PROTECTION IN THE UNITED STATES

OVERVIEW

Even though child abuse and neglect takes place all across America, in every community and locale, the infrastructure exists within each county and state to protect children. That is, we have the potential to intervene and protect every child. We can be proud of that—it is the hallmark of civilization. However, this was not always the case. Child protection in the United States has evolved slowly over our nation's history. In the earliest days of our nation, there was no protection of children at all. Later, it could best be described as piecemeal—one community might have a resource such as an orphanage or other residential arrangement for children, and the next community might not have anything. One state might have developed a juvenile court but be surrounded by other states that jailed young children in facilities along with adult offenders. As the public became aware of child protection issues, protections slowly were adopted by state after state, and later funding and incentives for child protection were provided by the federal government. Sadly, we cannot feel proud about our society's protection of Native American and African American children—indeed, non-White or minority children were historically denied the scant protection available to White children until fairly recent times. This chapter presents a quick historical overview of child protection in our country.

Childhood in the Colonial Era

Founding of Jamestown, Virginia, 1607. (The first English settlement in North America)
Landing at Plymouth Rock, 1620. (Pilgrims from the Mayflower establish a settlement)

Life was difficult for children in early America. How difficult, you ask? The Stubborn Child Law of 1646 in the Massachusetts Bay Colony allowed parents to execute their own male children over the age of 16 who were disobedient. A similar law was adopted by at least three other colonies. It was later modified to be less severe and expanded to include daughters (Sutton, 1981). Earlier, in 1642 Massachusetts had passed a more reasonable law allowing magistrates (local lay judges) to remove children from parents who were not viewed as training their children properly (Myers, 2006). Children had no rights and were considered the personal property of their parents or guardians—even well after the colonial period.

Life expectancy was short, estimated to be about 25 years in the early colony of Virginia; in the 1600s in New England, perhaps as many as 40% did not make it to adulthood. There was no central heating. If you wanted heat, you had to take an ax and chop firewood. There were no refrigerators, no electric or gas stoves, no washing machines or dishwashers, no hot showers. Indeed, baths were fairly rare, and one wore clothes for days at a time. If you wanted to plant crops, you had to hitch a plow to a mule or horse or break the ground yourself. If you wanted butter, you first had to milk a cow. After you waited for the cream to rise to the top, you would gather it and churn the cream for an hour or more. The grocery store might be 5 miles away, and you probably would walk there to buy things—if you had money. Bartering for things you might need was common. For instance, you might trade ham that you cured or a few chickens for the use of a neighbor's mule. A new dress would require you to buy a bolt of cloth and sew it yourself. There were no fast-food restaurants, no police riding around in patrol cars to protect you, no sidewalks or paved roads. Homes were lit with candles and often dark and damp. There was no electricity, no cell phones, no video games or television. The United States Postal Service didn't begin until 1775. Large families were common; farm families needed the extra hands to help. (Birth control pills in this country did not become widely available until the 1960s.)

Ideas about how to care for dependent children in society came from the English Poor Laws of 1601, which placed the initial burden on the families and then on the local community or charity available from churches. Neglected and dependent children might be apprenticed out or become **indentured servants** in other families—providing that they were not incapacitated or physically frail (Levine & Levine, 1992). This practice of making poor children indentured servants lasted until well into the 1800s. An indentured female child would, in exchange for room and board with the family, become a servant for them. Male children in this form of foster care often were required to work on farms.

As the population of colonial America grew, so did the number of people who needed financial support, food and shelter, and general oversight. These included individuals with mental illness or intellectual deficiencies, widows, dependent children, those with serious illness or injuries, the infirm elderly, and so on. Communities re-created the almshouse, the poor houses or workhouses, common in England, and these were often located on or near a farm. These were places where destitute families or dependent children could be provided shelter and food in return for their work. New York had an almshouse as early as 1653, and they were common by 1700. In theory, children could be cared for by others and could learn a trade there. Actually, however, children were often abused and mistreated and made to work for little or no pay in return for shelter and meager food (Myers, 2006).

Corporal punishment of children in early America was common. Historian Heywood (2001) has noted that Puritan preacher Cotton Mather coined the phrase "Better whipt, than Damn'd"—suggesting that this type of punishment by parents would guide the child toward living a virtuous rather than sinful life. Heywood (2001) also reports,

> A survey of the experiences of American children found that during the period 1750–99 every single boy and girl in the sample had been beaten with an instrument, ranging from a hickory stick to a horsewhip. Even during the nineteenth century, when advice manuals were beginning to move away from recommending corporal punishment, approximately three-quarters of the children experienced such punishments (p. 100).

Whipping children, even with belts, was not a rare form of discipline and was not considered illegal or abusive until fairly late in the 20th century. African American children were taught to be "especially careful in front of White people; adults believed that any misbehavior, no matter how slight, could engender the wrath of a White man or woman and lead to trouble for the whole family" (Jimenez, 2006, pp. 892–893).

Orphanages, where children could be better protected from adults who would take advantage of them, were slow to develop; the first to open was in New Orleans in 1728 and was run by a group of Catholic nuns. The first public orphanage opened in South Carolina in 1790—7 years after the American Revolution (Myers, 2006).

Looking through our 21st-century eyes, the need for orphanages might not make much sense. It is easy for us to forget that diseases we no longer fear (but still occurring in impoverished third-world countries) were very much active players in America during our country's early beginnings. Diseases such as typhus, cholera, tuberculosis, smallpox, typhoid, rheumatic fever, and scarlet fever claimed thousands of lives. Without food banks and charities maintaining food pantries for the poor and those down on their luck, adults and children could only beg so much from their neighbors. Individuals actually died from malnutrition.

Without antibiotics, even infections from small injuries could take lives. Antibiotics did not become available for the general use until the mid-1940s—about the same time as World War II. Hygiene in early America was difficult to practice, and even physicians didn't start washing their hands before surgery until the mid-1800s. Drinking water wasn't of the same quality as it is today; your drinking water could make you ill. Infant mortality was high, and many women died in childbirth. Body lice were common and particularly bad on sailing ships when clothes could not be washed.

Native American Children in Our Country's Early History

While television and movies often portray Native Americans as murderous barbarians, the truth is not all of them were hostile to early settlers. But it didn't take long for them to figure out that the White settlers were taking their game and destroying their hunting grounds as White settlements began popping up everywhere on their land. And it didn't take the settlers long to recognize that the Whites' muskets and guns were superior to the bows and arrows carried by the Native Americans. Both parties murdered the other, often with little consideration for the noncombatants—women and children. Conflict was inevitable, as the settlers wanted to push the Native Americans off the land so that they could farm and own it. Native Americans were viewed as heathens and savages because they weren't Christian and had different customs and lifestyles. This mindset created the view of Native Americans as less than human. They were infidels, disposable. As such, the individual Native Americans who chose to live in communities where they would encounter Whites were treated badly—harassed, intimidated, and bullied. Why would they live in close proximity to settlers? Many tribes were completely or almost completely wiped out—not from battles with the Whites so much as by the diseases the Whites brought with them for which the Native Americans had no prior immunity. Also, the settlers kept moving closer and closer to the Native Americans.

Despite treatment from the hands of Whites that at best could only be described as unfriendly and at worst as hateful and vicious, there were some Americans who attempted to improve the lives of Native American children.

The Choctaw Indian Academy was started in Kentucky in 1818 to teach Native American boys English, writing, and arithmetic. It closed a few years later and restarted in 1821 before closing for lack of funds in 1842. It had a record enrollment of 188 pupils in 1835.

Why did it close? President Andrew Jackson pushed for the Indian Removal Act of 1830, which granted tribes living in the eastern half of the United States land across the Mississippi River, where they would be under the "protection of the United States of America" (Office of the Historian, n.d.), in exchange for their traditional homelands.

Even though some Native Americans were intermarrying with Whites, farming, and not "warring" against settlers, their land was still very much desired as the population grew. After Andrew Jackson militarily defeated the Creek nation in 1814, he forced them to surrender their land constituting about half of Alabama and one fifth of Georgia. Settlers wanted land, and Indian tribes tried to appease the Whites when they could. Native American leaders were willing to give up some of their land in return for keeping some for themselves, although other tribes resisted (e.g., the Seminole Indian Wars). The Indian Removal Act provided financial incentives for the Native American to travel to the drier lands, such as in eastern Oklahoma. White leaders persuaded, bribed, and threatened to encourage Native Americans to vacate their homelands. Eventually, it is estimated that 50,000 Native Americans were strongly encouraged or forced to move from the part of the country where they had always lived.

Indian/Native American Residential Schools[1]

Boarding schools for Native American children began about the time of the Civil War, and one of the first, established by the Bureau of Indian Affairs, began in the state of Washington. These schools were part of a plan by often well-intentioned individuals to use the educational experience to assimilate Indian youth into mainstream America (Northern Plains Reservation Aid, n.d.).

Later, in 1879 the Carlisle Indian School in Carlisle, Pennsylvania, was formed. Church officials, missionaries, and local authorities took children as young as 5 from their parents and transported or had them transported many (sometimes hundreds of) miles away to Christian boarding schools; they forced others to enroll in Christian day schools on reservations. Those children sent to boarding schools were separated from their families for most of the year, sometimes without a single family visit. Parents caught trying to hide their children to prevent them from being kidnapped and sent to a residential school lost their food rations.

Virtually imprisoned in the schools, children experienced devastating abuses, from forced assimilation and grueling labor to widespread sexual and physical abuse. Captain Richard H. Pratt, an army veteran of the Indian wars, opened the federally sanctioned boarding school, the Carlisle School. His approach, summed up in his motto, was that one should "kill the Indian and save the man" (Bear, 2008).

Both the Bureau of Indian Affairs and church schools ran on bare-bones budgets, and large numbers of students died from starvation and disease because of inadequate food and medical care. School officials routinely forced children to do arduous work to raise money for staff salaries and "leased out" students during the summers to farm or work as domestics for White families. In addition to bringing in income, the hard labor prepared children to take their place in White society—the only one open to them—on the bottom rung of the socioeconomic ladder.

---

1. Note: There is no standard politically correct way to refer to people who were the first Americans. Some prefer to be known as Indigenous, others prefer American Indian, or Indian. Native American is used by many but that term could also be applied (although it usually isn't) to any person born in America. Tribal identity is also common and one could describe herself as Sioux or Kiowa, for example.

Physical hardship does not aptly describe the systematic abuse and assault on Native children and their culture. School staff cut off children's long hair, banned traditional clothing and customs, and expected all children to worship as Christians. A major goal of the acculturation process was to eliminate any use of their Native languages and force communication in English. They were given American names. Teachers created cruel punishments for uncooperative children, such as scrubbing wooden floors on hands and knees with toothbrushes or standing in line for hours without moving. One Navajo man reported, "I was forced to eat an entire bar of soap for speaking my language" (Smith, 2007). Reflecting the general societal contempt for Native Americans, in 1928 our northern neighbor, Alberta, Canada, passed legislation allowing school officials to forcibly sterilize Native girls; British Columbia followed suit in 1933. In a 2001 report, one author has estimated that 50,000 Native children died in the Canadian residential school system (http://citeseerx.ist.psu.edu/viewdoc/download?doi=10.1.1.468.89&rep=rep1&type=pdf). Although thousands of Native children are known to have died in the United States from malnutrition and mistreatment at underfunded Indian schools, there does not seem to be any official tally of their number. You can learn more about the Indian residential schools at https://www.npr.org/templates/story/story.php?storyId=16516865.

Child Protection Developments

The first reformatory for children was established in 1824 in Elmira, New York. This facility kept children convicted of crimes from being incarcerated with adults. In most states, however, children were punished or probated as though they were adults (Levine & Levine, 1992).

By the 1850s the Industrial Revolution required thousands of laborers in America's cities. The population surged from immigrants rushing to find better lives than they left behind as families moved from rural areas to cities. Safety precautions and procedures were minimal in factories, and machinery was often dangerous. Industrial accidents that left workers disabled were not uncommon. Unfortunately, factories did not provide workers' compensation, disability pay, or health insurance, and when the major wage earner was severely injured or killed, children often needed to find employment wherever they could to provide for their families and the expenses associated with living in cities.

Child care would have been unaffordable for many if not most families. Without extended families being nearby, child care might consist of locking the child in the apartment while parents worked or leaving them locked out on the street. If the major wage earner died or was disabled, orphanages were sometimes used even by single parents who could not make enough to care for their children. Unlike life in rural areas, moving to the city meant that families couldn't grow their own food and often didn't have family members or familiar and trusted neighbors around them to help with their needs.

Children's small hands were needed in industrial factories, but they were paid low wages even though working 10- to 16-hour days. There was no minimum wage. If they became injured, the factory or mine owners simply hired new children to replace them. Children worked in unheated factories and in extremely hot conditions. If they were late, they could be punished by the factory managers; orphans who were judged a risk of running away might be locked in leg irons. It took until 1918 for the last state to pass compulsory school attendance laws—although Massachusetts had a law on the books in 1852. Requiring students to attend school and get an education protected them from dangerous work and the exceedingly long workdays.

According to historian Heywood (2001), a study from the Royal Commission on the Employment of Children in 1843 found that that children as young as 6, 7, and 8 years of age were hired in England's hosiery factories and worked up to 12 hours a day. Similarly, as factories developed in America, very young workers were needed, and an investigating commission was shown "the enlarged joints, the cuts and callouses on the hands of a 6-year-old child to provide evidence of the work" (Heywood, 2001, p. 131).

Robert Owen, an owner of cotton and textile mills, traveled from Scotland to America in 1824 and started a utopian community in New Harmony, Indiana. Before coming to America, he discovered that 40% of his employees in New Lanark, Scotland, were under 13 years of age (Heywood, 2001). He later became known as a philanthropic social reformer and an advocate for improving the working conditions in factories.

In 1853 the New York Children's Aid Society was formed due to an estimated 30,000 children living on city streets begging, stealing, and scavenging for food in garbage. Charles Loring Brace was invited to head the organization. He viewed his position as a "city missionary for vagrant boys." There wasn't enough housing in cities, and he wrote about the influence of overcrowding with "half a dozen families … occupying one room, the old and young, men and women, boys and girls of all ages sleeping near each other" (Myers, 2006, p. 19). To improve their lives, the Children's Aid Society created industrial schools and night schools so that children could get an education. The society created lodging houses for homeless boys as well as kindergartens, reading rooms, Sunday School classes, baths, gymnasiums, and homes for children with chronic illnesses. Brace was among a large group of private philanthropists and concerned citizens who became known as the Child Saver's Movement. They advocated for the first juvenile court, services for homeless youth found on the streets of all the large cities, and child labor laws to prevent children from being mistreated by employers. They supported the orphan trains described next.

Orphan Trains (1853-1929)

Critical of the institutional placement of children, Brace believed that children would be better off in rural areas, where there was fresh air and an opportunity to enjoy outdoor activities. His notion was to take pauper children out of the overcrowded orphanages and almshouses and to place them with families outside of New York City in the rural areas of Pennsylvania and other eastern states. A bit later, children were placed in the Midwest and further out. Philosophically, he believed that life in an institution did not prepare children for life outside. Some of these children were orphans, but others had living parents who couldn't support them. Parents' permission was needed, and they often agreed with placement outside of the cities, believing that their children would be better off. Children were referred from the courts and other community agencies or individuals. Many were homeless, abandoned, dependent, or neglected—not all were orphans. The Children's Aid Society placed advertisements in newspapers along the route that the trains would travel in order to receive applications from families who were interested in obtaining a child.

Prior to being placed on the trains, children were bathed and given clean clothes and were accompanied by a representative of the Children's Aid Society all the way to their destinations. Once they arrived, interested families and individuals ("foster parents") were able to select a child that they liked. If the local citizens committee agreed that the family or individual was responsible and a good fit for the situation, then the child was allowed to go with them. The society remained the legal guardian of the child unless adopted and visited periodically and corresponded with children and their foster families. Older children could change their placements at will, and families could return children back to the society, too. Children not chosen in one town would ride the train again to the next town (with a Children's Aid Society agent) in hopes of being chosen. Children who had disabilities or were thought to be incorrigible were not participants. African American children were also excluded—possibly for fear that they might be treated as enslaved persons by their foster families. Orphan and dependent African American children were commonly informally adopted by family and friends. Involvement of the extended family created something of a safety net. Although it was by no means perfect, it did provide some protection from abuse and neglect for these African American children.

While there were criticisms of the orphan trains, several studies were very positive and indicated that the majority of children outplaced (outside of New York City) seemed to have benefited (Myers, 2006). The last orphan train sponsored by the Children's Aid Society of New York left the station in May, 1929. It is estimated that approximately 150,000 children were outplaced in foster care and adoptive families between the program's start and end (Cook, 1995). There became less need for the orphan train as states began developing their own foster home placements in-state and as the social work profession took off and social workers were able to work with families needing their assistance.

Several actual stories by children who were transported away from their homes as infants or children can be found at the website https://orphantraindepot.org/. Marguerite Thompson was one of those children who was placed, along with another child, in a family that used them as domestic laborers—despite their young ages. Prior to the development of Holiday Inns and Hilton Hotels, traveling businesspeople and salespeople would often rent rooms from families. The family that took Marguerite in as a family member used three of their bedrooms for salesmen. These were known as boardinghouses, and "boarders" could obtain their meals there as well.

Here is a portion of Marguerite's story:[2]

> [It] was a big two story house with 10 rooms, but we didn't have any electricity. The house was beautiful inside. I didn't have a bedroom of my own; I slept on the couch in the front room on a feather mattress Mama would take out of her closet every night. After a few weeks, she said I could do it myself. The boys had bedrooms upstairs. Teddy and I were not permitted to use the bathroom. We had to use the outside toilet, and on Saturday we would drag a galvanized bathtub from the back porch and put it by the cook stove. …
>
> When I was six, Teddy and I started school. When we came home from school, we had to wash the dinner dishes from noon. Then we had to go upstairs and make the beds, dust mop the floors and clean the bathroom. We didn't dare use the toilet, she said it took too much water. By the time we got through with that, it was time to set the table for supper. I always only had one helping put on my plate. Teddy and Charles always had milk to drink with their dinner, but she said I couldn't have any. …
>
> Once a year, Mr. McPhealy would come from the New York Foundling Home to see how I was getting along. I had to tell him fine. I would have to speak a piece for him, or poetry as it is called now. The name of it was "Looking on the Bright Side." Then I had to dance the Irish jig for him, and when I was through, I was excused. I would go outside and cry and wish he would take me back with him. I wanted to tell him the truth about how I was treated, but I couldn't. … I often wondered why Papa Larson didn't ever have anything to say about the way she treated me, but it seemed to me like she ruled the house." (https://orphantraindepot.org/history/orphan-train-rider-stories/marguerite-thompson/)

As more of the country began living in cities and more women began working outside the home, families began to have fewer children. Consequently, the largest number of children in orphanages was during the Great Depression of the 1930s, and their number slowly began to decline.

The legal principal in English common law of ***parens patriae*** (Latin for parent of the country) is the notion that the state has responsibility for those who are unable to care for or help themselves. In this country it was used in the 1850s in cases where guardians were appointed for young children who had inherited property. It was not until the 1960s, when the public began to be more educated about child abuse, that governmental agencies began relying on this principle in child protection cases in which it is necessary to remove abused and neglected children from harmful living environments (Jimenez, 2006).

---

2. "Marguerite Thompson's Story," https://orphantraindepot.org/history/orphan-train-rider-stories/marguerite-thompson/. Copyright © by National Orphan Train Complex

TABLE 1.1 KEY HISTORICAL LEGISLATION AND EVENTS IN CHILD PROTECTION

Year	Event
1646	Stubborn Child Law (Massachusetts)
1830	Indian Removal Act
1851	First Comprehensive Adoption Law (Massachusetts)
1853	New York Children's Aid Society founded; orphan trains begin
1863	Slavery abolished
1866	American Society for the Prevention of Cruelty to Animals founded
1875	New York Society for the Prevention of Cruelty to Children founded
1896	National Association of Colored Women
1899	First juvenile court
1909	First White House Conference on the Care of Dependent Children
1916	First federal child labor law (Keating–Owen Act)
1918	Compulsory school attendance
1921	Sheppard–Towner Act (funds for maternal and infant health care)
1929	Last orphan train
1929–1939	Great Depression
1935	Social Security Act signed (with some provisions for child welfare)
1938	Fair Labor Standards Act (minimum age of 16 for full-time employment)
1965	Medicare, Medicaid, and Head Start are created
1974	Child Abuse Prevention and Treatment Act
1978	Indian Child Welfare Act
1980	Title IV-E Adoption Assistance and Child Welfare Act
1994	Multiethnic Placement Act
1997	Adoption and Safe Families Act
1999	Foster Care Independence Act
2003	Amber Alert
2014	Preventing Sex Trafficking and Strengthening Families Act
2018	Family First Prevention Services Act

TEST YOURSELF

What social conditions could be found in the large cities such as New York, Chicago, and so forth that made the Child Saver reformers think that orphan trains were a good idea? Do not read below the dotted line until you are ready to see the answer.

- -

There were thousands of homeless youth roaming the streets who were cold, hungry, and often stealing to get food. Until Charles Loring Brace and his Children's Aid Society began to develop an early system of foster care, society had not responded with sufficient resources for the homeless or unsupervised children.

The Development of Legal Clout to Protect Children

Although the American Society for the Prevention of Cruelty to Animals (ASPCA) was founded in 1866, no private organization existed to provide protection for children. However, an urban missionary to the poor, Etta Angell Wheeler, became involved in the case of a child born to the widow of a soldier who died in the Civil War; the child was then indentured to the Connolly family at the age of 18 months. For 8 years the child, Mary Ellen Wilson, was horribly mistreated: not permitted to play with other children, routinely beaten with a leather whip, made to sleep on a piece of carpet on the floor.

Wheeler was able to see the child in a tattered dress with lacerations on the child's arms and legs; she immediately set about trying to find an organization to help her remove Mary Ellen from the home.

Wheeler received no help from the police or other organizations, and after 4 months approached Henry Bergh, the founder of the ASPCA. He sent an investigator out the next day and then contacted the attorney for his organization (Elbridge Gerry), who was able to find a legal means for police intervention.

Figure 1.1 Mary Ellen Wilson

Photographs of Mary Ellen show a child in great need of protection—even with a gash on her face where her keeper (Mrs. Connolly) had attacked her with scissors. The judge in the case allowed Mary Ellen to be removed, and she lived with Wheeler's family and enjoyed the rest of her childhood, marrying and giving birth to two daughters who attended college and became teachers. She died in 1956 at the age of 92.

There was a great deal of newspaper coverage of the story, and the case caught the public's attention—due both to the cruelty she had experienced and the "fact that she had been beaten by someone other than her natural parents, a circumstance that muted the old precept in favor of a parent's right to determine the nature and severity of a child's punishment" (Costin, Karger, & Stoesz, 1996, p. 57). The case also revealed that the existing hodgepodge system of private charities, "public relief," and indenturing children out was terribly inadequate—magnifying its failure to protect children. Mary Ellen was removed from the Connolly home in 1874.

Attorney Gerry began the New York Society for the Prevention of Cruelty to Children (NYSPCC) with the notion that it should have the powers of a law enforcement agency and would not be a typical social service organization. It was officially incorporated in 1875 and used its powers of threat of prosecution to rescue children and bring about better parenting techniques while also helping refer families for financial and other social resources. The NYSPCC was in many ways the forerunner of our modern child protection agencies, providing both temporary care and shelter for children removed from harmful homes and seeing that children got medical care and had their basic needs met. Other cities saw the value of child protection organizations, and they began spreading across the country.

Several factors began coming together that provided a boost to child protection efforts in early America. Slavery had been abolished in England in 1833 and in the United States in 1863, which made it much more difficult to support the notion of indentured servants and indenturing children. More restrictions were also being placed on employing children in factories because of the abuse going on there. Social reformers were successful in informing the public of the need to support charitable work for child protection and a larger role for government. However, a major obstacle was the well-established belief that the poor and "harshly disadvantaged persons were in their particular condition by reasons of personal fault" (Costin et al., 1996, p. 71). This perception is still existent among pockets of individuals today in our society. There are those who want to blame the poor and traumatized individuals with "invisible disabilities" like depression, post-traumatic stress disorder (PTSD), and addiction for not being able to get or hold jobs and pull themselves out of their problems.

Fortunately, in what is known as the women's right movement, as women began to voice their concerns in the latter part of the 19th century about their unequal status with regard to "being denied the right to own and manage their own property, escape a failed marriage, or hold guardianship and custody rights to their children" (Costin et al., 1996, p. 62), they also united on other social justice issues such as anticruelty-to-children campaigns, and women's right to vote (woman suffrage). The slow progression toward change is seen in that women didn't get the right to vote (the 19th Amendment) until 1920.

No Protection for African American Children

Life for African American children prior to the Civil War meant, in almost every instance, being an enslaved person and having no rights. Living standards for were generally substandard—cold in winter, and often children shared beds in a one-room cabin with their parents. Depending on their age, children of enslaved persons would commonly roam about plantations naked or nearly so until old enough to engage in some kind of work—but work began early. Many began working like an adult around age 10—although some began much earlier. They usually had no shoes, and whether they were adequately fed or suffered from malnutrition depended almost entirely on the plantation or landowner's financial situation and whether he was kind and benevolent or a miser. There was no school or education for enslaved children (or for adults), and it was illegal to educate them in most states. Hard physical labor was experienced, particularly by those growing up on rice or sugar plantations in the South. Beatings of adult enslaved persons occurred frequently, and their children did not escape this form of punishment. If enslaved persons became injured or ill, doctors were very expensive and not readily available. Infant and child mortality for African American children was twice the rate of White children (National Archives, n.d.).

There were few persons or institutions in their lives that protected enslaved African American girls from sexual abuse and rape, given the view that enslaved persons were property owned by a master. African American children were largely excluded from child welfare services in America, and what protection did exist for them was started years after the Civil War by African American churches or small local organizations such as Colored Women's Clubs (which became a national organization known as the National Association of Colored Women in 1896) and other voluntary organizations interested in interracial cooperation.

Wilma Peebles-Wilkins (1996) notes, "African American children were excluded from any meaningful and structured governmental care aside from the in-home services offered to former slave families by a few pre-Civil War private orphanages … and almshouses" (p. 137). Jimenez (2006) adds, "African American children were excluded from private orphanages until the 1960s, when they became known as residential treatment centers and opened up their doors to any children with foster care funding" (p. 899).

African American children did not benefit from the "child-saving activities" that settlement houses and organizations in cities employed to reach out to the "dependent, abused, neglected, or delinquent" children formed primarily for "poor Caucasian immigrant children" (Peebles-Wilkins, 1996, p. 137). The nation's racism and segregation can also be seen in the "practice of putting African American children in jail" well after the juvenile court system was established—even in Virginia "75 years after the practice was prohibited by state law" (Peebles-Wilkins, 1996, p. 137).

In fact, Peebles-Wilkins (1996) recounts the story of an 8-year-old in Virginia sentenced to 6 months in jail in 1914, but Janie Porter Barrett (a social reformer), appealed to the judge to send the child instead to the Weaver Orphan Home for Colored Children. Because the nation was slow to respond to the plight of African American children's need for foster care services, these children were either jailed or sent to reform schools (institutions for delinquents) because of a lack of the resources available to White children. What developed for dependent African American children were efforts arising in particular communities, such as the Carrie Steele Orphan Home (started by a maid working in the Atlanta Railroad Station who brought children seeking shelter in the railroad station into her home). It later became supported by the United Way as the Carrie Steele-Pitts Home and is still thriving in its provision of residential care.

The Industrial School for Colored Girls was opened in 1915 near Richmond, Virginia, and purchased by the Virginia Federation of Colored Women's Clubs. This organization was founded by Barrett, its first president, somewhere during 1907–1908. Even before starting the industrial school, Barrett had helped start a Child Welfare Department at the Locust Street Settlement House, where volunteers advocated for the removal of African American children from jail and assisted in finding them alternative placements. The school received consultation from the Child Welfare League of America (founded in 1921) and used a "cottage plan" instead of housing the children in a single building (Peebles-Wilkins, 1996).

After Barrett's death in 1948, the industrial school became known as the Barrett Learning Center. It was fully integrated in 1965, became briefly coed in 1977, and then became known as the Barrett Juvenile Correctional Center in 1978, serving only males. It closed in 2005.

> Janie Porter Barrett's biography is quite interesting. You might want to read more about her at https://socialwelfare.library.vcu.edu/settlement-houses/barrett-janie-porter-1865-1948-african-american-social-welfare-activist/.

Development of Juvenile Courts and Other Legislation

Although regular courts in Chicago had been treating juveniles separately from adults since before the Civil War, the first juvenile court in that city (and one of the first in the country) did not make its appearance until 1899. The juvenile court was less concerned with determining guilt and punishment and had more of a mindset of rehabilitation and guidance. It recognized that juvenile delinquency seemed to stem from the urbanization, industrialization, and poverty of the era as families became more uprooted and disorganized (Levine & Levine, 1992).

Jane Addams of Hull House was also supportive of the need for juvenile courts and probation officers, as she was quite concerned about the informal gangs of youth who moved throughout the city. In the early days of the Chicago juvenile court, probation workers were not civil service employees but were supported by private charities and organizations, churches and synagogues, and settlement houses. A great passionate advocate for juvenile courts (called the father of juvenile courts) was Judge Ben Lindsey. Although he straddled the era from post-Civil War to World War II, dying in 1943, he was a prolific writer, and some of his books are still available. You might want to read more about this colorful visionary. (See Additional Resources at the chapter's end.)

Along with social reformers becoming more successful in identifying areas where child protection measures were needed and the public becoming more enlightened and sympathetic came the passage of laws protecting children that are now so well accepted in our culture that they operate almost without our awareness or knowledge. The Massachusetts Society for the Prevention of Cruelty to Children (MSPCC) was especially effective in leading the way with these laws, which then were picked up and slowly enacted in other states. In 1851 the MSPCC helped Massachusetts pass the first comprehensive adoption law. Other child protective measures the MSPCC is credited with, according to an 1893 report by its "lead agent," are listed below:

- Guardianship laws (allowing the transfer of children away from unfit parents)
- A neglect law allowing children under 14 to be removed from parental control
- Nonsupport laws (punishment for parents not supporting their children)
- A law punishing parents who abandoned their infants
- Laws prohibiting the sale of liquor, tobacco, firearms, dangerous toys, and obscene materials to children
- Laws forbidding the exhibition of deformed children
- Restrictions on the number of hours children could work while school was in session and limiting work in dangerous occupations
- Laws requiring fire escapes and sanitary facilities in factories
- Laws preventing adults from using children as street beggars
- Prohibitions on children's entry into bars
- Special courts separating adult criminals away from juvenile offenders, truants, and children in need of protection
- Laws requiring children selling goods on the street to have a license
- Begging by children was made unlawful
- Abducting girls for "vicious purposes" was made unlawful
- Laws preventing children from sharing the same jail cell as adults and preventing incarceration in prison for children under age 12
- Licenses required for child care facilities (as cited in Myers, 2006, p. 40)

TEST YOURSELF

Besides the widespread publicity around the case of Mary Ellen Wilson, what legal change occurring in the 1860s made it possible for citizens to view forced work of children differently? Do not read below the dotted line until you are ready to see the answer.

Slavery had been abolished in 1863 under President Lincoln, and the concept of indenturing was slowly becoming less socially acceptable.

Child Protection in the 20th Century

By 1910 all states had laws against child sexual abuse, and most had laws against abandonment, desertion, and failure to support children. A recommendation of the White House Conference on the Care of Dependent Children in 1909 was that single mothers with small children should be granted financial assistance to allow the children to be raised at home instead of being placed in orphanages, foster care, or other less desirable places. Described as "mothers' pensions," the amounts granted were minimal and unfortunately many times were administered by punitive persons who assumed the worst about the mother's character. Women of color were usually denied mothers' pensions (Myers, 2006).

Humane societies and Societies for the Prevention of Cruelty to Children (SPCCs) numbered in the neighborhood of 350 across the nation in 1911–1912. However, their approaches to investigations and their work generally on behalf of children was not coordinated and could not be considered to follow uniform practice guidelines. Even the structure of these organizations differed a great deal, and they varied in terms of their effectiveness and the level of fighting spirit they exerted to protect endangered children (Costin et al., 1996). In fairness to them, most of these societies had a very small number of paid staff who, along with volunteers, were untrained or poorly trained. It was in the 1920s that the Child Welfare League began preparing standards for practice for foster care, but not until 1968 did it publish "standards for services to children in their own homes" (Costin et al., p. 93).

The federal government took several steps in the first part of the 1900s toward having a greater role for itself in protecting children with the creation of the Children's Bureau in 1912 with the broad mission of improving the lives of children and families, passage of the first federal child labor law (the Keating–Owen Act) in 1916, and passage of the Sheppard–Towner Act of 1921 to provide for greater maternal and infant health care. With the Great Depression (1929–1939), so many Americans were suffering from lack of employment and income that President Roosevelt's New Deal boldly addressed these problems with new programs, such as providing pensions to older adults (Social Security), assistance to the blind and victims of industrial accidents, unemployment insurance, and funding for public health problems.

With the passage in 1935 of the Social Security Act, Congress also created the Aid to Families with Dependent Children program as part of the Social Security Act—doing away with individual communities and private organizations needing to fund mothers' pensions. As the federal government assumed more responsibility for protecting children, the number of local (and private) SPCCs began to decline. This removed the issue of protection of vulnerable children from the visibility and awareness of most of the American public, since these organizations were no longer raising funds for their efforts. States did not, however, quickly gear up to replace the dwindling number of SPCCs in their communities.

In 1938 the Fair Labor Standards Act protected children from some of the harsh practices of the past by requiring an individual to be at least 16 to work full-time and at least 18 to work in hazardous sites or conditions (like mines). During World War II the Lanham Act of 1940 provided quality, low-cost child care in communities with defense industries so that mothers or parents could support America's war effort by working. Under the act, all families (regardless of income) were eligible for child care for up to 6 days a week, including summers and holidays.

An amendment to the Social Security Act in 1961 provided funds to states for foster care maintenance payments under Aid to Dependent Children, Title IV-A. Also, that year pediatrician C. Henry Kempe and colleagues (1962) published a study on the battered child that was widely publicized by many news outlets. The public became much more aware of child abuse, and many physicians realized that they needed to consider that possibility as an explanation for broken bones, bruises, burns, etc. Their professional paper was followed in 1968, by the publication of their book *The Battered Child*, which provided the professional audience and public with examples and photographs better preparing them to diagnose abuse and neglect. The book was widely read by child welfare professionals, social workers, and interested members of the general public.

The states began passing mandatory reporting laws in 1963 following the Kempe et al. (1962) article in the medical journal *JAMA*. Prior to that year, California was the only state where child abuse was specifically criminalized (Brown & Gallagher, 2014). In 1965 Democratic President Lyndon Johnson as part of his Great Society effort succeeded in getting Medicare and Medicaid addressed in Social Security amendments. Medicaid made medical care available to thousands of children and families living in poverty. Head Start began about this same time and gave very young children exposure to enrich their minds and prepare them for elementary schools.

By 1967 almost all of the states had assumed governmental responsibility for child protection. However, there was a stronger presence in cities than in rural areas. Even where there was an organized response, many communities did not have 24-hour coverage, and protective services were not available in every part of every state. Nonetheless, passage of the Aid to Dependent Children program was a giant leap forward in terms of ensuring that needy mothers and children could have shelter, food, and basic necessities. Initially, single fathers did not qualify but in 1961 states were allowed to extend benefits to families where the father was unemployed. However, many states added their own "man-in-the house rule" which prohibited families from receiving benefits if there was any adult male in the household. In 1968 the Supreme Court largely struck down those "rules."

In 1974 the Child Abuse Prevention and Treatment Act (CAPTA) provided funds for child abuse and neglect prevention, identification, prosecution, and treatment to both public agencies and nonprofit organizations for demonstration projects. The funding also supported training and regional multidisciplinary centers to conduct research and evaluation projects, technical assistance, and data-collection activities to improve the nation's response to physical and sexual abuse and to neglect. To receive CAPTA funds, states were required to have passed **statutes** (laws) defining and prohibiting child maltreatment, established mandatory reporting and reporting systems for child maltreatment, designated an agency for investigation of child maltreatment, provided statutory immunity for individuals making good faith reports of suspected child maltreatment, and protected the confidentiality of data generated by their reporting systems. While the federal government's greater role in child protection was vitally important, states still varied in their array of supported services and who was mandated to report. The most comprehensive of the mandatory reporting laws required all persons who have "reasonable cause to suspect abuse to report" (Brown & Gallagher, 2014, p. 38).

You can find a brief summary of each state's mandatory reporters of abuse at the Child Welfare Information Gateway at this link: https://www.childwelfare.gov/topics/systemwide/laws-policies/statutes/manda/.

By 1976 laws requiring professionals to report sexual abuse were present in all states.

In 1978 the Indian Child Welfare Act was enacted to reduce the number of Native American children removed from their homes for abuse or neglect. There was growing concern that these children too often were placed in non-Indian homes and losing their cultural heritage. The act gave preference to Indian families who wanted to provide foster care or to adopt. The act provided that for children living on reservations, only tribal courts could make decisions for abuse and neglect cases and that tribes were to be notified and had the right to intervene when the Native American child was living off the reservation.

In 1980 the large number of children in foster care prompted the Title IV-E Adoption Assistance and Child Welfare Act, which directed child protection agencies to avoid child removal if it could safely be avoided and to make reasonable efforts to reunite families. It also required permanency plans for moving a child back home or toward adoption with the termination of parental rights. This act further provided financial assistance to families who adopted as well as incentives for those adopting children with special needs. The act gave rise to family preservation programs such as Homebuilders and Family Builders.

Title IV-E provided funds to the states for the out-of-home care of children age 18 and younger removed from their parents' custody when these families would have been income-eligible under the old Aid to Families with Dependent Children program.

In the 1980s additional Title IV-E monies provided for independent living services for older foster youth to help them make the transition to adulthood. Training vouchers could be used for postsecondary education and vocational training.

In 1994 by the Multiethnic Placement Act (MEPA) was enacted to speed up the adoptive placements of children who might have been harder to place because of their race. It essentially restricted the ability of courts and agencies to take into account color, race, or national origin in making foster care or adoptive placement decisions. In other words, otherwise qualified persons could not be denied the opportunity to become a foster or adoptive parent because of the child's or the parents' race, color, or national origin. It also required plans from states for the recruitment of foster and adoptive parents that are reflective of the racial diversity of the children in care in that state.

Congress passed the Adoption and Safe Families Act in 1997 requiring firm guidelines for the length of time children can remain in foster care before returning them to their homes or requesting the change of the permanency goal and pursuing the termination of parental rights. There was a greater focus on outcomes, which led to Child and Family Service Reviews conducted by the Children's Bureau. This allowed states to compare their achievements against a national standard and to begin monitoring progress for improvement.

Taking up the issue of thousands of youths aging out of foster care each year without a permanent family of their own, Congress passed the Foster Care Independence Act in 1999. This act addressed the problem of children who had spent a significant portion of their lives in foster care and who may not have been prepared for independent living. The act extended the age of eligibility for federal funding to 21 and allowed states to enroll these now young adults in the state medical assistance program until 21. It also set aside funding for their education and training.

In 2003 President George W. Bush signed the Protect Act, creating the Amber Alert system—a nationwide system designed to quickly inform the public whenever there was a child abduction. The act also makes child pornography a criminal offense. No one can advertise, distribute, own, sell, or create any visual depiction (picture, drawing, cartoon, sculpture, or painting) that is, or appears to be, of a minor engaged in sexual intercourse that lacks serious literary, artistic, political, or scientific value.

In 2014 Congress passed Public Law 113-183, the Preventing Sex Trafficking and Strengthening Families Act, to address children most at risk of sex trafficking—those in foster care who run away.

Four years later, in 2018, Congress passed the Family First Prevention Services Act, which has a goal of keeping children in their families, where possible, to avoid the trauma of foster care. The act has several provisions that provide federal funding for increased prevention efforts for mental health and substance abuse prevention and treatment services, as well as in-home parent skill-based services for homes where children are at imminent risk of entering foster care. These services are also available for relatives able to assist the children, and pregnant or parenting teens. Additionally, federal funding will become available for children in qualified residential treatment programs or special treatment settings for pregnant or parenting teens, youth 18 and over transitioning from foster care to adulthood, and youth found to be or at risk of becoming sex trafficking victims. More support will be provided to relative caregivers; states must document how their foster care licensing standards accommodate relative caregivers, and family reunification services for children in foster care will be extended an additional 15 months for children once they return home from foster care. The act also extends independent living services to former foster youth up to age 23 and eligibility for education and training vouchers for these youth up to age 26. This comprehensive act will also establish an electronic case-processing system to expedite the interstate placement of children in foster care, adoption, or guardianship.

In conclusion, although our child protection system is not perfect and still varies considerably from community to community, it has come a long way from its historical beginnings. Yes, there is still more work to be done, and this will be discussed in more detail in the final chapter.

Main Points

Not everyone enjoys reading about the past. However, as philosopher George Santana once noted, "Those who cannot remember the past are condemned to repeat it." Earlier in our country's history, there was a shameful amount of discrimination against Native Americans and African Americans. We never want to become so focused on our own group—whoever that is—that we lose sight of those not in our "inner circle" who may need protection from exploitation and maltreatment. This chapter traces the evolution of child protection in early America from a period of having practically no protection for children of any kind in early America to legislation that we can be proud of.

- Society's understanding that children are little adults who can work long hours in factories and share jails with adults has changed over time.
- Many outstanding individuals, such as Janie Porter Barrett, created resources through the Colored Women's Clubs to provide shelter and facilities for needy children of color after the Civil War.
- Social reformers like Charles Loring Brace deserve a lot of credit for thinking "outside the box" and attempting to address the problems of orphans and neglected children with the Children's Aid Society and the orphan trains.
- Henry Bergh, founder of the American Society for the Prevention of Cruelty to Animals, had the courage to extend his resources to protect Mary Ellen Wilson in a case of child abuse the public really "got." Elbridge Gerry with the NYSPCC pushed the public's responsiveness even further.
- The passage of the Social Security Act of 1935 with the provision of Aid to Families with Dependent Children was a major milestone in our country's history. Other incremental acts followed.
- In 1968 a book by Kempe and Helfer (*The Battered Child*) once again reawakened the public to the problem of child maltreatment, and not coincidentally, legislation was passed. In 1974 it was the Child Abuse Prevention and Treatment Act. In 1978 the Indian Child Welfare Act addressed problems specifically affecting American Indian children and families.
- More recently the Multiethnic Placement Act removed some barriers for children in foster care, and the Adoption and Safe Families Act created guidelines to help agencies better monitor and manage children in foster care.
- The Family First Prevention Services Act is comprehensive, targeting existing services and prevention. Federal funding begins 2 years (FY 2020) after the legislation was signed.
- In conclusion, long strides have been made in creating measures that better protect our nation's vulnerable children.

Questions for Class Discussion

1. What is one thing you learned from this chapter that surprised you? Why?
2. What is one thing from this chapter that you would like to learn more about? Why?

3. Which one of the child protection actions or laws described in this chapter do you think was the most important? Why?

4. What do you think did more to help improve the lives of children: the orphan trains or the sensational case of Mary Ellen Wilson?

5. What ideas do you have about ways to better protect vulnerable children?

Self-Assessment for Personal Consideration

1. This chapter covered discrimination against African Americans and Native Americans. Although those events occurred in our country's past, how comfortable are you in working with families that are different from the one you grew up in?

| 1 | 2 | 3 | 4 | 5 | 6 | 7 | 8 | 9 | 10 |

Not comfortable   *Very comfortable*

Additional Resources

Allgeier, G. (2013). *Benjamin Lindsey: Father of the juvenile courts.* Palmer Lake, CO: Filter Press. Retrieved from https://history.denverlibrary.org/colorado-biographies/judge-benjamin-barr-lindsey-1869-1943

Children's Bureau. (n.d.). Children's Bureau timeline. Retrieved from https://cb100.acf.hhs.gov/childrens-bureau-timeline

Courtney, M. E. (2013). Child welfare: History and policy framework. In *Encyclopedia of Social Work.* New York, NY: Oxford University Press.

Husock, H. (2008, Winter). Uplifting the "Dangerous classes": What Charles Loring Brace's philanthropy can us teach us today. *City Journal Magazine.* Retrieved from https://www.city-journal.org/html/uplifting-%E2%80%9Cdangerous-classes%E2%80%9D-13071.html

Jalongo, M. R. (2006). The story of Mary Ellen Wilson: Tracing the origins of child protection in America. *Early Childhood Education Journal, 34*(1), 1–4.

McGowan, B. G. (2005). Historical evolution of child welfare services. In G. P. Mallon & P. M. Hess (Eds.), *Child welfare for the twenty-first century: A handbook of practices, policies, and programs* (pp. 11–50). New York, NY: Columbia University Press.

Roberts, D. E. (1999). Is there justice in children's rights? The critique of federal family preservation policy. *Faculty Scholarship at Penn Law, 587.* Retrieved from http://scholarship.law.upenn.edu/faculty_scholarship/587

References

Bear, C. (2008). American Indian boarding schools haunt many. NPR. Retrieved from https://www.npr.org/templates/story/story.php?storyId=16516865

Brown, L. G., & Gallagher, K. (2014). Mandatory reporting of abuse: A historical perspective on the evolution of states' current mandatory reporting laws with a review of the laws of the Commonwealth of Pennsylvania. *Villanova Law Review Tolle Lege, 59,* 37–80.

Cook, J. F. (1995). A history of placing-out: The orphan trains. *Child Welfare, 74*(1), 181–197.

Costin, L. B., Karger, H. J., & Stoesz, D. (1996). *The politics of child abuse in America.* New York, NY: Oxford University Press.

Heywood, C. (2001). *A history of childhood.* Cambridge, United Kingdom: Polity Press.

Jimenez, J. (2006). The history of child protection in the African American community: Implications for current child welfare policies. *Children and Youth Services Review, 28,* 888–905.

Kempe, C. H., & Helfer, R. E. (1968). *The battered child*. Chicago, IL: University of Chicago Press.

Kempe, C. H., Silverman, F. N., Steele, B. F., Droegemuller, W., & Silver, H. K. (1962). The battered child syndrome. *Journal of the American Medical Association, 181,* 17–24.

Levine, M., & Levine, A. (1992). *Helping children: A social history*. New York, NY: Oxford University Press.

Myers, J. E. B. (2006). *Child protection in America: Past, present, and future*. New York, NY: Oxford University Press.

Myers, J. E. B. (2008). A short history of child protection in America. *Family Law Quarterly, 42*(3), 449–463.

National Archives. (n.d.) What was it like to be a child slave in America in the nineteenth century? Retrieved from http://www.nationalarchives.gov.uk/documents/education/childhood-slavery-contextual-essay.pdf

Northern Plains Reservation Aid. (n.d.). History and culture: Boarding schools. Retrieved from http://www.nativepartnership.org/site/PageServer?pagename=airc_hist_boardingschools

Office of the Historian. (n.d.). Indian Treaties and the Removal Act of 1830. US Department of State. Retrieved from https://history.state.gov/milestones/1830-1860/indian-treaties

Peebles-Wilkins, W. (1996). Janie Porter Barrett and the Virginia Industrial School for Colored Girls: Community response to the needs of African American children. In E. P. Smith & L. A. Merkel-Holguin (Eds.), *A history of child welfare* (pp. 135–153). New Brunswick, NJ: Transaction.

Smith, A. (2007, March 26). Soul wound: The legacy of Native American schools. *Amnesty International Magazine*. Retrieved from https://lastshadetree.com/res-schools-ai.

Sutton, J. R. (1981). Stubborn children: Law and the socialization of deviance in the Puritan colonies. *Family Law Quarterly, 15*(1), 31–64.

Figure Credit

CHAPTER 2

CHILD ABUSE AND NEGLECT IN THE UNITED STATES

OVERVIEW

This chapter will introduce you to four broad categories of maltreatment commonly experienced by children. These are neglect, physical abuse, sexual abuse, and emotional abuse. While several forms of maltreatment may simultaneously occur within a family (known as **polyvictimization**), case vignettes will be used to illustrate each type of maltreatment separately. As you read about the various ways children are harmed or could potentially be mistreated under each category, keep fresh in your mind that these descriptions are not exhaustive or a complete and unabridged listing. That is, abuse and neglect can take many different forms that did not get a mention here. Just about any behavior or practice pushed to unreasonable excess can be harmful—and that is the issue. Is the child being harmed or at risk of being harmed? Five cases in this chapter will be used to demonstrate what a child protective services (CPS) worker might discover while investigating a case. Signs and symptoms accompany the definitions of maltreatment to help you assess the situations you may encounter. In a later chapter, we will examine the factors and dynamics contributing to the child maltreatment. This chapter also provides some estimates of the approximately four million U.S. referrals received each year alleging possible child maltreatment. Of that number, approximately 58% are investigated (or screened in) and of those investigated 17.2% are substantiated (the allegation is supported or indicated based on the state's child protection laws).

Neglect

The Cox Family

Marvin Cox is a 31-year-old White male who was raised in foster care. While Marvin was growing up, his parents were in and out of the home, and he spent quite a bit of time on the streets. Marvin made some decisions as an adolescent that he probably regrets and ended up serving time in prison. However, he is an adult now, and he and his girlfriend, Amy, have two young daughters. Amy grew up in California and is much younger than Marvin and relies on his support. They are not married but have been together for a number of years. However, Amy is becoming increasingly fed up with Marvin's inability to provide for the family. He is having a difficult time finding work in his rural community, and there are concerns that this frustration may lead to his relapse.

Although desperate to find a stable place to live, Marvin and his family have been living a transient lifestyle. They stay with people they meet or sleep on a friend's floor, but they never stay in the same place for very long. Most recently, they broke into an abandoned house by the lake that had been taken over by the bank for foreclosure. Marvin recognized that "squatting" in this home isn't a long-term solution, but he decided to risk it since they had nowhere else to go.

Last night, the local fish and game officer passed by, and Officer Smith noticed a light on inside the house that had been empty for quite some time. Smith and his partner crept up to the house to take a look, concerned that some type of criminal behavior may be taking place. Upon arriving, Smith noticed a unique odor that he was all too familiar with from prior encounters in his patrol area. He was immediately aware that the occupants of the house were cooking "meth" (methamphetamine). Looking through the broken side window, Smith and his partner could see Marvin and Amy in the kitchen wearing plastic gloves and standing next to a mound of overflowing trash bags, metal containers, and several 2-liter bottles. Realizing the production of meth produces potentially explosive materials and toxic gasses, Smith called for backup from the state police and local fire department to deal with the extremely dangerous situation. Thinking they might save the lives of the two adults, police officers kicked down the back door and entered the home.

Marvin and Amy were handcuffed, and as they attempted to spin a fanciful series of lies to explain what they were doing, two young girls with curly brown hair appeared in the hallway. They were dirty, wearing sagging diapers, and began crying when they saw the officers confronting their parents. Realizing the immediate safety concerns for the children, the first responders escorted the family outside, where they awaited the arriving fire department to detoxify the family and prevent an explosion in the vacant home. It was a chilly night, and one of the police officers wrapped the children in a blanket and held them until the child protection workers drove up.

The children were taken to an emergency foster home, where Mrs. Bell comforted them with soothing words as she changed their diapers and gave them each a teddy bear. She scrambled some eggs for the girls as they greedily ate a banana and pulled on her apron to hurry up her cooking.

After they wolfed down the eggs and drank their milk, Mrs. Bell exclaimed "Goodness!" Wiping their mouths with a napkin, she said, "You girls were starved to death!" She held them in her lap and rocked them while singing softly. Soon they were fast asleep..

Unfortunately, this situation is all too familiar for those working in child protection. Marvin and Amy are both responsible for meeting the needs of their children, and their inappropriate and dangerous behaviors placed both of their children in immediate risk of harm. **Neglect** occurs when a caretaker who is responsible for the supervision and well-being of an individual who is unable or incapable of taking care of themselves fails to provide the necessary care. The local child protective services agency may be called at all hours of the day or night; child protection is truly a 24/7 effort.

Definition of Neglect

Neglect of children is almost always described in terms of some type of failure—as when a parent or other person responsible for the child does not or cannot provide a safe environment with sufficient food, clothing, shelter, medical care, or supervision needed to keep a child healthy, safe, and able to develop normally. Some states include in their definition of neglect the failure to see that a child attends school (Child Welfare Information Gateway, n.d.).

TEST YOURSELF

Read the case a second time to see what evidence a child protection worker might find of parental neglect. Do not read below the dotted line until you are ready to see the answer.

- -

First of all, the parents are exposing the children to potentially harmful chemical fumes and the danger of explosion as they manufacture meth. This is illegal behavior that can result in possible prison terms and the loss of their children. Second, the children were dirty, in "sagging diapers," and did not seem to be properly clothed for a chilly night. Also, there was potentially dangerous garbage stored in the kitchen that the children could get into. Once in the emergency shelter, it was abundantly clear that the girls were hungry. Had they even been fed that day? Lastly, while it is not evidence in itself that the girls were neglected, having a father who has had substance abuse issues in the past and served time in prison is a concern. Is the father currently using? If so, then that would almost automatically raise the suspicion that the children likely were not receiving the care and attention they needed.

Types of Neglect

Physical/Environmental Neglect

Upon receiving a report of possible neglect, the child protection worker enters the home looking for unsafe, unsanitary, or possibly harmful environments. Many of these problems require only common sense to detect. For instance, if you step on the porch and the boards are so rotten you almost fall through, that's dangerous. If the windows in the house are broken out, that could make for a very cold winter and could actually be dangerous in northern states, with the possibility of frostbite to young fingers or toes. If you walk into the home and the place is overrun with cats (let's say you estimate 12 to 15, although there could be more hiding), and especially if the furniture reeks of cat urine and the litter boxes are overflowing or nonexistent, that's a major problem. Seeing evidence of mice droppings on kitchen counters or roaches is not good either. If the home does not have running water (because the water bills have not been paid or because of the rural area in which the home is situated), this is a *major* concern. You might be tipped off if the children seem to be especially dirty (faces, hands, arms, clothing) or if you see large plastic buckets in the bathroom (to flush the toilet).

PRACTICE TIP 2.1 Living in poverty and cultural considerations may be issues affecting the environmental conditions of the homes you visit. Saying this another way, if you are fastidious about order and cleanliness, you will notice its absence on many occasions. This does not necessarily mean that the parents are neglectful or poor housekeepers—they may simply have a different viewpoint than you on what's important. For example, a single mother working two jobs to feed her children may not have the energy to keep her home neat enough to entertain company, but she may always provide her children with hot meals and care passionately about their well-being. As an investigator, you will want to focus on actual evidence and concerns for the potential for harm to children. An unkempt or messy household may not in itself be important.

This is not to suggest that everyone has to have the same level of movie star hygiene, but infants and toddlers tend to put their fingers in their mouths and are more susceptible to diseases, for instance, carried by cats and dogs (such as roundworm and hookworm) and a parasitic infection carried by cats that could be harmful to the very young and those with impaired immune systems (toxoplasmosis).

Too many children sleeping in the same bed *might* be a concern; older children sleeping with younger ones *might* be a concern, too. However, these may not turn out to indicate anything but a family having too many children and not enough beds. You will likely want to probe and ask questions about any children sleeping with adults who are not their biological parents. Children who sleep with very young children who still wet the bed can contribute to children who smell of urine at school and get made fun of by other children. Thus, children who live in families where they are neglected can also find it difficult to develop friendships because they are shunned by classmates.

Children who look underweight for their age or appear undernourished, not enough food in the house or refrigerator, and lack of milk or supplement could suggest that a child's needs are not being met. Having food but not giving it to the child also constitutes physical neglect. This could also come about when the parent or guardian has a physical or mental disability and unable to cook or prepare meals for the child.

Neighbors might report adults who leave their children alone too long while they leave to shop or get a car repaired, etc. Their concerns are much more justified if the child is 5 years old and left to watch a 2-year-old than if a mature 12-year-old is left alone for 4 or 5 hours. However, some 12-year-olds might not be mature and could be scared to be by themselves—especially if they live in an isolated rural area or in a dangerous inner-city neighborhood where shootings are common. The context is often very revealing. A 2-year-old left unattended for long periods of time while the adult is out to a party is going to constitute neglect. The case of a 12-year-old left alone for the same amount of time may or may not indicate neglect. The assessment of the child protection worker will be very important in these situations.

It is almost impossible to describe all of the conditions that could signal a health and environmental hazard or show a lack of a concern and caring for a young child. The child protection worker who is investigating a possible neglect case must put himself or herself in the child's situation to see what is provided and what is missing. Generally, you won't have a checklist on a clipboard to follow. However, physical neglect often falls into these broad categories:

- Food or nutrition inadequacy, child is always hungry (under low nutritional environments, some children will eat paint chips, dirt, just about anything; this condition is known as *pica*)
- Lack of supervision or poor concern for safety
- Shelter or home environment inadequacy
- Poor hygiene, dirty or insufficient clothing, head lice.
- Lack of nurturing, lack of affection, or rejection of the child
- Educational neglect (not sending the child to school)

As the lists suggests, physical/environmental neglect can be much more than not providing adequate food, clothing, shelter, or protection (both from the elements as well as from too many pets or too many people in too small of an area). It also includes adult supervision. A 2- or 3-year-old should not be out walking down the highway at midnight, able to drink or consume adult beverages, or have access to dangerous chemicals like drain cleaners that are in open containers or cabinets at ground level. Very young children (e.g., 6-year-olds) should not be supervising or babysitting infants or toddlers while the adults go to the grocery store or out to party. There is a subjective element in all of this assessment in that some children asked to watch a toddler might be very responsible and mature despite their young age. In the Cox family case, there was no clear indication that the parents were emotionally abusing the children by saying mean or hurtful things to them. However, they were exposing them to dangerous chemicals and the possibility of an explosion as they manufactured meth. Further, the family broke into the house and therefore lacked legally appropriate shelter—so an argument could be made that parents were ignoring their children's needs for safety and protection. This would also be true if the parents allowed unsavory characters (those persons interested in buying drugs) into their "home." Isolating children, keeping them from society, is a form of neglect. Children should not be denied opportunities for cognitive stimulation by association with other children.

In the case at the beginning of the chapter, the two children were dirty, and there was a suggestion that they were in diapers needing to be changed. Depending on the weather, the season of the year, and the temperature inside the house, the girls may have been inadequately dressed. To push the example a little more, let's say that the children were 7 and 8—old enough to be attending school. If because the family is homeless and because the parents may be trying to avoid arrest (e.g., if there is an outstanding police warrant for their arrest), or if they were simply too "high" at times to see that their children got to school, then that could constitute educational neglect.

Neglect of Infants and Toddlers

Neglected children under the age of 2 may develop a medical condition known as **nonorganic failure to thrive** (NFTT), where the infant becomes severely underweight and possibly smaller than other children (on an objective scale used by pediatricians). Although there can be organic reasons, these children may also not receive an adequate level of nutrition to support their body's needs. This could come about because the parents are not skilled in feeding infants and don't administer the feeding properly by giving the child enough, because they don't have sufficient funds to buy formula, or because they have diluted the baby's formula to make it go further. In addition, angry and hostile parents who try to rush feeding or who don't truly want the child and are somewhat detached may find that the infant is not interested in feeding. Parents who forget or don't feed their infants regularly can also create this condition, which can contribute to a loss of weight and lack of growth. Children can die from NFTT.

Other ways that parental neglect may be detected in the very young include:

- Rashes and infections from sitting in dirty diapers too long
- Lack of affect (the child is listless, not laughing, smiling, or making noises that typical babies do, and doesn't make eye contact)
- Delayed or arrested development (poor muscle tone, inability to support self or move about like other babies of the same age)
- Babies left to sleep on soiled mattresses or cribs; no crib or place to sleep

Medical Neglect

States differ in their definitions of this form of neglect. **Medical neglect** often it means that the parents or guardian have not taken the child to a physician or clinic when there has been an accident (think: broken arm or leg), when the child has a chronic illness or acute illness that is not responding to home remedies or receives no treatment at all and the child looks very sick (pale or jaundiced complexion, not speaking or responding, wheezing or rattling in the lungs, high fever, etc.). Additionally, a few states define medical neglect as withholding medical treatment, nutrition, and water from a child not expected to live because he or she has a serious illness that may not be survivable. And in some states, not taking the child who has serious mental health concerns to a mental health counselor or clinic (think: a young child who is threatening suicide) could constitute medical neglect.

Emotional Neglect

Emotional neglect is a form of neglect where adequate attention, concern, affection are not given to the child. It may be part of a larger pattern of neglect that investigators find. Others may also refer to it as emotional abuse, psychological abuse, psychological maltreatment, emotional maltreatment, or even mental cruelty (Royse, 2016). However, emotional abuse is discussed in more detail later in this chapter. Unlike emotional neglect, emotional abuse is more like stabbing a child with hurtful words.

Emotional neglect is generally a consistent attitude or disposition—not a single event—that communicates rejection or being unwanted to the child. His or her developmental potential and worldview is affected. Think of it as a mental injury where a child begins to believe that he or she is stupid, unlovable, ugly, flawed, unwanted, or worthless.

A child who tries to get her mother's attention because she is hungry or thirsty and is ignored or told to "get away" experiences emotional neglect. The child who falls and hurts himself or plays with a sharp kitchen knife and accidentally cuts himself and is laughed at instead of treated and comforted experiences emotional neglect. The child who at breakfast knocks her milk over into her lap and is told to sit there in it for 15 minutes and not to talk for the rest of the day experiences emotional neglect. Adults who punish children by ignoring them and not talking to them for days at a time are emotionally neglectful.

Unlike physical abuse, there likely will be no bruises, broken bones, or anything visible that a camera might pick up other than perhaps a downcast, depressed look. The child may be anxious, fearful, (e.g., hiding behavior), overly quiet, shy, and slow to play with other children. Emotional neglect is often reported by investigators simply as neglect and it would not be uncommon for children who experience a lack of parental warmth to be lacking care in other areas as well.

Recognizing the Signs and Symptoms of Emotional Neglect

Young children who are experiencing emotional abuse/neglect may be:

- Withdrawn, nonverbal, passive
- Avoidant of the parental abuser
- Loners who don't interact with other children; have few friends
- Disrupters in the classroom or aggressive toward other children
- Noncompliant
- Low self-esteem, depressed affect
- At a risk for substance use and suicide attempts—if older
- Able to state that their parent(s) dislike them, don't want them

SUBSTANTIATED CASES OF NEGLECT, UNITED STATES, 2016*

Neglect:	74.8% of all substantiated cases
Medical Neglect:	2.1% of all substantiated cases

*U.S. Department of Health & Human Services, Administration for Children and Families, Administration on Children, Youth and Families, Children's Bureau. (2018). Child maltreatment 2016. Table 3–8.

Physical Abuse

Physical abuse is one of several types of abuse that we will discuss in this chapter. We start with an actual case that has been slightly changed to provide confidentiality to the family members.

Stevie Owens's Story

Stevie is an active 10-year-old African American male, full of energy and always going a mile a minute. He likes to play basketball and video games. His parents are separated, and he prefers to stay at his mom's house, where she and her fiancé often take him out to dinner and generally don't make him follow too many rules. Due to a court decision, Stevie spends every other weekend with his biological father, Richard. Richard is a hard worker and engages in semiskilled labor at a factory approximately 60 hours a week. He works overtime on purpose, because he wants to be able to pay his child support, and he has also just bought a brand-new red Camaro. Stevie and Richard get along okay, but Richard insists on structure and rules and has become frustrated with the laissez-faire attitude his ex-wife displays with respect to Stevie's upbringing. Richard's own parents engaged in traditional parenting techniques, where there were rules to follow, and respecting his family members was very important.

Last weekend Stevie and his father got into an argument. On his weekend visit, Richard had planned on taking Stevie out to the park to hit baseballs. As Richard went to the closet to get their equipment, Stevie showed his dad the brand-new cell phone his mother had bought for him. Stevie didn't want to go to the park; he wanted to spend time on Snapchat with his girlfriend. Richard became angry and berated Stevie for not wanting to go to the park so they could spend time together. That's when it happened. Stevie looked at his dad right in the eyes and said a four-letter curse word, starting with the F and ending with the word "you." Richard exploded. He grabbed the cell phone out of Stevie's hand and threw it on the floor. He yelled that Stevie was going to "learn some respect!" Taking off his belt, Richard held Stevie down and gave him several lashes across his buttocks and lower back.

Their disagreement had become a full crisis. Once released, Stevie shouted, "I hate you!" and ran to his room, slamming the door. After a few minutes, Richard calmed down and apologized through the door. With his father's permission, Stevie called his mother to pick him up. Once home, Stevie's mother heard Stevie's side of the story and saw the red welts on his backside caused by her ex-husband. She called the child protective service agency and reported Richard.

This situation provides an example of physical abuse. Today such disciplinary practices are much less acceptable than they were in years past. In his anger, Richard's decision to incorporate the use of an instrument (the belt) into his punishment of Stevie will very likely constitute child abuse by inflicting injury in an intentional act by a person in a caretaking role. Letting his anger get out of control has the capacity to lead to life-changing events that could change whether he would be able to continue to coparent Stevie.

Definition of Physical Abuse

Physical abuse is any nonaccidental injury. Typically, evidence in children are red marks or welts, bruises, lacerations or cuts, muscle sprains, or even broken bones. Actions that might cause such injuries are behaviors such as beating or whipping a child, punching, hitting, kicking, biting, slapping, or throwing a heavy object. More extreme behaviors could include choking, strangling, stabbing, scalding, suffocating, force-feeding, or poisoning. These actions only have to have the *potential* for injuring a child. For instance, turning the gas on in an oven and having a child stick her head in the oven for a brief might not actually injure the child, but it certainly has the potential for serious injury.

With infants unable to support their heads, there is a form of head trauma when there is a rough or violent whiplash shaking of the child. This is often known as the ***shaken baby syndrome***. Babies cry a lot, and because that is their only way of communicating, it can be terribly frustrating to parents and caregivers when the baby can't be comforted enough to stop its crying. When the adult has poor anger control, the infant might be shaken in such a way that permanent damage and possibly disability is caused.

TEST YOURSELF

Jim, a happy 12-year-old, complained that he was hungry as he was watching television in his biological father's home. His father yelled, "Heads up!" as he tossed Jim a large red apple from the kitchen. Unfortunately, as Jim turned to look as his dad, the apple struck him in the face, just missing his eye. The next day when he got back to his stepfather's and mother's house, his mother called the child protection authorities to report Jim's black eye. Does this black eye suggest physical abuse? Do not read below the dotted line until you are ready to see the answer.

Because Jim's father was not intentionally trying to hurt his son, it probably does not constitute physical abuse. Note that the case says the father "tossed" an apple. Of course, if the apple had been thrown overhand in an attempt to knock Jim out of his chair or in a state of anger, then it very well could be understood as physically abusive. Also, it might be important to learn if the father had been responsible for any previous accidents.

Accidents to children normally do not result in criminal charges of physical abuse unless there are accounts of a recklessness (such as placing a child on a lawnmower or in other potentially dangerous situations and not providing enough reasonable protection, support, etc.). Poor parental judgment where a child gets injured (e.g., allowing a 4-year-old to hold a lit sparkler) could be reported by neighbors as child abuse—and would need to be investigated.

Types of Physical Abuse

Injuries can be acquired if a child is pushed too high in a swing or pushed too hard while learning to ride a bike or if he or she is hit by a hard ball thrown too fast. A single incident like that probably doesn't constitute physical abuse unless the adult was deliberately trying to hurt the child. Sometimes there is a miscommunication, and the child might not be prepared for a sudden or strong push or simply might not be coordinated or skilled enough to catch a hard ball thrown overhand. Yes, adults and even parents can misjudge how strong a child is or his or her ability to hold on tight or position a baseball glove the right way to intercept a ball. Further, a parent might toss a child in the air softly but bungle the catch. Others might wrestle with their children and never hurt them. Minor bumps or bruises could result, and usually the adult learns to be more careful, but even the most cautious parent can accidently trip an unsteady toddler. Even the most protective parent might forget to move a hot pan or skillet onto the back burner so that a toddler can't reach it and spill its hot contents on him- or herself. Accidents happen in every family, and it is very likely that the vast majority of them were never intentional, were never intended to hurt a child. Physical abuse is specific to intention to harm. However, it may well be that a parent, especially one physically abused in childhood or one with anger control issues, *claims* the child's injury was an accident when it really was intentional. Some events will need to be sorted out by medical personnel *and* the child protection worker. Most children seem to be able to recognize whether the injury was intended and may be able to tell you accurately what happened in some detail. Other children may not want to talk, may not make eye contact, may act fearful, and remain watchful of the adult who injured them. This is especially concerning behavior for the investigator.

Recognizing Signs and Symptoms of Physical Abuse

Evidence of physical abuse can often be found on bruises to the body or fractures to bones. Children younger than 6 months do not normally acquire bruises on their own. Once they begin to pull up and walk, they may acquire bruises from running into things and falling down, with bruises showing on legs, knees, forehead, and so forth. Physicians Kodner and Wetherton (2013) describe the **TEN-4 rule**—which states that "bruising on the torso, ear or neck (TEN) in a child four years of age or younger or bruising of any region in a child younger than four months, requires further evaluation for abuse" (p. 670). Further, Kodner and Wetherton (2013) list important points to be covered when medically evaluating a suspicious injury. These are:

- Prior injuries, hospitalizations, medical illnesses, and conditions
- History of abuse toward child or others
- Recent social or financial stresses
- No explanation or vague explanations for injury
- Significant delay in seeking medical attention
- Details of explanation or child's history change dramatically over time
- Explanation is inconsistent with pattern, age, or severity of the injury
- Explanation is inconsistent with child's physical or developmental capabilities
- Child's history doesn't explain the injury
- Different witnesses provide alternative explanations for the injury.

When confronted, some parents will admit to being angry or under too much stress and that they lashed out at the child in an injurious manner, which they now regret. Some types of injuries leave characteristic marks. For example, using a whip, rope, electrical light cord, and so forth, if doubled can leave a loop-shaped welt in the shape of the instrument. Sometimes, a slap to the face or a spanking on the buttocks can leave a handprint, which can be captured if a photograph is able to be taken soon after. Cigarette burns leave a characteristic wound, as do bite marks. Bruises around the wrists or ankles can indicate the child was tied up.

Child protection investigators should become suspicious of explanations where the story doesn't match the injury. Medical personnel might also notice evidence of other fractures (from X-rays), old scarring, and untreated problems that usually would be brought to the attention of medical personnel. Anything like a record of previous fractures, scars, head injuries, and scalds to the child's bottom are very likely indications of physical abuse. Be aware that parents can hide previous injuries to a child by going to different hospitals or doctors so that a pattern isn't found in the child's chart. Also, be mindful that bruises and injuries to children may be hidden by clothing or even under underwear.

A recent study (Young et al., 2018) looked at whether infants 1 year old or younger were described with negative or developmentally unrealistic words by their parents. The researchers found that parents who described infants characterized with "one or more negative/unrealistic words had ten times greater odds of being classified as cases of abuse than those described with exclusively positive/neutral words" (p. 47). Clearly, listening to parents' descriptions of their children and their "accidents" may reveal whether the child is in a potentially dangerous situation.

Another thing to remember is that siblings are quite capable of physically abusing their brothers and sisters.

Behavioral Signs and Symptoms of Physical Abuse

Some children may show more signs of physical abuse, and some will show less. It is unlikely that the child will display every one of the possible signs.

- Depression
- Withdrawal from friends and social activities
- Poor (unbelievable) or inconsistent explanations of injuries
- Unusual shyness
- Avoidance of eye contact with adults or older kids
- Excessive fear of caretakers—this could be fear of the parent(s) or of a nanny or babysitter
- Antisocial behavior (older kids) like truancy, drug abuse, running away from home
- Seems overly watchful, on edge, as if anticipating something bad is going to happen
- Expresses a reluctance to go home
- Not comforted by parent or parent's presence (in younger children)
- Lack of interest in toys, play

SUBSTANTIATED CASES OF PHYSICAL ABUSE, UNITED STATES, 2016*

Physical Abuse: 18.2% of all substantiated cases

*U.S. Department of Health & Human Services, Administration for Children and Families, Administration on Children, Youth and Families, Children's Bureau. (2018). Child maltreatment 2016. Table 3–8.

Sexual Abuse

Mariana Martinez's Story

Mariana is a 14-year-old Latina female who could pass for someone in their early 20s. She is smart, funny, pretty, and independent. She has long dark hair and talked the owner at the tattoo parlor into giving her a tattoo of a butterfly on her ankle for free. She is currently in foster care, as the court removed her from her biological mother's care for issues related to truancy. She admitted she didn't find school very interesting and preferred to hang out and smoke cigarettes with her friends. Mariana is the only person in her family who speaks fluent English, as her parents both emigrated to the United States from El Salvador.

Her mother, Gloria, and her father, Ramon, do their best to provide support for Mariana, but they face significant language barriers and have an unfamiliarity with all of the requirements of full participation in American society. While Gloria and Ramon are actively participating in the ongoing case plan negotiated with the local child protective services agency, they live in constant fear of deportation, as they are both undocumented; they worry about what the U.S. government could do to them at any moment. Mariana's absences from school, curfew violations, and statements from her parents that she didn't listen to them and they couldn't make her go to school resulted in her being placed with a foster family. The child protection agency arranged for a Spanish-speaking social worker to provide family counseling so that the family could work toward reunification.

Mariana has been at the Flaherty foster home for approximately 1 year. She has built solid relationships with everyone in the home, especially with Mr. Flaherty. Considered to be rowdy and fun, Mr. Flaherty is not what one would perceive as the traditional foster parent. He rides a Harley and consistently takes Mariana out for rides on his motorcycle. They spend a significant amount of time together, and it has become apparent in the past several months that Mr. Flaherty has been behaving a bit differently. He recently started shopping for clothes at the newest hip clothing store in the mall and has become really interested in his appearance. The Flahertys have been foster parents for a number of years, and although it is difficult to find a home to meet the needs of teenage girls, there have been no prior reports of any inappropriate activity at the home.

While being transported by her ongoing child protective services professional to a supervised visit with her biological parents, everything changed. A song on the radio triggered Mariana to confide in her trusted caseworker by discussing her discomfort while at the Flaherty home. Through conversation, Mariana began to elaborate on the details of her relationship with her foster father.

She explained that she did not feel safe going back to the home and mentioned that at night Mr. Flaherty comes into her bedroom and kisses her on her neck. Mariana trusted her caseworker and said, "Honestly, nothing more has happened. There was one time when he attempted to reach his hand inside of my panties, but I made him stop." Realizing the immediate concern for her safety, her caseworker immediately called her supervisor and law enforcement to design a plan for moving forward.

Definition of Child Sexual Abuse

Child sexual abuse generally refers to sexual contact or exploitation of a minor child by an adult. The federal Child Abuse Prevention and Treatment Act, as amended by the CAPTA Reauthorization Act of 2010 is quite broad and, defines child abuse and neglect as, at a minimum, "any recent act or failure to act on the part of a parent or caretaker which results in death, serious physical or emotional harm, sexual abuse or exploitation"; or "an act or failure to act which presents an imminent risk of serious harm" (Child Welfare Information Gateway, n.d.).

Sexual abuse does not have to involve penetration; it can involve any act in which the child is used for sexual gratification. This could be touching the child under or over his or her clothing, asking the child to touch the adult's genitalia, having the child observe sexual acts (e.g., pornographic videos), or making pictures or videos of a sexual nature of children. Unfortunately, sexual abuse is not a respecter of persons and can even occur in the "best" homes—of foster parents, teachers, members of churches, police officers, and other well-respected individuals. The perpetrator can be a relative, live-in boyfriend, or someone considered part of the family (**intrafamilial abuse**); it is known as **incest** when a blood relative is involved. The perpetrator could also be a **pedophile** (someone who preys on children for sexual gain) who is not a family member—it could be a stranger or someone in a position to befriend and have frequent contact with the child. Law enforcement is likely to become involved in these cases.

Sexual abuse involving children often involves perpetrators who know the child (family member, neighbor, adult friend of the family), who may have opportunity to visit often (as in someone who watches the child while the mother works), or who lives close to the family (e.g., an older teen with proximity and access to the child). These individuals are usually careful to not raise suspicions but may seem to have a friendship or good relationship with the child. They may "behave affectionately most of the time, turning into a 'different person' during the abuse itself" (Von Hohendorff, Habigzang, & Koller, 2017, p. 54).

Sgroi, Blick, and Porter (1982) have described a five-stage model of the dynamics in these cases: (a) *engagement*: the offender befriends the child by giving gifts, playing games, or spending time together. The child is led to believe that he or she has a special relationship with the perpetrator—made special by the fact that the offender is older, wiser, and appears to genuinely care for the child; (b) *the sexual episode(s)*, which might be introduced gradually as a game the offender wants to teach the child or suddenly when the child is attacked unexpectedly; (c) *secrecy*, which is maintained by threats of potential harm or cessation of special privileges made possible by the offender; (d) *disclosure*, when the child reveals the abuse or it is accidently discovered; and (e) *suppression*, which may occur when the mother or other significant family member doesn't believe the child or when efforts are made to keep the child from interacting with the offender, but in either situation, the sexual abuse is still treated as a secret and authorities may not be notified (e.g., in the case of an offender closely tied to the family).

Von Hohendorff and colleagues (2017) have also described these stages in similar manner: (a) the preparation stage; (b) the actual episodes; (c) silencing; (d) disclosure or attempted disclosure; (e) repression, where effort is made to discount or undermine the victim's story; and (f) overcoming, when the abused child is believed, supported, protected, etc.

Part of the trauma occurring from sexual abuse is a sense of betrayal that a trusted individual has turned the child's world upside down—warping what the child thought he or she knew about that individual. Further, this affects the child's notions of the world being a safe place. There is also a powerlessness when the offender is an adult or respected family or community member and even when the offender is only 4 or 5 years older than the child but physically stronger. Powerlessness comes from the child's feeling that nothing can be done to prevent further episodes of abuse, because the offender has promised to hurt the child if he or she informs someone of their special relationship, or it could come about in the case of an older teen abusing a younger individual of the same sex and threatening to tell the child's friends that the victim is gay or a "slut" or other manufactured stories designed to humiliate the child. Powerlessness is also reinforced when responsible adults do not believe the child—leading to feelings of shame, guilt, low self-esteem, and depression.

Recognizing Signs and Symptoms of Sexual Abuse

As a professional in child protection, you might have occasion to suspect child sexual abuse or get a referral from child care workers or teachers who notice behavior such as a young child mimicking sexual intercourse with another child, having too much knowledge about adult sexual behavior, exposing him- or herself to other children, repeatedly rubbing his or her genitals or masturbating, frequently drawing genitalia, or attempting to masturbate others. Children do have curiosity about other children's genitals—and boys who have only brothers for siblings and girls who have only sisters in the home may show an interest in the differences found in the opposite sex. Six and seven year-olds may engaged in a "show me yours, I'll show you mine" game that is often normal unless it occurs too often or with much older children—and that might suggest the child has been sexually abused.

As a child protection worker receiving a referral for possible sexual abuse, medical professionals will very likely be involved. However, be aware that "most sexually abused children will not have signs of genital or anal injury, especially when examined nonacutely" (Adams, Farst & Kellogg, 2018, p. 225). That means that if the child was subjected to intercourse weeks ago but not recently, there may not be diagnostic physical findings of injury. Sensitive interviewing of the child to obtain details of a reported incident will be needed. In some cases, however, there could be evidence of sexually transmitted diseases (STDs) such as gonorrhea, chlamydia, or herpes. These STDs would not be normal findings in a prepubertal child. Your role in the investigation may well involve asking the child if he or she was encouraged to engage in unwanted or "secret" behaviors such as:

- Touching, rubbing, fondling, or kissing another person
- Forced nudity or exhibition of self or others (e.g., denied privacy in the bathroom, while dressing or undressing, etc.). This could include bathing with a family member or adult against one's wishes; having no door on the bathroom.
- Being forced to masturbate self or another person
- Having to share a bed with an adult or much older child who touches or relates sexually to child
- Being allowed to or forced to observe sexual acts or pornography, including hearing intimate conversations about sexual experiences or marital relations
- Being complimented for sexual features (e.g., being "well-developed")
- Sexual intercourse, oral-genital contact (may be explained as a game, trick, favor, or child might be threatened with loss of a pet, etc.)

Keep in mind that not every investigation will be **substantiated** (meaning confirmed or validated by the CPS worker). Sometimes when parents are separating, divorcing, or contesting child custody, one parent will claim another has done something like touched a child inappropriately while the child was bathing. Reports like this are sometimes made to try to gain some advantage over the other parent in a custody battle and could be completely fabricated.

SUBSTANTIATED CASES OF CHILD SEXUAL ABUSE, UNITED STATES, 2016*

Sexual Abuse: 8.5% of all substantiated cases

*U.S. Department of Health & Human Services, Administration for Children and Families, Administration on Children, Youth and Families, Children's Bureau. (2018). Child maltreatment 2016. Table 3–8.

Emotional Abuse

Michael Lombardo's Story

Michael is a soft-spoken 15-year-old boy with red hair. He enjoys reading and poetry and aspires to be a performer in the theater. He's had a hard time dealing with the loss of his mother, as she was his closest friend. She was patient and kind, his confidant and his biggest supporter. Michael has been working with a therapist from the community mental health center to process his grief since her death.

Michael's father is active-duty military, and it seems like he is often away from home—always deployed somewhere else. Michael's experience as a military brat has made it difficult for him to feel like he fits in, as his family moves often and it's hard for him to make long-term friends. He feels alienated from his father, and indeed, he is much different than his father, Bruce. Bruce fits the image of the "gung-ho" stereotypical military service member. He lifts weights, has tattoos, and is supremely self-confident. His buddies call him "Alpha dog," as he often makes decisions for the group. They like to spend the weekends drinking beer and watching football.

Due to feeling depressed, Michael began outpatient counseling. At a recent meeting with his therapist, Michael was abnormally uncommunicative. The therapist probed gently about what might be behind his silence. Michael eventually opened up and revealed the source of his current issues.

Michael said that his father repeatedly humiliates him in public, calling him a "sissy" and telling him that he had better "toughen up." Michael pulled out his cell phone and told his therapist to "look at this." He pulled up Bruce's Facebook account, where Bruce was soliciting women to take his son out on a date and stating that "no son of mine will be gay."

Michael revealed that he often cries at night, in his room, after incidents when Bruce's intimidation and psychological bullying seem too much to handle. Michael's self-esteem is very low. And although he wouldn't admit to having thoughts about taking his life, Michael's therapist is very concerned about that possibility. They discuss a no-suicide contract, where Michael promises to contact her or call 911 if he ever feels like hurting himself. With multiple guns in his home, she knows that he always has access to the means to end his life. She also lets him know that she is a mandatory reporter and that she is going to file a report for the local child protective service agency to investigate the potential emotional abuse in Michael's home.

Definition of Emotional Abuse

Emotional abuse can go by different names. It can be called psychological abuse, psychological maltreatment, emotional maltreatment, even mental cruelty. Generally, it is considered to consist of behavior such as name-calling, disrespect, threats, screaming, yelling, shouting, saying hurtful things, humiliating, and denigrating. These behaviors wound or damage the other person by attacking his or her self-esteem or security—although the abuser may not realize how much the barbed comments hurt.

Emotional abuse almost never is a single act. When we are angry, we can say things that we regret later. Sometimes we say things that we intend to be humorous that unintentionally hurt the other person. A sincere apology can often neutralize any harm resulting from our angry words or poor attempts at humor. However, emotional abuse is generally frequent, part of a pattern, or creates an unfriendly or hostile environment that is painful for the person targeted. Imagine a 12-year-old girl, Fatima, who is a bit overweight. Her grandmother begins calling her "Fatty" or "Fatty Fatima." What if at a birthday party the grandmother gave all the other children a large piece of cake and mound of ice cream but Fatima received a small dish of yogurt? What if she bought her granddaughter a beautiful outfit but a size too small? What if when Fatima offered to help with the dishes, her grandmother made her wash them all over again a second time but never required that of the other children?

Emotional abuse makes children feel chronically unloved or unwanted, worthless, or flawed. This can happen when the biological mother or father take new partners or remarry and the stepparent doesn't like or doesn't want the targeted child living in the home—possibly because it reminds him or her of the other biological parent and that relationship. While we might not want to believe that some parents would elevate and favor their children over other children in a marriage or relationship, it does happen. Just think about the fairy tale "Cinderella."

However, a single act or threat of a very hurtful act could also be enough to constitute emotional abuse. Imagine if Fatima's grandmother threatened to give Fatima's puppy, Roxy, poisoned meat if she didn't lose 10 pounds by Christmas. This is called terrorizing and is one of the types of emotional abuse listed below. Note that the specificity in these nine categories is much greater than the more succinct coverage earlier of emotional neglect.

Types of Emotional/Psychological Abuse (Behaviors)[1]

1. **Spurning:** Belittling, insulting, degrading, shaming, or ridiculing a child; singling out a child to criticize or punish; humiliating a child in public. Calling a child stupid, loser, crazy or other hurtful names.

2. **Terrorizing:** Committing life-threatening acts (e.g., killing a child's cat); making a child feel unsafe; setting unrealistic expectations with threats of loss, harm, or danger if they are not met; threatening violence against a child or child's loved ones or objects.

3. **Exploiting or corrupting:** Encouraging a child to develop inappropriate behaviors (like begging, serving as a courier for drug sales, involvement in adult activities like smoking, drinking).

4. **Denying emotional responsiveness:** Ignoring a child; refusing to talk to the child for long periods (e.g., for punishment); failing to express affection or caring for a child. No or little sensitivity to the child's needs.

5. **Rejecting:** Verbally making statements like, "I don't want you here," "Why don't you go live with your friends?" Allowing the child to get lost in a large department store and not looking for him or her. Locking the child out of the house for hours at a time. (However, this also constitutes neglect if the child is left out overnight or longer, because the child is not being protected by the shelter of the home and the adult.)

6. **Isolating:** Confining; placing unreasonable limitations on freedom of movement or social interactions, such as not allowing the child to go outside to play with other children; locking the child in his or her room for long stretches of time.

7. **Unreliable or inconsistent parenting:** When caretakers or parents are overly cruel or punitive in their punishments on occasions and not punitive on other occasions so that the child never knows what to expect from the parent. Sometimes there are loud emotional discharges, as when the adult has a volatile temper.

8. **Neglecting mental health, medical, or educational needs:** Ignoring, preventing, or failing to provide treatments or services the child needs. For example, not taking a child to a physician when the child has a high fever or other serious symptoms; keeping a child out of school for extended lengths of time as a punishment.

9. **Witnessing domestic violence:** Generally, this is against other family members; however, the individual can threaten to hurt the child also (Kairys, Johnson, & Committee on Child Abuse & Neglect, 2002).

The difficulty in recognizing emotional abuse is that the context is all important. For instance, a mother might say to a child who is misbehaving, "If you don't behave, I'm going to eat you alive." If the child goes right on with the behavior and the mother smiles as she then attempts to distract her child from whatever he or she was doing, then the child likely felt no fear and probably was not terrorized by the mother. If, on the other hand, the child has been severely bit on several occasions by the mother and immediately stops in his tracks or begins crying, then the child possibly was terrorized. To continue this a bit further, a mother or father could jokingly call a child "a little brat" if the two were playing a game and the child successfully outplayed or outmaneuvered the adult. This is different from calling a child "a little brat" several times a day or using that appellation instead of the child's name.

---

1. Adapted from Steven W. Kairys, Charles F. Johnson, and Committee on Child Abuse and Neglect, "The Psychological Maltreatment of Children—Technical Report," Pediatrics, vol. 109, no. 4. Copyright © 2002 by American Academy of Pediatrics.

Recognizing Signs and Symptoms of Emotional Abuse

Crosson-Tower (2014) has written:

Children who are emotionally maltreated by a parent or even siblings suffer feelings of being inadequate, isolated, unwanted, or unloved. Their self-esteem is low, and they consider themselves unworthy. ... Children respond to such messages in one of two ways: They fight back, becoming hostile, aggressive, and exhibit behavior problems, or they turn their anger inward, becoming self-destructive, depressed, withdrawn, or suicidal. (p. 200)

Children who are not yet verbal can still show signs of emotional abuse in their general affect. Here are some signs of emotional abuse that can be found in young children:

0 to 20 months old

- Passive, withdrawn, developmental delays cognitively and verbally

20 to 30 months old

- Negativity in play, lack of interest in social interactions with other children, socially avoidant of adults, deficits in memory (possible)

Children 3 to 4 years

- Delays in language development; difficulty in emotion discrimination; destroys toys or shows more anger than other children, negativity in play

Children 4 to 5 years

- Few interactions with other children, more aggressive and disruptive behaviors, possible delays in complex language skills, helpless outlook, difficulty discriminating emotions

Children 5 to 6 years

- Low self-esteem, insecure-avoidant attachment, poor peer relationships, angry, oppositional

Older children

- Few friends, peer rejection
- Low self-esteem
- Conduct problems
- Depression
- Substance use
- Suicide attempts

Other indicators children may have:

- Daytime anxiety and unrealistic fears
- Irrational and persistent fears, dreads, hatreds
- Sleep problems, insomnia
- Behavioral extremes
- Biting, rocking, head-banging, or thumb sucking in an older child (Kansas Department for Children and Families, n.d.; Naughton et al., 2013)

SUBSTANTIATED CASES OF EMOTIONAL ABUSE, UNITED STATES, 2016*

Emotional/Psychological Abuse: 5.6% of all substantiated reports

*U.S. Department of Health & Human Services, Administration for Children and Families, Administration on Children, Youth and Families, Children's Bureau. (2018). Child maltreatment 2016. Table 3–8.

Profile of Child Abuse and Neglect Cases, Federal Fiscal Year 2016

From the statistics already presented in this chapter, you have probably figured out that each state is required by CAPTA to report information annually to the National Child Abuse and Neglect Data System (NCANDS). This data then emerges sometime later as a report, which is available to the general public, researchers, planners, agencies, students, and so forth. At the time of this writing, the FFY 2016 was the most recent report available, but you may wish to look a more recent *Child Maltreatment* report. While we don't have the space to provide the detail here, one reason you might want to inspect these reports is because specific information is provided on each state.

Here is some summary data that provides a national view of the child abuse and neglect problem in the United States in FFY 2016 (October 1, 2015, to September 30, 2016). Further details can be found here: https://www.acf.hhs.gov/sites/default/files/cb/cm2016.pdf.

- Nationally, there were 4.1 million referrals on 7.4 million children alleging child abuse or neglect.
- Fifty-eight percent of the referrals were screened in and 42% were screened out.
- Professionals were responsible for triggering 65% of referrals, about 19% of these were educational personnel.
- Nonprofessionals (friends, neighbors, relatives) were responsible for 18% of referrals and another 18% came from "other" (e.g., anonymous, etc.).
- The percentages shown for each type of abuse or neglect sum to more than 100% because when there was a report of both neglect and abuse of a child, each got counted. However, if there were three different types of neglect, these only were counted in the neglect column once.
- The number of child fatalities from abuse or neglect are 2.36 per 100,000 children, or approximately 1,750 per year. Boys have a higher fatality rate than girls. The African American child fatality rates are twice as high as the rate of White children and three times higher than the rate of Hispanic children.
- Statistics are available by the age of the child. Children in their first year of life have the highest rate of victimization.
- American Indian or Alaska Native children have the highest rate of victimization, followed by African American children.
- For those cases that were not substantiated child abuse or neglect, the reasons could include not enough information to find the child, another agency was more appropriate, the child was older than 18, the child was already the responsibility of another agency, or no child abuse/neglect was assessed.
- *Polyvictimization* is a term used when the child has two or more types of maltreatment. In FFY 16, 86% of children were assessed as having a single type of maltreatment, and 14% had either more two or more different types of maltreatment or multiple reports. (However, it is certainly easier for a child protective services professional to identify physical abuse when it occurs and potentially more difficult to identify emotional abuse. It is assumed that there is much more polyvictimization than the records actually reflect. More on this topic in Chapter 4.)

You might also wonder who else besides teachers and school personnel most often reports suspicions of child maltreatment to the child protection professionals. Would it be medical personnel? Day care providers? You'll find your answers in Figure 2.1 below.

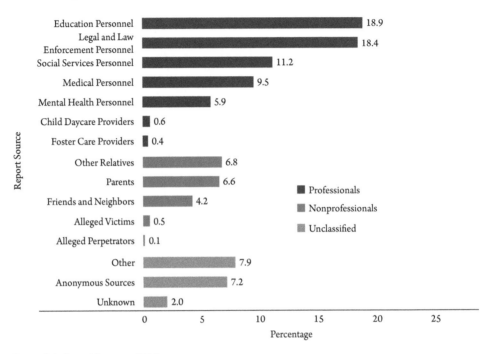

Figure 2.1 Report Sources, 2016
Professionals submitted the majority of screened-in referrals (reports) that received an investigation or alternative response.
Data are from the Child File. Based on data from 49 states. States were excluded from this analysis if more than 25% had an unknown report source. Numbers total to more than 100% due to rounding. Supporting data not shown.
Source: U.S. Department of Health & Human Services, Administration for Children and Families, Administration on Children, Youth and Families, Children's Bureau. (2018). Child maltreatment 2016. Retrieved from https://www.acf.hhs.gov/cb/research-data-technology/statistics-research/child-maltreatment

A Final Note

Here is an excerpt from a survivor's account of horrendous physical, emotional, and sexual abuse. While this chapter, for pedagogical reasons, discusses different types of abuse separately, child protection professionals will sometimes discover several forms of abuse or neglect occurring in the same severely dysfunctional family, as in the case below. This is a portion of "Anne's" story:

Anne's Story

There was a lot of screaming at the kids and physical abuse in our house. The six of us kids were slapped and whipped constantly—sometimes with a belt. Because of all the marks and bruises on us, our father was always worried that an accidental injury, if we fell or broke a leg somehow, would persuade the child protection authorities that we were abused. I'm convinced he wouldn't let us climb the trees around our house for that reason. ... Sometimes when he was unhappy with several of us kids he would grab two or three of us by our hair and pull us to where he would punish us.

Once he took me to his workshop in the basement, tightened my hand in a vice, and then slammed my thumb with a hammer ... he threatened to cut my toes off. I think he was afraid that I wouldn't wear my shoes outside and might step on a nail or something that would require a trip to the doctor. He really feared a doctor looking at us.

When I was very young, I was taken to the pediatrician because there was some foreign object in my vagina. The doctor thought that I had placed it there. He laughed and said that children sometimes do things like that. I don't remember what it was, but I have this feeling that maybe I didn't place it there.

When I was a little older, my father would drive me out to a secluded area and sexually abuse me in the car. Later he dispensed with all of that and would come into my room at night or catch me in the shower. The locks on our doors were such that he could open them from the outside even if they were locked.

To keep me from talking to anyone, he told me that he would be taken away and that I would be put in an orphanage where there were rats and no Christmas. He said that the family would have hard times because "mothers are too stupid to work." Mother didn't have good shoes to wear and I figured what he said was true—she couldn't get a job outside of the home.

I'm not certain that Mom knew what Dad was doing to me, but there are some things that I still don't understand. For example, one time I tried to tell my mother about some discomfort in my genital area and she said, "I guess you just didn't wash good enough." Why wouldn't she have taken more of an interest? Was she afraid what she might find?

I began drinking heavily in high school, and around my seventeenth birthday I was having blackouts and coming home drunk. I wasn't really punished for that. My parents didn't seem to notice. (Royse, 1994, pp. 51–52)

Main Points

This chapter introduces you to the four different types of child maltreatment commonly investigated by child protection professionals. Although each is different, you will likely find similarities in harm or damage they cause the child. Signs and symptoms are not always unique across these types. Whether physically, sexually, or emotionally abused or neglected, a child can develop low self-esteem, depression, and other manifestations. Keep in mind that the national statistics reported are summaries across the country. Individual localities or states may report a great deal more or less of one type of maltreatment that occurs nationally. The easiest types of maltreatment to confirm or substantiate will be neglect and physical abuse. You may find a few cases where there is only one type of abuse. However, it is not unusual in a dysfunctional home for there to be physical abuse, emotional abuse, and perhaps even neglect in terms of problems having sufficient food or shelter, etc.

- Neglect involves some type of inadequacy in a child's home, such as insufficient food/nutrition; inadequate hygiene, clothing, or shelter; or educational neglect when the child is not sent to school.
- Emotional neglect can also be called psychological abuse and psychological maltreatment, and although it may not leave marks or bruises on the skin, it does mental injury with actions that terrorize or emotionally reject, spurn, and isolate and with words that insult, denigrate, and so forth. Being witness to domestic violence in the home should also be thought of as psychological abuse.
- Signs and symptoms for each type of child maltreatment are listed to help in identifying children who have been abused or neglected.

- Physical abuse is always nonaccidental injury, although parents/caretakers may attempt to explain a child's injury as an accident. Be particularly alert when the details of stories (e.g., the child's version and the adult's version) don't match or when the adult changes the explanation.
- The TEN-4 rule suggests that professionals need to be suspicious of possible abuse when a child younger than 4 has injuries to the torso, ear, or neck and when any child younger than 4 months has bruising.
- Sexual abuse of children may involve a slow progression with stages of engagement, playing "games," and attempts by the adult to create a "special friend" relationship.
- Sexual abuse of children can include their exploitation, such as making videos of them naked or having them watch pornography with an adult. It does not have to involve sexual touching or penetration.

Questions for Class Discussion

1. What forms of abuse or neglect do you identify in Anne's story? Is there polyvictimization? Did other professionals in the community miss an opportunity to suspect problems with Anne or her siblings? Why do you think Anne was afraid ask for help while she was still living at home?

2. Let's say you are doing a home investigation and you find each situation below (but not all of them). How might you determine if the situation raises a level of concern to constitute child neglect? (a) The child is drinking a soft drink from a baby bottle. (b) In a pile beside the refrigerator, there is a small mountain of beer cans. (c) You see no picture books or toys for a 4-year-old child in the home. (d) A 4-year-old pulls his shoes off and runs out the back door into the weedy yard, where five or six dogs run up to greet him. (e) The family has been burning candles and cooking on a camp stove because they don't have the money to pay their overdue electricity bill. (f) A 25-month-old boy pulls his underwear off and runs through the house naked when company is visiting.

3. Opinion question: Is one form of abuse or neglect worse than another? Give a reason why you think so.

4. Opinion question: What type of emotional abuse do you think is the worst? Give a reason why you think so.

5. Janet went through elementary school, middle school, and through her junior year in high school without ever having a male friend or a date. While a senior, she met a foreign exchange student at a bowling alley, and after a few dates, he professed that he wanted to marry her. But what worried her was that while he said he wanted her for a wife, he also told her that she was the ugliest woman he had ever met. Janet is feeling ambivalent about what she should do. Discuss whether you think her boyfriend is emotionally abusive.

Self-Assessment for Personal Consideration

1. How confident do you feel in recognizing emotional abuse?

       1   2   3   4   5   6   7   8   9   10

   Not confident   *Very confident*

2. How confident do you feel in recognizing the symptoms a neglected child might show?

       1   2   3   4   5   6   7   8   9   10

   Not confident   *Very confident*

3. How comfortable would you be to talk with a child to talk about visible bruises?

       1   2   3   4   5   6   7   8   9   10

   Not comfortable   *Very comfortable*

Additional Resources

Calcaterra, R. (2013). *Etched in sand: A true story of five siblings who survived an unspeakable childhood on Long Island*. New York, NY: Morrow.

Rhodes-Courter, A. (2009). *Three little words: A memoir*. New York, NY: Atheneum.

References

Adams, J. A., Farst, K. J., & Kellogg, N. D. (2018). Interpretation of medical findings in suspected child sexual abuse: An update for 2018. *Journal of Pediatric and Adolescent Gynecology, 31*(3), 225–231.

Child Welfare Information Gateway. (n.d.). Definition of child abuse and neglect in federal law. Retrieved from https://www.child-welfare.gov/topics/can/defining/federal

Crosson-Tower, C. (2014). *Understanding child abuse and neglect*. Boston, MA: Pearson.

Kairys, S. W., Johnson, C. F., & Committee on Child Abuse & Neglect. (2002). The psychological maltreatment of children—technical report. *Pediatrics, 109*(4), e68.

Kansas Department for Children and Families. (n.d.). A guide to reporting child abuse and neglect. Retrieved from www.dcf.ks.gov/services/PPS/Documents/GuidetoreportingAbuseandNeglect.pdf

Kodner, C., & Wetherton, A. (2013). Diagnosis and management of physical abuse in children. *American Family Physician, 88*(10), 669–675.

Naughton, A. M., Maguire, S. A., Mann, M. K., Tempest, V., Gracias, S., & Kemp, A. M. (2013). Emotional, behavioral, and developmental features indicative of neglect or emotional abuse in preschool children: A systematic review. *JAMA Pediatrics, 167*(8), 769–775.

Royse, D. (1994). *How do I know its abuse? Identifying and countering emotional mistreatment from friends and family members*. Springfield, IL: Thomas.

Royse, D. (2016). *Emotional abuse of children: Essential information*. New York, NY: Routledge.

Sgroi, S. M., Blick, L. C. & Porter, F. S. (1982). A conceptual framework for child sexual abuse. In S. M. Sgroi (Ed.), *Handbook of clinical intervention in child sexual abuse* (pp. 9–37). New York, NY: Free Press.

Von Hohendorff, J., Habigzang, L. F., & Koller, S. H. (2017). "A boy, being a victim, nobody really buys that, you know?" Dynamics of sexual violence against boys. *Child Abuse & Neglect, 70,* 53–64.

Young, A., Pierce, M. C., Kaczor, K., Lorenz, D. J., Hickey, S., Berger, S. P., & Thompson, R. (2018). Are negative/unrealistic parent descriptors of infant attributes associated with physical abuse? *Child Abuse & Neglect, 80,* 41–51.

Figure Credit

Fig. 2.1: Source: https://www.acf.hhs.gov/sites/default/files/cb/cm2016.pdf.

CHAPTER 3

EXAMINING THE CAUSES OF CHILD MALTREATMENT

OVERVIEW

This chapter will summarize some of the main theories or explanations associated with child neglect, physical abuse, sexual abuse and emotional abuse/neglect. But don't think that it will be as simple as finding a single explanation—like substance abuse. While the use of drugs or alcohol may be an important contributor to the case you are assigned to investigate as a child protective services worker, it may only be a symptom of another problem or set of problems.

In brief, although each of the major types of child maltreatment can share some of the same factors or contributors, the explanations will be a little different. Do not look for one explanation to fit every case or every form of child maltreatment. Instead, adopt the role of a detective—what are the clues that best form an explanation for the abusive situation? As you read this chapter, you will learn not only about the factors most often involved but also how they may be combined with other circumstances. Sadly, there will still be cases where it is easy to describe the abuse that occurred but difficult to explain the "why" of the parents' behavior or their internal thought processes.

Neglect

Even though neglect is the most common form of child maltreatment, it can be difficult to establish conclusively that the caretaker or parent was neglectful. That is because neglect is generally not a single act or omission like forgetting to feed a child or provide clean clothes to wear to school on the one day when you overslept. Rather, neglect is usually considered to constitute a lack of caring behavior over time—a characteristic pattern of unconcern or lack of responsiveness to the child's needs. Another way of saying this is that neglect "occurs on a continuum without clear cut points to aid diagnosis" (Dubowitz, 2014, p. 444). What if the parents appear "neglectful" but simply don't make the same decision that you might make regarding your own children?

For instance, Vota (2017) has described a case where two children were dropped off at a local park to play at 4:00 p.m. on a Sunday afternoon and were instructed to leave the park at 6:00 p.m. for the 1 mile walk back to their home. Their ages were 10 and 6. When they didn't arrive home at 6:30 p.m., the parents began searching for them and eventually called the police. The police had picked up the children an hour into their play at the park and had them in protective custody. It was the first time the police had detained the children, but they had been intercepted once before on their walk home. The case occurred in Maryland, and in that state leaving anyone under the age of 18 unsupervised constitutes child neglect.

At this point, we are hungry for more details. Many questions come to mind: Did the children have to walk home through a dangerous neighborhood? Had other children in the neighborhood been abducted or threatened? Was the 10-year-old mature for her age? Did she have a cell phone she could have used if frightened? Finally, were the parents just plain irresponsible, or were they teaching their children to be independent and self-reliant? We would like to know what the parents were thinking.

This real case, and others like it—often of a parent leaving a child in a car to run into a grocery store or post office—will not, however, constitute the bulk of the neglect cases you may encounter as a child protective services professional. The majority of the cases you will encounter involve parents who likely have some sort of impairment or who have very challenging lives—often as a parent or parents living below the poverty line. As a rule of thumb, you usually won't have to guess or have an intellectual discussion about the merits of children walking home from a park. Even though lack of parental supervision is a category or subtype of neglect, generally the cases you will receive will be much more serious: a toddler walking down a busy highway or children playing with fire or firearms—incidents that suggest a serious abrogation of parental responsibility.

Sometimes a single parent has to make choices about working to provide for the children and leaving them unsupervised for a while (e.g., leaving them alone after school). This situation may never become an issue unless one of the children becomes hurt or harmed during the time when there was no parental supervision. As Hornor (2014) notes, "Poverty can affect the ability of the parents to provide adequate supervision" (p. 187).

WHAT IS A META-ANALYSIS? WHY IS IT USED?

A **meta-analysis** is an innovative kind of study that examines the results of multiple studies on the same topic in order to come to a conclusion about an intervention or phenomenon. It is not uncommon for studies to have flaws or limitations, and meta-analyses usually involve only the strongest studies to resolve uncertainty—for instance, when five studies find an intervention effective but three others find it ineffective. Meta-analyses use statistical procedures to understand the strength of the findings in the studies being appraised and to allow comparison.

In a meta-analysis of risk factors for child neglect that reviewed 36 studies, the authors found that there were multiple risk factors, and the most powerful predictors of child neglect were associated with parental characteristics. Among the strongest risk factors were "a history of antisocial/criminal offending, a history of mental/psychiatric problems, and low educational achievement" (Mulder, Kuiper, Van der Put, Stams, & Assink, 2018, p. 205). The authors also found evidence of intergenerational transmission of child neglect. Even though the effect was statistically small, the authors stated that "children raised by parents who experienced abuse and/ or neglect in their own childhood are at risk of being a victim of child neglect" (Mulder et al., 2018, p. 205).

In a separate study, some of the same colleagues as in the study above conducted another meta-analysis of 84 studies and found that parents who experienced maltreatment in their own childhood families were almost three times more likely to have child maltreatment in their current families, compared to those families without a history of child maltreatment (Assink et al., 2018).

In an earlier meta-analysis of 155 studies involving child physical abuse or neglect, Stith et al. (2009) found that the two strongest risk factors for neglect were parent–child relationships and parental perception of the child as a problem. Other risk factors included the parent's level of stress, parent anger/hyperreactivity, and parent self-esteem. Parent unemployment and family size were both moderately associated with neglect (but at a lower level with child physical abuse). The authors point out that while some studies have examined whether a child's behavior might contribute to child maltreatment, this study found that a parent's perceptions of a child's behavior were more strongly associated with maltreatment than "other indicators of child behavior" (Stith et al., 2009, p. 25).

Impaired Problem Solving

Certain medical and psychological conditions make it very difficult for parents and caretakers to be able to solve problems (e.g., a child crying from hunger or needing to be held), deal with hazards (e.g., a toddler playing with a screwdriver near an electrical outlet), and respond effectively to everyday life events (e.g., managing disagreements with children over appropriate bedtimes and completing homework). Azar, McGuier, Miller, Hernandez-Mekonnen, and Johnson (2017) describe the **executive functioning of cognitive skills** this way: "parents' ability to identify problems, generate and prioritize solutions, enact responses, and evaluate outcomes … skills are needed to be vigilant and respond to changing environmental cues … and be sensitive and flexible in response to child behaviors" (p. 10). Obviously, conditions that impair a caretaker's executive functioning would concern child protection authorities.

Examples of medical diagnoses that impair executive functioning include but are not limited to schizophrenia, bipolar disorder, depression, substance abuse, dementia, Alzheimer's disease, and so on. Individuals with these conditions may find it difficult to maintain employment, manage their money, administer medications properly, and feed and care for children who need assistance, provide adequate clothing, shelter, and so forth. These adults may have few and/or strained relationships with other adults and show lower levels of maternal warmth and responsiveness to children, talk with them less, and provide less cognitive stimulation. There often will be problems with or interruptions with their ability to provide adequate supervision of their children (Azar et al., 2017).

Parental substance abuse is almost always going to result in neglectful conditions because it affects every dimension of home life and interpersonal relationships. These parents place their own need for substances ahead of concerns about their child's or children's needs.

Extreme stress can also affect an individual's or a family's ability to carry out all of their responsibilities satisfactorily. What are causes of debilitating stress?

- Living in dangerous homes or neighborhoods (especially where street violence and neglect of children are common).
- Domestic violence and marital problems. In homes with domestic violence, the caregiver may be "abused to the point of being unable or unwilling to keep their abusers from also abusing the children. … In some cases, abused caregivers are afraid to defend the children because doing so might put the caregiver's or children's lives in danger or provoke more violence." Neglect in this type of situation

may be referred to as "failure or inability to protect the child from harm" (DePanfilis, 2006, p. 34). Also, see Joyce's 2016 article, "High-Conflict Divorce: A Form of Child Neglect," which explains that emotional neglect can occur when parents' anger, blame, inability to cooperate, and allegations of each other's maltreatment result in sabotaging parent–child relationships.

- Inadequate funds to pay for rent, utilities, food, medicines, etc.
- Single parent and/or caregiver burden (young children, family member with chronic illness or disability).
- Isolation from family support, friends, or community agencies.
- Engaging in criminal activities or living with someone involved in these activities.
- Life transitions (recovering from a serious accident or illness, loss of a job, death of a loved one, arrest of a partner or spouse engaged in illegal activities, being evicted).
- Job pressures (e.g., overbearing, controlling supervisors; production quota demands, etc.). Threat of losing one's job.
- Maltreatment in the caregiver's childhood coupled with any of the stresses indicated above (DePanfilis, 2006).

Families that concern child protection workers are those who know help is available but who are unwilling or refuse to access it. Individuals who have grown up in chaotic, dysfunctional homes may be less attentive to their children and have unrealistic expectations of them. It is possible that some of these individuals, having grown up in neglectful homes themselves, simply do not recognize that their own behavior or lack of action is neglectful. They may also have hostility toward their children and resent the expense and care required of a newborn or older children—especially those who may have special needs.

Keep in mind that any one stress or set of stresses or presence of risk factors does not imply that children in a family will be neglected. Healthy families can survive even when there are major stresses when the caregivers recognize and reach out for help or resources in order to provide for their children's needs. Being raised in an abusive or neglectful family does not mean that a new parent will abuse his or her children—the majority don't.

It is also important to keep in mind that although physical neglect may be very apparent when a child is dirty or smelly, dressed in unkempt or bedraggled clothes, underweight or hungry, or in need of medical attention (and these will be easy to identify), emotional neglect can also damage a child's self-esteem and have lasting effects into adulthood. This can be seen in the two cases below of adults reflecting back on their childhoods.

Marsha's Story

My father could not tolerate my disagreeing with his point of view. He always had to be the authority. We could just be talking and if I said something that he couldn't agree with, his face would turn red and he would shout, "You're crazy!" and glare at me until I would apologize. Then, he would return to his newspaper as if we had not been talking at all. He made me think I was crazy, and I began to doubt my honest feelings—never knowing when I had a right to question something I didn't like. I thought there was something wrong with my mind—it seemed to explain why he was so unhappy with me.

My mother had her own ways of putting me down and making me feel useless. She kept comparing me to herself. She liked to show me that I couldn't do things as fast or well as she could. She said she'd always done better than me when she was my age. She made me feel about as valuable as a dirty handkerchief. Anything I did, like vacuuming the carpet, she had to do over again. It seemed like she went out of her way to avoid giving me compliments.

(Royse, 1994, p. 11)

Ron's Story

My parents paid very little attention to me—where I went, who my friends were, or what we did. When I was 13, I had my first sexual experience with a man. He was 29. We dated off and on for several months. When I was 15, I began to date a 25-year-old man named Darren. He introduced me to a world of drugs, alcohol, and sado-masochism. Sex had no boundaries; I was taken to parties where young people (mainly boys 13 to 18) were passed around like peace pipes.

I would start drinking vodka as soon as I woke up in the morning and would take it to school with me. I would drink between classes and during lunch. After school, I would drink until it was time to find a party.

(Royse, 1994, p. 21)

The causes of the emotional neglect that both Marsha and Ron felt are challenging to diagnose. Marsha's mother was a college graduate; Ron's father was a physician. Seeing them simply as unskilled parents doesn't seem accurate enough. What both Marsha and Ron felt was a lack of emotional warmth and caring. Although Marsha grew up with both of her biological parents, perhaps Ron had a stepmother to whom he was not attached, but that does not explain why they would not have noticed the extent of his drinking, and they should have been very concerned with his dating much older guys. It is possible that one or both of his parents had drinking problems—that might explain how he had such easy access to alcohol. Perhaps both Marsha and Ron were unwanted children? As you work in child protective services, you may also come across cases where there is no easy explanation as to why the child or children are emotionally neglected or maltreated.

TEST YOURSELF

In the segment above on neglect, what were some of the examples of debilitating stress? Do not read below the dotted line until you are ready to see the answer.

Examples included: caregiver burden (chronic illness or disability), inadequate funds for the necessities of life, domestic violence, life transitions, and living in dangerous neighborhoods or homes.

Physical Abuse

Bob's Story

(A 75-year-old minister speaking about his childhood)

My stepfather was a physically and powerfully built man. One of my earliest memories involves his trying to teach me how to tie my shoes. We sat on the couch, and he showed me how he would tie a shoe. Then it was my turn. I didn't get it right and whoomp! He whacked me beside the head. He demonstrated the correct way to tie a shoe again, and when I couldn't reproduce the twin bows, whoomp! He knocked me in the head a second time. This went on each time until I finally learned the technique. I wasn't allowed to leave the couch, I couldn't run to my mother. She also didn't interfere. Each failure made my head rattle.

Although it doesn't come out in the short version of Bob's story, he went on to describe his stepfather being the son of immigrants to this country who spoke no English, a man who dropped out of school early, who sometimes struggled to find the right words for what he wanted to communicate. It is possible that some physical abuse stems from frustration with one's own abilities or with a child—and that this could trigger what others would call physical abuse. If this was the way that Bob's stepfather was raised by his father, social learning theory would suggest that this model of parenting could influence the stepfather's interactions with a child. In some families, harsh punishment, corporal punishment, and physical abuse are viewed as "normal" or as usually acceptable. These ways have been used in the family for generations; although unfortunate, they are familiar ways of "guiding" children who stray from adult expectations. Although corporal or physical punishment can be injurious to the child, such behaviors do not usually trigger phone calls to the child protection authorities by family members. In fact, most of us have heard the expression "Spare the rod and spoil the child," which is often connected with a biblical passage in Proverbs 13:24. The adage, based on the Bible verse, suggests that to help the child grow up to be a respected adult, caretakers shouldn't fear using physical discipline when the child misbehaves. This way of thinking may exist in some cultures and among some religious groups; however, physical punishment of children (whipping, etc.) is becoming tolerated much, much less in the Western nations of the world.

Too much stress such as illness of other family members, broken relationships (marital separation or divorce, widowhood), loss of employment, or being evicted can make people short-tempered. And in times like this, a child could be slapped, pushed, or shoved and receive a serious injury. While that would be unfortunate, the child protective services worker normally is going to look for *a pattern* of behavior or several past interactions that were too harsh or too punitive for the child.

Dr. Joel S. Milner is a giant in the field of assessing physical child maltreatment. The creator of the Child Abuse Potential Inventory (CAPI), a widely recognized measure for screening physical child abuse risk, he is a prolific researcher and author. Hundreds of studies have cited his articles on the CAPI, and it has been used extensively with U.S. Air Force personnel. There is research to support the following factors or contributors often associated with elevated child abuse scores on the CAPI or on other similar empirically validated instruments (Milner, 1994):

- Being a victim of abuse and observing abuse are related to high CAPI scores.
- Social isolation and lack of social support are related to high CAPI scores.
- Marital discord, lower levels of marital satisfaction, and family conflict are related to high CAPI scores.
- Adults who are more physiologically reactive (elevated heart rate, etc.) to child-related stimuli (e.g., crying children) and even non-child-related stimuli have elevated CAPI scores.
- Physical child abusers tend to have low levels of self-esteem and ego strength, and these are related to high scores on the CAPI.
- Parent-related and child-related stress are associated with higher scores on the CAPI.
- Physical child abusers and persons with high CAPI scores view children as exhibiting more problem behaviors. Further, they are less likely to consider mitigating factors.
- Parents with depression, anxiety, and anger (negative affect) have higher physical child abuse scores.

While the reader might desire a single-factor explanation for physical child abuse, that is not possible in most cases. Rather, a combination of factors seem to be involved. There can be environmental problems or stresses on the adult or family, but that explanation alone is not sufficient—most of the caregivers in similar situations do not abuse their children. Considering the family of origin history of the caregiver(s) provides another ingredient. When there was violence in their own families, caregivers may be affected by low self-esteem and depression, and as a result they may have fewer social contacts or a weaker social-support system. Having a relatively low self-esteem may lead individuals not only to experience rejection by peers but also to anticipate or expect rejection from their own children. The way these parents and caregivers *think* and *react* to children may add a final piece to the puzzle.

Milner's Social Information Processing Model

Milner (1993) has proposed a social information processing (SIP) model that involves cognitive perceptions and interpretations of a child's behavior. He argues that "physical child abusers, compared to nonabusers, engage in more automatic processing of child-related data in ambiguous and stressful situations" (Milner, 1993, p. 278). In other words, abusers and caregivers at risk of child physical abuse seem to process information in ways that increase the risk of aggression being directed at the child. In situations where the adult has high stress and a child misbehaves, makes a mess, or disappoints, the adult does not use control and reasoning but responds almost automatically and without awareness in a way that could be hurtful or abusive. Here are the stages that seem to set up a pattern of potentially abusive responses toward a child.

Stage 1: Perceiving What Is Occurring

Compared to other parents, parents who are physically abusive are not as aware of or attentive to their children. Thus, these parents may have problems with perception; for example, not perceiving differences in infant cues or appreciating the complexity of their children's needs or behaviors—being unable to recognize their children's emotional expressions. Under high stress, the caregivers may have less ability to distinguish between positive and negative behaviors—possibly because the child is viewed in a negative rather than a positive light.

Stage 2: Inappropriate/Inaccurate Expectations

The research supporting this stage suggests that mothers at high risk for physical abuse expect less compliance following discipline for a serious misbehavior and higher expectations that they would be able to address common and less problematic child behavior. Low-risk mothers had completely opposite expectations. For the high-risk parents, a child repeating a common misbehavior may confirm a discipline failure that the child is intentionally being annoying, defiant, or oppositional and "justify the use of power assertion techniques" (Milner, 1993, p. 284).

In this SIP model, abusive parents can expect or interpret even the minor transgressions of a child as having a hostile intent and being more wrong than nonabusive parents view it. One might say potentially abusive parents are biased against viewing children's behavior as normal or as the result of an innocent mistake or accident.

Stage 3: Information Integration and Response

This stage allows for the consideration of mitigating factors. In Milner's example of little Johnny spilling his milk because his brother bumped him, the abusive parent doesn't seem to consider the mitigating factor of bump from brother because of biases or distortions held about child behavior. High-risk parents may not have the ability to integrate mitigating information. Also at work is that in considering how to respond to the incident, abusive parents seem to have fewer appropriate child management strategies to draw on. Some research suggests that abusive parents use punishment as a predominant strategy and are less flexible in their ability to find an appropriate discipline strategy. Abusive parents tend to have lower rates of interaction with their children, which may follow from less positive views of children.

Stage 4: Response Implementation and Monitoring

Abusive parents seem to differ in their skill set needed for effective, nonabusive parenting. This may be due to expected noncompliance, rigidity in what they consider effective correctional measures, or simply inability to draw on other solutions that are not physically abusive. They also are not successful in accurately monitoring the effects of the discipline they administer. The parent's own emotional state (anger, stress) may produce an automated response/type of discipline, which appears to be an inability to control their anger; they do not appear to be able to access a more controlled processing of the situation.

Parents who demonstrate clinically elevated levels of anger not only rated children's behavior and ambiguous behavior (where intent or mitigating factors are present) as more intentional and blameworthy, they engaged in more harsh or coercive parenting practices than parents without high levels of anger (Pidgeon & Sanders, 2012, as cited in Crouch et al., 2018). Ateah and Durrant (2005) found that mothers' anger was a significant predictor of physical discipline even after statistically controlling for the parent's belief in the value of corporal punishment and perceptions of the seriousness/intent of the child's behavior. According to Crouch et al. (2018), such findings "suggest that at-risk and abusive parents may have difficulty regulating their affective states" (p. 100). Indeed, in their study, Crouch and colleagues (2018) discovered that parents

> who reported less ability to regulate their thoughts, feelings, and behaviors when upset tended to obtain higher CPA [child physical abuse] risk scores. This finding is especially poignant when one considers the myriad of challenges faced by parents on a daily basis (e.g., whining, temper tantrums, noncompliance, competing demands), and the fact that such parenting challenges often evoke negative affect (e.g., frustration, irritation, anger). (p. 104)

Other research has linked the parents' negative experiences in their own early family environments with emotion regulation and executive functioning difficulties (Bridgett, Kanya, Rutherford, & Mayes, 2017). Executive functioning, a higher order cognitive process, includes the following skills: "strategic planning, flexibility of thought and action (switching), inhibition of inappropriate responses, generation of new responses (fluency) and concurrent remembering and processing executive-loaded working memory" (Henry, Messer, & Nash, 2012, as cited in Kirke-Smith, Henry, & Messer, 2016, p. 518). A recent article has found that perceptions of poor behavior in children were a strong predictor of physical child abuse risk. When a child was perceived as behaving poorly (stage 1), and the parent felt the situation was out of control and discipline deserved (stage 2), there was an increased risk for physical child abuse. Physical child abuse risk also increased the more the parent felt anger. Thus, it was not the child's behavior alone that increased the risk of physical abuse (Rodriguez, 2018).

These SIP stages do not provide a complete explanation for physical child abuse because other factors such as alcohol or drug use, mental illness, and so forth may also be involved, which can affect cognitive processing abilities and silence any internal prohibitions against hurting children.

TEST YOURSELF

Which of the statements below seem to be characteristic of parents who physically abuse their children? Do not read below the dotted line until you are ready to see the answer.

    a. *possess low self-esteem*
    b. *have been abused themselves as children*
    c. *not consider mitigating factors when evaluating a child's misbehavior*
    d. *all of the above*

- -

The prior segment on physical abuse describes each of these three statements as being characteristic of parents who physically abuse their children.

Sexual Abuse

The Offender

Men are much more likely to be reported for child sexual abuse (CSA) than women. In most societies around the world, women are socialized to be nurturers. Women may be more empathic in recognizing a child's pain, and children may have greater dependency needs on their mothers or mother figures than on males, which creates involvement and positive engagement with the child. So it is possible that there are fewer reports of female abusers because of their maternal roles.

However, McLeod and Craft (2015) have reported that research over the years suggests that 15% to 20% of the CSA cases reported nationally to child protective services involve women as the abusers. This contrasts with other research showing that only about 1% of incarcerated sexual offenders in this country are women (U.S. Department of Justice, 2007). Similarly, this percentage corresponds with a Canadian criminal rate of 1.67% reported by Weinsheimer, Woiwod, Coburn, Chong, and Connolly (2017).

The discrepancy in the handling of these CSA cases in criminal court appears to be due to mediation in the adjudication of these cases. McLeod & Craft (2015) found in their study that female offenders accessed substance abuse services at much higher rates than males and were more likely to receive counseling and mental health services, as well as case management and family preservation. Thus, authorities may be more "likely to view female sexual offending behavior more as a mental health issue, in contrast to male offending behavior which could be viewed more as a criminal one" (McLeod & Craft, 2015, p. 411).

Other factors can also come into play. Women also may be able to mask sexual activities with a child through normal contact such as bathing and dressing; further, boy victims might be less likely to report (Crosson-Tower, 2014). Women may not always be independent (sole) abusers as much as men are, but they can be co-offenders or accomplices with a man—especially when substance abuse is involved. There may be mental health issues in these situations as well.

WHAT IS A PEDOPHILE?

In the popular press and sometimes in legal proceedings, the term *pedophile* is applied to those who are sexually attracted to prepubescent children. However, Tenbergen et al. (2015) identified two studies that indicate only about half of those who sexually abuse children are pedophilic. Sometimes these individuals are referred to as being "fixated" (on children). The other half of child abusers appear to be individuals who usually have or look for an adult partner but who may take advantage of an opportunity for a "replacement partner" or "surrogate" at times (Tenbergen et al., 2015, p. 2). Some men who are sexually attracted to children appear to be able to restrict their desire for sexual contact with children to a fantasy life associated with viewing child pornography—which is aggressively prosecuted as a serious crime in this country.

To understand who commits CSA, we first start with a potential offender. Research indicates the offender is at risk for committing child abuse because of prior abuse (usually sexual abuse) in his or her childhood family of origin. Studies suggest a link back to the perpetrator's family of origin—especially where a strong relationship (attachment) between the child and the parent(s) or caregiver did not develop. Infants attach to their mothers when their needs are met and when there is emotional and physical closeness. Children have difficulty attaching (have insecure attachment) when the caregiver doesn't meet the child's needs (e.g., is neglectful) or doesn't do it in a way that is caring and that makes the child feel safe and secure. Sex offenders have described their parents "as being affectionless and controlling and presenting a host of problems such as substance abuse, psychiatric problems, delinquent behaviors, and a host of victimization" and a "high turnover of individuals in a parent/ caregiver role as well as the prolonged absence—if not abandonment—by at least one parent" (Martin & Tardif, 2014, p. 375.) Further, "Available findings suggest that sex offenders evolve in a family environment marked by dysfunction, deficiencies, and unfulfilling relationships, which likely offers little support for the development of adaptive intimacy dispositions" (Martin & Tardif, 2014, p. 376).

Children whose primary caregivers were attentive, caring, and trustworthy develop expectations that others in future relationships will respond similarly. However, children denied healthy emotional intimacy may have problems with emotional regulation, difficulties with intimate relationships, and distorted views of individuals. These individuals may not be able to recognize the feelings of others or to feel empathy toward their victims by correctly identifying what the child is feeling.

Both the secure and insecure types of attachment produce an internal working model (IWM) for children. The IWM has been described as a template for the child's future relationships in that IWMs "define the individual's self-image and shape his or her expectations of care and stability in future relationships" (Grady, Levenson, & Bolder, 2017, p. 434). Children with secure attachment have higher self-esteem and stable relationships as adults.

Individuals who experienced insecure attachment tend to have low self-esteem, poor interpersonal skills, and possibly increased vulnerability to sexual victimization in their youth by any adults who shower them with attention and special favors. Years later, as poorly socialized adults, the adults who were CSA victims may have an incapacity to have satisfactory relationships with adults and have sexual gratification needs met with partners of the same age. These problems may lead the adults to have fantasies about or actively consider having sexual activities with minors—especially when there is loneliness in their adult lives and great desire for a sexual relationship. The factor of blockage was suggested by Finkelhor (1984) for when men could not meet their sexual needs with adults and may follow, he hypothesized, from a lack of social competence and effective self-regulation resulting from insecure attachment.

Some researchers have explored what is called the sexually abused–sexual abuser hypothesis. This notion is that those who experienced sexual abuse as a child are likely to become perpetrators. And indeed, there does seem to be an association between these. Stirpe and Stermac (2003) report that 61% of CSA offenders claimed to have an experience of CSA themselves. Similarly, 55% of incarcerated CSA offenders reported having a childhood CSA experience in a different study (Smallbone & Wortley, 2001). Studies comparing adult sexual abuse (ASA) offenders to child sexual abusers reveal that once again the CSA offenders have reported they were more often victims of CSA than the ASA offenders. In a meta-analysis of studies comparing adult sex offenders against non-sex offenders on sexual abuse history, 16 of 17 studies reported greater odds of the sex offenders having experienced sexual abuse; however, they did not differ on history of physical abuse or emotional abuse or neglect. Further, 12 of 15 studies found that sex offenders against children had more CSA experiences in their youth than sex offenders against adults had. In 8 of 9 studies, the sex offenders against adults had more physical abuse in their backgrounds than the CSA offenders (Jespersen, Lalumiere, & Seto, 2009). Research has found a correlation between insecure attachment and sexual offending in adolescence and adulthood. Thus, childhood attachment patterns and childhood sexual abuse seem to predict adult patterns (Grady et al., 2017).

The problem with latching on to a single-factor explanation is that not all of those who experience CSA go on to perpetrate this offense against children. The terms *correlation* and *association*, often found in scientific investigations of child abuse, simply mean that two factors tend to go together. Association doesn't mean causation or sole cause—it is better to think of the terms as identifying possible contributors to a problem. So although statistically there may be correlation or association between being the victim of childhood sexual abuse and being identified as a perpetrator of childhood sexual abuse, the existing research does not prove that prior victimization causes or creates a perpetrator. To understand this point, consider that there are many female victims of CSA but many fewer female than male sex offenders (Jespersen et al., 2009).

What is it about childhood CSA experiences that may contribute to sexually offending a child? First, their experiences may distort their thinking about the acceptability of sexual activity with children, creating **cognitive distortions.** These are thinking errors that would include normalizing attitudes or beliefs supportive of CSA that allow perpetrators to view their behaviors in a favorable way. One example of a distortion (denial) might be that children aren't harmed by genital touching. This cognitive distortion has been reported by the majority of *female* CSA offenders (Gannon & Alleyne, 2013). Another distortion might be projecting blame—saying that the child caused it by flirting or acting "sexy."

Other writers on the topic describe **scripts** or mental representations that the child might have learned from an abuser. These scripts enable "individuals to interpret sexually relevant behaviors and function as a guide in sexual encounters" (Ward & Siegert, 2002, p. 332). Thus, the sexually abused child may acquire a script that accepts children as appropriate partners for adults. Such scripts may then form the basis for these adults to become sexually aroused by children—viewing them as sexual objects.

Because the sexual abuse of children occurs before the child has the maturity to process what is occurring, such children can become sexualized early. Beard et al. (2017) phrased it this way: "Early partner sex increases the young victim's interest in sex" (p. 102). Sexual preoccupation occurs in child sex offenders (Sullivan & Sheehan, 2016). The study by Sullivan and Sheehan (2016) found that some abusers enjoyed the power and control they had over children, and any theory attempting to explain the sexual abuse of children must involve the presence of and interaction of multiple factors. Experts agree that it is "a multifaceted phenomenon that may manifest when different factors converge: victim, offender, situation, and culture" (Clayton, Jones, Brown, & Taylor, 2018, p. 192).

TEST YOURSELF

What is the connection between sexual abuse and insecure attachment? Do not read below the dotted line until you are ready to see the answer.

When there is not a strong, secure attachment between parent and child, the child can grow up with low self-esteem, which increases the risk of sexual victimization by those who give the child gifts and attention and manipulate him or her. Also, adults who sexually abuse children may have been abused themselves or at least had insecure attachment with a parent figure, which results in emotional regulation difficulties and perhaps difficulty forming relationships with adults—perhaps resulting in fantasies about minors that they can control.

Putting All the Factors Together

The Offender

We started with a notion of the offender or possible offender who as a child may have had an insecure attachment to a parent or caregiver. Because of that problem, the child may have increased vulnerability to sexual abuse. If the child becomes a victim of sexual abuse, then many, but not all, may develop an IWM of the world and cognitive distortions favorable to the consideration of sexual activities with children, given the "right" set of conditions.

If these adults find it difficult to form adult relationships because of their social deficits or inability to trust or be open to others but are attracted to children either sexually or to control and have power over them, these adults might be a step closer to committing CSA.

What follows is a summary of some of the conditions and factors that may either predispose or not prevent an individual from considering or using a child as a sex object for personal gains. Figure 3.1 illustrates how sexual abuse might occur, as is explained in the text below.

Predisposing Factors

Certain conditions or situations might present opportunities that allow the potential offender to spend time alone with a child. For instance, the offender could be unemployed and left with children for prolonged periods each day to watch or babysit. The risk of potential sexual abuse is increased if the home is in a very rural or isolated area without other adults coming and going. Smallbone and Wortley (2001) talk about a "capable guardian" who might act as a protecting factor against those who might attempt the sexual abuse of a child. Living in a household or neighborhood where the adults wouldn't be concerned or even notice another adult spending too much private time with a child, or where there was a great deal of alcohol or drug abuse, could create a predisposing factor because of the absence of a capable guardian. Too many people living in too small of a space may also give opportunities, with shared bedrooms or beds, to have intimate contact with a child.

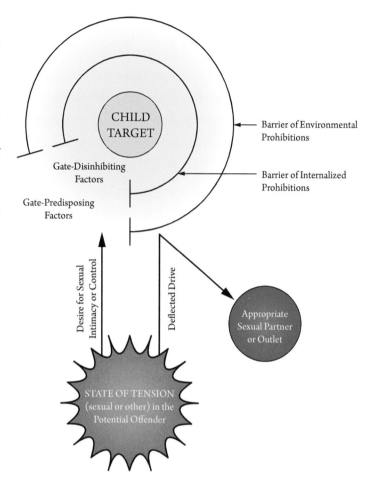

Figure 3.1 Model Representing Factors and Gateways in Child Sexual Abuse

Another predisposing factor can be the adult who is in an unsatisfying or dysfunctional marriage. With no adult sexual outlet, cognitive distortions about the acceptability of children as sexual objects, loneliness in one's adult relationship(s), and the availability of children, could help "set the stage" for abuse. Some cases of CSA involve men who are not necessarily sexually attracted to children; they occasionally become offenders when they do not have access to an adult sexual partner. Ward and Siegert (2002) use the phrase "situational opportunism" (p. 330), which seems to characterize accurately the situation that some predisposing factors create.

It is also possible that some mothers' own developmental histories of abuse and/or neglect have created conditions where they are emotionally distant from or emotionally neglectful toward the child, absent (e.g., military service, working), or physically ill. Crosson-Tower (2014) summarizes earlier work by Johnson (1992) describing mothers of incest victims in one group who are withdrawn or impaired and who push daughters into a wife's role within the family, starting with household tasks. Daughters can harbor anger toward the mother for not protecting them from the sexual abuse, and mothers (once replaced) can harbor resentment toward the daughter. Mothers can also believe themselves to be powerless in the father-tyrant's home. Mothers can be "ill equipped to nurture effectively, so great are their own needs. Or their own incestuous childhoods may rob them of the ability to face or intervene in the pattern that is being repeated (Joyce, 1997; Strand, 2000)" (Crosson-Tower, 2014, p. 147).

In a recent study of father–daughter incest, a team of researchers had this to say about the relevance of the mother's own incestuous victimization:

> Based on the results of our study, we believe that the generation-to-generation transmission mechanism is a result of the adult FDI [father–daughter incest] victim-daughter modeling her behaviors with her husband on her mother's behaviors with the FDI victim's own father. So, if the daughter fights with her own husband (like her mother) and she is unaffectionate with her own husband (like her own mother), she reproduces the same two risk factors that set her up for FDI in her own nuclear family, and she sets her own daughter up for FDI (thereby passing the incest along to the next generation through a mechanism that depends on nothing more than the FDI victim's modeling her behaviors on her mother's behaviors). (Beard et al., 2017, p. 100)

While the literature on CSA discusses "maternal role abdication" and other wife/mother behaviors such as avoiding having sex with their husband/boyfriend or emotional unavailability to these individuals and others within the home, the reader is reminded that the sexual abuse of children involves several (if not many) interacting factors. Mothers who bring their own issues into a marriage or relationship are not solely or more to blame. However, they may unconsciously have a role that they don't recognize.

Disinhibiting Factors

Even though the stage might be set for CSA, there is widespread societal prohibition of CSA. It very possibly takes another set of conditions to "open the gate" or "lower the walls" protecting the child from sexual abuse. One factor that might overcome internal inhibitions could involve the adult's drinking to the point of intoxication or the use of substances to get "high." Either situation dulls the rational, decision-making part of the brain and serves to weaken the conscience. Some forms of mental illness, dementia, impulse disorders, or even extended sessions viewing pornography might also create conditions where reasoning and judgment are affected, possibly allowing the abuser to attend more to internal arguments favorable to CSA than to thoughts in opposition.

Wrap-Up

The two key findings of a study conducted by Beard et al. (2017) were that dysfunction in the parents' relationship allowed a young daughter to fill the father/stepfather/boyfriend's needs emotionally and then sexually. The researchers go on to state this about FDI:

> Removal of the perpetrator-father from the home often fails to protect the FDI victim-daughter from additional CSA because she is very likely to find other adult male sexual partners before she reaches 18 years of age. ... One likely mechanism for such an undesirable outcome is that the FDI victim's mother's relationship with each new partner she brings into the home reproduces the dysfunctional relationship she had with the FDI victim's father in the original nuclear family. In support of this idea, our study showed that a new male partner in the home before the participant reached 18 years of age increased the risk of FDI by 4.8 times. (Beard et al., 2017, p. 102)

TABLE 3.1 **CHILD MALTREATMENT TYPE COMBINATIONS SUBSTANTIATED CASES, 2016**

Maltreatment type combinations	Maltreatment type (number)	Maltreatment type (percentage)
SINGLE TYPE	–	–
Neglect includes medical neglect	423,007	63.0
Other/unknown	20,258	3.0
Physical abuse	74,548	11.1
Psychological or emotional maltreatment	15,504	2.3
Sexual abuse	44,468	6.6
TWO TYPES	–	–
Neglect and "other"/unknown	23,182	3.5
Neglect and physical abuse	34,606	5.2
Neglect and psychological maltreatment[1]	12,858	1.9
Neglect and sexual abuse[2]	9,079	1.4
Physical abuse and "other"/unknown	681	0.1
Physical abuse and psychological maltreatment[3]	5,109	0.8
Physical abuse and sexual abuse[4]	1,430	0.2
Sexual abuse and psychological maltreatment[5]	425	0.1
THREE TYPES	–	–
Neglect, physical abuse, and psychological maltreatment	3,176	0.5
Neglect, physical abuse, and "other"/unknown	1,207	0.2
Neglect, physical abuse, and sexual abuse[6]	980	0.1
REMAINING COMBINATIONS	**1,104**	**0.2**
National	671,622	100.0

Source: U.S. Department of Health & Human Services, "Maltreatment Type Combinations, 2016," Child Maltreatment 2016, pp. 45, 2016.
Note: Based on data from 51 states.
1. Includes 155 victims with a combination of neglect, psychological maltreatment, and "other"/unknown.
2. Includes 359 victims with a combination of neglect, sexual abuse, and "other"/unknown.
3. Includes 24 victims with a combination of physical abuse, psychological maltreatment, and "other"/unknown.
4. Includes 26 victims with a combination of physical abuse, sexual abuse, and "other"/unknown.
5. Includes 9 victims with a combination of sexual abuse, psychological maltreatment, and "other"/unknown.
6. Includes 1 victim with a combination of neglect, physical abuse, sexual abuse, and "other"/unknown.

While it is theoretically possible that intense family therapy and marital therapy could preserve a family where incest has occurred, a meta-analytic review of treatment outcomes of sexual offenders against children found only a small number of studies of sufficient rigor to include. The authors conclude, "Published research with acceptable quality cannot support the claim that psychological treatment of convicted SOAC [sexual offenders against children] reduces recidivism" (Gronnerod, Gronnerod, & Grondahl, 2015, p. 286). And this was despite the offenders being in psychotherapy for an average of 48 weeks and an average follow-up period of 6.8 years. Instead of trying to prove the effectiveness given the problems associated with conducting this type of research with an offending population, the authors recommend focusing on "developing and studying local but comprehensive child sexual victimization prevention programs" (Gronnerod et al., 2105, p. 285).

Somewhat along the same line, but different, Beard et al. (2017) recommend:

> Our present study regarding risk factors for FDI suggest that a more fruitful approach to actually preventing CSA within the nuclear family (before it occurs) would be to provide information to all parents about the dangers of continuing to live within a problematic marriage and the importance of either finding help designed to improve the marriage or terminating the marriage by means of a divorce. (p. 104)

These thoughts relate to the child protection worker this way: While you will be working to actively investigate and protect children from harm, you will also be thinking about ways to prevent future abuse and the conditions that create the mix of ingredients that make it possible. It is important to be aware of research about interventions and new developments in the field and to be an evidence-based practitioner. Let knowledge guide your practice, not personal feelings, hunches, or personal judgment,

Finally, although we, the authors of your textbook, believe that your understanding of the possible contributors and causes of neglect, physical abuse, and sexual abuse is facilitated by examining these types of maltreatment separately, Table 3.1 actually reveals that the child protection worker will often be dealing with cases where more than one type of maltreatment is present. With experience, you will soon see that similar factors tend to be involved—no matter the type of maltreatment. Chief among those factors will be neglectful or adverse childhood experiences that occurred in the parents' (or caretakers') own childhood that have significantly affected their ability to parent appropriately.

Main Points

This chapter discussed research and current thinking about what factors are associated with various forms of child maltreatment. Although some contributors to abuse or neglect will be predominant and stand out in some cases more than others, at times an explanation linking to a single cause may be difficult to determine. However, research suggests that across all types of child abuse and neglect, individuals who are responsible are likely to have been victims themselves of child maltreatment.

- Neglect is the most common form of maltreatment.
- Parents who experienced maltreatment in their own families are much more likely to have child maltreatment in their current families.
- Milner's social information processing model (SIP) proposes that physically abusive parents have cognitive interpretations and inappropriate expectations about children that are different from parents not as likely to abuse. They may have more automatic processing of events that don't allow them to consider mitigating factors when a child is thought to be misbehaving.
- Milner's construction of the Child Abuse Potential Inventory has revealed the usefulness of objective instruments for assessing and better understanding adults who may be at risk for maltreating children
- Sexual abuse of children also seems to be associated with one's own experience of being abused, being denied emotional intimacy, low self-esteem, and insecure attachment as a child. Perpetrators seem to form cognitive distortions that allow them to justify and engage in inappropriate sexual contact.

- No single explanation seems adequate to explain sexual abuse, but there may be predisposing factors such as an adult in a dysfunctional marriage or being left alone with a child for long periods of time, coupled with disinhibiting factors that remove one's inhibitions, such as drinking, substance use, etc.

Questions for Class Discussion

1. The text cites an author noting that "poverty can affect the ability of the parents to provide adequate supervision." How else might poverty affect what parents can provide to their children? Brainstorm as many ways as are relevant.
2. Which type of maltreatment do you find it easiest to explain? Neglect, physical abuse, or sexual abuse—and why?
3. Which type of maltreatment do you find it most difficult to explain?
4. Does the social information processing (SIP) theory seem like a valuable explanation too you? What kinds of questions might you use to see if the caretaker's thinking fits the described stages?
5. What do you make of the types of maltreatment and combinations shown in the national data in Table 3.1?

Self-Assessment for Personal Consideration

1. How confident are you in your ability to identify factors related to child neglect?

   1   2   3   4   5   6   7   8   9   10

   Not confident   *Very confident*

2. How confident are you in your ability to identify factors related to physical abuse?

   1   2   3   4   5   6   7   8   9   10

   Not confident   *Very confident*

3. How confident are you in your ability to identify factors related to sexual abuse?

   1   2   3   4   5   6   7   8   9   10

   Not confident   *Very confident*

Additional Resources

Center on the Developing Child at Harvard University. (2013, October 31). In brief: The science of neglect [YouTube video]. Retrieved from https://www.youtube.com/watch?v=bF3j5UVCSCA

Dr. Phil. (2016, June 20). Daughter describing sexual abuse by father: "I was brainwashed" [YouTube video]. Retrieved from https://www.youtube.com/watch?v=tWYFV60WfIQ

Klika, J. B. & Connte, J. R. (2017). *APSAC Handbook on child maltreatment.* Thousand Oaks, CA: Sage Publications.

Royse, D. (2016). *Emotional abuse of children: Essential information.* New York: Routledge.

Tedx Talks. (2017, January 17). A "normal" life. When child abuse is normal | Luke Fox | TEDxCalPoly [YouTube video]. Retrieved from https://www.youtube.com/watch?v=vSTUSxdGaMo

References

Assink, M., Spruit, A., Schuts, M. Lindauer, R., Van der Put, C. E., & Stams, G. J. J. (2018). The intergenerational transmission of child maltreatment: A three-level meta-analysis. *Child Abuse & Neglect, 84*, 131–145.

Ateah, C. A., & Durrant, J. E. (2005). Maternal use of physical punishment in response to child misbehavior: Implications for child abuse prevention. *Child Abuse & Neglect, 29*, 169–185.

Azar, S. T., McGuier, D. J., Miller, E. A., Hernandez-Mekonnen, R., & Johnson, D. R. (2017) Child neglect and maternal cross-relational social cognitive and neurocognitive disturbances. *Journal of Family Psychology, 31*, 8–18.

Beard, K. W., Griffee, K., Newsome, J. E., Harper-Dorton, K. V., O'Keefe, S. L., Linz, T. D., ... & Nichols, A. N. (2017). Father-daughter incest: Effects, risk-factors, and a proposal for a new parent-based approach to prevention. *Sexual Addiction & Compulsivity, 24*(1–2), 79–107.

Bridgett, D. J., Kanya, M. J., Rutherford, H. J. V., & Mayes, L. C. (2017). Maternal executive functioning as a mechanism in the intergenerational transmission of parenting: Preliminary evidence. *Journal of Family Psychology, 31*, 19–29.

Clayton, E., Jones, C., Brown, J., & Taylor, J. (2018). The aetiology of child sexual abuse: A critical review of the empirical evidence. *Child Abuse Review, 27*, 181–197.

Crosson-Tower, C. (2014). *Understanding child abuse and neglect*. New York, NY: Pearson.

Crouch, J. L., McKay, E. R., Lelakowski, G., Hiraoka, R., Rutledge, E., Bridgett, D. J., & Milner, J. S. (2018). Do emotion regulation difficulties explain the association between executive functions and child physical abuse risk? *Child Abuse & Neglect, 80*, 99–107.

DePanfilis, D. (2006). *Child neglect: A guide for prevention, assessment and intervention*. Washington, DC: Office of Child Abuse & Neglect.

Dubowitz, H. (2014). Child neglect. *Pediatric Annals, 43*(11), 444–445.

Finkelhor, D. (1984). *Child sexual abuse: New theory and research*. New York, NY: Free Press.

Gannon, T. A., & Alleyne, E. (2013). Female sexual abusers' cognitions: A systematic review. *Trauma, Violence, & Abuse, 14*(1), 67–79.

Grady, M. D., Levenson, J. S., & Bolder, T. (2017). Linking adverse childhood effects and attachment: A theory of etiology for sexual offending. *Trauma, Violence, & Abuse, 18*(4), 433–444.

Gronnerod, C., Gronnerod, J. S., & Grondahl, P. (2015). Psychological treatment of sexual offenders against children: A meta-analytic review of treatment outcome studies. *Trauma, Violence & Abuse, 16*(3), 280–290.

Hornor, G. (2014). Child neglect: Assessment and intervention. *Journal of Pediatric Health Care, 28*(2), 186–192.

Jespersen, A. F., Lalumiere, M. L., & Seto, M. C. (2009). Sexual abuse among adult sex offenders and non-sex offenders: A meta-analysis. *Child Abuse & Neglect, 33* (3), 179–192.

Joyce, A. N. (2016). High-conflict divorce: A form of child neglect. *Family Court Review, 54*(4), 642–656.

Joyce, P. (1997). Mothers of sexually abused children and the concept of collusion: A literature review. *Journal of Child Sexual Abuse, 6*(2), 75–92.

Kirke-Smith, M., Henry, L. A., & Messer, D. (2016). The effect of maltreatment type on adolescent executive functioning and inner speech. *Infant and Child Development, 25*, 516–532.

Martin, G. M., & Tardif, M. (2014). What we do and don't know about sex offenders intimacy dispositions. *Aggression and Violent Behaviors, 19*, 372–382.

McLeod, D. A., & Craft, M. L. (2015). Female sexual offenders in child sexual abuse cases: National trends associated with Child Protective Services system entry, exit, utilization, and socioeconomics. *Journal of Public Child Welfare, 9*, 399–416.

Milner, J. S. (1993). Social information processing and physical child abuse. *Clinical Psychology Review, 13*, 275–294.

Milner, J. S. (1994). Assessing physical child abuse: The Child Abuse Potential Inventory. *Clinical Psychology Review, 14*(6), 547–583.

Mulder, T. M., Kuiper, K. C., Van der Put, C. E., Stams, G. J. J., & Assink, M. (2018). Risk factors for child neglect: A meta-analytic review. *Child Abuse & Neglect, 77*, 198–210.

Rodriguez, C. M. (2018). Predicting parent–child aggression risk: Cognitive factors and their interaction with anger. *Journal of Interpersonal Violence, 33*(3), 359–378.

Royse, D. (1994). *How do I know it's abuse? Identifying and countering emotional mistreatment from friends and family members*. Springfield, IL: Thomas.

Smallbone, S., & Wortley, R. (2001). *Child sexual abuse: Offender characteristics and modus operandi* Canberra, Australia: Australian Institute of Criminology.

Stirpe, T. S. & Stermac, L. E. (2003). An exploration of childhood victimization and family of origin characteristics of sexual offenders against children. *International Journal of Offender Therapy and Comparative Criminology, 47*, 542–555.

Stith, S. M., Liu, T., Davies, C., Boykin, E. I., Alder, M. C., Harris, J. M., ... & Dees, J. E. M. E. G. (2009). Risk factors in child maltreatment: A meta-analytic review of the literature. *Aggression and Violent Behavior, 14*, 13–29.

Strand, V. C. (2000). *Treating secondary victims: Intervention with the nonoffending mother in the incest family.* Thousand Oaks, CA: Sage.

Sullivan, J., & Sheehan, V. (2016). What motivates sexual abusers of children? A qualitative examination of the spiral of sexual abuse. *Aggression and Violent Behavior, 30,* 76–87.

Tenbergen, G., Wittfoth, M., Frieling, H., Ponseti, J., Walter, M., Walter, H., … & Tillmann, H. C. K. (2015). The neurobiology and psychology of pedophilia: Recent advances and challenges. *Frontiers in Human Neuroscience, 9,* 344.

U. S. Department of Health & Human Services, Administration for Children and Families, Administration on Children, Youth and Families, Children's Bureau. (2018). *Child maltreatment 2016.*

U. S. Department of Justice. (2007). Female sex offenders: A project for justice programs. Office of Justice Programs, Center for Sex Offender Management.

Vota, N. (2017). Keeping the free-range parent immune from child neglect: You cannot tell me how to raise my children. *Family Court Law Review, 55*(1), 152–167.

Ward, T., & Siegert, R. J. (2002). Toward a comprehensive theory of child sexual abuse: A theory knitting perspective. *Psychology, Crime & Law, 8,* 319–351.

Weinsheimer, C. C., Woiwod, D. M., Coburn, P. I., Chong, K., & Connolly, D. A. (2017). The usual suspects: Female versus male accused in child sexual abuse cases. *Child Abuse & Neglect, 72,* 446–455.

CHAPTER 4

INVESTIGATIONS: THE CHILD ABUSE/ NEGLECT INVESTIGATOR'S ROLE

OVERVIEW

When you think of the word *investigator*, what comes to mind? Maybe something to do with law enforcement or the FBI. In child protection, trained professionals investigate allegations of child maltreatment on a daily basis. Actually, a national study estimated that 37.4% of children experience a child protective services investigation by the time they are 18 years old (Kim, Wildeman, Jonson-Reid, & Drake, 2017). In this chapter, we will walk through the child protective services investigation process with the hypothetical Perkins family and we will follow them in the next two chapters as the case moves from the investigation phase to the provision of ongoing services and, finally, permanency for the children. The CPS investigator "sets the table" for all future interactions, beginning a trajectory of involvement with the agency for the substantiated cases. Specific tips for best practice will be illustrated for real-world implementation. An overview of associated court processes will also be discussed.

Tonya: The CPS Investigator

Today was going to be a good day, Tonya just knew it. When she arrived at her office, she felt confident and motivated to make a difference. Tonya had always known that she wanted to work in child protection, a desire that had been in her heart since spending time in foster care as a child. She was determined to make a difference in her community and had moved back to her home county after earning her degree in social work. She was an advocate, a survivor, and the face of the local agency. Today was going to be a good day!

Arriving at the office, she waved at her colleagues and made her way to her desk with her customary Frappuccino. She had worked for the agency for almost 2 years and was becoming comfortable with her daily routine. Her agency delivered specialized services, meaning that she and several colleagues were only assigned to investigations associated with the alleged maltreatment of children—other colleagues were responsible for the long-term provision of ongoing services.

Wanting to knock out a few phone calls before the workday began to get busy, she made her way to her office and sat down at her desk. Taking a sip from her Frappuccino, she heard her supervisor shout, "Hey Tonya, I have something for you." Tonya walked down the short hallway with butterflies building up in her stomach. She was excited but nervous. What would she be assigned?

Once inside the supervisor's office, Tonya was handed documentation—a police report—that had been received by the agency. While involved in a criminal investigation, the local police department became privy to some very concerning behavior related to the safety of two young girls in the area. The supervisor confirmed that the agency had formally accepted the allegation as a child protective services investigation, assigning it to Tonya.

"Drop everything else today," the supervisor said as she opened the next file folder on her desk. Tonya grabbed her laptop and her Frappuccino and left for the police department to dig into the allegations.

The Child Protection Process: Steps to Be Taken

Child protection generally involves the phases of the investigation, ongoing services, and aftercare. In this chapter, we will focus only on the investigation. Chapter 5 will address ongoing services, and Chapter 6 will discuss the process of achieving permanency. Throughout these chapters, we will follow one hypothetical family's involvement with the child protection agency from the beginning (investigation) to the end (aftercare). While this chapter will focus on the CPS investigator's role, additional information about the process of involvement with the child welfare system can be found at this website: https://www.childwelfare.gov/pubPDFs/cpswork. pdf#page=7&view=Summary.

The Investigation

CPS investigators are truly the face of the agency. They are often the first professionals to contact at-risk families and the direct link between vulnerable populations and safety. As detailed by Stanley (2010), the CPS investigator will actively build knowledge and construct an impression of risk through assessment, consultation, and analysis. Investigators must deliver information that families may not want to hear during difficult times. Investigators are on the front lines, navigating legal mandates and capturing highly sensitive information. This position has both real and perceived authority and comes with great responsibility. CPS investigators will never have to wonder whether they have ever made a difference in the lives of children—they do!

Referral and Acceptance

How do people become involved with the child welfare system? Generally, an event triggers the involvement of a citizen and the child protection agency. Possibly a car accident, an incident at school, or maybe an outburst by a parent in the parent's own home. The event reveals the assumed or alleged maltreatment of a child by a parent or caretaker. Child protection is inherently associated with concerns about (usually adult) behaviors potentially violating **statutes** (laws) designed to protect children.

For all intents and purposes, involvement with the child welfare system is initiated through what is called a **referral**. A referral is the reception of a formal report (often made anonymously) by someone alleging the maltreatment of a child by their caretaker. However, sometimes referrals can be made by **mandated reporters**, or those who are legally required to report the suspicion of child maltreatment (e.g., teachers, social workers, therapists, medical personnel, law enforcement, etc.).

Although the federal government provides guidelines for policies associated with reporting the suspected abuse of a child, the majority of the specifics are left to the states (Steen & Duran, 2014). In addition, key variables have been found to influence the occurrence of reports of child maltreatment. In one study, King et al. (2017) indicated that Black families are more like to be investigated than White families. In another, Menard and Ruback (2003) identified a higher occurrence of reports of CPS child sexual abuse in rural counties.

How might the agency receive a referral? Referrals can be made face-to-face, by phone, via paper documentation, or through electronic communication. Telephone communication can improve the quality of the report, as the agency representative may be able to ask the caller additional questions that may be beneficial. However, some individuals feel uncomfortable using the telephone and prefer to expedite the process through a written report or by submitting their allegations through an electronic web portal (if available). It is also possible that someone from the local area could drop an anonymous letter in a mailbox identifying a child at a certain address and alleging maltreatment. Individuals can also walk into a brick-and-mortar local office and ask to see someone to share details about a possible situation involving child maltreatment. Additionally, law enforcement can also direct a copy of a report of their involvement with a family to the child protective agency to begin the investigative process.

Social media or television can also initiate reports of child maltreatment. Years back, an individual from Alaska went on a *Dr. Phil* show entitled "Angry Moms" to ask for "help." Through video footage made available, she was shown forcing her child to drink hot sauce as a form of discipline. Public outcry resulted in a formal investigation and criminal charges. More can be found in this article: https://nypost.com/2011/08/24/woman-convicted-of-child-abuse-in-hot-sauce-ploy-to-get-on-dr-phil/. One thing is for certain, child protection agencies will be the recipient of allegations of child maltreatment, and they can come from just about anywhere.

Regardless of how the referral was communicated, agencies utilize either a centralized or decentralized reporting system. A **centralized reporting system** is where the agency has one main unit that collects and screens all referrals and then assigns accepted reports to the local agency for involvement. A **decentralized reporting system** is where the local agency not only receives and screens the referral but moves forward with the investigation if accepted. In this model, the professional who screens the initial referral may also be assigned to facilitate the investigation.

Research has shown a similar rate of overall referrals between centralized and decentralized systems but identified that centralized systems are significantly more likely to "screen-in" or accept a referral that alleged the maltreatment of a child (Steen & Duran, 2014).

What information is collected on the referral? Commonly, required information includes demographic information on the approximate age(s) of the child(ren), location, background, and any details (date, time, reactions, witnesses) about the specific events associated with the alleged maltreatment. The professional processing this report is well aware of the criteria needed to meet the statute for acceptance (meeting the criteria for investigation), based on the type of offense and relevant agency policy. The individual making the report can remain anonymous. On one hand, it is helpful for the CPS investigator to have information identifying the **reporting source**, as that person may have additional information or details related to the investigation if able to be contacted again. On the other hand, some individuals may refuse to provide personal information because they are concerned about their own safety. If the reporting source does provide his or her personal information, it is kept confidential. However, it is always possible that a court order by a judge could potentially force the release of this sensitive information should the case go to trial.

Irrespective of how the agency receives the initial allegations of child maltreatment, the allegations are screened by the agency and a decision is made. By **screening**, we mean that the agency must formally evaluate if the collected information has met the statutory guidelines for acceptance and involvement. If the allegations do not meet the criteria for acceptance, the agency may file this information should other allegations be made in the future. If it does meet the criteria for acceptance, the case will be distributed to an investigator like Tonya.

Assignment and Preparation

Tonya arrived at the local police department. She felt a strange vibe, as a number of officers were waiting on her arrival. It was explained to Tonya that an individual in the community had just been charged with burglary after recently breaking into a home and stealing jewelry, TVs, and a video camera. After stealing the video camera, this individual found some concerning footage on the camera and immediately drove to the police station to turn himself in and to clear his conscience about what he had seen. The disturbing footage identified the sexual abuse of two young individuals by their caretakers. As Tonya watched the video, she recognized the individuals on the film. It was Rodney and Angela Perkins and their daughters, a family she had investigated in the past. It was difficult to watch, but the video affirmed evidence of the sexual assault of both Rebecca and Renee Perkins by their father and the complicity of their mother. The date stamp on the video revealed that it was recorded approximately 3 weeks before. Recognizing an imminent risk to the safety of both children, Tonya developed a plan with law enforcement to initiate a formal investigation and immediately assure the safety of both of the children. Tonya noted the current home address of the family and made a phone call to the children's school where both Rebecca and Renee were present. Tonya had a few hours before school was out. She called a coworker to help her out. Accompanied by law enforcement, they met at the school to begin their investigation by speaking to both of the girls in private.

Depending on the structure of the agency, the worker may be part of a **generalist team**, in which each team member not only conducts investigations of child abuse but also provides ongoing services after the completion of the investigation. Tonya works on a specialized team, in which each worker had specific job duties (e.g., investigator, ongoing services worker, etc.). After the investigation is completed, her supervisor typically assigns the case to a coworker, who will then have primary responsibility for providing ongoing services. There are pros and cons to working on a **specialized team**, and researchers are now beginning to investigate whether this agency structure has any influence on the outcomes for children (Smith, Fluke, Fallon, Mishna, & Decker Pierce, 2018).

Engaging in a child protective services investigation is quite a responsibility. In Tonya's scenario, she needed to collaborate with law enforcement, a common practice in many areas (Jordan et al., 2011). However, it is important to understand that there are two different paths with respect to the child protection investigation. The child protective services investigator may request assistance from law enforcement, and criminal charges may result, but a child protective services investigation is a separate entity from criminal matters. At times these two separate paths may align, but the child protective services investigator will routinely investigate allegations of child maltreatment that never involve criminal charges, law enforcement, or criminal court. The reason for this is that the child welfare system is a civil system and has a different court structure than the criminal court system. Further, criminal courts have a much higher standard of evidence. While research has shown that the collaborative aspect of working in partnership with other agencies involved in a child abuse investigation can be stressful (Powell, Guadagno, & Cassematis, 2013), building relationships with law enforcement and other professionals in your area is a key component for effective practice.

Receiving a new case can often bring a rush of adrenalin because of the need to move quickly to prevent children from further harm; it's also important to realize that it can result in stress or anxiety (Tehrani, 2018; Waterhouse & McGhee, 2009). Before immediately taking off on a new investigation, take time to prepare yourself. This will make a world of difference and will truly benefit you once you are in the field.

It is likely that your agency will use an electronic computer system to manage prior reports of investigations. The ability to search for prior reports and collect preliminary information will help you make informed decisions throughout the assessment process. Also, you may be able to access an online portal or reach out to law enforcement counterparts to access other data about past criminal actions associated with the individuals involved in your investigation. Wouldn't it be helpful to know if Rodney Perkins had current criminal charges for assault or domestic violence, for example, before you went to his home? A wealth of knowledge may also be obtained by reaching out to your colleagues in the office.

For instance, perhaps a veteran colleague previously had an open case with this family on a different matter—the colleague might be able to supply information that would increase the effectiveness of your interviews and also keep you safe during the investigation. The reality is, you are about to walk into a stranger's life and become a part of a potentially difficult process. What do you need to know about that situation? Social media can be an avenue for quickly accessing valuable information about current behaviors or the whereabouts of individuals associated with your investigation. You would not be directly communicating with individuals through this medium, but many social media accounts offer public information, and the click of a few keys can sometimes reveal information that can be of great value when assuring the safety of a child.

The point is, proactively searching for valuable tidbits of information can improve the effectiveness of your assessment strategy. Keep in mind, though, if your investigation suggests imminent risk of harm to a child or that the child is currently being mistreated, you may not be able to take the time to collect thorough information before pursuing contact with those involved in the allegations. Depending on the severity of the abuse, it may be more important to facilitate face-to-face contact immediately with the alleged victim than taking time to look for information on the Internet. When the problem is not considered urgent, technology can definitely be a friend, and an ounce of work on the front of the case can offset a pound of problems on the back.

Initial Contact

After a formal allegation of abuse has been received and the agency has accepted the report as indicating that it meets the criteria for an investigation, the case is assigned, and it's time to **initiate the investigation**. What does this mean? To initiate the investigation means making initial face-to-face contact with the alleged victim. Depending on the law or statute, the amount of time that you have to initiate your investigation will be based on the nature of the allegations and the level of risk associated. Not all allegations have the same level of risk, and it is important to understand that you will need to prioritize which individuals you should contact first. For example, a report identifying possible educational neglect for a 12-year-old in the community may result in a low-risk report that may not need to be addressed within 24 or even 48 hours to make face-to-face contact with the child.

On the other end of the spectrum, allegations of high-risk harm require a faster response from the agency. For a referral alleging the sexual abuse of a child in the community, you might need to initiate the investigation within the hour. Agency policies and state statutes assist with time frames, and it is important to know and comply with agency guidelines associated with contacting the alleged victim.

Tonya was familiar with the school system and had worked hard to develop a level of rapport with the principal and counselors. After arriving at the elementary school, she notified the principal that she had been assigned an investigation alleging child sexual abuse and requested contact with both Rebecca and Renee Perkins. Following agency policy, she presented her agency identification badge and documentation supporting her legal authority to interview both children due to a current investigation of child sexual abuse. Then she and Sgt. Smith from the police department were led to a discrete room, where they patiently waited to speak with the girls, one at a time.

Rebecca arrived first, a 7-year-old Caucasian female with red curly hair. She was nervous, asking "Am I in trouble?" and then "Where's Renee?" Through the course of this face-to-face contact, Tonya reassured her and asked open-ended questions in an age-appropriate format to collect information from Rebecca relevant to the allegations. Quickly, it became clear that Rebecca had concerns about her own safety and home environment. Rebecca eventually spoke of inappropriate touching and affirmed the behaviors found on the home video that was collected by law enforcement. Tonya wrote notes as she spoke with Rebecca, wanting to have good documentation and also thinking of a plan to assure Rebecca's safety.

After talking with the school guidance counselor about Rebecca's behavior in school, Tonya and Sgt. Smith spoke with her older sister, Renee. Renee presented differently, anxious and uncooperative at first. Tonya had to adjust her delivery with respect to speaking with Renee, as Renee continually asked to be able to go back to class and was initially resistant to speaking with her. Renee was an 11-year-old Caucasian female with dark hair. She was tall, smart, and appeared mature for her age. After Tonya engaged with Renee about her interests in playing softball and their pet dog, Renee began to warm up and was more comfortable answering questions about life in her family. Tonya introduced the allegations in a general, nonthreatening way. Avoiding Tonya's eyes, Renee confirmed that she and her sister had been involved in sexuality activity with their father. "He made us do it," she said. She had not told anybody because she was embarrassed and didn't want the family to "get in trouble." Tonya did not push to get all of the details and specifics of the sexual abuse with either Rebecca or Renee, as she knew that there would be a formal forensic interview with the girls at the Child Advocacy Center in the near future that would get into this.

THE CHILD ADVOCACY CENTER

The first Child Advocacy Center was established in 1985. Child Advocacy Centers utilize cross-agency and multidisciplinary collaboration to respond to serious abuse investigations. A few reasons that the Child Advocacy Center is helpful is that it helps to minimize trauma and distress and allows for specific tasks associated with the child abuse investigation to be conducted in a professional and child-friendly location. Typical professions involved in the Child Advocacy Center are law enforcement, child protection, mental health therapists, medical personnel, and advocacy specialists. Further, Child Advocacy Centers provide the opportunity for a child to be forensically interviewed only one time. While the possibility of multiple child interviews leading to higher rates of criminal conviction has been explored (Block, Foster, Pierce, Berkoff, & Runyan, 2013), there are significant concerns about retraumatization and distress associated with requiring child victims to continually describe their abuse. Today there are 795 Child Advocacy Centers that are members of the National Children's Alliance, and their model is also being employed in Europe, Canada, and Australia. Child Advocacy Centers have been found to improve substantiation rates and investigation efficiency (Brink, Thackeray, Bridge, Letson, & Scribano, 2015; Herbert, Walsh, & Bromfield, 2018; Smith, Witte, & Fricker-Elhai, 2006; Wolfteich & Loggins, 2007).

Given the presence of video footage and the verbal disclosure of child sexual abuse by Rebecca and Renee, Tonya knew that this was a serious situation and that she needed to speak with her supervisor and immediately begin designing a plan to assure their safety. Tonya and the school personnel made arrangements to keep both Rebecca and Renee at school until Tonya completed a couple of tasks. She asked the school not to release the girls to their parents but to immediately reach out to school security and call law enforcement if Rodney or Angela came to pick them up. After speaking with her supervisor, Tonya knew she would very likely be petitioning the court on behalf of the children later in the afternoon.

Field Interviews: Safety, Strategies, and Access

Investigating child maltreatment involves unique challenges as child protective services professionals balance both "care" and "control"—which are likely to produce tension (Turney, 2012). There are also concerns about working with involuntary clients who may be less apt to cooperate. Further, researchers have identified that violence from clients is a genuine concern for those working in child protection (Shin, 2011). Be that as it may, it is important to keep in mind that the child protective services investigation is a fluid process involving many decisions, and there are ways you can maximize your effectiveness and safety.

Know your policies, and be flexible. Be clear about who you need to contact, how they should be contacted, and when this contact should occur. Best practice results in interviewing the alleged victim in private, before anyone else is contacted. The alleged victim should be approached in an area where a private conversation can be held and, if at all possible, away from the alleged perpetrator. This minimizes the potential for pressure or bias and hopefully assures the integrity of the interview.

Implementation of this ideal approach to data collection is not always possible. Imagine that you are Tonya in this scenario. However, you were unable to contact the children at school before they boarded the bus for home. This would mean you would have to arrive at the Perkins family home and try to speak to each girl and parent separately about the allegations of child sexual abuse. How challenging would it be to conduct an investigation in this circumstance? How would you feel if you were a parent and someone arrived at your home and said, "Excuse me, can I speak to your child in private to ask them about a report alleging their sexual abuse?"

PRACTICE TIP 4.1 Though not always necessary, consider bringing law enforcement or a coworker with you when interviewing relevant parties in the field. Also, if there is no private space for the interview, attempt to find a place more remote, possibly talking to the child alone on the front porch, for example. Explain to the family that you have a job to do and that their cooperation will assure that this is less stressful on the child. You can also mention that even though they may not want to cooperate with this involuntary investigative process, it is in their best interest to do so.

It is important to decide who to interview, and in what order. A little bit of strategy is involved. For example, if in our scenario there were pending criminal charges associated with Mr. Perkins, law enforcement may want to schedule a forensic interview at their headquarters, and Mr. Perkins could choose to bring an attorney. This type of interview would be in a predetermined location, at a set time; he may be read his rights, and it may be recorded. However, the majority of contacts by the child protective services investigator will occur in the field. This means that the majority of the time, you will interview and speak with individuals in locations like the school, a jail, or the community. This is a unique and exciting part of being an investigator. Each day is different, and you will be able to use your skill set in a number of scenarios. At times, interviews will be spontaneous or conducted with little planning. At other times, they will be predetermined.

One commonality in this process will be having contact with families in their residences. Meeting with individuals in their home is important. Specifically, access to the home offers a great opportunity to observe living conditions and assists the investigator by offering a candid view of the family's home environment. Engaging a family at their residence is the "bread and butter" of child protection and also affords the family an opportunity to provide "evidence" that may help refute the allegations.

On the other hand, it is important to consider a number of factors. For example, who owns the residence? Who lives there? How long have they lived there? Are there firearms? Are there any aggressive pets that may present a safety hazard? And further, is there likely to be illegal substances or other criminal contraband? While you may remain safe during the majority of your trips into people's homes, always be proactive. Your safety should always be of the utmost concern; if you are not willing to prioritize your own safety, no one else will.

PRACTICE TIP 4.2 Take steps to become familiar with the area that you will be traveling to. This will help you feel more comfortable and become more efficient in practice. Use Google Maps or Google Earth to view the location beforehand. Sometimes addresses change, and it may be helpful to get an idea of the neighborhood layout from an aerial view before leaving in your vehicle. Possibly ask a coworker or a colleague if they are willing to go with you to the location. If unavailable, seek insight from coworkers or community partners about the area to assess for any previous involvement and safety risks. It is possible that the fire department or local ambulance has been there and can provide an accurate idea of the surroundings before you arrive. Reach out to law enforcement and ask about any prior involvement with the family. See if they would be willing to conduct a "standby" and meet you at the residence for support. Make sure that you back your vehicle into the residence drive so that you can leave in a hurry if necessary. Let someone else know where you will be. Leave a paper trail by signing out or sending an e-mail to a colleague or supervisor so that they will know where you are when making home visits. Carry a cell phone. After a few months on the job, you will become well versed in this process and have a good understanding of the dynamics and potential areas for concern.

Also, your appearance matters. Wear comfortable yet professional clothes. Keep away from flip-flops or sandals and wear closed-toed shoes or boots. Refrain from wearing fancy jewelry and any hooped earrings. These may present a safety risk, and we always want to have a professional and respectful presence when entering someone's home and representing the agency. Bring a camera and possibly a tape measure to help with taking pictures of the home or any bruises, etc.

Conducting investigations is a primary function of child protection agencies. Operating in the community and having legal access to individuals in their private homes is a privilege and a significant responsibility. It must be taken seriously, and individuals may respond in a variety of ways. When people feel desperate or threatened, anything is possible. Taking steps to ensure your safety is always worth the effort.

After speaking with her supervisor about the current status of the investigation with the Perkins family, Tonya planned to drive to the home of Rodney and Angela Perkins to attempt to conduct a face-to-face interview. Due to the comprehensive nature of the unfolding events and the likelihood of immediate court involvement, Tonya brought a coworker and Sgt. Smith. She wanted to make sure that she collected as much information as possible in a short period and wanted to be safe as she went about her duties.

When they arrived at the Perkins's mobile home, the door was wide open. Tonya knocked on the side as loud as possible and then loudly identified herself and the agency. Initially, it did not appear that anyone was there. However, multiple needles, drug residue, and other signs of drug paraphernalia were in plain sight. Tonya bit her lip and resolved to overcome her nervousness. Clearly, this home was unsafe, and the Perkins family seemed to be involved with illicit activity. She called out again.

Although it seemed like an eternity, a minute or so later, Tonya heard a noise from the back of the home. Rodney and Angela emerged and walked unsteadily to the door. The bright light from outside seemed to bother them, and as they squinted to see their visitors, Tonya noticed the dark circles under their eyes. Angela rubbed her itchy inner arms and unconsciously revealed needle marks. Both adults were likely under the influence of some type of substance. Seeing the police officer, Angela invited the visitors into the mobile home. Sgt. Smith watched Rodney go to the sink and try to find a clean glass for water.

Tonya invited Rodney to join the conversation. There was a place for him on the couch littered with candy bar wrappers and used tissues. He shook his head that he didn't want to join them and stayed at the sink. When he appeared to be trying to wash something down the sink, Sgt. Smith called for backup.

Tonya spoke loud enough that Rodney and Angela could hear about the allegations. Angela began sobbing as she tried to light a cigarette. Rodney still looked unsteady and seemed to be trying to clear his head—almost as if he was unable to believe what he was hearing. Given their seemingly impaired cognitive functioning, Tonya realized that while she notified the parents that they were being investigated, she would be unable to conduct thorough interviews at this time. As another patrol car arrived, Sgt. Smith informed Rodney and Angela that they were being arrested and charged with child sexual abuse and possession of illegal drugs. He handcuffed them both and led them out of the mobile home.

It could have been a dangerous situation, and Tonya was glad that she had the support of law enforcement and her coworker. She took pictures of the living room and the kitchen to provide documentation on the prevailing safety risks and to verify that the living room on the videotape was also the same as the living room in the center of their residence.

Rodney and Angela were notified of their Miranda rights and responsibilities outside in the presence of the second officer and were informed by Tonya that she would be immediately filing a petition in civil court to allege the child sexual abuse of Rebecca and Renee Perkins with the local county prosecuting attorney.

As Rodney and Angela sat in the police cruiser to be taken to the county jail for processing, Tonya called her supervisor and advised her of the situation. She then had limited conversation with Angela and Rodney and neither could think of an appropriate family member to take immediate care and custody of the girls. Given the significant safety issues for the girls and the fact that Rodney and Angela were headed to jail, it was likely that Rebecca and Renee would potentially end up in foster care.

The Investigative Assessment

The investigative risk assessment relies on the comprehensive collection of observations, evidence, documentation, and clinical judgement. While it is unreasonable to expect the CPS investigator to be able to predict human behavior, research has produced objective ways to measure risk to children through inventories and scales that may be of supplemental value to the investigation (Leschied, Chiodo, Whitehead, Hurley, & Marshall, 2003). These may have been developed within your agency or by other researchers. (Chapter 7 contains more discussion about assessment.)

Realize that your personal observations and perspective matter in a way that can't always be captured on paper-and-pen assessment questionnaires. In a study of 200 child protection workers, respondents with a "pro-removal" attitude made higher risk assessments and were more likely to recommend child removal (Arad-Davidzon & Benbenishty, 2008). Unconscious bias or predetermined perceptions could lead an investigator to assess more risk than another investigator might see. The use of standardized processes or instruments may help eliminate any implicit bias.

Decision making in child protection is complex and contextual, and current research is dedicated to exploring avenues for improving decision making by implementing and evaluating the use of standardized assessment tools as a way to objectively supplement professional judgment (Alfandari, 2017; Dettlaff, Christopher Graham, Holzman, Baumann, & Fluke, 2015; Nyathi, 2018).

The purpose of the investigative assessment is to use any and all resources to make a thorough determination of whether the allegations received meet the criteria for further action by the agency. Just because there are allegations does not mean that maltreatment has occurred. Just imagine if someone filed a report on you because they didn't like you and had malicious intent to embarrass you. Such things actually happen. Nonetheless, the child protective services investigative assessment must be comprehensive and detailed. It is both a **process** and a **product**, and there is a lot at stake.

The process portion can be understood as investigators conducting interviews, collecting documentation from any relevant community members or providers, and doing everything within their power to complete a thorough investigation. The assessment is also a product, which your agency may refer to as an investigative report or assessment report. This formal report is very important for a number of reasons because it will likely be held on file for an unlimited time.

In today's child welfare agencies, investigative workers enter documentation in their computers in real time. This improves accessibility and can result in long-term backup for future use and immediate review. Whether located on a server or in a paper file, this investigative report will be accessible in the future, and any effort you can make to produce a detailed, thorough, and comprehensive report is well worth the effort. (It is not uncommon for families to come back through CPS agencies with new allegations.)

An additional example of accessing a previous investigative report could be if a child aged out of the foster care system and wanted more information about his or her upbringing or biological family. Or a child protection worker in a different county may need immediate information because a family of interest has moved across the state. Finally, it is always possible that a client chooses to file a lawsuit or an appeal about an action taken by the agency. A detailed report will affirm that the investigative worker and supervisor followed policy and will protect against a nuisance type of litigation.

Documentation

When discussing the necessity for thorough and detailed documentation, remember the phrase "if it's not documented, it didn't happen." Never have truer words been spoken about a professional activity. As we mentioned above, your formal report may exist in some type of media for many years. Once it is submitted and approved, you will probably not be able to change anything. Focus on contributing accurate and thorough details, in spite of any challenges with time constraints or other relevant concerns.

The assessment report is usually divided into sections. The *narrative portion* is based on the chronological trajectory of events after receiving the allegations. This narrative will include the reports of interviews from individuals that you spoke with, their location, what was discussed, and any additional information that might be relevant to the allegations. Your supervisor should be able to read your narrative and visualize the process and decisions made throughout. This narrative should also include identification of times that you met with your supervisor to process the decision making throughout the investigative process. If there are any relevant court hearings, they should also be described in this section. When you think about the assessment report, the narrative is an overview of the process that the investigator intentionally and purposefully went through while conducting the investigation.

In addition to the narrative, it is likely that your assessment report will include a section where the *individuals* identified in the report are each described. In the Perkins case, Tonya would describe observations separately for Rebecca, Renee, Rodney, and Angela. The investigative worker can then focus on describing, at a micro level, several key factors that will be pertinent for each individual, including age, address, education, cognitive functioning, physical health conditions, etc.

Additionally, another section will likely describe the *family* and its level of functioning and dynamics. For example, this would be a place to talk about everyday life events and challenges that the family is having. Substance abuse in the Perkins family would be one key issue, but there may have been others. Perhaps the parents were not sending the two girls to school on a regular basis. Or maybe Rodney and Angela Perkins have been involved in domestic violence for a number of years.

PRACTICE TIP 4.3 Given the possibility of distractions at the local office, consider taking a few minutes to find a parking lot for typing your field notes into a laptop immediately after interviewing clients in the field. Not only will this give you protected time to produce a detailed report while it is fresh in your mind, it will improve your efficiency in the investigative process. Think about your vehicle as a mobile work station. Keep a small plastic filing cabinet in the trunk stocked with forms and documents that you frequently use. Not having to return to the office to get a single form for a signature will truly save you hours each month. You may want to use dictation software to save your field notes into word processing software for safe backup and eventual insertion into the server. This is a quick and easy time-saver, and having your narrative backed up to a electronic document eliminates any problems if the server crashes while you are busy typing. See if your agency has its policy manual online or uses a mobile app, which will help you address questions when you are new in your position and in the field.

Collateral Contacts

Collateral contacts in a child protective services investigation refers to secondary or additional individuals who can confirm facts or details key to the investigation and provide depth to the assessment. Collateral contacts can help solidify an assessment that has identified the maltreatment of a child and can also serve as a support in refuting the allegations when abuse is not likely to have occurred. Collateral contacts are important, and a quality assessment involves as many collateral interviews as necessary. It is possible that your agency may require a certain number, but the point is to intentionally add context and depth to your assessment. In Tonya's case with the Perkins family, an example of a collateral interview that would contribute to the investigation would be interviewing the school guidance counselor. This individual may be able to speak about the Perkins's family dynamics, daily routines, the girls' progress in school, and their physical and mental health. Similarly, teachers, preachers, extended family members, neighbors, mental health therapists, law enforcement officers, or any additional social service providers may have information relevant to the assessment. There are many possibilities; use your knowledge to identify key familial and community members who may strengthen your assessment. Investigating child maltreatment should always be taken seriously, and reaching outside the original family to capture information from others can make the assessment take longer but ultimately better protects the child.

Decision Making

Child protective services investigations do not last forever. At some point, a decision must be made about the results of your investigative work. Information has been collected, interviews have been conducted, and documentation has been collected from a number of sources. While you may get up to 45 days to complete your formal report (it depends on agency policy), practically speaking, a decision will most likely be made long before that time. Throughout the entire investigative process, professionals are actively considering options that would provide safety and stability for the vulnerable victims. Investigations are concluded by making objective decisions based on the prevailing risk factors and information collected.

Decisions in child welfare often occur through multidisciplinary and collaborative team decision making (McConnell, Llewellyn, & Ferronato, 2006; Nouwen, Decuyper, & Put, 2012). Decision making is an integral component of working in child protection, as this important and complex professional activity influences future courses of action for the child and family (Nyathi, 2018).

In the case scenario, Tonya would have to make a decision with her supervisor long before those 45 days. It is clear that there were far too many risks to allow the children to go home from school on that day. Therefore, Tonya and her supervisor would have to make a decision for the children's safety almost immediately. To review, law enforcement had video footage of child sexual abuse, and both of the children disclosed that they were victims of child sexual abuse. Drugs and drug paraphernalia were found at the home, and both parents appeared to be under the influence. Further, Rodney and Angela were both taken to jail and charged with child sexual abuse and possession of illegal drugs.

The seriousness of this case requires the investigative worker to expedite the investigative decision. Two questions that the CPS investigator must address are (a) Is there a preponderance of evidence that child maltreatment has occurred? and (b) Do I have enough evidence to meet the state's statute for this type of maltreatment?

When deciding to conclude a child protection investigation, there are several options. In the Perkins case, Tonya and her supervisor found a **preponderance of evidence** (that is, extensive, overwhelming, not minimal) that Rebecca and Renee experienced maltreatment. In other words, there was sufficient evidence to affirm the occurrence of child sexual abuse. Agencies may then use language that calls this a **substantiated**, **confirmed**, or **indicated** investigation. Regardless of the chosen terminology, a substantiated report means that the agency's investigation resulted in enough evidence to meet the statute that the child was abused or neglected.

STATE STATUTE: AN EXAMPLE

It is critical that your findings conform with state statute. On occasion defendants of the agency's actions will appeal the findings or conclusion of the investigation. Thus, you must always be clear on the violation and have sufficient evidence to defend your decisions. While you cannot predict human behavior, you can follow policy, provide comprehensive documentation, reach out to collateral partners, and always err on the side of the safety of the child.

Several risk factors have been found to influence the probability of substantiating an allegation. In a large-scale study evaluating a total of 501,060 substantiation decisions, Victor, Grogan-Kaylor, Ryan, Perron, and Gilbert (2018) found that the identification of parental substance misuse and domestic violence in the course of the child protection investigation significantly increased the odds of substantiation. Also, the social outrage associated with higher numbers of child fatalities has been identified as a key contributor for influencing the substantiation of reports of child maltreatment (Jagannathan & Camasso, 2017).

What if Tonya did not find enough evidence to substantiate the investigation? Most likely she would deem the investigation **unsubstantiated** or **unfounded,** and this would result in the closure of the investigation and termination of the family's involvement with the agency. However, there can be a middle ground where the agency may use an alternate method to initiate preventive services with a family and not actually substantiate the investigation. The purpose of this approach is to encourage the family to cooperate with the agency in a longer term capacity to improve their functioning and overall health. Keep in mind that the substantiated report of child maltreatment is something that will likely follow someone around for the rest of his or her life and could present barriers for employment; for instance, if the person becomes listed on a child abuse registry. Decisions about families are serious, and the repercussions must always be weighed in terms of protecting the child.

As a review, a general overview of the key steps involved in the CPS investigation are as follows:

1. Agency receives a formal referral that alleges the maltreatment of a child.
2. Agency screening results in the decision to accept the report as a CPS investigation.
3. Report is assigned to a CPS investigator.
4. Investigator considers avenues for preparation before initiation.
5. Investigator makes initial contact with the alleged victim within time frame.
6. Investigator conducts field interview and makes collateral contacts.
7. Investigator completes the assessment and writes up a detailed report.
8. Investigator and supervisor make the formal decision regarding the findings and whether ongoing services or court involvement are necessary.

TEST YOURSELF

As the face of the agency and a professional in a position of authority, public perception is an important factor that influences the experience of the CPS investigator. How might public perception affect you as a CPS investigator?

Lawrence, Zeitlin, Auerbach, Chakravarty, and Rienks (2018) developed a scale that you may want to read and think about. Specifically, it explores the constructs of respect, blame, and stigma. These areas are important to consider, as they have a direct influence on the investigator's job experience and longevity. More information can be found here:

Lawrence, C. K., Zeitlin, W., Auerbach, C., Chakravarty, S., & Rienks, S. (2018). Measuring the impact of public perceptions on child welfare workers. *Journal of Public Child Welfare*, 1–18.

Involuntary Services and Court Involvement

With a preponderance of evidence supporting the occurrence of child sexual abuse, an immediate decision had to be made. Tonya and her supervisor were able to get a quick meeting with the county prosecuting attorney at 11:00 a.m. to file a petition in civil court and request the emergency custody of Rebecca and Renee. Unable to find an appropriate relative, the agency requested that the girls be placed in out-of-home care and in a state-approved foster home.

Presented with the petition later that afternoon in his office, the judge agreed that the risk was too great for the children to remain in the custody of their parents, and an emergency custody order was granted to the state through the CPS agency for the children to be placed in foster care. Tonya was given a copy of the signed court orders and informed that the family's emergency removal hearing would occur within 3 days. The judge reminded her that the parents had a right to participate in that hearing, and arrangements would be made to transport them to the hearing from the jail if they were still incarcerated.

Child protection agencies share an inherent relationship with the court system, fundamental to the provision of child protective services (Gupta-Kagan, 2016; Wattenberg, Troy, & Beuch, 2011). Child protection is involuntary or statutory, meaning that services are legislatively mandated when the situations put children at risk of harm or continued harm.

The court experience for the child protective services worker can be an opportunity to feel good about the investigative work and doing one's job of protecting children from harm. However, it can also produce anxiety and may result in feeling vulnerable—even attacked during cross-examination by the defendant's attorney. Regardless, understanding the court process and becoming familiar with the purpose of these hearings are key to feeling comfortable in your role as a child protective services professional.

PRACTICE TIP 4.4 Specific behaviors can help you be more effective and confident in the courtroom as a CPS worker. Make sure you are prepared. Do your homework and consider practicing your testimony beforehand if needed. Breathe, relax, and possibly meditate to clear your mind and focus before your hearing. Turn off your cell phone and don't fidget around with any objects (e.g., playing with your hair). Use appropriate body language, sit up straight, and take command of the situation. You know the information and evidence you have obtained. If you make a mistake, own it. Next time you can use this as a lesson learned to become more confident and effective.

The next section of the chapter will provide an overview of some of the common hearings typically associated with working in child protection. It will provide a quick illustration of how these court hearings are involved with the investigation and then become a part of the responsibilities of the ongoing services worker (which will be covered in Chapter 5). Not all involvement with families will result in court interaction. Further, not all court interaction (e. g., filing a petition alleging abuse) involves the emergency removal of children from their parents' custody. However, the information below will assist in your understanding of the court processes.

Court Proceedings

Table 4.1 provides an illustration of the steps likely to occur in terms of court proceedings if an investigative worker filed *only* a petition of abuse or neglect alleging the maltreatment of a child in a family—where it was *not felt necessary* to request a change of custody for the children. With these cases the agency would not feel that there is enough of a concern to request that the children be removed from their parents' custody but wants to hold the family accountable through court involvement due to recommendations for their participation in ongoing services for long-term improvement.

TABLE 4.1 COURT PROCESSES—PETITIONS WITHOUT AN EMERGENCY CUSTODY ORDER

Hearing	Purpose
Initial hearing	An investigation results in necessary court interaction, without requesting a change in custody.
Adjudication hearing	A trial to determine whether there is evidence to support the petition alleging neglect or abuse by the caretaker(s).
Dispositional hearing	If adjudicated, this hearing is focused on a review of the case plan and any relevant visitation/contact.
Review hearings	Periodic review of a case to evaluate family safety, stability, and progress on the case plan. Case closure is an option.

Table 4.2 furnishes an example of what happened with the Perkins children. When a case presents with risks too great to leave the children in the custody of their parents, the agency will consider requesting a change in emergency custody. As you remember, Tonya made her way to the courthouse to initiate a court petition alleging the sexual abuse of Rebecca and Renee Perkins *and* to request an emergency custody order from the judge. After a morning of interviews and meetings with law enforcement, school personnel, and her supervisor, Tonya met with the county prosecuting attorney, and this official also agreed that the risks were too great for the girls to remain in the care and custody of their parents. The county attorney then approached the judge with this information, along with the petition alleging abuse.

Moved by the evidence shared in the petition and Tonya's description of her visit to the Perkins home, the judge signed an emergency custody order immediately placing the girls in the custody of the state. Given that an appropriate relative was not found or identified, the girls were placed in state foster care. Keep in mind that emergency custody is temporary and not permanent. That is why the first court hearing in Table 4.2 is called the emergency removal hearing. The emergency removal hearing is held quickly, likely within 72 hours, and is where decisions about custody and placement are the primary focus (more about this below).

TABLE 4.2 COURT PROCESSES-PETITIONS WITH AN EMERGENCY CUSTODY ORDER

Hearing	Purpose
Emergency removal hearing	An investigator presents evidence, and parents can challenge the petition and custody/placement of the child. A judge makes decision about placement and custody of child.
Adjudication hearing	A trial to determine whether there is evidence to support the petition alleging neglect or abuse by the caretaker(s).
Dispositional hearing	If adjudicated, a review over custody and placement of child occurs. A review of the case plan, any relevant visitation/contact, and the child's permanency.
Review hearings	Periodic review of a case to evaluate family safety, stability, visitation/contact, and progress on the case plan. Also, a review of the child's placement and custody toward permanency.
Permanency hearing	At 12 months the court will review the child's permanency goal and with respect to the Adoption and Safe Families Act and possibly make a change (e.g., adoption instead of reunification).
Termination of parental rights hearing	This hearing is a special trial where the agency will present evidence to support the court moving forward with the termination of parental rights. This often happens in a different court and only happens after the child's permanency goal has been changed from reunification at the permanency hearing. Termination of parental rights must occur before adoption takes place.

*Please review https://www.childwelfare.gov/pubPDFs/cwandcourts.pdf for additional information.

The main difference between Tables 4.1 and 4.2 is that in Table 4.2 there is an emergency removal hearing to determine if the children should continue in the custody of someone else (i.e., the state or a relative) or be returned to the custody of their parents. When children are removed from their homes in this process, they are placed in what is called out-of-home care (OOHC). Foster care is a common type of OOHC. Due to the significant legal implications associated with the change in custody, there is far greater oversight and court involvement (e.g., more hearings) when a child is removed from the custody of his or her parents and placed in OOHC. From the beginning, child protective service agencies work toward a permanent solution whenever children are placed in OOHC. As we will explore in Chapter 6, the Adoption and Safe Families Act (ASFA) guides these decisions, seeking reunification with the family as a primary option if appropriate. If not, the other end of the spectrum could result in the termination of parental rights and permanent legal separation.

The child protective services worker is supported by the county attorney or prosecuting attorney in court. Again, some of the terminology may vary in different parts of the country. Regardless, you are the key ingredient in this mixture and will need to be prepared and ready to testify under oath when requested. With experience, court hearings become familiar and are understood as an empowering avenue for advocacy and protection. Although family members will change and allegations and circumstances will be different, for the most part local attorneys and judges have the same roles, and this continuity will assist in your confidence and effectiveness.

Initial Hearing/Emergency Removal Hearing

Court and legal involvement in the civil court system begins with the CPS worker approaching the county attorney or prosecuting attorney in the local area to initiate a petition to allege the dependency, neglect, or abuse of a child. However, in Tonya's case, Rodney and Angela Perkins were also facing concurrent criminal charges that occurred independent of their involvement with the child protection agency. Criminal proceedings take place in a different court with a different level of evidence, different proceedings, and generally more public access. Court involvement in the child protection system is primarily kept out of the public eye for many reasons, with the chief one being preventing the release of confidential and sensitive information about the children. Arguments have been made that this "secret court" could benefit from public access, but the benefits may not outweigh the consequences of this dramatic change (Leggett, 2014).

The first hearing in this court involvement process is either called the initial hearing or the emergency removal hearing. As mentioned, this depends on the level of risk and if a change of custody has already occurred. Although Tonya pursued an emergency custody order and the children were placed in the custody of the state government by the judge, the emergency removal hearing was still required, and the Perkins parents had the right to argue, if they wished, for their children to be returned.

This first hearing generally results in the child protective services worker presenting evidence of the maltreatment (or substantial risk of maltreatment) of a child. As mentioned above, this can occur with or without the emergency removal of the children. For example, in a different case the child protection agency may feel that the risk to the children is low enough that it is not in the best interest of the child to request removal from the home. In these cases the CPS agency may feel it is necessary to initiate ongoing services (e.g., outpatient therapy, homemaker services, etc.) with the family by going to court to increase the chances that the family will comply. **Homemaker services** can be provided to stabilize homes where an assigned staff person travels to the client's home and assists with meal planning and possibly meal preparation, cleaning the home environment, helping the caretaker with organization, budgeting, and basic child care as necessary. Decisions about placing children in foster care are very important and not taken lightly, as not all children do well in foster homes away from their families. Homemaker services may help improve a home or the care of children enough to prevent placement in foster care.

The initial hearing or emergency removal hearing (depending on the circumstances associated with the investigation) will begin with formalities associated with the assignment of legal representation. By law, all respondents in a civil court hearing of this nature will have legal representation. Respondents may choose to pay for their own attorneys, or the court may assign these based on the respondents' financial circumstances. As we saw in the scenario above, the investigative worker will be represented by the county or prosecuting attorney.

The parents will each be assigned a defense attorney. It is important that each parent has his or her own legal representation, because Rodney and Angela may decide that it is in their best interest not to align. That is, they could have different charges against them, and one parent could attempt to mitigate his or her offense by blaming the other parent. Also, each of the children will be assigned their own guardian ad litem. The **guardian ad litem, or GAL** (highlighted in Chapter 11), is a term used to identify an attorney who is assigned to represent and advocate for the interests of the child—serving an essential role in the court process (Mabry, 2013).

The court assignment of legal representation may initially seem a bit confusing, but this is a quick and standard process that only takes a few minutes and occurs each and every time you begin the court process with the family. Courts have a number of reliable and familiar attorneys who can be called on. After a few months on the job, you will probably recognize several attorneys in court who specialize in this type of work.

The investigative worker will generally testify under oath to the contents of the petition, which will describe the evidence supporting the alleged maltreatment of the children. The respondents to the petition (the parents or legal guardians) will have an opportunity to challenge the allegations, and the judge will make a determination on the merits of the allegations and the parental response. It is possible that a parent could admit to the petition and choose to move forward with ongoing services although that is a rare circumstance.

The primary purpose of this hearing is for the parents to be notified of their rights—they have a right to challenge the allegations. Also, if the children have been removed from the custody of the parents, this hearing will require the judge's decision about whether to return the children to the care and custody of their caretaker(s) or to continue with the OOHC plan or relative placement.

Adjudication Hearing

The adjudication hearing is a trial where the child protection worker and CPS agency legal representation go on record through testimony to assert their findings and provide evidence that identifies the maltreatment of a child. The adjudication can be scheduled at the initial hearing or the emergency removal hearing but typically occurs much later (normally within about 45 days). At times, those parents or caregivers with allegations against them work with their attorneys and come to an agreement. They may admit to allegations, and the adjudication hearing will be a lot quicker. At other times, the adjudication hearing may consist of a number of professionals testifying, and the hearing could take quite some time.

Popular movies and television programs provide examples of taking the witness stand and going through the process of cross-examination. To a certain degree, these representations may capture the essence of this process. The investigative worker will likely testify, and community partners (e.g., physicians, therapists) may also be asked to provide relevant testimony. Make no mistake about it, the child protective services investigator is the cornerstone of the adjudication and needs to be prepared to take questions from the defense attorneys, GAL, county attorney, and judge.

Although it may vary in your geographic area, a common level of evidence associated with child protection findings is the *preponderance of the evidence* criterion. What this means is that the court must decide that it is more likely than not that the abuse of a child has occurred. In practical terms, that means that the scale would have to be tipped by at least 51% confidence that the child was neglected/abused.

A quality and thorough investigation may lead to a client's (respondent's) admission of culpability. For example, clients that you work with may recognize the obvious nature of the evidence against them and that taking the witness stand and trying to challenge the allegations would be pointless. Rodney and Angela Perkins could plead guilty to their criminal charges (in criminal court), and if so, they would likely admit to the allegations in their civil court hearing, as criminal proceedings have a much higher level of evidence associated. However, that decision is based on legal consultation with their assigned attorney(s). If their attorney(s) recommend a strategy to challenge the allegations, they may pursue a full-on adjudication trial.

The adjudication hearing is a critical step in the protection of children and setting the trajectory for their safety. It is an exhilarating experience but also one that can produce some anxiety. It is intense, but you will be prepared. It will be important to be authentic and honest, and if you don't know the answer then just say so. The adjudication is an opportunity for you to showcase the hard work and attention to detail you have utilized while following agency policies. It is possible that the court will rule against your allegations, and the case could be immediately closed. It is also possible that this hearing could provide for the long-term stability and protection of vulnerable children needing assistance.

Dispositional Hearing

If adjudicated, a dispositional hearing will occur and focus on the treatment prescribed to the family in an ongoing capacity. The dispositional hearing will occur after the adjudication, but the specific time frame is highly contingent on agency policy and on the situational needs of the family. If the children were placed in OOHC and removed from the custody of their parents, the dispositional hearing will also involve a review of the children's permanency and stability and an evaluation of the progress of their visitation with their parents. The ongoing caseworker will likely have a large role in the dispositional hearing, as usually the investigative worker would have passed this case on to a colleague who specializes in ongoing services by this time (more about this in Chapter 5.

After the completion of her investigation in our scenario, Tonya's supervisor will assign ongoing involvement with the Perkins family to a colleague who specializes in ongoing services. While the inner workings of case management with the family in an ongoing capacity will be described in Chapter 5 it is appropriate to provide a glimpse of this next phase. When a child has been removed from the custody of his or her parents, the dispositional hearing will identify timelines defined by the ASFA. The dispositional hearing establishes future reviews on the family's progress on the negotiated case plan. Working toward the reunification of their children with the family (if applicable) will remain the priority.

Review Hearings

Review hearings can be quite general in nature, as their purpose is not as specific or intentional as that of the adjudication or disposition hearings. Nonetheless, they are very important. Review hearings can occur continually and over a prolonged period. A review hearing may be placed on the **court docket** (a listing of all the cases before the court). This will serve as a reminder to review the case on a continual basis for progress. A common example of this would be if a family had made progress (e.g., in therapy or completed recovery) and the ongoing caseworker was interested in asking the court for permission to allow the children overnight visitation. Regardless, the primary purpose of a review hearing is to evaluate the family's progress on the negotiated case plan. Additionally, the review hearing can examine the appropriateness of the children's placement and custody, especially if they are still in OOHC.

Permanency Hearing

As we will explore in Chapter 6, the ASFA was designed to expedite children in foster care into an appropriate form of permanency. Initially, the focus is always on attempting to reunify the family. There is a fundamental belief that the family is the best place for raising a child, unless there are conditions that make this not in the best child's interest. The permanency hearing occurs when the child has been in OOHC for 12 months, and it provides an opportunity for the agency to submit evidence to the court about the progress that the family has made toward reunification. The family's progress should be evident, one way or another. The permanency hearing is important because it may provide the agency an opportunity to request that the court change the goal from family reunification to another form of appropriate permanency (e.g., adoption) when there is a lack of progress or improvement in a family's situation. If a permanency goal is changed from reunification to adoption, the agency would then begin the process of seeking to terminate the parental rights of each relevant party (involved child). However, if there is adequate evidence that the family is making progress, continuance toward reunification should occur.

Termination of Parental Rights Hearing

Often called the TPR hearing, this proceeding has the potential to erase the legal relationship between a child and his or her parent(s). There is quite a bit of focus on this hearing, and rightfully so. It usually takes place in a separate court system, like a circuit court, for example. However, it is a civil hearing and has significant ramifications—children cannot be adopted until their parental rights are terminated. Because this hearing is consequential, it can require a large amount of time and may result in service appeals.

It is likely that the investigative specialist and the ongoing services worker will both provide testimony at the TPR hearing. Depending on the child's mental health and cognitive functioning, the child may be asked to testify. At this point, the agency has likely worked with the family for well over a year and possibly several years. The TPR hearing makes it clear that the agency is moving forward on a different path to permanency, given the parents' inability or unwillingness to make substantial progress.

During the hearing, the agency will provide the court with as much evidence as possible to indicate that it is in the child's best interest to terminate and sever the legal relationship with his or her parents/caretakers forever. The respondents will have the opportunity to testify and challenge the agency, including the cross-examination by their legal representatives. The child's GAL remains a key player in this event, and it is always in the agency's best interest to be fully aware of the GAL's intentions before the hearing commences. While the termination of parental rights does not always occur, if the court does affirm the termination of parental rights, the involvement with the family immediately changes. For example, many agencies have a permanency team that will begin to work with the child and any specific needs he or she may have. The case plan will now exclude the biological family or caretakers and focus solely on the needs of the child and long-term permanency goals. We will get into this more in Chapter 6.

Completing the Investigation and Transition

Families become involved with child protection for many reasons, but the investigation and the initial assessment begins the trajectory. In this chapter, Tonya began the process of working with the Perkins family, and we will follow their journey in the next two chapters. Although it may seem as if there are many hearings for each case, there can be some CPS worker overlap in court hearings. For example, if Tonya has an emergency removal hearing a couple of days after the filing of the initial petition, it is likely that her supervisor may send the ongoing services worker to the hearing to become familiar with the case that may soon be coming his or her way. Further, as the Perkins children will be placed in foster care, it is important that a case plan and visitation plan be developed and negotiated with the family as soon as possible. Basically, you don't have 45 days to wait for the completion of your assessment report to begin implementing needed services and considering the implementation of any approved visitation.

Even after the case has been assigned to the ongoing specialist and Tonya's investigation has been completed, Tonya still needs to be able to testify at any necessary hearing (e.g. adjudication, disposition, etc.). Having an understanding and awareness of this process and being able to adjust and accommodate as necessary is an important skill that you will use throughout your career.

Removal and Placement in Foster Care

An emotional aspect of working in child protection involves the process of removing children from their parents or caretaker. The media sometimes portrays child protective service workers as "baby snatchers," and some individuals have even maliciously suggested that CPS professionals supposedly earn a commission for children that are placed in foster care. Rest assured, nothing could be further from the truth. The reality is that decisions must be made to assure the safety of a vulnerable child. No doubt, the process of removing a child is something that you will never forget. However, let's be clear. A court order removes the child; it is not the decision of the investigative child protective services worker. To say this another way, there is a checks-and-balances system in place whenever there is consideration for out-of-home arrangements.

Being supportive, honest, and transparent with children through this sensitive process can make the transition easier. A qualitative study exploring children's views of transition to foster care found that while the pain of separation was evident, children referred to their CPS investigator as a "very nice" or "regular person, just like anyone else" and were consistently informed that the abuse was "not your [the child's] fault" (Bogolub, 2008, p. 93).

As you work with the foster parents at the agency to assure a smooth transition, it is critical to provide them with as much information as possible (when appropriate). Can you imagine taking care of several children in your home but not knowing that one has an affinity for starting fires? It is vital to go into as much detail as you are able to attempt to assure the effective preparation of these foster parents so they can meet the needs of the child. The investigative worker has an important opportunity to make sure that the foster parent feels appreciated and taken seriously—key areas found to influence much needed foster parent retention (Randle, Ernst, Leisch, & Dolnicar, 2017).

Do everything you can to show warmth and care for the child and assure him or her that things will be fine in the foster home. Use your skills to think of ways that would help the child feel cared for and safe. If the foster home or placement doesn't work out (called a **placement disruption**), it does not mean that the child will immediately be going home. If there are challenges or problems associated with the child being placed in a foster home, efforts will be made to rectify any problems that occur, if at all possible. Sometimes the child will be moved to a different foster home or to relative care if appropriate.

Obtaining the signed emergency custody orders, Tonya and her supervisor picked Rebecca and Renee up from school and began discussing the new foster home where the girls would be going. Tonya did her best to provide an age-appropriate discussion of the need for a temporary foster home and to give other needed details about their family. It wasn't easy, but Tonya did her best. Renee was upset and continually asked who would be able to take care of her dog. Rebecca, on the other hand, was far less emotional and stated that she was "ready to go." Rebecca's only request was for some food since she was hungry.

This was not the first time that Tonya had a role placing children in OOHC. She knew that her current investigation and upcoming testimony at the emergency removal hearing would likely mean long-term involvement for the children with the local child protection agency. Knowing of its importance to Renee, Tonya called the foster parent and asked if she was willing to accept Renee's small dog for a brief time. When she agreed, Tonya shared this news with Renee, who became overwhelmed with joy, immediately resulting in a happier child. Tonya took both of the girls through the drive-through at McDonald's for some food and ice cream, and although she had to pay out of her own pocket, she felt that it was money well spent.

Tonya and the girls arrived at their new foster home, and Tonya took the time to walk through the house with Rebecca and Renee and answer questions. She was open and honest. Tonya let the girls know that they will soon have an ongoing services worker who would be there to help them and work with their family toward reunification, if at all possible. After helping the girls become comfortable in the home, Tonya was exhausted. Before driving home, she sat in the air-conditioning in her vehicle for a few minutes and took deep breaths to unwind a bit.

She knew her involvement had changed the course of the girls' lives. She felt confident in her abilities but also felt the weight of this responsibility. Had she done the right thing? Correctly followed all the agency's procedures? She believed so. Once she had seen the video footage of Rebecca and Renee being sexually abused, she knew she would do everything within her power to make things better. Tonya was an advocate, an agent of change, and someone who was determined to stop this cycle of abuse. She turned on some music and made her way home. She was looking forward to dinner but first was going to put on her sneakers and take a slow jog through the Arboretum.

Main Points

This chapter introduces you to the actual processes involved with carrying out an investigation of alleged child maltreatment. The investigative worker has a very vital role and a great responsibility to collect credible evidence. In some instances, there is insufficient evidence of maltreatment or harm to a child. Other times, as in Tonya's case, the evidence supporting the allegation of sexual abuse is quite strong. The court's involvement and required processes will likely be new to you and something you will become quite familiar with in your career in child protection.

- Child protection agencies receive reports of alleged maltreatment of children, and these can come from many different sources.
- After an initial agency screening of the report or allegation to ensure that it meets the criteria necessary for acceptance, it will be assigned to a CPS professional to conduct an investigation—generally within 24 to 48 hours.
- Investigative specialists interview families and others in the community (collateral contacts) to assess situations or circumstances that may be harmful or helpful to children. The authority for the investigation is supported by state statute and agency policy.
- Investigative specialists complete a comprehensive assessment with a focus on documenting their evidence and safety for the children. The investigative assessment is both a process and a product.
- Agency supervisors play key roles in reviewing allegations, assigning investigations, supplying consultation, and decision making and planning that would result in any continuation of services for the family.
- Court hearings and processes are a routine part of child protection work. Initiating a petition of child abuse or neglect begins the trajectory of involvement for the family.
- If removal or out-of-home care is necessary for the children, the Adoption and Safe Families Act directs practice with respect to family reunification.
- Placing children in foster care can be difficult for them and their parents; however, it is never done unless it is in the child's best interest.

Questions for Class Discussion

1. How might it be different to work on a team with generalist responsibilities vs. one that is specialized?
2. Would you prefer to work as a specialist or a generalist worker? Why?
3. Discuss some safety concerns associated with investigating child maltreatment that were not mentioned in the text.
4. Are there any mobile apps or software programs that you feel could help CPS investigators in their course of duty?
5. How do you think the two Perkins girls felt about being separated from their parents? Do you think they would be relieved? Worried? Conflicted?

Self-Assessment for Personal Consideration

1. How comfortable are you with conducting a child abuse investigation?

1	2	3	4	5	6	7	8	9	10

   Not comfortable   *Very comfortable*

2. How comfortable are you with the idea of testifying in court?

1	2	3	4	5	6	7	8	9	10

   Not comfortable   *Very comfortable*

Additional Resources

Chaiyachati, B. H., Asnes, A. G., Moles, R. L., Schaeffer, P., & Leventhal, J. M. (2016). Gray cases of child abuse: Investigating factors associated with uncertainty. *Child Abuse & Neglect, 51*, 87–92.

Child and Family Services Reviews. (n.d.). Information portal: Investigation. Retrieved from https://training.cfsrportal.acf.hhs.gov/section-2-understanding-child-welfare-system/3012

Child Welfare Information Gateway. (n.d.). Investigation. Retrieved from https://www.childwelfare.gov/topics/responding/iia/investigation

Dawe, S., Taplin, S., & Mattick, R. R. (2017). Psychometric investigation of the Brief Child Abuse Potential Inventory in mothers on opioid substitution. *Journal of Family Violence, 32*(3), 341–348.

DePanfilis, D., & Salus, M. K. (2003). *Child protective services: A guide for caseworkers.* Washington, DC: US Department of Health and Human Services. Retrieved from https://www.childwelfare.gov/pubpdfs/cps.pdf

Simon, J. D., & Brooks, D. (2017). Identifying families with complex needs after an initial child abuse investigation: A comparison of demographics and needs related to domestic violence, mental health, and substance abuse. *Child Abuse & Neglect, 67*, 294–304.

United States. (2006). *Photo-documentation in the investigation of child abuse.* Washington, DC: Office of Juvenile Justice and Delinquency Prevention.

References

Alfandari, R. (2017). Systemic barriers to effective utilization of decision making tools in child protection practice. *Child Abuse & Neglect, 67*, 207–215.

Arad-Davidzon, B., & Benbenishty, R. (2008). The role of workers' attitudes and parent and child wishes in child protection workers' assessments and recommendation regarding removal and reunification. *Children & Youth Services Review, 30*(1), 107–121.

Block, S. D., Foster, E. M., Pierce, M. W., Berkoff, M. C., & Runyan, D. K. (2013). Multiple forensic interviews during investigations of child sexual abuse: A cost-effectiveness analysis. *Applied Developmental Science, 17*(4), 174–183.

Bogolub, E. B. (2008). Child protective services investigations and the transition to foster care: Children's views. *Families in Society: Journal of Contemporary Social Services, 89*(1), 90–99.

Brink, F. W., Thackeray, J. D., Bridge, J. A., Letson, M. M., & Scribano, P. V. (2015). Child advocacy center multidisciplinary team decision and its association to Child Protective Services outcomes. *Child Abuse & Neglect, 46*, 174–181.

Dettlaff, A. J., Christopher Graham, J., Holzman, J., Baumann, D. J., & Fluke, J. D. (2015). Development of an instrument to understand the child protective services decision-making process, with a focus on placement decisions. *Child Abuse & Neglect, 49*, 24–34.

Gupta-Kagan, J. (2016). Child protection law as an independent variable. *Family Court Review, 54*(3), 398–412.

Herbert, J. L., Walsh, W., & Bromfield, L. (2018). A national survey of characteristics of child advocacy centers in the United States: Do the flagship models match those in broader practice? *Child Abuse & Neglect, 76*, 583–595.

Jagannathan, R., & Camasso, M. J. (2017). Social outrage and organizational behavior: A national study of child protective service decisions. *Children and Youth Services Review, 77*, 153–163.

Jordan, N., Yampolskaya, S., Gustafson, M., Armstrong, M., McNeish, R., & Vargo, A. (2011). Comparing child protective investigation performance between law enforcement agencies and child welfare agencies. *Child Welfare, 90*(2), 87–105.

Kim, H., Wildeman, C., Jonson-Reid, M., & Drake, B. (2017). Lifetime prevalence of investigating child maltreatment among US children. *American Journal of Public Health, 107*(2), 274–280.

King, B., Fallon, B., Boyd, R., Black, T., Antwi-Boasiako, K., & O'Connor, C. (2017). Factors associated with racial differences in child welfare investigative decision-making in Ontario, Canada. *Child Abuse & Neglect, 73*, 89–105.

Lawrence, C. K., Zeitlin, W., Auerbach, C., Chakravarty, S., & Rienks, S. (2018). Measuring the impact of public perceptions on child welfare workers. *Journal of Public Child Welfare*, 1–18.

Leggett, Z. (2014). Opening up the family courts in the name of public interest, but at what cost? *Journal of Criminal Law, 78*(3), 202–206.

Leschied, A. W., Chiodo, D., Whitehead, P. C., Hurley, D., & Marshall, L. (2003). The empirical basis of risk assessment in child welfare: The accuracy of risk assessment and clinical judgment. *Child Welfare, 82*(5), 527–540.

Mabry, C. R. (2013). Guardians ad litem: Should the child's best interests advocate give more credence to the child's best wishes in custody cases? *American Journal of Family Law, 27*(3), 172–188.

McConnell, D., Llewellyn, G., & Ferronato, L. (2006). Context-contingent decision-making in child protection practice. *International Journal of Social Welfare, 15*(3), 230–239.

Menard, K. S., & Ruback, R. B. (2003). Prevalence and processing of child sexual abuse: A multi-data-set analysis of urban and rural counties. *Law and Human Behavior, 27*(4), 385–402.

Nouwen, E., Decuyper, S., & Put, J. (2012). Team decision making in child welfare. *Children and Youth Services Review, 34*(10), 2101–2116.

Nyathi, N. (2018). Child protection decision-making: Social workers' perceptions. *Journal of Social Work Practice, 32*(2), 189–203.

Powell, M. B., Guadagno, B. L., & Cassematis, P. (2013). Workplace stressors for investigative interviewers of child-abuse victims. *Policing: An International Journal of Police Strategies & Management, 36*(3), 512–525.

Randle, M., Ernst, D., Leisch, F., & Dolnicar, S. (2017). What makes foster carers think about quitting? Recommendations for improved retention of foster carers. *Child & Family Social Work, 22*(3), 1175–1186.

Shin, J. (2011). Client violence and its negative impacts on work attitudes of child protection workers compared to community service workers. *Journal of Interpersonal Violence, 26*(16), 3338–3360.

Smith, C., Fluke, J., Fallon, B., Mishna, F., & Decker Pierce, B. (2018). Child welfare organizations: Do specialization and service integration impact placement decisions? *Child Abuse & Neglect, 76*, 573–582.

Smith, D. W., Witte, T. H., & Fricker-Elhai, A. E. (2006). Service outcomes in physical and sexual abuse cases: A comparison of Child Advocacy Center-based and standard services. *Child Maltreatment, 11*(4), 354–360.

Stanley, T. (2010). Working at the nexus of risk: Statutory Child Protection. *International Journal of Interdisciplinary Social Sciences, 5*(6), 87–97.

Steen, J. A., & Duran, L. (2014). Entryway into the child protection system: The impacts of child maltreatment reporting policies and reporting system structures. *Child Abuse & Neglect, 38*(5), 868–874.

Tehrani, N. (2018). Psychological well-being and workability in child abuse investigators. *Occupational Medicine-Oxford, 68*(3), 165–170.

Turney, D. (2012). A relationship-based approach to engaging involuntary clients: The contribution of recognition theory. *Child & Family Social Work, 17*(2), 149–159.

Victor, B. G., Grogan-Kaylor, A., Ryan, J. P., Perron, B. E., & Gilbert, T. T. (2018). Domestic violence, parental substance misuse and the decision to substantiate child maltreatment. *Child Abuse & Neglect, 79,* 31–41.

Waterhouse, L., & McGhee, J. (2009). Anxiety and child protection—implications for practitioner–parent relations. *Child & Family Social Work, 14*(4), 481–490.

Wattenberg, E., Troy, K., & Beuch, A. (2011). Protective supervision: An inquiry into the relationship between child welfare and the court system. *Children & Youth Services Review, 33*(2), 346–350.

Wolfteich, P., & Loggins, B. (2007). Evaluation of the Children's Advocacy Center model: Efficiency, legal and revictimization outcomes. *Child & Adolescent Social Work Journal, 24*(4), 333–352.

CHAPTER 5

ONGOING SERVICES: THE WORKER'S ROLES

OVERVIEW

A substantiated investigation of child maltreatment will likely result in the child protection agency opening a case to provide ongoing services to the family. These services will be focused on addressing the high-risk behaviors and developing strategies to ensure long-term safety, stability, and permanency for the children. In this chapter, we direct our attention to the role of the ongoing caseworker, the development of the family case plan, facilitating services, and strategies for best practice. Ongoing case management is the backbone of working in child protection, and we will continue to examine the Perkins family scenario to illustrate how the case plan is developed and implemented.

Chad: The Ongoing Caseworker

Out on a monthly client home visit, Chad received a text message from his supervisor that Tonya's case had a scheduled emergency removal hearing. Chad was asked to attend and informed that he would be the ongoing caseworker for the family. As an ongoing caseworker, Chad was a specialist in family reunification and the facilitation of comprehensive services. A good team player, he was someone that his colleagues could count on. Checking his busy schedule, he made a few phone calls and made his way to the courthouse, arriving right before the hearing.

Seeing Tonya, Chad shot her a smile across the courtroom and began to take notes as the situation unfolded. As directed by the local county attorney, Tonya testified to the allegations of the child sexual abuse of Rebecca and Renee Perkins and informed the court of the pending concurrent criminal charges for the parents. Rodney and Angela Perkins were present, wearing orange outfits and handcuffs, but declined to testify. However, they both made a formal request that the children be placed with Rodney's mother, Dorothy Perkins, in Bentonville, Arkansas, instead of remaining in state foster care. Without an appropriate local relative, the girls were kept in foster care pending the results of an out-of-state relative home evaluation. The necessary adjudication hearing was scheduled for 45 days out. Chad knew that the request for a relative home placement in Arkansas through the Interstate Compact on the Placement of Children (ICPC) could take some time, but he was ready to expedite the process.

Knowing that it would be a busy afternoon, Chad wanted to speak with his supervisor and the foster parents and have a conversation with Tonya about the Perkins family. He made his way into an auxiliary court room to meet with Rodney and Angela and their attorneys and introduced himself as their ongoing caseworker. Chad mentioned that he would probably be working with them for quite some time, facilitating services with the family to address the high-risk behaviors in their home and promote family stability and reunification if possible. Chad let Rodney and Angela know that he was looking forward to meeting Rebecca and Renee today at the foster home, and he scheduled a meeting with them for the following day at the county jail to begin the process of developing a family case plan.

THE ICPC

The Interstate Compact on the Placement of Children (ICPC) established procedures for the placement of children across state lines. Developed in 1960, this formal contract developed procedural guidelines that are used among all 50 states, the District of Columbia, and the Virgin Islands. Children may have appropriate family members outside of the state where they live, making this collaborative framework a valuable option for achieving appropriate permanency. While the initiating court retains jurisdiction, the receiving agency provides ongoing protective services and oversight until the case is closed or services can be terminated. More information can be found at the following websites:

http://icpcstatepages.org/
https://www.csg.org/NCIC/InterstateCompactforthePlacementofChildren.aspx
https://www.childwelfare.gov/topics/permanency/interjurisdictional/icpc/

Ongoing Child Protection Services

Following the completion of the child abuse investigation, the child protection agency may conduct ongoing services when there is a need to reduce the risk associated with future harm (Lwin, Fluke, Trocmé, Fallon, & Mishna, 2018). We described the responsibilities of the child protective services investigator in Chapter 4, but in Chapter 5 we will illustrate the role of the ongoing caseworker by looking further into the Perkins family case and integrating Chad, the specialized ongoing caseworker. This important position may be known by different terms (e.g., case manager, ongoing caseworker, caseworker); individuals working in this capacity are responsible for the facilitation and evaluation of a number of intentional processes. The ongoing caseworker may have several responsibilities with a case, but it is important to begin this discussion by explaining roles this professional does not have. The ongoing caseworker is not an attorney, is not a law enforcement officer, nor is the caseworker a therapist, a mind reader, or a magician. The ongoing caseworker is a specialist and the catalyst for improving the health and safety of families who have experienced neglect, abuse or dependency.

While there are common and transferrable skills between working as a child protection investigator and as an ongoing caseworker, there are some differences. For starters, investigators are generally only involved with families for a limited time. Investigations must be expedited, and it is quite possible that the child protective services investigator may only see or speak with a client one time. This is a significant contrast with the ongoing caseworker, who will need to establish professional working relationships with clients that may last for several years.

An essential belief guiding the implementation of ongoing services is that family participation will result in better outcomes (Hollinshead, Kim, Fluke, & Merkel-Holguin, 2017). This belief is critical when understanding your role as an ongoing caseworker. That is, you may be working with individuals who have been involuntarily assigned services, and they may not be particularly motivated to work on their issues—with you or with the agency. Additionally, you may work with a family that has experienced recent trauma and is possibly facing concurrent criminal charges. The investigation may have been unpleasant, and now you are responsible for picking up the pieces and helping the family rehabilitate. Ongoing casework is valuable and rewarding—affording the professional an opportunity to be a part of positive family transformation.

Family Case Planning

Delivering ongoing services with families involved with the child protection system involves the pursuit of family empowerment *and* the implementation of child protection. These goals may seem at times to be competing with each other (Gentles-Gibbs, 2016) and must be understood.

It is possible that some of your ongoing cases will be concerned with low-risk behaviors (e.g., truancy) and may not have court involvement. Also, some cases may include families who voluntarily agree to needed services. However, a good portion of your cases will involve significant maltreatment, possibly generational family abuse, and will necessitate both placement of the child in foster care and ongoing court involvement. Related to this last circumstance, the ongoing caseworker will need to be clear on legal liabilities, ongoing court orders, and the legal rights of individuals involved with this process. But as was discussed in Chapter 4, you will have colleagues, supervisors, and attorney support as you move through that process. Remember, you are not operating alone but as part of a team in a position of real authority while working with the family to promote a healthy environment and establish long-term stability.

SOLUTION BASED CASEWORK

Focusing on the use of evidence-based practice in child protection, an effective model of delivering ongoing case management is Solution Based Casework. This acclaimed child welfare practice model is especially valuable for the ongoing caseworker, as it highlights partnership with the family, focusing on everyday life events and developing solutions that target prevention skills. Dr. Dana Christensen and his colleagues facilitate training models for implementation, and peer-reviewed research continues to evaluate the effectiveness of using this practice model. More about Dr. Dana Christensen and Solution Based Casework can be found here:

https://www.solutionbasedcasework.com/

Christensen, D. N., Todahl, J., & Barrett, W. G. (1999). *Solution-based casework: An introduction to clinical and case management skills in casework practice.* New York, NY: Aldine DeGruyter.

Pipkin, S., Sterrett, E. M., Antle, B., & Christensen, D. N. (2013). Washington State's adoption of a child welfare practice model: An illustration of the Getting to Outcomes implementation framework. *Children and Youth Services Review, 35*(12), 1923–1932.

Van Zyl, R., Barbee, A. P., Cunningham, M. R., Antle, B. F., Christensen, D. N., & Boamah, D. (2014). Components of the Solution-Based Casework child welfare practice model that predict positive child outcomes. *Journal of Public Child Welfare, 8*(4), 1–46.

Development of the Case Plan

As the ongoing caseworker, you will be involved in implementing change through the development and facilitation of a family case plan. If you are a specialized ongoing caseworker, you were probably assigned the case after the completion of an investigation by one of your colleagues. If you are a **generalist worker**, one who may both investigate and be an ongoing caseworker, you may complete the investigation of child maltreatment and continue with the ongoing services for the same family by yourself. Regardless, high-risk behaviors will have been identified with evidence creating a rationale for agency involvement, and the goals and tasks forming the family case plan must revolve around the high-risk behavior associated with opening the case in the first place.

The purpose of developing the **family case plan** is to design a "blueprint" for service delivery. While the ongoing caseworker has the freedom to mediate the formation of the case plan with the family at a predetermined time and location (e.g., at the courthouse after a hearing), ongoing caseworkers may also choose a more flexible option and conduct this conference meeting during a routine family home visit (more on this later). Irrespective of where the case-planning conference is held, it is critical that an agreement is developed between the agency, with the ongoing caseworker as its representative, and the family. The case plan is an official document that may be reviewed in court and is a plan for long-term involvement. It is a contract between the family and the agency, and it details the steps that need to be taken for developing a healthy future for the family—one free from future abuse or neglect. If there is court involvement, the case plan will need to be reviewed and accepted by all appropriate attorneys and the judge. It will be filed in the courthouse and will be utilized to evaluate progress and also to expedite agency action and court involvement. Research has suggested a positive effect on timely reunification when ongoing caseworkers involve parents in child welfare-related decisions and activities (Yampolskaya, Armstrong, Strozier, & Swanke, 2017). Something this important must have your supervisor's approval and will be highly detailed and specific.

The ongoing caseworker will be the expert in developing and facilitating this case plan and will draw on a knowledge of the services available in the geographical area. It is very important that the ongoing caseworker identifies and communicates any possible barriers associated with potentially recommending services to the family. Imagine that you agreed to participate in treatment but later found out that the treatment facility was 75 miles away and expensive. What if you realized that your ongoing caseworker knew this beforehand and did not choose to let you know up front? Lack of transparency in this situation would possibly be unethical and would negatively affect a person's relationship with the ongoing worker. If you are an ongoing caseworker, do not withhold relevant information about services when designing a case plan.

The family case plan is only effective for a certain length of time. It is continually evaluated and can be adjusted as necessary. An example could be that the family has made significant progress, resulting in court-ordered reunification. Nonetheless, with some cases, your agency will likely have a formal review process where the ongoing caseworker and supervisor will periodically monitor or assess progress within the family to determine if ongoing services should be adjusted or if they are still necessary.

Deciding on Strategies for Implementing Change in a Case Plan

Designing a case plan to address a family's prevailing issues and create a path for a safe future is a logical process. However, case plans benefit from a knowledge of pragmatic strategies for implementing needed change that comes from having prior experience in child welfare, as a rule. Supervisors and veteran CPS professionals can help the new worker develop good, workable case plans. Strategies must be specific, individualized, and contextually relevant. While the family must be viewed as a holistic unit, each relevant individual has his or her own responsibilities and needs that must be considered.

Let's quickly review the Perkins family case from Chapter 4. You'll remember that a burglar had broken into the home and stolen, among other items, a video camera that contained footage of two young girls being sexually abused by their parents. The thief was so disturbed by what he saw that he turned himself and the camera into the police, who contacted the child protection agency. The investigative worker recognized the family from prior involvement.

The overarching issue in the family was the occurrence of child sexual abuse. This significant issue influences the family as a unit yet also has implications for every family member. A brief example of a possible case plan for the Perkins family with a focus on Mr. Perkins is shown below.

PERKINS FAMILY CASE PLAN

FAMILY GOAL: The family will ensure the children's safety and well-being, and they will be free from sexual abuse.

FAMILY TASKS:
1. Each parent will attend individual therapy sessions to gain an understanding and address the issues that allowed the sexual abuse of their children to occur.
2. *The parents will visit and support their children during placement in foster care.*
3. The parents will help their children develop appropriate trust through visitation and through following recommendations of the therapist.
4. The ongoing caseworker will consult with the therapist monthly on the parents' progress.

GOAL for Mr. Perkins: Mr. Perkins will understand what constitutes sexual abuse, the harm it does to children, and stop abusive behavior.

TASKS for Mr. Perkins:
1. Mr. Perkins will complete a psychological assessment and comply with the recommended treatment.
2. Mr. Perkins will complete a substance abuse assessment and comply with the recommended treatment.
3. Mr. Perkins will have no unsupervised or physical contact with his children until permission is granted.
4. Mr. Perkins will follow all court orders.

Continuation of the Case

Chad arrived at the county jail to meet with Rodney and Angela Perkins to develop a case plan and work toward family reunification. He met with Rodney first and then Angela. During both meetings, Chad focused on the serious nature of the allegations and affirmed that due to a court no-contact order, there would not be any visitation or contact of any kind with the children at this time. Also, Chad explained the implications of the Adoption and Safe Families Act; he let Rodney and Angela know that after 15 of 22 months in foster care, the state agency could request to change Rebecca and Renee's permanency goal to another form of permanency (e. g., adoption) if the parents do not address their issues. However, at this point, the agency was entirely focused on the primary goal of reunification, and Chad made it clear that he was going to work with them in an ongoing capacity to address the high-risk behaviors involved with the family and work to ensure the children's long-term stability and safety.

Chad had to meet with the parents separately at the jail. There were similarities in the two meetings but also some differences. Specifically, Rodney presented as upset and frustrated and claimed that he was going to be "let out tomorrow." Regardless, Chad continued to thoroughly explain the purpose of the case plan but found it difficult to earn Rodney's "buy-in." Although Rodney seemed to finally agree to the components of the case plan, he made it clear that he was "innocent" and would be let out of jail in the near future. Rodney never asked about his children and kept mentioning that he did not like Chad's colleague, Tonya, as he felt she was mean and "hateful."

Angela presented differently; she was quiet but asked questions about her children. Chad spent significant time assuring her that be believed the girls would do well at their current foster care placement and advised that he had submitted an ICPC request to Arkansas for potential placement of the girls with Rodney's mother in Bentonville, Arkansas. Angela appeared to take some responsibility for her behaviors and mentioned that she believed that she and Rodney could become better parents. She wanted to take care of their kids again, although she knew it wouldn't be right away. Chad had worked with many families with similar issues before and left the jail feeling positive about beginning to work with the Perkins family.

Engagement and Facilitation

After beginning the process of involvement with the family, the ongoing caseworker will be the key link in facilitating service delivery and evaluating outcomes. One of the key ingredients to successful case planning is getting the investment of the involved parties. As mentioned earlier, this may be particularly difficult when family members are mandated to participate in services as part of the case plan. Involuntary clients (because they have little choice once their children are removed) may not be excited to work on their issues and begin the implementation of services. However, a critical step is identifying this "elephant in the room" and being authentic as you move into service provision. With time, you will learn techniques and strategies about how to reframe difficult and common circumstances to hopefully increase the buy-in of those families you are working with. Besides the involuntary aspect, it is possible that you are working with a family that has a long history with the agency. If so, they may have already formed negative perceptions about working with child protection professionals that influence their attitudes and interest about working together.

A practice tip here is to recognize any hard feelings they may still retain; be up front and respond to their concerns or issues with the agency, if possible. You can remind them that this is a new case, a new set of circumstances, and you are a professional who is not "out to get them." Alternately, you may be working with a family who has never had any involvement with the agency and is unfamiliar with what exactly may be expected of them. Take the time to answer their questions as well. Be honest and authentic. Authenticity means that if you do not have the answer, you let them know that you will try to find the answers to their questions. Keep your promises.

Newer workers sometimes attempt to answer questions that they may not be able to answer. Realize, though, that it will not take long for a client to recognize if you give bad information, and it will damage your credibility and negatively influence your ability to begin the vital process of engagement. **Client engagement** refers to the process of client participation with the agency (or reestablishing interconnectedness with the family unit). Research has validated the importance of engagement in child protection work, and its positive influence on case outcomes.

A mixed-methods study by Gladstone et al. (2011) demonstrated the positive association between worker–client engagement and positive case outcomes; it also identified the parents' ability to trust their worker as one of the top two self-reported reasons for positive change. Cheng and Lo (2016) completed a longitudinal study with nationally representative records of 3,185 children and their parents and identified collaborative engagement as one of the five specific variables positively associated with parents' progress on the case plan. Without a doubt, engagement is important, but what are the skills and strategies to accomplish it?

In a Canadian study, Gladstone et al. (2014) examined 131 worker–parent dyads from 11 child welfare agencies and identified casework skills that should be emphasized when working to establish engagement. These were including parents in case planning; being caring and supportive; and providing praise for efforts, ideas, or achievements. In a qualitative study in Illinois, a sample of parents involved with the child protection system identified positive communication skills, competency, and the provision of support (concrete or emotional) as the three main components for successful worker engagement during child protection intervention (Schreiber, Fuller, & Paceley, 2013). Also, a recent study by Damiani-Taraba et al. (2017) identified key caseworker skills (e.g., involving parents in planning, locating appropriate services, returning phone calls, etc.) that influenced client engagement and promoted collaboration and positive case outcomes.

In the next section, we will explore the interplay between the ongoing caseworker's responsibilities and the formation of a dynamic relationship with the family unit and community partners.

Working with the Family

Families are unique, and you will have the opportunity to develop professional relationships with individuals that you may not have ever come across otherwise. Working in child protection affords the individual the opportunity to engage with a diverse population of individuals with different beliefs, customs, and traditions. One commonality is that you will be working with at least one child and his or her legal caretaker in each case. The endangered child could be very young or a teenager, and the caretaker a single parent, a more traditional family, or a grandparent or other relative. In the Perkins family scenario, Chad is working with two children who are currently in foster care. While this occurs somewhat frequently, you may find that the majority of cases on your caseload involve children who remain in their homes of origin or are placed with relatives close by. Each family of origin or foster family can have a context or unique micro culture that you will need to learn, as it may influence how you work with it to achieve the goals of the family case plan.

A few examples for consideration are the number of children in each case, their relationship with one another, and how this may or may not influence their safety and well-being. If you are working with a family with one child, it will be much different than attempting to facilitate ongoing services with a family with multiple children. Further, siblings may have different biological fathers or legal relationships that will need to be considered. While keeping siblings together is almost always the primary plan, it is possible that this could negatively influence the child's health and well-being. Think about working with a family in which an older child molested a younger sibling. It is highly unlikely that an agency would recommend keeping these two children together—at least for the time being.

It may also be possible that children in a case have divergent paths and very different needs that should be considered. Or a specific behavior could emerge that could negatively influence the children's safety and stability. What if Angela Perkins began blaming Renee Perkins for causing Renee's own sexual abuse and the family's problems? The ongoing caseworker should gather as much comprehensive information as possible about the family's dynamics before beginning services. Keeping abreast of any new information or changes associated with family dynamics will assist the ongoing worker in directing and managing the right set of services to expedite positive family outcomes.

Working with the Community

Individual members of the family involved in the case plan will have their own specific needs apart from those of the family as a whole. These may not always be completely known at the time of developing the case plan. Child protective agencies are heavily reliant on service provider partners in the community; CPS workers cannot provide all of the comprehensive services required by a range of family problems.

All CPS professionals will hopefully have access to mental health therapists, medical providers, foster parents, and a functional court system no matter where they are physically located within the United States. Other valuable community partners may include the local library, school social workers and guidance counselors, food banks and clothes closets, the fire department, and law enforcement. Community providers are the backbone of ongoing services in child protection.

Given our scenario with the Perkins family, let's imagine that Angela later reveals to Chad that she has been the victim of domestic violence. However, what if the local area does not have any therapists who have an expertise in that area? Seeking to revise the case plan to address this issue, Chad would need to reach out—possibly outside the community or county—to see what options were available. However, transportation and ability to pay could be barriers.

In an optimal situation, Chad would have multiple effective and court-approved options for services in the local area to present to Angela. However, challenges associated with turnover at local agencies and limitations related to services in certain areas are often an unfortunate reality. That is, key staff known to be especially skilled or competent may change jobs and be replaced by less experienced staff. Or the most skilled expert could be located in a private practice the client cannot afford. At times, you may have little choice if only one agency provides a particular service.

It is critical for the ongoing caseworker to know as much as possible about the availability and details associated with each type of service in the area. Having a good understanding of the length of treatment, services provided, cost, and initiation processes for beginning treatment are important. (Many ongoing workers keep a resource file of information about their most used or favorite community partners.) Consider the availability of concrete services (e.g., financial assistance, public transportation, etc.) in your area. Integrating these supports can quickly help build trust between you and the family by addressing these apparent needs. Being informed about the availability of community services and operating from a position of professional competence is sure to increase engagement with the family and positively influence progress on the case plan.

GENOGRAMS AND ECO-MAPS: PRACTICAL TOOLS

Making sense of the family's structure and involvement in the community are both critical for the ongoing caseworker. Consider using genograms and eco-maps as tools to assist in this process. The genogram is designed to provide a visual representation of the family tree, so to speak. This can afford the ongoing caseworker the opportunity to visualize familial relationships, demographic information, and additional data such as levels of education; physical or mental health concerns may also be entered to provide context to the family. The eco-map is similar but provides a visual representation of the family's involvement with systems. Creating a visual illustration of the systems (e.g., church, school, medical doctor) involved with the family can be helpful as a baseline and also as a visual indicator of progress throughout the case. Technology can be your best friend in this effort, as the utilization of software programs or smartphone applications can make quick work of their creation.

Case Continuation: The Perkins Adjudication Hearing

After posting bail and eventually returning to their home, Rodney and Angela Perkins arrived at the adjudication hearing at the local courthouse. The adjudication hearing had been moved back for several months, due to the pending criminal charges. Related to the placement of Rebecca and Renee Perkins, this extra time afforded Arkansas the ability to complete its ICPC home evaluation on Dorothy Perkins and have the formal report ready for the hearing.

Given the pending criminal charges and the video footage of inappropriate sexual activity with the children, Rodney and Angela both realized that their behavior produced a preponderance of evidence, and they admitted to child sexual abuse as alleged in the child protective services petition.

Chad presented an approved ICPC home evaluation for Dorothy Perkins from Bentonville, Arkansas. Dorothy had traveled to the courthouse for the hearing, and with the approved home evaluation and no objection by the children's GAL, the court ordered placement for Rebecca and Renee Perkins at the home of Dorothy Perkins in Bentonville, Arkansas. Chad informed the court that he was facilitating ongoing services with the family and that a formal copy of the case plan would be presented to the court at the disposition hearing.

Given the extreme nature of the pending criminal charges, Chad's recommendation for continued no contact between the children and their parents was ordered by the judge. A date was set for the disposition hearing, and random monthly drug screens were also ordered for Rodney and Angela. After the hearing, Chad made his way to the local foster home to discuss Rebecca and Renee's move to Arkansas. A safety plan was also developed and discussed with Dorothy Perkins to assure the well-being and stability of the children while in her care. Chad went over the necessity for compliance with all court orders and visitation agreements, and portions of the case plan were shared to help her understand that the girls would need to be involved and compliant with ongoing courtesy services in Bentonville, Arkansas.

Monthly Home Visits and Contacts

Usually, the ongoing caseworker will visit each child and parent involved in the case at least monthly. This contact can be during a home visit, a trip to a treatment facility, contact at the local jail, or by requesting a courtesy interview if a child on your caseload is outside of the local area and, for instance, living in another state. Known as a protective factor, the effects of worker–family contact are now being quantitatively explored with respect to their influence on potential risk of subsequent child maltreatment (Halverson, Russell, & Kerwin, 2018).

Normally, most monthly contacts involve a visit to the family's primary residence. Home visiting is an integral part of ongoing child protection services—part of a strategy developed long ago to monitor and check on families, with primary interest in following those responsible for the maltreatment and those who received the brunt of it (Chaiyachati, Gaither, Hughes, Foley-Schain, & Leventhal, 2018). Visitation affords the ongoing caseworker the opportunity to observe stability inside the home and assess for improvement in any relevant and contextual family factors. Home visits are important, yet they occur in *sites of uncertainty* (Pink, Morgan, & Dainty, 2015). Keep in mind that you will be invading an individual's private space, and this could be met with pushback. While safety issues and strategies for best practice in visitation will be identified later, there are a number of reasons and factors that may influence *how* you choose to facilitate a home visit.

If the case was opened due to an environmental neglect situation (e.g., where the family had a home that was rampant with head lice and rodents), the primary purpose of the home visit might be to arrive unannounced and assess for any environmental improvement. If an unannounced visit is not necessary to check on progress, another approach might involve possibly scheduling visits to minimize your travel time from one part of the city or county to another. Sometimes you might delay a visit to a nonoffending caretaker or a foster parent in order to accommodate medical or therapy appointments. This is within your decision-making capacity. At times, unannounced home visits are deemed necessary, but realize that if no one is at home, you will have to take the time to come back on another occasion.

Since Rebecca and Renee were placed with their paternal grandmother, Dorothy Perkins, Chad would not need to commute to Arkansas for monthly visits. Instead, he will be able to rely on a protective services worker (courtesy services) from the state of Arkansas to conduct monthly visits and submit timely documentation about both of the Perkins girls to him.

PRACTICE TIP 5.1 Become familiar with the key staff at the local jail and at the local inpatient treatment facilities. You may want to align multiple clients' monthly visits on the same date, one after another. This will save you travel time and make it much easier to manage your other responsibilities. Also, consider working with coworkers to tag team monthly visits. If they have a visit at the jail, see if they are able to help you out by making contact with your client (if appropriate and approved). What that means, for instance, is that Chad could have a meeting with Rodney at the jail, and while he was there, conduct a face-to-face monthly visit for one of his coworkers' clients who is also at the jail. Keep in mind that this does not remove responsibility for visiting that the other ongoing worker would have; however, at certain times colleagues can help with managing multiple cases and responsibilities happening all at once.

Visitation

Research shows that consistent and appropriate visitation positively influences family reunification (Haight, Kagle, & Black, 2003; McWey & Cui, 2017). **Visitation** can be broadly defined as the intentional and direct interaction between children and their parents or caretakers once separated. In child protection services, visitation is generally between the child in foster care and his or her parent(s) or caretaker during the reunification process, but you may have cases where you are involved in facilitating the rebuilding of a relationship between a child still in the home and his or her parent/caretaker.

Visitation can take place in a lot of different ways, but without a good reason or a court order, it must occur. It should occur frequently and appropriately, and visits must always be in the child's best interest. Visitation may occur through a phone call, in the agency's office, or in a face-to-face setting such as a church, restaurant, or other public place. Depending on the contextual issues, the ongoing caseworker is involved in overseeing and coordinating the visitation.

If you are working with a family that is involved with the court, visitation is likely to be a key ingredient in these hearings. It is common for the court to take the "crawl before you walk, walk before you run" strategy by starting visitations in a highly structured environment and moving slowly toward more flexibility. However, if you are working with a family without court oversight, there is much more freedom for the ongoing caseworker to arrange visitations and determine their frequency, location, and so forth.

Initially, Rodney and Angela Perkins were not approved to have any type of visitation with their girls. However, a natural place to begin contact later would be with supervised phone calls to the children in Arkansas. After positive reports from the children's therapists and little or no concern about any potential negative effects of the contacts, Chad would be able to consider moving to actual face-to-face visitation. If the children were locally placed in foster care, a common logistical progression could involve starting with supervised visitation in Chad's local office. If that went well, visitation might be allowed at a local park or relative's home. The ongoing caseworker continually assesses if the contact is in the child's best interest. The ongoing caseworker is going to note how the children feel after the visit—whether they are upset or happy and wanting to see their parents or caretaker again.

The Perkins case is unique in that the children were placed out of the state and pending court orders did not allow parental contact. It is always important to keep in mind that visitation has the capacity to trigger earlier traumas and could negatively affect the child's progress. When the family all seems invested in reunification and is making good progress, the agency may seek approval for trial weekend or overnight visits as the last step. At that point, the agency should be convinced that there are minimal safety risks.

Visitation isn't only between children and their caretakers. It may be evident that a child could greatly benefit from having contact with other family members as well (e.g., an aunt stationed in the military overseas whom they have not seen in a long time.) With approval, the child could periodically engage in video chats and reestablish a relationship with this individual using technology. It is also possible that children may benefit from contact with any other siblings from whom they have been separated or the other set of grandparents. In our scenario, Rebecca and Renee are placed together. But what if they weren't? It would be helpful to explore the possibility of keeping their family connections healthy. There are a variety of reasons why siblings may sometimes be separated; however, numerous avenues are available for appropriate contact between siblings (and sometimes other relatives, too), and this is important.

Not all of your cases will result in the separation of children from their families, but some will. Visitation will be a common topic of discussion in court hearings and an invaluable component in the assessment progress. On one hand, visitation may afford the family the opportunity to act appropriately and demonstrate a healthy level of functioning. On the other, visitation often can clarify the need for decisions to permanently separate a family.

TEST YOURSELF

While safety and permanency are measurable objectives for ongoing child protective services, child well-being is a much broader and complex concept. If a judge asked you to describe the elements of child well-being, what would you say?

- -

Jones, LaLiberte, and Piescher (2015) examined multiple existing frameworks to define child well-being in child protection and identified social functioning, cognitive functioning, behavioral/emotional functioning, and physical health and development as key domains for consideration. More information can be found here:

Jones, A. S., LaLiberte, T., & Piescher, K. N. (2015). Defining and strengthening child well-being in child protection. *Children and Youth Services Review, 54,* 57–70.

Working as the Ongoing Specialist

In this section of the chapter, we will describe the individual traits, techniques, and strategies that will help you work effectively as an ongoing caseworker. Although it may seem like a lot to ask, as an ongoing caseworker you will be responsible for planning and implementing services, monitoring, and evaluating progress on the negotiated components of the formal family case plan. You will be simultaneously responsible for a number of unique cases, but there will be some similarities related to your monthly and ongoing responsibilities (e.g., scheduling home visits, face-to-face contacts, visitations, checking with service providers, preparing court documentation, etc.).

Nonetheless, the ongoing caseworker is truly the facilitator of the comprehensive case plan designed to improve the long-term stability and permanency of the family. In the next section, we will discuss skills and techniques that will help the ongoing caseworker improve efficiency and effectiveness.

Interpersonal Characteristics and Competencies Needed

Frontline child protection teams are composed of professionals who possess a diversity of experience, education, background, and opinion. They draw on their skill set and use their own blend of personality characteristics and experience to guide them in practice. Remember, ongoing casework is distinct in that the child protective services professional will be a significant part of the family's life for an extended time (generally months but could be a year or longer). Recognizing this, there are several characteristics and personal competencies that will assist the professional in effectively managing the responsibilities of being an ongoing caseworker.

Specific interpersonal abilities are important for the ongoing caseworker, as they promote the effective interaction with others. First, the effective ongoing caseworker should have a *positive attitude*. You should be prepared to experience disappointment and frustration with some cases, but you cannot give up on these families. Recognize that meaningful change may take time; you are working to make a difference in human lives.

Additionally, having a *strong work ethic* is important. Ongoing casework consists of many actions (e.g., completing paperwork for clients or the court) that are time critical. The job is not always nine to five. Scheduling visits some distance from one's office or home eats up a lot of travel time and requires you to manage time well. You may not always be able to receive overtime or "comp" time, but you cannot worry about that. You will find that on some days you may not be finished when the clock says it is time to go home. You will be finished when your tasks for the day are done. Why? Because you aren't making plastic widgets—you are working to make a difference in human lives.

Effective ongoing caseworkers must be able to *collaborate*, as they will be facilitating services with a number of community partners, and teamwork truly promotes success. Finally, effective ongoing workers must be *good listeners* and remain *patient*. You will be a large part of the family's life for a significant period of time. Being a good listener and remaining patient builds rapport and forms a solid professional relationship for the long term. This is especially important if you may need to deliver difficult information, like telling a family that the agency is going to pursue the termination of parental rights.

In addition, the effective ongoing caseworker must be competent in several areas. Important areas of competency for the ongoing caseworker include organization, paying attention to detail, having strong communication skills (written and verbal), and being able to navigate when things are ambiguous. More than anything, the effective ongoing caseworker must be *organized*. Scheduling, arranging meetings, keeping track of timelines, and documentation are a daily *responsibility*. If you are not an organized person by nature, please seek professional development in this area, as it is truly a key to effective ongoing practice. Further, *paying attention to detail* is another important competency. As the saying goes, the devil is in the details. A simple typo or error on a court report could result in spending several hours to fix a simple issue. Or having a wrong birthday on paperwork when seeking to place a child in a specialized treatment facility may result in the child being refused for treatment. Additionally, having strong and effective *communication skills* (written and verbal) is a necessity. The ongoing caseworker is the facilitator and will be responsible for leading, guiding, and directing a variety of continuous professional services. Clear and concise communication that is respectful and professional will make your job much easier and help you better serve clients and community partners. If you need help in this area, consult with your supervisor for help. Know what is expected in the official forms you will complete. Finally, the ongoing caseworker must be able to *navigate the gray* (when things are vague and lack clarity). Basically, you will be involved in making decisions throughout your professional relationship with the family. At times, you may not have all of the information you feel like you need. While you should have access to supervisory consultation, small decisions with real implications will often arise and must be addressed immediately (e.g., transportation decisions for scheduled visitation); the effective ongoing caseworker must be ready to navigate this circumstance. Don't form opinions prematurely. Let the evidence (or lack of it) speak. As a professional, you must be nonjudgmental and objective.

Table 5.1 summarizes the qualities and competencies needed by ongoing case workers. Briefly, you will save time and better serve your clients and team if you have a positive attitude and a strong work ethic, and are collaborative, a good listener, and patient. Additionally, you can better work with families and protect yourself from appeals and frustration by being organized, paying attention to detail, having strong communication skills, and being able to navigate the gray and remain objective.

TABLE 5.1 INTERPERSONAL SKILLS AND COMPETENCIES

Interpersonal Skills	Competencies
Positive attitude	Organizational ability
Strong work ethic	Attention to detail
Collaborative	Communication skills
Good listener	Ability to navigate the gray
Patience	Able to be objective

Documentation

A mainstay of working as an ongoing caseworker will be creating, collecting, and managing different forms of documentation. For example, you will need to keep up with the case plan, notifications from community service providers, court reports and legal documentation, and information from ongoing face-to-face contacts, home visits, and phone calls. If you were working with the Perkins family in an ongoing capacity, each month it is likely that you would conduct a home visit at the foster home to see both of the girls, perform a home visit to see Rodney and Angela, and collect information from service providers to document familial progress on the case plan. Additionally, you might want to obtain school and medical records each month, as well as progress notes from the therapist. Also, you may periodically receive e-mails from attorneys or the court, like Renee and Rebecca's GAL. Also, detailed notes of consultation with agency personnel and your supervisor must be kept. As mentioned in Chapter 4, the saying "if it's not documented, it didn't happen" is especially relevant for the ongoing caseworker. Thorough, comprehensive, and detailed documentation of every aspect of services and progress with the case will help you remain effective and assure that you are following agency procedures and policy.

Many child protection agencies use an electronic system to collect and store documentation and records, yet some also use a supplementary hard file that is kept in a local office. The utilization of mobile and web access to a database system for case management in child protection is debated and utilized in some locations, but there are concerns about data protection and privacy (Edstrom, Moreau, & Sire, 2013). Regardless of the storing mechanism used by your agency (paper file, electronic server, remote access, etc.), ongoing caseworkers receive a consistent flow of important documentation that must be recorded and accounted for. Further, you will receive phone calls, e-mails, and other tidbits of information on a daily basis related to a variety of cases. These also must be accurately documented and become part of the case file. Recent evidence suggests that the median number of cases an ongoing CPS worker handles is about 55 cases per year (Edwards & Wildeman, 2018). With that being said, how would you as the ongoing caseworker effectively manage the continuous paperwork associated with a number of different cases?

Consider the following organizational strategies suggested to help you save time and remain efficient: Set up your office to help you remain productive. Consider creating a separate hanging file folder for each of the families on your caseload. If you receive a phone call about a different case while you are writing up a report on another, quickly make a note about the call and place it in the paper hanging file. If a colleague walks in with mail about a different case, read it, and if it's not a priority, place it into the appropriate family case file for the time being.

Strategically plan your work with "protected time" at the end of the month for completing all documentation. Consider gathering each family's file and heading to an empty conference room to lay out all of the information. Organize by family and chronological order. Make piles that you can go through one at a time when you return to your office and begin entering these important records into the system. This strategy uses your time wisely, reduces anxiety, and assists when you receive various phone calls about some aspect of different cases.

Alternatively, some ongoing caseworkers create word documents for each family and supplement them with new information—say, when an important phone message is received. A quick blurb is entered for safekeeping until it can be inserted later into the agency's server. Keep in mind, though, that electronic documentation must be backed up and highly organized. And this strategy might not be as effective for time management as using a paper note system.

Clearly, if you receive a crisis phone call or become aware of time-sensitive requirements, then you will act accordingly. However, a good portion of your job responsibilities involves managing documentation about your cases. Develop a strategy that works for you. Your time is valuable, and you cannot isolate yourself from the families you are working with for two or three days to catch up on your documentation. Prioritize your efforts to take care of the most important things first. Remember, these records will potentially be available forever and have the capacity to influence future decisions taken to protect vulnerable populations. Any effort to make sure that your records are excellent is worth the time.

PRACTICE TIP 5.2 Given the importance of comprehensive and thorough documentation when working in an ongoing capacity, the use of dictation software is often valuable. Medical doctors use this frequently when documenting their work with patients in an office or hospital setting. As an ongoing caseworker, you can dictate notes from a home visit while in the car or use dictation software in your office to complete a thorough investigation or court report. Make sure that you back up your electronic information, as servers do crash and this frustrating experience could result in problems for your clients. Finally, if you have a case in court, consider saving each electronic court report by date. Then you could use the former electronic document as a template for the next hearing and not have to start over when making adjustments.

Scheduling and Organization

As previously described, monthly home visits and other frequent contacts are an important piece of effective ongoing casework. To save time, it is important to consider tips for scheduling and remaining organized with multiple clients. As previously noted, depending on your caseload, you could have a number of visits to make, and some could be outside of your local area. For example, the Perkins girls were currently placed in another state. Additionally, you would need to meet with Rodney and Angela at their place of residence. Further, you would likely be responsible for ongoing and monthly contact with a variety of service providers in the community related just to that case.

To assure that all of these integral parts of the case plan are working properly and that there is appropriate documentation, consider developing an accountability grid. The benefit of this strategy is that the ongoing worker can have a visual aid in helping recognize what is needed and when it is needed. This monthly accountability grid serves as a checks-and-balances guide for ensuring compliance with all of your monthly responsibilities.

Start the grid by identifying each person that you need to visit. (This can also assist in keeping track of your mileage connected with visiting. Agencies might reimburse travel mileage for such job responsibilities.) Further, this grid could have a column for court dates and important deadlines such as for case plans. The grid can be as detailed as you need it to be. Efforts like this to organize your responsibilities will save time and help you better serve your clients.

Demographics				Travel		Documentation			Court/Case Plan	
Case	**Type**	**Name**	**Address**	**Miles RT**	**Frequency**	**Scheduled HV**	**Completed**	**Entered**	**Court Appt.**	**Case Plan Due Date**
1	OOHC	Perkins	Denver, CO	6	1/mo	7/22/19			11/10/19	9/23/19
	OOHC	Perkins	Bentonville, AR	ICPC	1/mo	Courtesy			11/10/19	9/23/19
2	OOHC	Valdez	Denver, CO	9	1/mo	7/18/19			10/10/19	8/19/19
	OOHC	Valdez	Ft. Collins, CO	128	1/quarter	Courtesy			10/10/19	8/19/19
3	In-Home	Jones	Denver, CO	19	1/mo	7/22/19			N/A	8/20/19
4	In-Home	McIntyre	Denver, CO	12	1/mo	7/15/19			N/A	8/13/19
	In-Home	McIntyre	Brighton, CO	42	1/mo	7/15/19			N/A	8/13/19

Figure 5.1 **Example of an Accountability Grid**

ACCOUNTABILITY GRID

Let's imagine that the accountability grid above was developed by Chad as an ongoing caseworker in Denver, Colorado. This portion of it allows us to see four of his cases, two of which include children in foster care (out of home) and two living at home. For the Perkins family, Chad is responsible for two monthly home visits on behalf of the family. The first one is with Rodney and Angela and is in Denver, Colorado, approximately a 6-mile round-trip from his local office. The second visit is with Renee and Rebecca in Arkansas. In Chad's case with the Perkins family, he will obtain monthly courtesy supervision for the girls in Arkansas through the ICPC. In his Valdez case, we can see that he has a child in foster care in Fort Collins, Colorado. Rather than driving 128 miles per month for one home visit, he has arranged for courtesy supervision and only drives to see the child face-to-face once a quarter. The grid documents the scheduling and completion of his home visits and when this related documentation is entered into the server. Finally, Chad uses the grid to track the dates for his upcoming court appointments and case plan reviews. As you can see, creating a simple accountability grid can be quite effective in helping the ongoing worker manage his or her responsibilities.

When scheduling, make a genuine effort to remain aware of people's work schedules and the schedules related to children's school responsibilities and their extracurricular interests (e.g., playing in the school band). If at all possible, try to arrange your visits and contacts so that your clients do not have to miss work and the visits don't place any unwarranted burden on them to participate. Aligning your visits so that everyone is able to maintain their responsibilities and extracurricular interests is good practice and could be very important in helping stabilize families. The more familiar you are with your community resources, service partners, and family circumstances, the better able you will be to schedule to increase your effectiveness and save time as an ongoing caseworker.

PRACTICE TIP 5.3 As described in Chapter 4, your vehicle can be a mobile workstation. Consider purchasing an inexpensive file cabinet and placing it in the trunk of your vehicle. There you can keep resource guides for community partners that would be helpful in providing details about each program, fees, and a description of the services provided. Having contact information for various community partners can save you a significant amount of time while in the field. Additionally, keeping different and relevant agency forms in your vehicle can help prevent having to drive back to the office for something a client might have to sign (like a release for medical information) and can save you time. You may also wish to keep trash bags, gloves, an inexpensive camera, and measuring tape for documentation in pictures. Having access to these items when in the field will save you time.

Safety and Service Delivery

Frontline child protection workers operate in the field. They visit apartment buildings, health facilities, business establishments, and especially people's homes on a daily basis. Ferguson (2018) notes that each home establishes its own practice domain, influencing how complex interactions may occur between the practitioner and client. While it is at times humbling to have access to the private personal lives of those you are working with, it is also a great responsibility. To establish yourself as a professional, it is important to dress appropriately, act in a measured and objective manner, and keep your safety in mind while working in a new home or neighborhood.

Related to professional attire, ongoing caseworkers may know that they will be in court all day every Monday and will dress accordingly. Caseworkers must make wise decisions related to their professional attire when they are out in the community and entering people's homes. It may be perfectly appropriate to wear *stilettos* in court, but on a home visit they might result in the client developing an elitist perception that could set up a barrier or lack of trust for someone living in poverty. Think about it. What impression might you get of an individual walking through your front door with fancy high heels? What would you think of a CPS worker in shorts and a Coors Light T-shirt? Look professional and think safe. Wear flat shoes with solid soles, and if you work in a rural area, you may want to have a trusty pair of boots.

It is important that the ongoing caseworker does not become *too* familiar with the family. Since you will be working with this family for possibly a year or longer, you may become comfortable and be tempted to self-disclose at times. While choosing to acknowledge that you have children of your own may be helpful to build a rapport and develop a sense of commonality, mentioning your children's names, their teacher's name, their school, where you live, or inviting a client's child over for a play date can immediately destroy your professional boundaries.

Taking steps to protect your safety is as important for the ongoing caseworker as for the investigator. Keep your agency informed about home visits and how long you should be gone. If you have any reason to expect a hostile situation may arise, contact law enforcement or a coworker to accompany you.

Once in strange homes, do not place yourself in a vulnerable position. Sit or stand close to the door so that you can exit quickly, if necessary, without being cornered. If there is an aggressive dog, ask your client to restrain it before you arrive. Or, upon arrival, sit in your vehicle and honk the horn to announce your presence and wait in the car until the dog is put away.

Once inside, explore the whole home as a matter of practice. Taking a walk-through can provide valuable insight to the way the family lives. You may be able to identify areas for improvement—or you could find drug paraphernalia. If something like that is discovered, don't make a big deal of it, and exit the home as soon as you can.

PRACTICE TIP 5.4 Those working in child protection are primarily female (Barth, Lloyd, Christ, Chapman, & Dickinson, 2008; Griffiths, Royse, Culver, Piescher, & Zhang, 2017), but whether male or female, it is important to remain diligent in your awareness of being in a vulnerable position when alone with a child. There is an explicit vulnerability for adults when alone with a child. Child protection professionals must protect themselves from any suggestion or allegation of inappropriate conduct.

Let's say that Chad is meeting with Rebecca at her foster home, where she was placed due to sexual abuse. While best practice requires Chad to meet with the child in private to assure the child has the freedom to communicate freely, he may not want to do it behind a closed door. Weather permitting, Chad might choose to speak with her on the front porch or walk out into the front yard to have a conversation. Irrespective of your age or gender, take steps to protect yourself from possible allegations. Make decisions that are defensible and document who you spoke to and where. Small tips like this will prevent you from any unintended consequences from working with families who are in a desperate situation and may attempt to thwart or stymie the child protection agency.

The Perkins Disposition Hearing

Having worked with the Perkins family for several months, it was time for the disposition hearing. This case was rather unusual, as Rodney and Angela had returned home from jail and were still facing criminal charges, while Rebecca and Renee had been placed out of state with Dorothy Perkins in Bentonville, Arkansas. Arriving with a copy of the negotiated case plan and of a formal report recommending that the no contact order stay in place at this current time, Chad was greeted by the children's GAL, who mentioned that Dorothy Perkins was on the phone and needed to talk to him immediately. When Chad picked up the phone, Dorothy blurted out that she wanted him to "come pick up these kids. They aren't welcome anymore!"

He attempted to console Dorothy and communicate with her, but she cut short their conversation and said that if Chad didn't arrive by noon tomorrow, she would take the girls to the local child welfare agency and drop them off. She was unreasonable and gave him no reason why she no longer wanted her grandchildren in her home. This was the first notion Chad had that this placement was going to disrupt. Chad advised Dorothy that he would contact her again after the hearing and asked her to be patient.

Chad presented the court with this new information, and Rodney and Angela used the information as an opportunity to request that the children be returned home. After deliberation, the court ruled that the children would reenter foster care locally rather than being placed in the home with Rodney and Angela. However, against the agency's recommendation, the court did approve of supervised visitation as long as Rodney and Angela were compliant with random drug screens. Chad made a phone call to his supervisor to notify her about the pending changes in the family and also reached out to his favorite colleague, Tonya, and asked her if she would be willing to get on a plane first thing tomorrow morning and help him transport the girls back from Arkansas. Tonya was a team player and agreed, laughingly saying, "Chad, you owe me one!"

Ongoing Supervisory Consultation

Ongoing caseworkers will meet regularly with their supervisors for routine case evaluation and to assist in case-related decision making. This supervision is a little different from the investigative specialist, who may only engage in supervisory consultation in a more time-limited and acute fashion (e.g., making after-hours decisions after arriving at a home with an active meth lab). The ongoing caseworker will engage in strategic and planned case consultation with his or her supervisor regarding each of his or her cases. Effective supervision is widely associated with positive outcomes and is an important component in child protection practice (McCrae, Scannapieco, & Obermann, 2015; Saltiel, 2017; Zinn, 2015). Having this resource is important and should not be undervalued. Some agencies may subscribe to a more top-down approach with strong supervisor input to decision making, while other agencies will have supervisors in a shared or horizontal style of decision making (Falconer & Shardlow, 2018). You may encounter both types of supervisors during your career in child protection.

Beyond having routine monthly consultations, ongoing caseworkers may ask supervisors for their suggestions when preparing for an upcoming court hearing, when the worker is considering recommending a change in visitation status, or after receiving an unfavorable report about a client's progress from a community partner. It is important to document key decisions in these important meetings (Wilkins, 2017).

A Change of Course

While unsure about how the meeting might go, Chad prepared the visitation room in the local agency and arranged for the foster parent to drop off Rebecca and Renee for the supervised visit with Rodney and Angela. The girls had not spoken to their parents in several months, so Chad spoke with the girls first, and they expressed their anxiety about meeting with their parents. However, Chad used age-appropriate language to explain that the parents had requested the meeting and that it was natural for the girls to feel nervous. He reassured them that he would be just behind the two-way mirror to watch the interaction and support them throughout the 1-hour visit.

Chad made his way to the front of the office to meet with Rodney and Angela to discuss the parameters for appropriate behavior during the visit. For instance, they were not to discuss any specifics about the ongoing case or their pending criminal charges during the visit. While neither Chad nor the children's therapist felt that this contact was in the girls' best interests at this time, a court order had to be obeyed. Further, visitation is a critical component toward family reunification, and that is currently the court ordered permanency goal with the Perkins family, in spite of any current concerns about the adult family members.

Chad arrived at the front lobby and could not believe his eyes. Rodney and Angela were both arguing, somewhat unsteady on their feet, and appeared intoxicated. Chad quickly exited and asked his supervisor to witness their behavior. He was unwilling to allow contact between Rodney and Angela and their children, given his concerns about their apparent intoxication. The supervisor agreed with Chad's decision.

Chad informed Rodney and Angela that they would not be seeing their children that day. Both of them denied being under the influence of any medication or narcotics but not with as much heat and outrage as he had expected. As an experienced caseworker, Chad knew what he was observing and requested that the parents complete a drug screen at the agency across the parking lot. Although protesting and still denying there was a problem, both parents eventually left the building when the supervisor handed them a copy of the court order requiring random drug screens.

About an hour later, Chad received a phone call from the technician at the lab advising him that Rodney showed up at their facility to take his drug screen with a freshly shaven head that was scuffed up by cuts from a razor. Evidently, Rodney had gone into their bathroom with a razor and shaved his entire head because he suspected that the agency would ask for a sample of hair for the drug screen. Hair follicle drug screens provide accurate results of drug usage over a period of time. The technician laughed, saying, "I guess Rodney didn't know that I could remove his underarm hair and find out the same information." In the end, Rodney and Angela both tested positive for using methamphetamines.

Chad and his supervisor created a new plan for the county attorney to put this case back on the docket for a permanency hearing. Chad had been working with the family for over a year now, and Rodney and Angela Perkins were not making progress. Even though he was a little troubled by the grandmother's wanting the girls out of her house, Chad had the objective information he needed to request a change of course with the case and to move forward with a different form of permanency on behalf of Rebecca and Renee Perkins.

Main Points

In contrast to the investigative worker, the ongoing caseworker has the responsibility to oversee the family's involvement with community resources such as rehabilitation from substance abuse, mental health counseling, and so forth. Ongoing caseworkers are an integral factor in this process, having many responsibilities to ensure the family case plan is faithfully implemented.

- Ongoing services are usually initiated following a substantiated investigation of child maltreatment. They are designed to address the high-risk behaviors and reduce or eliminate their reoccurrence.
- Ongoing caseworkers may be specialists or generalists in units where they also conduct investigations.
- Each opened case within the child protection agency will have its own family case plan, which serves as the basis for reunification (when out-of-home care is necessary) or as a "blueprint" for restoring the family's functioning to a level where there is minimal concern about the children's safety or well-being.
- Common responsibilities for ongoing casework include monthly home visits, contact with community partners, ongoing case evaluation, participation in court hearings, and supervisory consultation. Visitation is usually a major activity and a key component of the case plan.
- Interpersonal skills such as having a positive attitude and a strong work ethic, being able to collaborate, being a good listener, and being patient will help you work effectively with families needing services.
- Competencies such as being organized, paying attention to detail, having strong communication skills, and being able to navigate the gray and remaining objective will help you effectively facilitate services when serving as an ongoing caseworker.
- Using an accountability grid and taking steps to be safe and organized are proactive ways to save you time and energy.

Questions for Class Discussion

1. Would you prefer to be an investigative worker or an ongoing caseworker? Why?
2. What concerns do you have about being an ongoing caseworker?
3. What skills might be helpful for the ongoing caseworker to have?
4. Are there additional smartphone apps or technological resources that could help the ongoing caseworker stay organized? What might help you to stay organized?

Self-Assessment for Personal Consideration

1. How comfortable would you be in the position of ongoing caseworker?

   1   2   3   4   5   6   7   8   9   10

   Not comfortable   *Very comfortable*

2. How comfortable would you be informing the Perkins family that their visitation was canceled because of their apparent intoxication?

   1   2   3   4   5   6   7   8   9   10

   Not comfortable   *Very comfortable*

Additional Resources

Degarmo, J. (2018). *Foster care survival guide: The essential guide for today's foster parents*. Ocala, FL: Atlantic.

Harrison, K. (2004). *Another place at the table*. New York, NY: Tarcher/Penguin.

References

Barth, R. P., Lloyd, E. C., Christ, S. L., Chapman, M. V., & Dickinson, N. S. (2008). Child welfare worker characteristics and job satisfaction: A national study. *Social Work, 53*(3), 199–209.

Chaiyachati, B. H., Gaither, J. R., Hughes, M., Foley-Schain, K., & Leventhal, J. M. (2018). Preventing child maltreatment: Examination of an established statewide home-visiting program. *Child Abuse & Neglect, 79,* 476–484.

Cheng, T. C., & Lo, C. C. (2016). Linking worker-parent working alliance to parent progress in child welfare: A longitudinal analysis. *Children and Youth Services Review, 71,* 10–16.

Damiani-Taraba, G., Dumbrill, G., Gladstone, J., Koster, A., Leslie, B., & Charles, M. (2017). The evolving relationship between casework skills, engagement, and positive case outcomes in child protection: A structural equation model. *Children and Youth Services Review, 79,* 456–462.

Edstrom, J., Moreau, A., & Sire, X. R. (2013). Lessons from Senegal's Database System for Case Management for child protection: A pilot project on web-based and mobile technology. *IDS Bulletin: Institute of Development Studies, 44*(2), 69–81.

Edwards, F., & Wildeman, C. (2018). Characteristics of the front-line child welfare workforce. *Children and Youth Services Review, 89,* 13–26.

Falconer, R., & Shardlow, S. M. (2018). Comparing child protection decision-making in England and Finland: Supervised or supported judgement? *Journal of Social Work Practice, 32*(2), 111–124.

Ferguson, H. (2018). Making home visits: Creativity and the embodied practices of home visiting in social work and child protection. *Qualitative Social Work, 17*(1), 65–80.

Gentles-Gibbs, N. (2016). Child protection and family empowerment: Competing rights or accordant goals? *Child Care in Practice, 22*(4), 386–400.

Gladstone, J., Dumbrill, G., Leslie, B., Koster, A., Young, M., & Ismaila, A. (2011). Looking at engagement and outcome from the perspectives of child protection workers and parents. *Children and Youth Services Review, 34*(1).

Gladstone, J., Dumbrill, G., Leslie, B., Koster, A., Young, M., & Ismaila, A. (2014). Understanding worker-parent engagement in child protection casework. *Children and Youth Services Review, 44,* 56–64.

Griffiths, A., Royse, D., Culver, K., Piescher, K., & Zhang, Y. (2017). Who stays, who goes, who knows? A state-wide survey of child welfare workers. *Children and Youth Services Review, 77,* 110–117.

Haight, W. L., Kagle, J. D., & Black, J. E. (2003). Understanding and supporting parent–child relationships during foster care visits: Attachment theory and research. *Social Work, 48*(2), 195–207.

Halverson, J. L., Russell, J. R., & Kerwin, C. (2018). Effect of worker contacts on risk of child maltreatment recurrence among CPS-involved children and families. *Child Abuse & Neglect, 82,* 102–111.

Hollinshead, D. M., Kim, S., Fluke, J. D., & Merkel-Holguin, L. (2017). Factors associated with service utilization in child welfare: A structural equation model. *Children and Youth Services Review, 79,* 506–516.

Jones, A. S., LaLiberte, T., & Piescher, K. N. (2015). Defining and strengthening child well-being in child protection. *Children and Youth Services Review, 54,* 57–70.

Lwin, K., Fluke, J., Trocmé, N., Fallon, B., & Mishna, F. (2018). Ongoing child welfare services: Understanding the relationship of worker and organizational characteristics to service provision. *Child Abuse & Neglect, 80,* 324–334.

McCrae, J. S., Scannapieco, M., & Obermann, A. (2015). Retention and job satisfaction of child welfare supervisors. *Children and Youth Services Review, 59,* 171–176.

McWey, L. M., & Cui, M. (2017). Parent–child contact for youth in foster care: Research to inform practice. *Family Relations, 66*(4), 684–695.

Pink, S., Morgan, J., & Dainty, A. (2015). Other people's homes as sites of uncertainty: Ways of knowing and being safe. *Environment and Planning, 47*(2), 450–464.

Saltiel, D. (2017). Supervision: A contested space for learning and decision making. *Qualitative Social Work, 16*(4), 533–549.

Schreiber, J. C., Fuller, T., & Paceley, M. S. (2013). Engagement in child protective services: Parent perceptions of worker skills. *Children and Youth Services Review, 35*(4), 707.

Wilkins, D. (2017). How is supervision recorded in child and family social work? An analysis of 244 written records of formal supervision. *Child & Family Social Work, 22*(3), 1130–1140.

Yampolskaya, S., Armstrong, M. I., Strozier, A., & Swanke, J. (2017). Can the actions of child welfare case managers predict case outcomes? *Child Abuse & Neglect, 64,* 61–70.

Zinn, A. (2015). A typology of supervision in child welfare: Multilevel latent class and confirmatory analyses of caseworker-supervisor relationship type. *Children and Youth Services Review, 48,* 98–110.

CHAPTER 6

PERMANENCY: THE WORKER'S ROLES AND ASFA OPTIONS

OVERVIEW

Foster care is designed to be temporary, a stop on the road to permanency. This chapter will provide an overview of the processes involved in working with families who have been separated by the foster care system and after the court determines that reunification is not in the child's best interest. Implications and timelines associated with all approved forms of permanency set by the Adoption and Safe Families Act will be described, and the chapter will follow the Perkins family case vignette with Rebecca and Renee going through the adoption process. Roles and responsibilities of the ongoing caseworker will be examined, as a specific focus on meeting the child's needs, and the importance of utilizing additional support mechanisms as a key element of effective service delivery and aftercare services will be discussed.

Pursuing Permanency for Rebecca and Renee

On his way to the courthouse, Chad reflected on his lengthy professional relationship with the Perkins family. Today was a big day; he would be testifying and recommending that the court change the permanency goal from reunification to adoption for Rebecca and Renee. Chad had worked diligently to provide Rodney and Angela with the resources to rectify their issues and reunify with their children. However, minimal progress had been made on the case plan, and the girls had remained in foster care for the last 15 months. It was time to move forward, as Rebecca and Renee deserved a stable and healthy future with a "forever" family.

Walking into the courtroom, Chad noticed Rodney and Angela and waved to them. Represented by their attorneys, they gave him a quick glance to acknowledge his presence. Chad had butterflies in his stomach, but this was his chance to advocate for the long-term safety and well-being of Rebecca and Renee.

Considering the magnitude of this event, Chad's supervisor and Tonya were both present as well. Tonya, the investigative specialist who initially worked with the Perkins family, took the stand first. She testified about the substantiated investigation of child sexual abuse and effectively navigated through the cross-examination of Rodney and Angela's attorneys. Chad was up next, and he discussed the lack of progress on the case plan and supported his position with evidence. He testified to multiple failed drug screens and the child sexual abuse criminal charges that Rodney and Angela had recently pled guilty to. He stated that Rodney and Angela had not completed their substance abuse assessments and that they were unwilling to cooperate with the agency in completing the recommended mental health treatment.

Chad was clear, confident, and able to illustrate the instability and familial issues that continued to place the girls at risk. He made a formal recommendation to the court—basically that the agency believed it was no longer in the children's best interest to pursue reunification with their parents and that an appropriate relative was unable to be found. He requested that the court formally change the permanency goal of Rebecca and Renee to adoption.

Rodney and Angela's attorneys provided a rebuttal to the testimonies and asked for additional time to improve their situation and reunify the family. However, the GAL gave a passionate testimony about how he also believed it would not be in the children's best interests to ever return to the care and custody of Rodney and Angela Perkins.

The court then ordered the permanency goal of Rebecca and Renee Perkins to be changed from reunification to adoption. Rodney and Angela were upset, realizing that the agency would now be pursuing the termination of their parental rights.

Chad left the courtroom relieved that the necessary ordeal was over. From this day forward, he knew that that he would be almost entirely focused on the needs of the two girls for the future. He knew that Rebecca and Renee had been relatively stable at Bob and Tina Is it supposed to be Wells's or Wells'? foster home, but he was unsure of the Wells's ability or interest in adopting the girls. Rebecca and Renee had experienced profound trauma and sexual abuse. They needed understanding parents with patience and a dedication to see that they got the therapy and services that they needed. Chad was also determined to do anything in his power to assure the long-term stability and health of Rebecca and Renee, and this path was about to begin by preparing for the termination of parental rights (TPR) hearing.

The Importance of Permanency and the ASFA

Permanency refers to "a legally permanent, nurturing family for every child involved in the system" (Child and Family Services Reviews, 2019). Achieving permanency is a key goal for the child welfare system, focused on ensuring meaningful and enduring connections for the involved children (Salazar et al., 2018). As you remember from earlier, not all investigations result in ongoing services, and not all open cases with ongoing services result in children being removed from their parents by the court and placed in foster care. However, when the court determines that the risk is too great for children to remain in their homes, foster care is a temporary intervention—one that is designed to ensure the safety and stability of the child while the agency works toward an appropriate form of permanency. Achieving permanency is a fundamental goal of the child welfare system and is explicitly described in the Adoption and Safe Families Act. In this chapter, we will explore the approved options for permanency and explore what it might be like to work with a family through this process.

The Adoption and Safe Families Act of 1997 is a monumental piece of legislation that was enacted to expedite the timely permanency of children who are in foster care. Developed in response to children becoming "lost in the system," the ASFA was designed to ensure oversight, accountability, and responsibility. A significant component of the ASFA is the required annual permanency hearing, which occurs within 12 months of the child entering out-of-home care (Moye & Rinker, 2002).

The ASFA identifies five options as approved permanency for children in out-of-home care, including reunification with parent, permanent relative placement, adoption, legal guardianship, and a planned permanent living arrangement. The primary permanency goal under the ASFA is the reunification of a child with his or her parents, when appropriate. However, if after 15 months in foster care the family has made only limited progress on the case plan or there are other aggravating factors to consider (e.g., criminal charges, etc.), the agency may request a change of permanency goal from the court.

To illustrate the importance of securing appropriate permanency, it is valuable to examine the characteristics of children recently in foster care. According to the Adoption and Foster Care Analysis and Reporting System (AFCARS), it is estimated that 442,995 children were in foster care on September 30, 2017, with 52% identifying as male and averaging 8.4 years of age (Children's Bureau, 2018). They entered foster care for a number of reasons, and while these categories are not mutually exclusive, 62% were due to neglect and 36% to a parent or guardian's drug use. AFCARS is the only ongoing federal data set that collects information on children in foster care—important information for understanding trends associated with this population. More information on AFCARS can be found on the AFCARS website: https://www.acf.hhs.gov/cb/research-data-technology/reporting-systems/afcars.

Achieving timely permanency is in the child's best interest. This is made very clear when the research is explored. Children in foster care have often been subject to adverse childhood experiences, creating a risk for their mental health (Hambrick, Oppenheim-Weller, N'zi, & Taussig, 2016). In a study that analyzed data from the National Survey of Children's Health, Greiner and Beal (2017) found an association between foster care and poor mental health in children. In addition to affecting mental health, foster care has also been associated with other issues. A systematic literature review examined the outcomes of 32 quantitative studies and found that when compared with the general population, children who grew up in foster care had greater challenges with criminal involvement, substance abuse, health, housing, income, employment, and education (Gypen, Vanderfaeillie, De Maeyer, Belenger, & Van Holen, 2017). While it is unlikely that we'll ever be able to do away with foster care, shorter stays versus longer stays are better for the child.

Helping children obtain timely permanency is also important because research shows that children who age out of the foster care system face a high risk for incarceration, homelessness, unemployment, educational deficits, food and income insecurity, and mental health disorders (Fowler, Marcal, Zhang, Day, & Landsverk, 2017; Lockwood, Friedman, & Christian, 2015). According to Lockwood et al. (2015), over 20,000 children age out of the system each year without reaching a permanent family placement; adolescents, children spending extended time in foster care, and children with a diagnosed disability face a higher risk of problems. Unstable placement (i.e., frequent moves) is a barrier to children achieving permanency (Stott & Gustavsson, 2010). Recognizing the detrimental effects of placement instability, Koh, Rolock, Cross, and Eblen-Manning (2014) analyzed data from the Illinois Department of Children and Family Services. Comparing groups of children with two or fewer placements during an 18-month period with those experiencing three or more moves during the same time frame, the researchers identified caregiver commitment, the absence of the child's mental health diagnosis, and placement with a relative caregiver as the key factors influencing placement stability (Koh et al., 2014).

On an individual level, Akin (2011) identified demographic characteristics, the clinical needs of the child, and the child's continuity and connections as three main predictors of achieving permanency. On an agency level, a study in Colorado found that timely and consistent administrative case reviews with effective interventions positively influenced permanency and the amount of time in out-of-home care (Whitaker, 2011).

Researchers are also using "big data" and sophisticated quantitative methods to examine the probability of predicting foster children achieving permanency. A study by Elgin (2018) used data from a national administrative data set of 233,633 foster children to create a "boosted tree" model that predicted the odds of achieving permanency with a 97.66% accuracy. The authors highlighted the importance of using available data to assist in developing strategies that will confidently identify areas for using limited resources to benefit at-risk populations (e.g., specific barriers or services that can help with achieving permanency). While this strategy is likely to remain at the forefront of future research considerations, it is designed to supplement and not replace "traditional decision-making processes" (Elgin, 2018, p. 164) at child welfare agencies. Further, Murphy, Van Zyl, Collins-Camargo, and Sullivan (2012) developed the Child Permanency Barriers Scale to uniquely investigate the contribution of four factors that influence the achievement of permanency for children in foster care (i.e., kinship, placement and matching, adequate services and resources, and communication and collaboration). Tools that supplement the child welfare worker in facilitating the process to permanency are worth consideration and will likely remain a focus in the future.

Permanency Options: An Overview

The Adoption and Safe Families Act was designed to expedite permanency, and this landmark piece of legislation continues to guide practice. While some may argue that the ASFA creates a false dichotomy between the rights of children and their parents (Stein, 2000), an effective practitioner must have a good understanding of why it was implemented and how it guides policy and practice. Table 6.1 identifies the five approved forms of permanency under the ASFA and is followed by a detailed look at each option and its purpose.

TABLE 6.1 **AFSA PERMANENCY OPTIONS**

Option	Purpose
I. Reunification with parent	Initial goal, when in best interest of child.
II. Permanent relative placement	If unable to reunify with parent, placement with a suitable relative is the least restrictive option.
III. Adoption and the termination of parental rights	When it's not in the best interest for the child to return home and there is not an appropriate or suitable relative. Parental rights must be terminated first.
IV. Legal guardianship	Often used when an unrelated caregiver is able to take custody (e.g., teacher or basketball coach).
V. Planned permanent living arrangement	Uncommon, and mostly considered when children are close to age 18 and have no other appropriate options for permanency.

I. Reunification with Parent

Reunification is the process of reuniting a child with parents after the child has been removed by the court. Reunification is widely known as the primary permanency goal when children are in out-of-home care. As discussed in Chapter 5, services by the child protection system are designed to reunify the family, as this is almost always the initial permanency goal for a child. In this chapter, we will focus on the trajectory of Rebecca and Renee's path to permanency after the court has determined that reunification and relative placement are no longer an option. However, our discussion about the approved options for permanency under the ASFA will begin with the "gold standard" of family reunification.

Reunification is the preferred permanency option, based on the fundamental belief that children should be raised by their parents when possible. Research is making strides not only in identifying factors that negatively affect family reunification but also in designing evidence-based strategies to improve its occurrence. Fernandez and Lee (2011) explored factors that negatively influence parent–child reunification, finding that parental substance abuse, domestic violence, experiencing abuse/neglect, and having high risks in the social environment were all meaningful contributors.

Additionally, financial stability and socioeconomic status have been identified as key factors in reunification. Esposito et al. (2017) examined longitudinal data from 39,882 children in foster care between 2002 and 2013 and found that socioeconomic vulnerability (identified by unemployment, lack of education, and lower income levels) decreased the likelihood of the reunification for children placed in out-of-home care.

Specialized training models are also showing value in facilitating family reunification. Recently, Akin and McDonald (2018) investigated the effects of Oregon's Parent Management Training model, an evidence-supported parenting intervention program that focuses on delivering in-home services to individual families where parents are identified as the agents of change. Curriculum is designed to help address child and adolescent antisocial behavior through five core processes: (a) positive involvement, (b) skill building, (c) supervision and monitoring, (d) problem solving, and (e) appropriate discipline. Evaluation of this model has found a positive influence on the reunification of children in out-of-home care, especially related to those with serious emotional and behavioral problems.

Seeking a better understanding of the priorities of the professionals who are involved with these decisions, Jedwab, Chatterjee, and Shaw (2018) conducted a thematic analysis of 284 caseworkers. They found the most critical factors to ensuring successful family reunification hinged on the safety of the child and the provision of services and support to the birth family. While reunification will almost always be the immediate and primary focus for permanency, the next option is to pursue the extended family and explore the option for permanent relative placement.

II. Permanent Relative Placement

Permanent relative placement is a preferred option for children who have been removed from their homes and placed in out-of-home care, primarily because it is the least restrictive of all out-of-home placements. Permanent relative placement may also be called kinship care and is focused on placing a child with someone with a close connection. According to the Child Welfare League of America (1994), **kinship care** is defined as "the full-time nurturing and protection of children who must be separated from their parents, by relatives, members of their tribes or clans, godparents, step-parents, or other adults who have a kinship bond with a child" (p. 2).

Depending on your state or province, kinship care may also include those who are not related through blood, marriage, or legal relationship. Recently, there has been a push to include "fictive kin" as an approved avenue for permanent relative placement. **Fictive kin** may include neighbors, friends of the family, teachers, or even someone from church. Currently, a total of 28 states and the District of Columbia and Guam consider placement with fictive kin when an appropriate relative is not found (Child Welfare Information Gateway, 2018). At times, kinship care is broken down into two categories: informal and formal. The major difference has to do with custody and financial support. **Informal kinship care** involves a relative taking care of a child without the involvement of the court system and possibly not receiving external financial support for the child, such as Temporary Assistance for Needy Families.

Formal kinship care involves the relative obtaining permanent legal custody through court involvement when the child is in foster care. While there are challenges associated with differences in terminology and context, efforts are being made to develop kinship care policies that improve the transparency and consistency associated with this important permanency option (Berrick & Hernandez, 2016). Permanent relative placement and kinship care are important and are often much less complicated or detrimental options for placing a child in a safe home when they cannot be reunited with their parents.

When compared with other children in foster care, research has shown that kinship care is a viable option for the well-being of children. Specifically, Winokur, Holtan, and Batchelder (2018) systematically reviewed data from 102 studies and reported that when compared with children in foster care, children in kinship care experienced fewer mental health disorders and had fewer behavioral problems. They experienced fewer placement disruptions, had better well-being, and had similar reunification rates.

III. Adoption and the Termination of Parental Rights

Adoption is a permanency option that can only be pursued after the termination of parental rights, when the legal status between the child and parents (either biological or prior adoptive parents) is permanently severed. The termination of parental rights is a strong legal mechanism for protecting a child and is undertaken when there is little hope for family reunification because of unresolved problems in the family unit. For this reason, it has been called the "civil death penalty"—because of the seriousness of this action. Keep in mind that we are talking about parental rights, not custody.

Custody can usually be given back to the parent unless there is a termination of parental rights. The termination of parental rights means that a parent is no longer legally associated with the child—and has no right to contact the child in any way, shape, or form. The termination of parental rights may occur in one of two different ways: voluntarily or involuntarily. After working with a child welfare professional for a time, it is possible that parents may voluntarily decide to give up their rights. Examples of this could be that they are aware of their inability to meet the needs of their child and feel that the child's needs could be better met by a different caretaker. However, child protection professionals can also pursue the involuntary termination of parental rights, where a court hearing would determine whether this should be allowed. The termination of parental rights opens the door for the avenue of adoption, but the agency must wait until all court processes are complete until moving a child's adoption forward.

The termination of parental rights is appropriate whenever the court determines it would not be in the best interest of the child to reunify with the family and there also is no option with an appropriate relative. Unless there are extreme circumstances, the ASFA prohibits the child welfare agency from pursuing the termination of parental rights unless the child has been in out-of-home care for 15 of the past 22 months. This gives the CPS agency ample time to work with the parents toward reunification. At the annual permanency hearing, the goal must change from reunification to adoption before the termination of parental rights can be pursued. Examples of grounds for pursuing the termination of parental rights include the following:

- Abandonment of the child
- Termination of parental rights on another child

- Sexual abuse of a child
- Extreme emotional/psychological abuse of a child
- Violent crime against a child
- Severe or chronic abuse or neglect
- Significant and long withstanding parenting incapacity due to mental illness
- Significant and long withstanding parenting incapacity due to substance use

The Adoptive Process

After the termination of parental rights has been finalized, adoption can be pursued. Adoption is the process of an individual who is not the biological parent assuming the full responsibilities of a raising a child and obtaining all legal rights for the child. There is a process to adoption, generally following these steps:

1. In a hearing, the court changes the child's permanency goal from reunification to adoption.
2. In a hearing, the court orders the termination of parental rights.
3. A goodbye visit is considered (see below).
4. A permanency (or adoption) worker and the ongoing caseworker begin to look for possible adoptive families.
5. Children begin to make contact with potentially adoptive families.
6. In a hearing, families formally adopt children.

Children begin the path to permanency by closure with their former parents and building relationships with their new adoptive family. The ongoing caseworker will remain a vital part of this process, beginning with the decision about having a goodbye visit. A **goodbye visit** is a purposeful event that is planned to secure closure with a child's parents. A goodbye visit is a difficult and emotional experience that can present a number of challenges. Specifically, it will be the last time that their former parents and the child will be seeing each other, likely creating feelings of discomfort and anxiety. The ongoing caseworker must consider the developmental capacity of the child when facilitating this event, possibly involving the child's therapist in preliminary discussions to assure the best possible outcome. Additionally, there will be a detailed conversation beforehand with the parents about the expectations and purpose of the visit to minimize any negative impact or behaviors. Beyond this preparation, it is important to consider the location. It is a good idea to have the goodbye visit at the local agency and have multiple staff members available if any issues arise. For many reasons, this event sometimes produces desperate behaviors (e.g. parents trying to grab the child and run out or possibly making ugly comments that could have long-standing consequences). However, steps can be taken to minimize their occurrence and allow the family the opportunity to achieve closure and give the child permission to move forward with his or her life.

After closure with the former parents, the adoptive process moves forward. The next step involves the ongoing caseworker locating and identifying an approved adoptive family for consideration. Sometimes, foster parents become the adoptive parents. However, this is not always the case. Adoptive parents come from diverse backgrounds. They may be professionals in the community or individuals whose children have grown and left home. Individuals may choose to become adoptive parents for religious reasons or a number of other reasons.

After an appropriate adoptive family has been identified that may be a good fit for meeting the child's needs, the ongoing caseworker will consider arranging an initial meeting. This first-time visit may include a couple of hours at the local park with the direct supervision of a known party (e.g., the ongoing caseworker). Based on this experience and consultation with the child, a second and less structured meeting may be designed to provide the child an opportunity to continue building attachment and developing a relationship. The process is designed to go slow to give the child an opportunity to build a trusting relationship and familiarity with the adoptive parents. If all goes well, the child will visit the home of the potentially adoptive parents, and this could include an overnight stay.

Adoption is a process that is often portrayed in television and in the media. For example, the movie *The Blind Side* was based on the life of Michael Oher, who was placed in foster care due to his mother's substance abuse. Michael was adopted by the Tuohy family and became a pro football player and Super Bowl champion. Adoption involves transition, change, and adjustment, on the part of the child and the adoptive parents.

Of the approximately 250,000 children exiting foster care in the federal fiscal year 2017, 24% of those, or 58,104, were adopted. Infants are in great demand by couples interested in adoption. This can be seen in Table 6.2 below (Children's Bureau, 2017).

TABLE 6.2 INFANTS' ENTRANCE INTO FOSTER CARE AND ADOPTION, 2017

Children Waiting to Be Adopted			Age at Entry into Foster Care		
Age	Number	Percent	Age	Number	Percent
Less than 1 year	4,639	4%	Less than 1 year	50,076	19%
1 year	11,978	10%	1 year	20,117	7%
Total	16,617	14%	Total	70,193	26%

Note that while almost one-fifth of all the children entering foster care nationally are less than a year old, those waiting to be adopted under age 1 year constitute only 4% of all the children in foster care. Such a dramatic reduction in the children waiting to be adopted does not happen for any other age group. If you are curious, you may want to examine the data for other age groups (https://www.acf.hhs.gov/sites/default/files/cb/afcarsreport25.pdf).

Pregnant teens, single women, those who have become estranged from the father of their child, and women who have been sexually assaulted but do not wish to have an abortion may start the process of putting their child up for adoption before the child's birth. The birth mother still must go through a court process terminating her parental rights before the infant would become available for adoption.

You may want to know more about the adoption laws in your state. Do you think you could now, at your age, adopt a child? Some states say "any adult" can adopt, others say any "reputable adult." Still other states provide more guidelines, such as any adult who is "at least 25 years old and living with his or her spouse." (See sidebar on additional adoption information below.)

You may have wondered about what kind of approval processes are used to assure the appropriateness of the adoptive family. An adoptive family must be approved through a home study, which includes a **comprehensive background check** to learn of any past encounters with law enforcement or CPS, as well as a thorough review of the home. Also, the family must be financially stable, willing and able to meet the needs of the child. The specific requirements for a home to become approved in your state as well as answers to the questions of who can adopt, who may be adopted, and who may place a child up for adoption can be viewed in the web links also found in the adoption information sidebar below.

ADDITIONAL INFORMATION ON ADOPTION

State Laws on Adoption
This website (https://www.childwelfare.gov/pubPDFs/parties.pdf) provides answers to three common questions:

1. Who may adopt?
2. Who may be adopted?
3. Who may place a child for adoption?

Home Study Requirements for Prospective Parents in Domestic Adoption
This website https://www.childwelfare.gov/pubPDFs/homestudyreqs_adoption.pdf answers questions such as the following:

- Who must be studied?
- What agency or person will conduct the study?
- What qualifications are required for adoptive parents?
- What is involved in a home study?
- What grounds can there be for withholding approval for adoption?
- What is the timeline by which home studies must be completed?
- What are the requirements of a postplacement study?

IV. Legal Guardianship

Legal guardianship is another approved permanency option under the ASFA, whereby a caregiver takes legal custody of a child, yet the termination of parental rights does not necessarily occur. For example, if a teenager's parents were killed in a car wreck, it may not be in the teen's wishes or best interest to seek adoption. A legal guardian could be assigned by the court to help with the management of any monies or property inherited, as well as to meet any needs and provide for the child. The legal guardian could involve a basketball coach, church member, teacher, etc. Legal guardianship may be a better option in states that do not recognize "fictive kin" as a viable permanent relative placement option.

V. Planned Permanent Living Arrangement

A planned permanent living arrangement (PPLA) is the final approved option for permanency under the ASFA. However, this is one of the most uncommon and is not often considered. For all intents and purposes, a PPLA occurs when all other options are not feasible. A PPLA means that the agency has considered all other permanency options (e.g., reunification, permanent relative placement, termination of parental rights and adoption, and legal guardianship), and none are in the child's best interest. An example of a PPLA would be a child who is closing in on the age of 18 and is already in a treatment program that provides for the child's needs and helps him or her develop the skills needed to live as an adult. A PPLA allows the court to choose exactly what this "permanent living arrangement" is and identify how it suits the child's needs. According to the Child Welfare Information Gateway (2016), if changing the permanency goal to a PPLA, 30 states require documentation of a compelling reason, and 12 states require that the child must be at least 16 years of age.

Strategies have been implemented to improve the permanency of older youth in foster care with the goal of a PPLA. The Multisite Accelerated Permanency Project involves the utilization of permanency roundtables to facilitate an exchange between experts within and outside of the child welfare agency, helping identify individualized strategies and barriers toward achieving permanency (White et al., 2015). A PPLA is a unique permanency option, one that you will rarely see when working in child protection.

Emancipation and Aging Out

Emancipation is included in this section, though it is not an approved permanency option under the ASFA. Emancipation means that the child has aged out of the system and the court has declared the individual's independence and release from custody.

Basically, we are talking about those who reach the majority age of 18 without achieving permanency and obtain a court order to be released from care. While it is possible that a child under the age of 18 may also be emancipated from the court, this is not likely and would only happen in unique circumstances. Further, child protection agencies are hesitant to support the emancipation of youth in foster care, as the child would immediately leave thousands of dollars of unused benefits on the table. That is, if the child had agreed to remain in care after the age of 18, he or she would have been eligible for assistance with college and housing until age 26. To collect these benefits, some states require the youth to work at least 80 hours a month. More information can be obtained at this website, which provides some state-by-state information: http://www.ncsl.org/research/human-services/extending-foster-care-to-18.aspx. Courtney and Hook (2017) have shown a positive association between extending foster care and earning an education, finding a 46% increase in the odds of educational attainment for each additional year in foster care. Even with the significant benefits to remaining in foster care, it's a tough sell to youths who have been involved with the constant oversight from the child protection agency. It is not hard to imagine why they are ready for "freedom" and aspire to leave the constant supervision of foster parents and CPS agency involvement. About 8% of children and youth exiting foster care each year are emancipated (U.S. Department of Health and Human Services, 2017). Unfortunately, as mentioned earlier, aging out of foster care is associated with significant risks to the child's health, well-being, and future.

Research has identified factors that influence the path to emancipation, including teenage pregnancy. Several studies suggest that adolescents in foster care may not have good knowledge about sexual and reproductive health and may experience difficulty accessing related information and services. King and Van Wert (2017) reported in a study of over 30,000 girls who spent time in foster care after their 10th birthday that 18% gave birth as an adolescent. Those who entered foster care when they were 15 and 16 had the highest rates of childbirth. Girls who had been in foster care for 1 year or less had much higher birthrates than girls who had been in foster care at least 5 years. Placement in a nonrelative home or group home produced higher rates than when living in kinship care homes, and girls who had ever run away from a foster care placement experienced twice the birthrates of those who had not run away. Thus, placement instability is a risk factor associated with higher rates of pregnancy when care providers have not yet had the time to build strong relationships with the girls in their homes.

King, Putnam-Hornstein, Cedarbaum, and Needell (2014) have also written about the relationship between placement instability and adverse outcomes:

> This finding also comports with qualitative research that suggested that girls in foster care who choose to give birth do so because they believe that parenting will provide a sense of stability, increased attachment and permanence, and the opportunity to be successful in ways their own parents and the foster care system were not. (p. 183)

TEST YOURSELF

What are the major reason that child protection agencies do not often encourage emancipation of teenagers? Do not read below the dotted line until you are ready to see the answer.

Because there are benefits (up to $5,000 per year academic year) for foster youth to use for attending college or training for a career, plus funds for housing and opportunities to stay connected to agency resources and learn skills like budgeting that they may need for living on their own. See https://www.acf.hhs.gov/cb/resource/chafee-foster-care-program.

This program serves youth who are likely to remain in foster care until age 18, youth who, after attaining 16 years of age, have left foster care for kinship guardianship or adoption, and young adults ages 18 to 21 who have "aged out" of the foster care system. The new Family First Prevention Services Act extends eligibility for education and training vouchers for these youth to age 26.

Will the Foster Parents Adopt?

Arriving at the Wells foster home, Chad was ready to discuss the future and explore their intentions to adopt Rebecca and Renee. Chad had worked with Bob and Tina Wells for a number of years, and they were his favorite foster parents. They were always willing to go above and beyond to meet the needs of the children placed in their home. Tina was small in stature but an energetic advocate for children, a volunteer at the local domestic violence shelter, and someone who you would want on your side if you were in an argument. Bob was a little more relaxed than his wife. He was a retired engineer, and although he was soft-spoken, people listened when he talked.

Chad informed the family that the court had changed Rebecca and Renee's permanency goals from reunification to adoption and that the termination of parental rights hearing was scheduled in 2 months. The girls had been there for well over a year; they were stable and seemed to be doing well, and he was hoping that the Wellses would be interested in adoption. He had faith in Bob and Tina and did not want to uproot the children from their placement if at all possible.

Tina was open and honest, letting Chad know that Rebecca's recent behaviors of not engaging with other children and seeming sad all the time were puzzling. Bob related several instances of trying to help Rebecca with school work when she was struggling and she just left it and walked away. He took the rejection personally and was not sure that they would be able to commit to an adoption. Chad recalled that earlier in the week he had met a therapist in the community who had just relocated to the area and who had an extensive history in working with children with reactive attachment disorder. Chad spoke with the foster family and offered to make a specialized referral for treatment for Rebecca with hopes that this would help address her behavior. Bob and Tina had always received good advice from Chad; they agreed to see if this specialized treatment would help Rebecca. Chad let the family know that he would set up services tomorrow and thanked them for their consistent support and care of the girls.

The Worker's Roles

Child protection professionals can have many roles and responsibilities. As you remember, Tonya was assigned as the investigative worker for the Perkins family but was only involved with them for a very limited amount of time. Her primary focus was to complete a thorough assessment and determine the amount of risk associated with the children's safety and well-being.

After the completion of the investigation, Tonya's supervisor assigned the case to Chad to facilitate ongoing services with the family. Chad's primary focus was to arrange the services and resources needed by the girls and their parents. The goal was to prevent reoccurrence of the child sexual abuse and to work toward family reunification at that point. As an ongoing caseworker, he had been involved with the family for at about a year and a half. In the balance of this chapter, we will continue to follow the journey of the Perkins girls to see more of the worker's specific roles and responsibilities when children have been placed in out-of-home care and the court has determined that reunification is no longer in the girls' best interest.

A Balancing Act

In many ways, providing ongoing services when seeking a different form of permanency than family reunification feels like a balancing act. For a number of months, Chad had discussed the agency's commitment to reunifying the Perkins family at each home visit, court hearing, and phone call. However, this had all been transformed by the court order changing the permanency goal of Rebecca and Renee from reunification to adoption. While he was still responsible for ongoing services with the parents, at least until the termination of parental rights was finalized, the change of permanency goal meant that he also was in the somewhat awkward predicament of needing to focus on the potential adoptive placement for the girls. Children in foster care are often caught in the middle of two families, and the interplay between these relationships may be complex and tense (Chateauneuf, Turcotte, & Drapeau, 2018). To complicate matters a bit, sometimes families appeal the findings of a termination of parental rights, and that battle may stretch out for a long time. Or the court may decide not to terminate parental rights in spite of the agency's recommendations—although it seemed a safe bet the court wouldn't do that in the Perkins case.

Despite any uncertainties, the ongoing caseworker must remain professional, transparent, and entirely focused on the needs of the child. Once families have been involved with the agency for a significant amount of time, there should not be many surprises.

Working with Foster (Resource) Parents

A significant source of support when working with children to achieve permanency is the availability of foster parents (sometimes known as resource parents). Foster parents are a critical component in child protection and help provide the stability and safety needed by children placed in out-of-home care. Foster parents also assist with transporting children to and from visitations; getting them to medical, therapy, and other appointments; overseeing their schoolwork and performance; and making sure their overall health and well-being are attended to.

Research has shown that foster parents play an important role in children achieving permanency and in the effective delivery of services. Katz, Lalayants, and Phillips (2018) used quantitative data from the National Survey of Child and Adolescent Well-Being II (NSCAW II) to examine the influence of out-of-home care caregivers on permanency outcomes for children in foster care. While controlling for child- and parent-level characteristics, this longitudinal study found that the availability of caregiver respite services and caregivers' communication with caseworkers predicted permanency for children in foster care.

Foster parent characteristics and behaviors also significantly influence placement stability and permanency outcomes. With respect to LGBTQ youth, foster parent acceptance is vital in developing an environment of inclusion and affirmation (McCormick, Schmidt, & Terrazas, 2016). This is increasingly important, as a recent study estimates that approximately 15.5% of children involved with the child welfare system identify as gay, lesbian, or bisexual and are at a higher risk of having mental health concerns (Dettlaff, Washburn, Carr, & Vogel, 2018). Further, Patterson et al. (2018) used comprehensive data-collection methods to prioritize and identify essential competencies that helped resource parents promote permanency and increase well-being. While the findings are quite exhaustive, important competencies included using trauma-informed parenting, building trusting relationships, assisting in maintaining connections, helping with emotional regulation, and being adaptable to the child's needs.

Children who have been in a certain foster home for a significant amount of time may have developed a quality relationship with their foster parents. For that reason, it is important to consider foster parents with established relationships as a potential adoptive family. While not all foster parents may be interested, exploring this option might be a valuable avenue for achieving permanency.

The Permanency Worker

An additional asset when working toward permanency is the permanency (adoption) worker. The permanency worker becomes involved with the child in an administrative and supportive fashion to the ongoing caseworker after the court has changed the child's permanency goal from reunification to adoption at the annual permanency review hearing. The essential responsibilities include gathering the child's hospital records, educational records, and any other personal and relevant legal documentation. Collecting and organizing this material is helpful in expediting the termination of parental rights hearing and preparing the child for adoption. This adoption specialist saves the ongoing caseworker many hours of data collection and organization. Consider for a moment what you might want to know about a child that you were considering adopting? This information is what the permanency worker helps collect. Additionally, these documents can become important to adopted children when they reach the age of 18 or older and request their early records.

> After returning from lunch, Chad was called to the front desk. He was greeted by Monica, with a great big smile. Monica was the adoption specialist for the agency and had stopped by the local office to collect some preliminary information about Rebecca and Renee Perkins. She informed Chad that she was working to prepare all necessary documentation for the upcoming termination of parental rights hearing. Monica was bubbly and energetic, having worked for the agency for a number of years. She enjoyed her job and was passionate about helping the ongoing caseworker assist children in finding a forever family.

Intensive and Specialized Ongoing Services

Intensive and specialized ongoing services are an important consideration for children who have been in out-of-home care and are working toward an alternate form of permanency. Children come into foster care for a variety of reasons, and the associated trauma and difficulties involved with being in foster care itself can present issues. As mentioned earlier, these circumstances may present a barrier in keeping a foster home placement or in finding a permanent home.

In his discussion with the Wells foster family, Chad heard their concerns about Rebecca's sadness and often withdrawal when she actually needed support or assistance. She rarely smiled and seemed very irritable at times. While Dorothy (the girls' grandmother) did not give an explicit reason for why she requested that Chad pick up the girls from her relative placement in Arkansas in Chapter 5, it is not uncommon for children in foster care who have received neglectful parenting to need therapy. Chad recognized that foster parents' description of Rebecca seemed to fit the category of **reactive attachment disorder**. Chad made a mental note to call a child therapist who worked with children with this disorder when he got back to the office. It is always important to have a list of resources and to have a grasp on the services that are available (or unavailable) in your service area. In Chapter 9 we will focus on special populations and the challenges of providing them with stability and long-term well-being. It is the ongoing caseworker's role to identify and facilitate any intensive and specialized services that children need to support their permanency.

Group Homes and Residential Care

An additional form of intensive and specialized ongoing services can also consist of group homes and residential care. While it may be a preference for your agency to initially seek a traditional foster home for out-of-home care, group homes and residential care facilities offer specialized treatment for a number of reasons. These may be viable options for youth with specific needs (e.g., extreme behavioral and mental health problems, substance abuse, teenage pregnancy, sexual offenses, etc.). Group homes and residential care have specially trained staff that meet the needs of children in a highly structured environment. Normally, they are not permanent solutions.

Group homes and residential care can be a purposeful intervention that can result in the child's return to a traditional foster care home upon program completion. An example may include a teenage boy with anger and behavioral issues who needs a highly structured residential care program that could help him acquire self-management and social skills. Another example could be a teenage girl exhibiting promiscuous behavior who continues to run away from her caretaker and uses illicit substances. Group homes and residential care are costly and likely to require an additional level of approval and justification. They are only considered after other avenues have been exhausted or found ineffective. Unfortunately, some children with a high level of needs may end up staying in a group home or residential care instead of being placed in a traditional foster home—but that would never be the ideal goal.

Independent Living Skills

Independent living skills are designed to help prepare children in foster care for their future. Child welfare agencies proactively engage their youth in foster care by facilitating trainings and services that are designed to assist them in becoming self-sufficient adults when they are eventually released from the supervision of the agency.

Independent living skills are taught based on the child's age and level of maturity. Younger teens may focus on developing "soft" independent living skills designed to assist in thinking, communication, problem solving, personal hygiene, and time management. Older youths will begin developing the skills of everyday living, such as completing laundry, cooking, managing a checkbook, applying for a job, and paying bills. Also, independent living skills for teens may include assistance with applying for student loans, obtaining a Social Security card or driver's license, taking college entrance exams, or earning a GED.

Ideally, an individualized plan relative to a child's cognitive level of functioning and his or her specific needs will be developed. When children are in a traditional foster home, it is likely that your agency will have a specialized worker who is responsible for facilitating these trainings. If children are placed in a group home or residential care, trainings for skills needed for independent living will likely be conducted by the facility's own staff.

While the need to prepare children in foster care with the skills that they will need to become autonomous adults is clear, research has shown some concerns in its implementation. Thompson, Wojciak, and Cooley (2018) used data from the NSCAW II to simultaneously explore the perceptions of foster care alumni living independently and children currently in foster care. Their findings reveal that most of the respondents denied receiving the necessary resources to develop independent living skills. Additionally, a study by Katz and Courtney (2015) collected self-reported feedback from youth transitioning to adulthood from foster care; the major unmet need in independent living skills was preparation in the area of finance (e.g., being trained to use a budget). While there are a number of effective supports that can assist the ongoing worker in preparing foster children and teens for living more independently, there are also some tips that can assist in keeping children in good foster families so that they don't try to launch out on their own too early.

Preventing Disruptions and Postplacement Services

After achieving permanency, aftercare services will be implemented to prevent adoption disruptions and reentry to foster care. **Aftercare** refers to the strategic involvement of extended resources, after the agency has closed the case and terminated services. Having a sound strategy for aftercare services is important; an adoption disruption and reentry to foster care is especially problematic, as it begins the trajectory of court involvement all over again and forces the child to begin developing new attachments and seeking a new form of permanency. A common reason for adoption disruptions is that the adoptive parent did not have the support or skills needed to meet the specific needs of the child. In order to proactively address this significant issue, the ongoing caseworker should create a comprehensive plan for aftercare services that will address any issues that might affect the child's long-term stability and well-being. Even with the formal agency involvement ending and the case being technically closed by the agency, following through with necessary ongoing services is necessary. For example, Chad may work with the adoptive parents to assure that Rebecca and Renee both continue treatment with their mental health therapists, etc. Beyond meeting the individual needs of the child, support mechanisms can be put in place for the adoptive family. Examples include receiving an adoption subsidy and health insurance for the child. While placement discontinuity and adoption disruption are a significant concern (White, 2016), disruptions only occur in about 15% of children who were adopted or going into guardianship (Rolock & White, 2017).

PRACTICE TIP 6.1 When working with children who have been in out-of-home care and are seeking an alternate form of permanency besides reunification, it is important to remain patient. Many of the decisions made will be permanent, and it is likely that individuals involved in this process may become quite emotional at times. Recognize that moving from a family reunification goal to a different form of permanency may create inherent conflicts that may influence the health and well-being of the child as well as of the biological or former family and foster family.

Always be open and transparent, acknowledging if you are not the expert or do not have the answer. You will be waiting on the finalization of important court hearings, and this tension will likely be palpable. Utilize any and all supports in this process, including the foster parents, independent living skills coordinator, permanency worker, and specialized treatment options that may assist you in meeting the child's needs and achieving permanency. Become an expert on these resources, building professional relationships with these individuals and letting them know how much you appreciate their efforts.

Consider utilizing the child's therapist as an effective tool for delivering difficult information and having difficult conversations. The child should have had a stable therapist who has been a part of his or her life for a significant time, and utilizing the therapist's professional support should be beneficial to the child's well-being.

Continue to keep excellent documentation and records, and maintain quality relationships with court personnel. The GAL is a key element in the important court hearings associated with achieving permanency (e.g., annual permanency review hearing, termination of parental rights, adoption).

Lastly, if children obtain a change in placement (e.g., group home, foster home, adoptive home), it is likely that they will experience a barrage of questions by their new classmates in school. Consider helping these children develop a *cover story* that can explain their background and prevent their having to explain hurtful past incidents. This must be age-appropriate and brief, leaving out any detrimental details that may be problematic. Helping them be prepared to tell their story in a safe and positive way may significantly help their mental health and adjustment in a new school.

Seeking a Forever Home

At the conclusion of the TPR hearing wherein Rodney and Angela's parental rights were terminated, Chad realized that he had a voicemail from Tina Wells, who asked him to stop by their home after the hearing. When Chad arrived, Tina began to cry and explained to him that she was overwhelmed with the progress that Rebecca had made since involvement with her new therapist. Tina and Bob both thanked Chad and mentioned that his ability to secure these specialized services had changed their outlook on adoption.

Tina reached for the photo album on the coffee table and asked Chad, "Did you know that I was adopted?" Chad had no idea. Tina showed Chad a picture of Ms. Jenkins, who adopted Tina when she was 13 years old. Tina explained to Chad that Ms. Jenkins gave her a second chance when nobody else would and that she didn't know where her life would be today without her. Reaching for a tissue, Tina, with Bob silently nodding in agreement, notified Chad that they were ready and willing to adopt both Rebecca and Renee Perkins.

A few weeks later, the big day arrived, and Chad couldn't help but feel excited. He dropped by the office and picked up Tonya and Monica, then headed to the courthouse for the adoption hearing. Monica was artistic and had created monogrammed T-shirts for Rebecca and Renee that included their new initials, as the Perkins girls were about to have a new last name. Arriving at the courthouse, Rebecca and Renee both ran up to Chad and immediately gave him a big hug at the same time. They seemed genuinely happy and at peace. Chad was part of their journey. Memories rushed through his mind as he recalled the challenges along this path. But this was a new day! It was the beginning of their new life, and Rebecca and Renee had finally found their forever family.

Main Points

When children are placed in out-of-home care and the court has decided that reunification is no longer an option, the ongoing caseworker facilitates the path to permanency for the child.

- The Adoption and Safe Families Act of 1997 directs involvement with families when children have been placed in out of home care.
- The ASFA has five approved options for permanency (i.e., reunification, permanent relative placement, adoption, legal guardianship, and planned permanent living arrangement).
- Reunification is the primary permanency goal for children who are placed in out-of-home care.
- Permanent relative placement is the least restrictive option for permanency when reunification is not appropriate.
- After 15 of 22 months in out-of-home care, the ASFA permits the child protection agency to pursue changing the permanency goal and seeking the termination of parental rights. Adoption can only be pursued after the termination of parental rights (voluntary or involuntary).
- Emancipation or aging out of foster care are associated with many negative outcomes.
- Specialized support and aftercare services are vital to the stability and permanency of children exiting foster care.

Questions for Class Discussion

1. Which permanency option(s) might be easier to accomplish? Why?
2. Which permanency option(s) might be harder to accomplish? Why?
3. What strategies might the ongoing caseworker use to solidify an adoptive placement?
4. Give an example of a situation that could result in a foster child's placement in a group home or residential care.
5. Describe some independent living skills that you feel are very important to develop as a child approaches the age of 18.

Self-Assessment for Personal Consideration

1. How comfortable would you be with conducting services with a biological family after letting them know that you will be requesting a change of permanency goal from reunification to adoption?

   | 1 | 2 | 3 | 4 | 5 | 6 | 7 | 8 | 9 | 10 |

   Not comfortable   *Very comfortable*

2. How comfortable are you with children being adopted by families that are different (e.g., race, ethnicity, religion, sexual identity, etc.)?

   | 1 | 2 | 3 | 4 | 5 | 6 | 7 | 8 | 9 | 10 |

   Not comfortable   *Very comfortable*

Additional Resources

Francesca, Z., & Ghahremani, S. (2007). *My family, my journey: A baby book for adoptive families.* San Francisco, CA: Chronicle Books.

Graham, K. E., Schellinger, A. R., & Vaughn, L. M. (2015). Developing strategies for positive change: Transitioning foster youth to adulthood. *Children and Youth Services Review, 54,* 71–79.

Malm, K., Vandivere, S., Allen, T., DeVooght, K., Ellis, R. … & Zinn, A. (2011). *Evaluation report summary: The Wendy's Wonderful Kids Initiative* (Executive summary, Dave Thomas Foundation for Adoption, Columbus, OH). Retrieved from https://www.davethomasfoundation.org/library/wwk-research-executive-summary.

Meyer, A. S., McWey, L. M., McKendrick, W., & Henderson, T. L. (2010). Substance using parents, foster care, and termination of parental rights: The importance of risk factors for legal outcomes. *Children and Youth Services Review, 32,* 639–649.

Purvis, K. B., Cross, D. R., & Sunshine, W. L. (2007). *The connected child: Bring hope and healing to your adoptive family.* New York, NY: McGraw-Hill Education.

References

Adoption and Safe Families Act, P.L. § 105–89 (1997).

Akin, B. A. (2011). Predictors of foster care exits to permanency: A competing risks analysis of reunification, guardianship, and adoption. *Children and Youth Services Review, 33,* 999–1011.

Akin, B. A., & McDonald, T. P. (2018). Parenting intervention effects on reunification: A randomized trial of PMTO in foster care. *Child Abuse & Neglect, 83*, 94–105.

Berrick, J. D., & Hernandez, J. (2016). Developing consistent and transparent kinship care policy and practice: State mandated, mediated, and independent care. *Children and Youth Services Review, 68*, 24–33.

Chateauneuf, D., Turcotte, D., & Drapeau, S. (2018). The relationship between foster care families and birth families in a child welfare context: The determining factors. *Child & Family Social Work, 23*(1), 71–79.

Child and Family Services Reviews. (2019). *Achieving permanency.* Retrieved from https://training.cfsrportal.acf.hhs.gov/section-2-understanding-child-welfare-system/3030

Children's Bureau. (2018). *The AFCARS report* (Report, US Department of Health & Human Services, Washington, DC). Retrieved from https://www.acf.hhs.gov/sites/default/files/cb/afcarsreport25.pdf

Child Welfare Information Gateway. (2016). *Court hearings for the permanent placement of children.* Washington, DC: Children's Bureau.

Child Welfare Information Gateway. (2018). *Placement of children with relatives.* Washington, DC: Children's Bureau.

Child Welfare League of America. (1994). *Kinship care: A natural bridge.* Washington, DC: Author.

Courtney, M. E., & Hook, J. L. (2017). The potential educational benefits of extending foster care to young adults: Findings from a natural experiment. *Children and Youth Services Review, 72*, 124–132.

Dettlaff, A. J., Washburn, M., Carr, L., & Vogel, A. (2018). Lesbian, gay, and bisexual (LGB) youth within in welfare: Prevalence, risk and outcomes. *Child Abuse & Neglect, 80*, 183–193.

Elgin, D. J. (2018). Utilizing predictive modeling to enhance policy and practice through improved identification of at-risk clients: Predicting permanency for foster children. *Children and Youth Services Review, 91*, 156–167.

Esposito, T., Delaye, A., Chabot, M., Trocme, N., Rothwell, D., Helie, S., & Robichaud, M. J. (2017). The effects of socioeconomic vulnerability, psychosocial services, and social service spending on family reunification: A multilevel longitudinal analysis. *International Journal of Environmental Research and Public Health, 14*(9), 1040.

Fernandez, E., & Lee, J.-S. (2011). Returning children in care to their families: Factors associated with the speed of reunification. *Child Indicators Research, 4*(4), 749–765.

Fowler, P. J., Marcal, K. E., Zhang, J. J., Day, O., & Landsverk, J. (2017). Homelessness and aging out of foster care: A national comparison of child welfare-involved adolescents. *Children and Youth Services Review, 77*, 27–33.

Greiner, M. V., & Beal, S. J. (2017). Foster care is associated with poor mental health in children. *Journal of Pediatrics, 182*, 404.

Gypen, L., Vanderfaeillie, J., De Maeyer, S., Belenger, L., & Van Holen, F. (2017). Outcomes of children who grew up in foster care: Systematic-review. *Children and Youth Services Review, 76*, 74–83.

Hambrick, E. P., Oppenheim-Weller, S., N'zi, A. M., & Taussig, H. N. (2016). Mental health interventions for children in foster care: A systematic review. *Children and Youth Services Review, 70*, 65–77.

Jedwab, M., Chatterjee, A., & Shaw, T. V. (2018). Caseworkers' insights and experiences with successful reunification. *Children and Youth Services Review, 86*, 56–63.

Katz, C. C., & Courtney, M. E. (2015). Evaluating the self-expressed unmet needs of emancipated foster youth over time. *Children and Youth Services Review, 57*, 9–18.

Katz, C. C., Lalayats, M., & Phillips, J. D. (2018). The role of out-of-home caregivers in the achievement of child welfare permanency. *Children and Youth Services Review, 94*, 65–71. doi:10.1016/j.childyouth.2018.09.016

King, B., Putnam-Hornstein, E., Cederbaum, J. A., & Needell, B. (2014). A cross-sectional examination of birth rates among adolescent girls in foster care. *Children and Youth Services Review, 36*, 179–186.

King, B., & Van Wert, M. (2017). Predictors of early childbirth among female adolescents in foster care. *Journal of Adolescent Health, 61*, 226–232.

Koh, E., Rolock, N., Cross, T. P., & Eblen-Manning, J. (2014). What explains instability in foster care? Comparison of a matched sample of children with stable and unstable placements. *Children and Youth Services Review, 37*, 36–45.

Lockwood, K. K., Friedman, S., & Christian, C. W. (2015). Permanency and the foster care system. *Current Problems in Pediatric and Adolescent Health Care, 45*(10), 306–315.

McCormick, A., Schmidt, K., & Terrazas, S. R. (2016). Foster family acceptance: Understanding the role of foster family acceptance in the lives of LGBTQ youth. *Children and Youth Services Review, 61*, 69–74.

Moye, J., & Rinker, R. (2002). It's a hard knock life: Does the Adoption and Safe Families Act of 1997 adequately address problems in the child welfare system? *Harvard Journal on Legislation, 39*(2), 375–394.

Murphy, A. L., Van Zyl, R., Collins-Camargo, C., & Sullivan, D. (2012). Assessing systemic barriers to permanency achievement for children in out-of-home care: Development of the Child Permanency Barriers Scale. *Child Welfare, 91*(5), 37–71.

Patterson, D., Day, A., Vanderwill, L., Willis, T., Resko, S., Henneman, K., & Cohick, S. (2018). Identifying the essential competencies for resource parents to promote permanency and well-being of adolescents in care. *Children and Youth Services Review, 88*, 457–466.

Rolock, N., & White, K. R. (2017). Continuity for children after guardianship versus adoption with kin: Approximating the right counterfactual. *Child Abuse & Neglect, 72*, 32–44.

Salazar, A. M., Jones, K. R., Amemiya, J., Cherry, A., Brown, E. C., Catalano, R. F., & Monahan, K. C. (2018). Defining and achieving permanency among older youth in foster care. *Children and Youth Services Review, 87*, 9–16.

Stein, T. J. (2000). The Adoption and Safe Families Act: Creating a false dichotomy between parents' and childrens' rights. *Families in Society-the Journal of Contemporary Human Services, 81*(6), 586–592.

Stott, T., & Gustavsson, N. (2010). Balancing permanency and stability for youth in foster care. *Children and Youth Services Review, 32*(4), 619–625.

Thompson, H. M., Wojciak, A. S., & Cooley, M. E. (2018). The experience with independent living services for youth in care and those formerly in care. *Children and Youth Services Review, 84*, 17–25.

Whitaker, T. (2011). Administrative case reviews: Improving outcomes for children in out-of-home care. *Children and Youth Services Review, 33*(9), 1683–1708.

White, C. R., Corwin, T., Buher, A. L., O'Brien, K., DiLorenzo, P., Kelly, S., & Morgan, L. J. (2015). The Multisite Accelerated Permanency Project: Permanency roundtables as a strategy to help older youth in foster care achieve legal permanency. *Journal of Social Service Research, 41*(3), 364–384.

White, K. R. (2016). Placement discontinuity for older children and adolescents who exit foster care through adoption or guardianship: A systematic review. *Child and Adolescent Social Work Journal, 33*(4), 377–394.

Winokur, M. A., Holtan, A., & Batchelder, K. E. (2018). Systematic review of kinship care effects on safety, permanency, and well-being outcomes. *Research on Social Work Practice, 28*(1), 19–32.

■ CHAPTER 7

RISK ASSESSMENT FOR MALTREATMENT: FURTHER INFORMATION AND RESOURCES

OVERVIEW

In Chapter 4 we "walked" through the investigative process to give you a general idea of how it starts and proceeds. However, there is much more to say and learn about risk assessment. After all, the Perkins family case represented only one specific kind of allegation although there were other problems. To prepare you for other scenarios that you will encounter in child protection, a layer of additional information is provided.

This chapter functions as a valuable resource for the practitioner focused on risk assessment as part of the investigation process or for the professional wanting to measure improvement as a result of intervention. Assessing for risk is an inherent component that is integral to both the initial and ongoing process of service provision. Instruments such as those identified in this chapter can assist the investigator in gathering objective information regarding the initial allegation and will assist the ongoing caseworker in examining progress made and risk of future harm.

Scenarios in this chapter address common ones that as a child welfare professional you will likely encounter in your career. They illustrate circumstances and factors that influence the assessment of risk. A distinction will be made between the practitioner's *concerns* about risk and *evidence* of risk. While this chapter cannot provide an all-inclusive listing of every possible assessment instrument or contingency that the child welfare professional will encounter, the risk assessment process is so critical to child protection that it merits additional discussion after the student or new CPS employee has a good understanding of the key content provided earlier. This chapter does not provide an explicit step-by-step guide but elaborates on both the finer points and practical aspects of risk assessment to better prepare you to be a CPS professional.

Risk Assessment Revisited

Earlier in the text, we explored the case of the Perkins family to illustrate the investigative process. This chapter will not describe the actual steps involved in this process but will provide the reader with a contextual understanding about risk assessment. However, before we begin the practical application material, we will make another attempt at emphasizing the importance of risk assessment in child protection.

Broadly speaking, risk assessment in child protection refers to the systematic evaluation of factors that either contributed or have the potential to contribute to the maltreatment of a child. Risk assessment is the heart of the investigative process; the investigator must determine whether child maltreatment has occurred and can be substantiated or if there is a high enough level of risk that it certainly could occur in the future. In an ongoing capacity, risk assessment is useful for evaluating progress and continually estimating the prevalence of factors that could influence the probability of future child maltreatment.

Risk assessment in child protection is focused on the occurrence of child maltreatment, yet similar strategies are used in other professional fields. For example, insurance companies strategically evaluate the potential impact of negative factors when creating policies. Specifically, a homeowner's policy may consist of the insurance agency collecting background information on behalf of the client, assessing for crime rates in a neighborhood, distance from the fire department, the average price of homes in the neighborhood, and other salient sources of data to decide what rate to charge. Similarly, a life insurance company may require a physical examination to determine the health of the applicant and any preexisting conditions before writing an individual policy.

Another example would be that of weather forecasters, who each day utilize historical data, scientific technology, and other avenues to best predict the probability of severe weather. These examples are analogous to the practice of risk assessment, but the process in child protection is much different.

In child protection, risk assessment will result in evaluating factors that may literally result or have resulted in the abuse of a child. As described by Van der Put, Assink, and Van Solinge (2017), risk assessment is "crucial" in preventing maltreatment by assisting the agency in facilitating services when high-risk cases have been identified. Risk assessment with a less than comprehensive approach could result in leaving a child in an unsafe situation. Also, an unsatisfactory risk assessment evaluation could result in the agency facilitating services that may not best address the prevailing issues faced by the family.

Decision making in child protection is challenging, as practitioners face barriers and uncertainties throughout this process (Bartelink, Van Yperen, & Ten Berge, 2015). While it is unreasonable to expect anyone to be able to predict human behavior with great accuracy, there must be a rationale to show how decisions were made. The risk assessment process gathers evidence to support conclusions. Very few times will you walk into a situation where it is clear and evident that abuse has occurred (e.g., by client admission, video or photographic evidence, etc.), so using such techniques to support your decisions is especially important when working investigations. The good news is there are many objective measures to support you in assessing risk, as we will see in this chapter.

The necessity to understand and evaluate the circumstances and contributing factors that place children at a higher risk for the occurrence of child maltreatment cannot be emphasized enough. Comprehensive risk assessment has remained the primary evaluative mechanism that guides the involvement of child protection agencies across the country. As identified by Cash (2001), risk assessment in child protection is both "art" and "science," and we will begin this chapter by exploring how these two paths converge.

Sophisticated Research Approaches to Risk Assessment

Two very sophisticated approaches to risk assessment in child protection found in the literature are the **actuarial approach** and the **consensus-based approach** (Mendoza, Rose, Geiger, & Cash, 2016). Actuarial risk assessment is focused on limiting biases when estimating future harm, described as a "statistical procedure for estimating the probability that a critical event, such as child maltreatment, will occur in the future" (Coohey, Johnson, Renner, & Easton, 2013, p. 151). In contrast, consensus-based approaches use clinical decision making and consider the practice wisdom of the practitioner, where "workers rate selected characteristics that were originally identified by consensus among experts and these factors are then processed using professional judgement rather than according to a standard algorithm" (Barber, Shlonsky, Black, Goodman, & Trocmé, 2008, p.177).

Child welfare agencies are often tasked with more and given less. Many operate in an environment of competition for scarce resources, with increasing demands. For this reason, there is an increased interest in the improvement of risk assessment techniques that support decisions that must be made in this line of work (Cuccaro-Alamin, Foust, Vaithianathan, & Putnam-Hornstein, 2017).

Robust explorations continue to investigate this trajectory. Mendoza et al. (2016) used secondary data to examine records from 2,178 families, exploring the risk assessment process with respect to utilizing measurements in both the clinical and actuarial dimensions. The study focused on worker decisions about substantiation and services, and findings illustrated the complex interplay between both of these methods. Possibly serving as a springboard for improving the development of future instruments that could encapsulate both dimensions, the article provided examples of evidence-based instruments for each approach. See Table 7.1.

TABLE 7.1 CLINICAL AND ACTUARIAL INSTRUMENTS FOR RISK ASSESSMENT

Examples of evidence-based clinical instruments

- The Washington Risk Assessment Matrix (WRAM)
- The California Family Assessment Factor Analysis (CFAFA or Fresno Model)
- The Child at Risk Field System (CARF)
- The Child Emergency Response Assessment Protocol (CERAP)

Examples of evidence-based actuarial instruments

- The Children's Research Center's Actuarial Models for Risk Assessment

For more information, please review:
Mendoza, N. S., Rose, R. A., Geiger, J. M., & Cash, S. J. (2016). Risk assessment with actuarial and clinical methods: Measurement and evidence-based practice. *Child Abuse & Neglect, 61,* 1–12.

In a similar fashion, a meta-analysis by Van der Put et al. (2017) examined 27 different risk assessment instruments across 30 independent studies, assessing for validity in predicting child maltreatment. Findings from the study identified actuarial instruments as outperforming clinical instruments and that the onset of maltreatment was better predicted than its reoccurrence.

Predictive analytics and predictive modeling are being utilized in a number of locations to evaluate and improve risk assessment and decision making in child protection (Cuccaro-Alamin et al., 2017; Daley et al., 2016; Gillingham, 2016; Russell & Macgill, 2015; Schwartz, York, Nowakowski-Sims, & Ramos-Hernandez, 2017; Thurston & Miyamoto, 2018). Given the advances in technology, and that child maltreatment was estimated to result in a $2 trillion economic burden in the United States in 2015 (Peterson, Florence, & Klevens, 2018), the development of predictive analytics and modeling is an increasing area of focus for the future of child protection (Russell, 2015).

While the value of utilizing predictive analytics is understood, there are skeptical viewpoints. Specifically, researchers have identified that analytic strategies must utilize established criteria that focus on reliability, validity, equity, and usefulness (Russell, 2015). Also, research has shown that caution must be taken, as predictive modeling could quite literally open a Pandora's box through "false positives" and mistakenly identify individuals as "potential child abusers" (de Haan & Connolly, 2014).

COMPREHENSIVE FAMILY ASSESSMENT

Recently, child welfare has explored the development and utilization of the comprehensive family assessment (CFA). The CFA is a process, not a tool, and helps child welfare agencies understand the "big picture." In 2007 the Children's Bureau supported the development, implementation, and evaluation of comprehensive family assessments that are designed to assist in understanding the functioning of each individual family and identifying factors that could influence child maltreatment. Guidelines have been developed for this focus on a family-centered and culturally competent approach that includes the perspectives of multiple family members and obtains a holistic view of the family's safety. Researchers evaluating the effectiveness of these assessment strategies (Smithgall, Jarpe-Ratner, Gnedko-Berry, & Mason, 2015), and state and local examples can be found at the following website:

https://www.childwelfare.gov/topics/systemwide/assessment/family-assess/famcentered/

Practical Application

If you are working as a child welfare practitioner, your local agency will have a set of practice standards that will guide your assessment process with families. You will be able to use your practice wisdom and experience to assist in this effort. Empirically based and objective information you collect will fortify the decisions that you will have to make.

A comprehensive assessment is thorough and considers a number of factors. Remembering Cash's (2001) description of risk assessment in child welfare as an art and a science, we can understand that practice wisdom is the art portion and that the use of empirically based instrumentation is the science part. Sometimes your assessments will draw largely on what you have learned in your training and experience, and at other times you may employ an objective measure to undergird your impressions.

What do you look for when assessing families for risk factors associated with child maltreatment? We will begin by providing an appropriate contextual framework to help the practitioner assess the family using a holistic, ecological, and empirically based assessment (Cash, 2001). Then we will explore risk assessment in several common scenarios.

An Ecological Perspective

Attributed to Urie Bronfenbrenner (1979), the ecological systems theory is of particular value in social work practice—especially when considering risks associated with child maltreatment. The ecological perspective helps us view each person in his or her environment, providing a framework for the contributions of various influences and serving as a main theoretical approach for understanding families who live in a complex system (Cash, 2001).

Individual or micro-level factors for consideration will include the physical, psychological, and spiritual dimensions that may be particularly relevant in the assessment of risk. While your role in the risk assessment process will not be that of a medical professional, it is valuable to be able to look for visible evidence of injury such as bruises, lacerations, and physical impairments, sickness, or disease. Similarly, you will consider individual mental health or illness and influencing factors. Mental health is the absence of cognitive or emotional problems that can affect an individuals' ability to function effectively in their environment and make decisions about their lives.

While you will not likely be in a clinical diagnosis role, understanding red flags and what to look for is important. Related to risk assessment, a standard exploration will include asking questions to appraise any risks associated with the psychological health and well-being of the individuals you are investigating. Additionally, understanding basic human development is key, as certain behaviors should be appropriately viewed through this developmental context. An example might be that you receive allegations of malnutrition in a 4-year-old. In this situation it would be helpful to recognize an underweight child and appropriate to ask questions about diet, eating habits, and discipline at mealtimes and to verify that nutritional foods are available and given to the child. Participation in a religious community might be a resource in tough times.

Mezzo-level factors are important to examine and likely will include relationships, customs, power differentials, roles, and responsibilities. Remember, when working in child protection, you will always be involved with a child (or children) and some type of legal caretaker. Their relationship is important to understand and evaluate. Beyond this, there could be many different familial relationships, arrangements with siblings, and the inclusion of extended family members that would be important to understand. Assessing for problems and strengths associated with these relationships is a key component in risk assessment. Relationships that are fluid and change suddenly (e.g., through divorce) can disrupt a family's functioning. Understanding daily routines, who makes decisions, and odd or inappropriate relationships is a critical component in the assessment process. In a sexual abuse investigation, it would be helpful to know if the parent has a paramour living in the home. Understanding the sleeping arrangements of the children is important, too.

On a macro level, structures with large and broad implications—such citizenship, socioeconomic status, legal difficulties, policies, and other factors—affect families. Macro-level structures are important to consider, as practitioners in child protection may need to advocate for change in or work to implement strategies to alleviate conditions that are affecting families.

The three levels of the ecological framework do not occur in a vacuum, and they influence each other. For example, if the father of a child has a mental illness (micro level), his individual circumstances could directly influence his ability to provide appropriate supervision and parenting of his children (mezzo level). For this reason, it is critical to identify how the family is impacted with regard to the micro, mezzo, and macro level. The ecological perspective helps us assess for concerns and collect evidence in our assessment process.

A study by Cash (2001) analyzed the state of risk assessment in child welfare and provides an overview of factors found in the literature that place children at a higher risk of child maltreatment. While this study is several years old, it provides useful information and informs practice.

On a micro level, parental factors such as depression, psychopathology, antisocial behaviors, low self-esteem, substance abuse, and a lack of self-control were identified as placing children at a higher risk of maltreatment. Micro level factors associated with children that increased risk included premature birth, medical fragility, younger age, and disability status. On the mezzo level, having a lack of resources, having increased levels of familial stress, and living in an environment that does not shield against these stressors were factors that elevated risk. Related to the macro level factors, socioeconomic status and living in poverty were identified as key contributors to a heightened level of risk for child maltreatment.

Despite the importance of understanding risk factors, families are unique and must be viewed individually. For example, you may be working with a parent with no prior history who engages in extreme alcohol use, becomes intoxicated, and drives their vehicle off the road with a child in the backseat. While it is clear that we cannot predict human behavior perfectly, if you are asked to investigate, you will be responsible for producing a thorough and comprehensive risk assessment that documents the presence of both concerns and evidence of harmful or potentially harmful behavior.

Concerns vs. Evidence

Assessment in child protection involves two separate groupings of potential indicators of risk to the child or family. The first of these can be called **concerns**. Concerns are subjective, referring to worries or conditions that may be apparent and are believed to be problematic for safe family functioning. Concerns are red flags, possibly something that you just can't put your finger on. These might include a client's erratic behavior during an interview, inappropriate nonverbal behaviors, avoidance of eye contact, or a feeling that an explanation is not truthful. However, concerns aren't necessarily indicative of abuse or that a home is hazardous or unsafe.

TEST YOURSELF

What factors do you think protect against child abuse?

- -

There is more than one response you can make to this question. You might want to see what the Children's Bureau has suggested:

https://library.childwelfare.gov/cwig/ws/library/docs/capacity/Blob/107035.pdf?m=1&r=1&rp-p=10&upp=0&utm_campaign=&utm_content=&utm_medium=aprilspotlight&utm_name=&utm_source=govdelivery&w=+NATIVE%28%27recno%3D107035%27%29

You also might want to read one or both of these articles:

Putnam-Hornstein, E., Needell, B., & Rhodes, A. E. (2013). Understanding risk and protective factors for child maltreatment: The value of integrated, population-based data. *Child Abuse & Neglect, 37*(2–3), 116–119.

Slack, K. S., Holl, J. L., McDaniel, M., Yoo, J., & Bolger, K. (2004). Understanding the risks of child neglect: An exploration of poverty and parenting characteristics. *Child Maltreatment, 9*(4), 395–408.

On the other hand, **evidence** refers to objective facts or verification of important details. Evidence is the gold standard, what we seek to find when working in child protection. Evidence carries significant weight and is useful when attempting to affirm or disprove allegations of maltreatment and when working with families in an ongoing capacity. An example of evidence is actually seeing and taking pictures of lacerations on a child's backside. Or obtaining medical records from the hospital that identify the presence of a sexually transmitted disease in a young child. Formal tools for measurement can also serve as evidence in the investigation of child maltreatment. They can assess client progress in an ongoing case plan or be used when working with community providers (i.e., mental health services). Integrating evidence into your assessment can be important if you have to testify in court or if your records are subpoenaed as a part of an appeal.

Practice wisdom and the documentation of subjective concerns is standard practice in child protection, but integrating evidence as **evidence-based practice** is truly best practice. Evidence-based practice refers to a combination of drawing on a systematic review of the research, the client's individual circumstances and preferences, and the practice wisdom of the professional. Evidence-based practice has been utilized in public health and medicine for quite some time, and efforts are being made to integrate this into practice in child protection (Kessler, Gira, & Poertner, 2005; Horwitz et al., 2014; Walsh & Reutz, 2015). A comprehensive risk assessment collects information from multiple sources, strives to integrate as much evidence as possible, and utilizes the practice wisdom of the practitioner to inform decision making.

Situational Risk Assessments for Child Maltreatment

With the prior information about risk assessment as a backdrop, we can now present specific information associated with assessing risk with the most common allegations made to child protection agencies: abuse, neglect, dependency.

Abuse

Abuse is an overarching theme that includes physical, emotional, or sexual abuse. Abuse is often much different than neglect or dependency, as it generally includes an intentional or nonaccidental act of harm.

Physical Abuse

> Allegation: A second-grade boy, age 8, arrived at school today with parallel vertical bruise marks across his lower back. When asked about where they came from, he initially was unwilling to talk. However, he eventually said that he was "bad" and that "daddy did it to me."

Child physical abuse is probably the most indisputable form of abuse you will encounter when working in child protection. Physical abuse refers to the intentional harm to a child. Physical abuse usually involves hitting, whipping, slapping, shaking, or other actions that inflict harm to an infant or child. Physical abuse can be related to anger issues, domestic violence, or a parent attempting to discipline. Certain caretakers may not understand that the corporal punishment they received as children is no longer socially accepted. For instance, the caretaker might use a belt to whip the legs of a child. Discipline techniques may also be a part of a family's cultural dynamics.

Other examples could include a caretaker getting into a fistfight with a teenager. The age of the child is important, as newborn children and toddlers are very fragile and vulnerable. An infant with colic may cry so much at night that an exhausted parent shakes the child in exasperation. Shaken baby syndrome is an extreme form of physical abuse that can have detrimental outcomes for the rest of the child's life. Also, a parent could pull or twist a child's leg or arm, resulting in a spiral fracture. The occurrence of a spiral fracture will almost always be found only through an X-ray in a medical setting.

PRACTICE TIP 7.1 Physical abuse refers to the intentional physical harm to a child. Areas for consideration should revolve around firsthand accounts of the activities and include the perceptions of any eyewitnesses or relevant third parties as well as medical documentation. Seek to include photographic evidence that will either confirm or refute the allegations. It is important to have an understanding about the intentionality of the actions. It is always possible that the behavior was simply an accident, and if so, we need to be able to identify the basis for that assumption.

It is important to evaluate the family's form of discipline and understand the child's age and chronological development. For example, a family spanking a 6-year-old with an open hand on the bottom might not cause any marks or harm. However, spanking a 15-year-old should be considered unreasonable and problematic. Additionally, when caretakers integrate the use of belts, switches, electrical cords, and so forth into corporal discipline techniques, this quickly becomes abuse. The use of physical discipline often occurs during times of high stress, and this can amplify the use of force. A good question to ask the family when assessing for use of discipline, as modeled by Dr. Phil on his television show, is "how is that working for you?" Sometimes a quick self-reflection may serve to assist the individual in understanding that a discipline technique that uses physical force is not actually successful anyway. Try to learn from the family about how their culture may view discipline and whether this aligns with the statutory requirements in your state or region.

Another important factor for assessing for physical abuse is whether the injury was in a critical area (e.g., head, stomach, groin, kidneys). For example, if the child has a bruise on the head or abdomen, medical attention should be sought immediately. However, having a bruise on the back of the left leg might not be as concerning. These factors need to be taken into context for the assessment. Also, evaluate prior events of high stress in which the caretaker did not engage in physical contact. Is this a one-time occurrence, or might this be a frequent experience for the child?

Gather photographic evidence when possible. Take pictures of bruises, cuts, scrapes, or other ways that you can affirm or disprove the allegations. However, in some cases visual indicators of physical abuse will not always be present. For example, a lethargic infant may need evaluation from a community partner (e.g., physician or emergency medical service).

Since physical abuse is often associated with anger, the child protection worker should make efforts to assess for relationships in the family that might include domestic violence. Unfortunately, domestic violence is underreported but often a reality in many families that we will work with in child protection.

TABLE 7.2 EXAMPLES OF MEASURES RELATED TO CHILD PHYSICAL ABUSE[1]

Child Abuse Potential (CAP) Inventory (Physical Abuse)
Milner, J. S., Gold, R. G., & Wimberley, R. C. (1986). Prediction and explanation of child abuse: Cross-validation of the Child Abuse Potential Inventory. *Journal of Consulting and Clinical Psychology, 54*(6), 865–866. (Note: This instrument is for use with parents or prospective parents.)

Childhood Trauma Questionnaire (CTQ-SF)
Bernstein, D. P., Stein, J. A., Newcomb, M. D. Walker, E., Pogge, D., Ahluvalia, T. ... Zule, W. (2003). Development and validation of a brief screening version of the Childhood Trauma Questionnaire. *Child Abuse & Neglect, 27*, 169–190. (Note: Contains a physical abuse measure. See fuller description in Table 7.4.)

---

1. **Chapter note:** Even though we have provided a number of objective instruments that might or could be used by CPS professionals, you may not find one "right off the shelf" to your liking. This is not unusual. In fact, there are an almost dizzying variety of instruments that seem to complicate decision making rather than simplify it. For instance, in the article by Oh et al. (2018), instruments were screened by "adversity categories, target populations, administration time, administration qualifications and method, and reliability and validity" (p. 564). Additionally, information is provided on those that are free or must be purchased. Even if you select an adversity category like sexual abuse, you will discover that some researchers approach the problem from a measurement of frequency of the event, others focus on severity, and still others want to explore the range or specific type of sexual maltreatment. There are also differences in the vocabulary used or reading level. Some definitely would not work for very young children.

All of this is to say that, despite our intentions to give you a good idea of the variety and types of objective instruments that exist, you may still come away frustrated and discouraged. Fortunately, university libraries have available many powerful search engines for locating useful instruments. If you are unsure how to begin, you may want to see what you can pull up with Google using terms such as "instrument, measure, scale, or questionnaire, index, or inventory" and then the topic of interest like "physical abuse." Reference librarians are also very helpful.

Also note that there are a variety of instruments for assessing trauma symptomatology in children. However, these would more likely be used by mental health professionals than investigators.

Sexual Abuse

Allegation: During the course of a routine medical checkup by her pediatrician, a 7-year-old girl tested positive for a sexually transmitted infection.

Child sexual abuse refers to a variety of behaviors that result in a child becoming involved in sexual behaviors or exposed to sexual activity. It can refer to the sexual exploitation of a child, prostitution, production of child pornography, or being exposed to graphic sexual material. The key factors in child sexual abuse is that it is illegal and inappropriate, given the age of the child who is unable to provide any type of legal consent to these activities, and the perpetrator is a legal caretaker or someone in a caretaking capacity (e.g., babysitter, family friend, etc.).

Child sexual abuse can involve fondling, molesting, or intercourse. Indirectly, a caretaker could expose a child to sexual material, sexual relationships or actions, or any other graphic sexual content. Child sexual abuse is a significant issue, and there are profound long-term implications with this type of maltreatment.

In our allegation, we received a report of a child who had been at a regularly scheduled medical checkup and was identified to have a sexually transmitted infection. This is a clear example of inappropriate sexual conduct, as there is no other way that this could have potentially occurred. While this type of scenario could occur, it is more likely that you will need to assess for child sexual abuse when the situation is much less clear. For example, fondling outside of a child's clothes is not likely to leave any physical evidence. The child protection worker will often seek consultation from medical providers when working in this role.

PRACTICE TIP 7.2 When assessing for child sexual abuse, it is absolutely necessary to evaluate and understand important relationships with the child. Determine who has access to the child and whether the child is left unsupervised with certain individuals. It is important to obtain separate firsthand accounts from the child, alleged perpetrator, and any relevant third parties. You may be working with law enforcement, as child sexual abuse is a crime. Sometimes law enforcement may lead these investigations. Make sure to consult with your supervisor when working on child sexual abuse investigations. This is a volatile situation, and their practice wisdom may be especially helpful. Seek consultation from medical providers. Know whether your region has a Child Advocacy Center to assist in a child-sensitive forensic interviews and medical evaluation during this process.

Consider working with a colleague or medical professional to have medical or photographic evidence to assist you in the assessment. Never take pictures of a child's private area alone—leave this to a medical professional or specially trained law enforcement officer, if possible. Take steps to facilitate your investigation without further traumatizing the child. When the situation seems to require that you need photographs of bruising or bite marks or other indicators on or near the child's genitals, remember that this is an invasion of privacy, and even if it is needed for evidence, we need to always proceed with deliberate caution (e.g., coworker as witness).

Understand the allegation well. How might the investigation be different if a 15-year-old female was suspected of having a sexual relationship with her 19 year-old "boyfriend" as opposed to her caregiving uncle? Statutory definitions in your region may guide you in making decisions in some scenarios.

Child sexual abuse influences the mental health of the child. It is important to assess for any cognitive delays, emotional trauma, anxiety, or additional stress that could be associated with the abuse. Integrating a mental health provider as a valuable component in the assessment process is best practice. Assuring that the child has ongoing treatment moving forward is a necessity.

Discussing child sexual abuse with the family can be awkward, to say the least. Having difficult conversations about highly sensitive and personal experiences can make even the most seasoned professional uncomfortable. Sometimes, this may result in a reactive response from the client that is more reflexive than reasoned. Be prepared for strong emotions to arise. Examine the family's culture, as it could be possible that generational sexual abuse is a reality in this family and a cycle that must be broken. Child sexual abuse is a significant problem in society, and Table 7.3 includes examples of instruments for assessing child sexual abuse.

TABLE 7.3 EXAMPLES OF MEASURES RELATED TO CHILD SEXUAL ABUSE

Six items from the Childhood Trauma Questionnaire (CTQ)
Bernstein, D. P., Fink, L., Handelsman, L., Foote, J., Lovejoy, M., Wenzel, K. ... Ruggiero, J. (1994). Initial reliability and validity of a new retrospective measure of child abuse and neglect. *American Journal of Psychiatry, 151* (8), 1132–1136. (Note: See a fuller description in Table 7.4.)

Six items from the Child Abuse and Trauma Scale (CATS)
Sanders, B., & Becker-Lausen, E. (1995). The measurement of psychological maltreatment. Early data on the child abuse and trauma scale. *Child Abuse & Neglect, 19,* 315–323. (Note: This instrument contains measures for negative home environment/neglect, punishment, and sexual abuse.)

Six and 15 items from the Early Trauma Inventory-Self Report (ETI) & (ETI-SF)
Bremner, J. D., Bolus, R., & Mayer, E. A. (2007). Psychometric properties of the Early Trauma Inventory-Self Report. *Journal of Nervous and Mental Disease, 195* (2), 211–218.

Listing of other child sexual abuse measures
Hulme, P. A. (2007). Psychometric evaluation and comparison of three retrospective, multi-item measures of childhood sexual abuse. *Child Abuse & Neglect, 31,* 853–869. (Note: Many of the items found above contain language that very young child may not know.)

Emotional Abuse

Allegation: A 16-year-old girl in tears confided to the school counselor as she revealed cut marks on her wrists that her mother has "pushed her to the edge." When asked about the specifics, she mentioned that her mother verbally assaults and embarrasses her on purpose, and that she "can't take it anymore."

The emotional impact of child maltreatment is traumatic, and you can expect that children you work with will be at a significantly higher risk of emotional problems. Trauma has a negative impact on the health and well-being of children and negatively influences their development. As has been described throughout the book, a standard approach in child protection is to arrange for mental health services for children as needed.

The allegation in this section explicitly revolves around parental emotional abuse of a child. Emotional abuse is a highly specialized form of investigation, and it is likely that you will need the testimony of a qualified mental health professional (e.g., licensed clinical social worker, psychologist, psychiatrist, etc.) to be able to affirm that emotional abuse did in fact take place. Their testimony may include what the child has described to the practitioner or the diagnosis or treatment that resulted from the presumed abuse. For practical purposes, agencies may choose to screen allegations of emotional abuse under the category of neglect, as it is less precise and affords the agency a broader avenue for providing a preponderance of evidence.

When assessing for the emotional abuse of a child, it is important to realize that each individual handles situations differently. Whether you are working in an investigative or ongoing capacity, assessing for the emotional health of children will be a primary function in your job position. Further, it is not likely that you will be involved in making any clinical assessment or diagnosis when working in child protection.

PRACTICE TIP 7.3 Assessing for emotional abuse will involve speaking to the child and relevant third parties. If the child is younger than 7 years old, it may be difficult to collect valuable information through a one-on-one interview. However, if the child is 13 or 14 years old, he or she will be able to describe specific taunts, hurtful names, threats and fear-producing behavior, humiliation, lack of emotional responsiveness and so forth. Sometimes their trauma may hinder communication, and children can just shut down.

It is important to speak with caretakers and nonoffending parents, neighbors, school counselors, therapists, coaches, or anyone else who could possibly provide a description of the child's emotional well-being. Has the child seen a therapist? Can anyone provide details about specific events or behaviors that may be relevant to understanding this situation?

Given the uses and abuses of social media, you may be asked to investigate an allegation of cyberbullying. Additionally, traditional (threatening, intimidating) bullying may also come from a school setting; a school counselor could be helpful in these situations. Emotional abuse is a highly specialized avenue and will likely require the consultation and contribution of a mental health therapist. Table 7.4 provides examples of measures related to child emotional abuse that may be helpful.

TABLE 7.4 MEASURES RELATED TO CHILD EMOTIONAL ABUSE AND ADVERSIVE EVENTS

Exposure to adverse childhood events (abuse, neglect, household dysfunction)
Oh, D. L., Jerman, P., Boparai, S. K. P., Koita, K., Briner, Bucci, M. ... Harris, B. (2018). Review of tools for measuring exposure to adversity in children and adolescents. *Journal of Pediatric Health Care, 32*(6), 564–583. (Note: This article identifies 32 different instruments, screens them along various dimensions, and recommends 14 of them.)

Maltreatment and Abuse Chronology of Exposure (MACE) scale
Teicher, M. H., & Parigger, A. (2015). The "Maltreatment and Abuse Chronology of Exposure" (MACE) scale for the retrospective assessment of abuse and neglect during development. *PLOS One, 10*(2), 1–37. (Note: This instrument is very comprehensive and contains 8 different dimensions: emotional neglect, nonverbal emotional abuse, verbal abuse, physical maltreatment, physical neglect, sexual abuse, witnessing interpersonal violence, and witnessing violence to siblings.)

Childhood Trauma Questionnaire (CTQ)
Bernstein, D. P., Ahluvalia, T., Pogge, D., & Handelsman, L. (1997). Validity of the Childhood Trauma Questionnaire in an adolescent psychiatric population. *Journal of the American Academy of Child & Adolescent Psychiatry, 36*(3), 340–348. (Note: This instrument seems to be the most widely used to measure psychological maltreatment/emotional abuse. The short form contains five subscales measuring emotional abuse, emotional neglect, physical neglect, physical abuse, and sexual abuse.)

Adverse childhood experiences (ACEs)
Felitti, V., Anda, R. F., Nordenberg, D., Williamson, D., Spitz A. M., Edwards V. ... Marks J. S. (1998). Relationship of childhood abuse and household dysfunction to many of the leading causes of death in adults: The adverse childhood experiences (ACE) study. *American Journal of Preventive Medicine, 14*(4), 245–258.

UCLA Post-Traumatic Stress Reaction Index (UCLA PTSD-RI)
Steinberg, A., Brymer, M., Decker, K., & Pynoos, R. (2004). The University of California at Los Angeles post-traumatic stress disorder reaction index. *Current Psychiatry Reports, 6*(2), 96–100.

Trauma Symptom Checklist for Children (TSCC)
Briere, J. (1996). *Trauma Symptom Checklist for Children (TSCC), Professional Manual.* Odessa, FL: Psychological Assessment Resources.

Neglect

Allegation: Law enforcement receives a phone call about two young children who are playing dangerously close to traffic and repeatedly running into the street. Upon arrival, they found a 5-year-old boy and his 7-year-old sister—both left unsupervised by their parents and alone at the residence for approximately 6 hours.

While abusive behavior is a main reason that child protection agencies will become involved with families, neglect is also an important category. Neglect refers to the failure of a caretaker to provide for the needs of a child and is the most prevalent form of child maltreatment (Stowman & Donohue, 2005). Neglect is much broader than specific forms of abuse (i.e., physical, emotional, sexual) and generally encompasses the safety, supervision, nutrition, or physical and mental health needs of a child. In the allegation, two children were left alone and unsupervised and ended up playing in the street. The investigation could reveal that a lack of parental supervision placed the children at risk of harm or death by having access to a street that is traversed by moving motor vehicles.

Child neglect could also refer to an infant who is **failure to thrive**. Failure to thrive means that a newborn is not having his or her nutritional needs met, and it is important for the child protection worker to assess whether this is due to the parents not knowing how to care for an infant or to other circumstances, such as a child having an undiagnosed medical problem. Nobody is born with the inherent knowledge of how to be an excellent parent—this is something that needs to be learned. As you are involved with working with families, it is important to ascertain whether their lack of knowledge is a contributing factor or if there are other issues (e.g., not wanting the child and not attending to him or her).

An additional circumstance related to neglect can create a sticky situation. For example, a pregnant mother might use illegal substances that could directly and negatively influence the health of her unborn child. Once the infant is delivered, the hospital may call the child protection worker to a meeting. Was this behavior on the mother's part deliberately abusive or a case of neglect, where the child's needs simply were not given a high priority? While this may be splitting hairs, the goal is to make sure that the child is protected and their needs are met. Collecting robust information from multiple sources can assist the agency in making a good decision moving forward.

When assessing for neglect, one must always pay close attention to environmental and macro-level factors. As mentioned earlier, poverty is a significant contributor to child maltreatment. Keep in mind, however, that it is not illegal to live in poverty, and child protection agencies are not tasked with the judgment of how others choose to live their lives. Poverty can make it much more difficult for families to assure that the nutritional, hygienic, safety, and supervisory needs of children are met.

Chronic neglect refers to an ongoing deprivation or failure to meet the needs of the child. Chronic neglect could be a learned behavior or an established cultural practice (e.g., not seeing the importance of education and not sending children to school) by a family that has lasted for generations. A recent study by Logan-Greene and Jones (2018) examined administrative child welfare data (n = 2,074) to identify risk factors and found that families with chronic neglect were younger, had more children, were more likely to have children under the age of 1 year, and had increased rates of domestic violence, more mental health problems, and cognitive impairment.

PRACTICE TIP 7.4 Neglect is, unfortunately, a common occurrence in child protection. As mentioned above, there are a variety of contextual details that must be understood.

Related to supervisory neglect, it is important to start with understanding the context of the occurrence. In the initial allegation in this section, in which two young children were left unsupervised, we would need to understand if this was a one-time occurrence or if the lapse in supervision occurred frequently. Speaking with neighbors and family members will be important, as you will need to understand who was responsible for the lapse and whether the caretaker is capable and able. Are there mental or physical health factors that are barriers to appropriate and consistent supervision? Is there a lack of understanding about its importance? Perhaps an educational component would be helpful for addressing this issue and preventing its recurrence.

Related to environmental neglect, it is important to capture photographic evidence of unsafe or dangerous issues that could impact children. Examples would be head lice, roaches, too many animals inside the house, broken doors and windows, lack of working plumbing, etc. Are children getting baths? Medical records of dog bites, infections, and so on can help determine whether a problem is recent or has happened in the past.

Related to neglecting the needs of a child, situations must be assessed in context. For example, if a child was failure to thrive, it would be important to immediately integrate medical assistance and obtain medical documentation to provide evidence of risk and/or improvement in the future. If the child had a specialized medical condition (e.g., juvenile diabetes) and the parents were failing to provide the care needed, it would also be important to collaborate with medical professionals to assess for risk and progress.

As we noted earlier, the category of neglect is quite broad, yet it is unfortunately a common path that involves many families and child protective service agencies. Table 7.5 identifies a number of instruments that may be helpful when assessing for neglect.

TABLE 7.5 EXAMPLES OF MEASURES RELATED TO CHILD NEGLECT

Child Neglect Questionnaire (CNQ)
Stewart, C., Kirisci, L., Long, A. L., & Giancola, P. R. (2015). Development and psychometric evaluation of the Child Neglect Questionnaire. *Journal of Interpersonal Violence, 30* (19), 3343–3366.

Home Accident Prevention Inventory (HAPI)
Tertinger, D. A., Greene, B. F., & Lutzker, J. R. (1984). Home safety: Development and validation of one component of an ecobehavioral treatment program for abused and neglected children. *Journal of Applied Behavior Analysis, 17*(2), 159–174.

Multidimensional Neglectful Behavior Scale-Child Report (MNBS-CR)
Kantor, G. K., Holt, M. K., Mebert, C. J., Straus, M. A., Drach, K. M., Ricci, L. R., ... Brown, W. (2004). Development and preliminary psychometric properties of the Multidimensional Neglectful Behavior Scale-Child Report. *Child Maltreatment, 9*(4), 409–428.

Dependency

Allegation: A 6-year-old boy is without parental care, as his mother was just pronounced dead at the scene of a fatal car accident. His father has been in prison for the past 3 years, serving a 30-year sentence.

In addition to abuse and neglect, dependency is the third main reason that child protection agencies become involved with families. In our allegation, the child no longer has parents to provide care. It is clear that the child protection agency must take steps to immediately address the absence of parents. For pedagogical reasons, this is a clean and clear example. However, in real life these situations are almost never this simple.

Dependency is sometimes an option that the court will choose when the child is beyond the control of the parent. For example, it is possible that a parent feels a child's behavior is too much to handle. Maybe the parent reaches out to the school counselor, or a child's neighbor concerned about discipline practices such as locking a teenager out of the house calls law enforcement. For whatever reason, dependency can sometimes become a "catch-all" where the court becomes involved in initiating an open case on behalf of the child.

The main understanding necessary with dependency is that the situation is presumed to be at no fault of the parent. Some children are beyond their parents' ability to control when they engage in theft, abuse substances, refuse to attend school, and so on. However, as the old adage goes, "every coin has two sides." It is entirely possible that the parents' own alcohol or substance use has contributed to strained relations with the child over a long time period. Even though this factor might be present, it is difficult to hold parents accountable if there is a presumption that the problem is with the child and is not a fault of the parent. Regardless, dependency is an important avenue for protecting children and assuring that their needs are met.

PRACTICE TIP 7.5 Dependency is a unique situation that sometimes occurs in child protection. Issues of concern flow from the family and its possible lack of resources; at the same time, some overarching factors should be considered. If the CPS agency is involved in dependency because the child literally has no source of parental support, that is far different than a child who is beyond the control of the parents. Assessing the behavior of the child is a critical component in any child protective services involvement— especially if the child is beyond parental control. In such a scenario, the CPS worker would have concerns about fragile or broken relationships between the child and parent or caretaker, or any other integral familial components.

It is important to understand the child's problematic behavior. For example, common behavioral issues for teenagers include talking back to their parents and seeking independence. However, it is more concerning if a child is sexually perpetrating on younger children, lighting fires, or deliberately trying to and seriously injuring others. Being able to understand the context and capture the intensity of the behaviors is important. Table 7.6 lists a number of instruments for assessing the behavior of children, which are especially important in this scenario but could be utilized throughout the process of working in child protection.

TABLE 7.6 EXAMPLES OF MEASURES FOR ASSESSING CHILD BEHAVIOR

Behavioral Assessment System for Children (BASC)
Sandoval, J., & Echandia, A. (1994). Behavior Assessment System For Children. *Journal of School Psychology, 32*(4), 419–425.

Eyberg Child Behavior Inventory (ECBI)
Eyberg, S. M., & Ross, A. W. (1978). Assessment of child behavior problems: The validation of a new inventory. *Journal of Clinical Child Psychology, 7*(2), 113–116.

The Child Behavior Checklist (CBCL)
Achenbach, T. M., & Edelbrock, C. S. (1984). *Child Behavior Checklist.* Burlington: University of Vermont.

(Continued)

Ohio Scales for Youth (the Ohio Scales)
Ogles, B., Melendez, G., Davis, D., & Lunnen, K. (2001). The Ohio Scales: Practical outcome assessment. *Journal of Child and Family Studies, 10*(2), 199–212.

Strengths and Difficulties Questionnaire (SDQ)
Goodman, R. (1997). The Strengths and Difficulties Questionnaire: A research note. *Journal of Child Psychology and Psychiatry, 38*(5), 581–586.

Additional Assessment Areas for Consideration

Throughout this chapter, we have examined risk assessment and its important place within child protection, and we also explored commonly found circumstances that occur when working in child protective service. To wrap up this chapter, we are going to explore other areas for assessment that may be helpful when working with families.

Parenting, Familial Involvement, and Progress

In just about any aspect of working in child protection, you will be involved with families who may need to improve their functioning and minimize the risk of child maltreatment. The parent is truly a key ingredient in the safe family, and it is important to understand that some of our clients did not have healthy parents themselves as role models. Additionally, they may have been the recipient of negative parenting strategies as a child that could have influenced how they relate to their own children. We know that objectively evaluating progress is important, and there are a number of assessment tools that may help in assessing families trying to become healthier. Table 7.7 provides a few examples of measurements that could be used to evaluate parenting, familial involvement, and progress.

TABLE 7.7 EXAMPLES OF INSTRUMENTS RELATED TO FAMILIAL INVOLVEMENT AND PROGRESS

Child Adjustment and Parent Efficacy Scale (CAPES)
Morawska, A., Sanders, M. R., Haslam, D., Filus, A., & Fletcher, R. (2014). Child Adjustment and Parent Efficacy Scale: Development and initial validation of a parent report measure. *Australian Psychologist, 49*(4), 241–252.

Child and Adolescent Burden Assessment (CABA)
Messer, S. C., Angold, A., Costello, E. J., & Burns, B. J. (1996). The Child and Adolescent Burden Assessment (CABA): Measuring the family impact of emotional and behavioral problems. *International Journal of Methods in Psychiatric Research, 6*(4), 261–284.

Parenting Stress Index (PSI)
Abidin, R. R. (1997). Parenting Stress Index: A measure of the parent–child system. In C. P. Zalaquett & R. J. Wood (Eds.), *Evaluating stress: A book of resources* (pp. 277–291). Lanham, MD: Scarecrow Education.

Parent-Child Conflict Tactics Scales (CTSPC)
Straus, M. A., Hamby, S. L., Finkelhor, D., Moore, D. W., & Runyan, D. (1998). Identification of child maltreatment with the Parent-Child Conflict Tactics Scales: Development and psychometric data for a national sample of American parents. *Child Abuse & Neglect, 22*(4), 249–270.

Evaluation of Child Welfare Services

Client satisfaction is an important component in program evaluation, helping agencies measure service quality, detect problems, and remove obstacles that may be barriers to effective service delivery (Royse, Thyer, & Padgett,

2016). Showing this importance, Fraser and Wu (2016) completed a systematic review of research reports published from 2003 to 2013, and found 58 different measures of consumer satisfaction in social welfare and behavioral health. However, there are legitimate biases associated with interpreting data from clients—especially related to clients in child protection, where service delivery is often involuntary. Therefore, clients might not have chosen to become involved with the agency. Further, services in child protection may be court-mandated, and this may influence the perception and responses of the respondent.

Specifically related to child welfare services, Ayala-Nunes, Jiménez, Hidalgo, and Jesus (2014) completed the first systematic review to identify and analyze measures for assessing family feedback from 1980 until 2013. In total, the authors identified 13 studies that included eight instruments. While the feedback of clients in child protection must always be understood in the appropriate context, it is necessary to remain objective and seek to improve our service delivery. After all, we are working to eliminate child abuse and to protect vulnerable populations. Table 7.8 identifies several assessment options that have been designed to provide consumer feedback about services in child welfare.

TABLE 7.8 EXAMPLES OF MEASURES RELATED TO CHILD WELFARE SERVICES

Family Feedback on Child Welfare Services (FF-CWS)
Ayala-Nunes, L., Jimenez, L., Hidalgo, V., Dekovic, M., & J., S. (2018). Development and validation of the Family Feedback on Child Welfare Services (FF-CWS). *Research on Social Work Practice, 28*(2), 203–213.

Parent Satisfaction With Foster Care Services Scale (PSFCSS)
Knapp, S. A., & Vela, R. H. (2004). The Parent Satisfaction With Foster Care Services Scale. *Child Welfare, 83*(3), 263–287.

The Parents With Children in Foster Care Satisfaction Scale (PCFCSS)
Harris, G., Poertner, J., & Joe, S. (2000). The Parents With Children in Foster Care Satisfaction Scale. *Administration in Social Work, 24*, 15–27.

Culturally Relevant Assessment for Client Satisfaction
Mundy, C. L., Neufeld, A. N., & Wells, S. J. (2016). A culturally relevant measure of client satisfaction in child welfare services. *Children and Youth Services Review, 70*, 177–189.

Main Points

Because risk assessment is so important in child protection, this chapter was included to give readers additional resources for obtaining objective information for making those tough decisions requiring solid evidence. Although we did not suggest it earlier, it could be that parental attitudes or perspectives about disciplining or raising their children as revealed in an instrument like the Child Abuse Potential Inventory could help justify CPS involvement—even if there were no photographs or other "hard" evidence of physical abuse. Think of this chapter as a "booster shot" to help you further identify ways of thinking about concerns with a family and the evidence that might be gathered to affirm or disconfirm an allegation of child maltreatment.

- Risk assessment is systematic and comprehensive, involving multiple possible causes or influences.
- An ecological perspective helps the worker contemplate influences that may occur at the micro, mezzo, or macro level.
- Concerns during an investigation are somewhat subjective; that is, one worker might pick up on a client's sneer or inappropriate laugh that a coworker did not notice or wasn't troubled by.

- Concerns are like hunches or a sense that a client is lying. Concerns may pan out with further investigation or the use of an objective instrument, or they may just remain concerns in the written record.
- Evidence is objective, not subjective. Therefore, it carries more weight in a legal proceeding. Objective evidence might be photographs of a child's injury, medical records, and instruments to assess things like a child's depression or trauma symptoms.
- Physical abuse refers to intentional harm to a child. Physical evidence is often available.
- With sexual abuse, the CPS worker will likely be working with both medical professionals and law enforcement.
- It is difficult to obtain evidence of emotional abuse, and as a result, it might be easier to attempt to demonstrate that the child might be neglected.
- Neglect is a very broad category, and the possible ways of neglecting a child are too numerous to list. Many forms of neglect are easy to document.
- Dependency allegations can involve a child with no living parents or children who are incorrigible and beyond a parent's control. Parents can petition courts to do something to help them manage a minor who is destructive, violent, involved in criminal activity, etc.

Questions for Class Discussion

1. How do you feel when you are asked to complete an attitudinal test or some paper-and-pencil instrument that might give another person some "window" into understanding how you think or what issues you might have? Do you think clients might have some of the same feelings? Do they have a right to feel this way during an investigation?
2. Would you always have the same concerns about a specific type of allegation? For instance, in cases of a child acting out sexually, would you tend to always believe that an adult was responsible for the abuse as opposed to an older sibling?
3. As a new CPS worker, how accurate do you think your concerns will be during your early investigations? What concerns do you think an experienced worker might develop over time that you might not initially have? (Consider discussing this relative to a particular type of abuse investigation.)
4. Choose an article to read about one of the assessment instruments listed in this chapter. Can you see using it as a CPS worker? Why or why not?

Self-Assessment for Personal Consideration

1. How comfortable would you be with asking a client to complete an objective assessment instrument?

   1   2   3   4   5   6   7   8   9   10

   Not comfortable   *Very comfortable*

2. How comfortable do you think you would be asking a child for permission or reassuring a child that it was all right, in the nurse's office, to take a picture of an injury that might have been caused at home?

   1   2   3   4   5   6   7   8   9   10

   Not comfortable   *Very comfortable*

Additional Resources

- More information about the Comprehensive Family Assessment (CFA):
  https://www.acf.hhs.gov/sites/default/files/cb/family_assessment.pdf
  https://www.childwelfare.gov/pubPDFs/familyassessments.pdf
  https://www.childwelfare.gov/topics/systemwide/assessment/family-assess/

- Additional instruments for measuring various issues related to child trauma and child protection can be found at the National Child Traumatic Stress Network: https://www.nctsn.org/search?query=All+Measure+Reviews

- Another source of small, rapid assessment instruments for measuring different dimensions of child and family life can be found in Corcoran, K., & Fischer, J. (2013). *Measures for clinical practice and research: A sourcebook.* New York, NY: Oxford University Press.

References

Ayala-Nunes, L., Jiménez, L., Hidalgo, V., & Jesus, S. (2014). Family feedback in child welfare services: A systematic review of measures. *Children and Youth Services Review, 44,* 299–306.

Barber, J. G., Shlonsky, A., Black, T., Goodman, D., & Trocmé, N. (2008). Reliability and predictive validity of a consensus-based risk assessment tool. *Journal of Public Child Welfare, 2*(2), 173–195.

Bartelink, C., Van Yperen, T. A., & Ten Berge, I. J. (2015). Deciding on child maltreatment: A literature review on methods that improve decision-making. *Child Abuse & Neglect, 49,* 142–153.

Bronfenbrenner, U. (1979). *The ecology of human development.* Cambridge, MA: Harvard University Press.

Cash, S. J. (2001). Risk assessment in child welfare: The art and science. *Children and Youth Services Review, 23*(11), 811–830.

Coohey, C., Johnson, K., Renner, L. M., & Easton, S. D. (2013). Actuarial risk assessment in child protective services: Construction methodology and performance criteria. *Children and Youth Services Review, 35*(1), 151–161.

Cuccaro-Alamin, S., Foust, R., Vaithianathan, R., & Putnam-Hornstein, E. (2017). Risk assessment and decision making in child protective services: Predictive risk modeling in context. *Children and Youth Services Review, 79,* 291–298.

Daley, D., Bachmann, M., Bachmann, B. A., Pedigo, C., Bui, M. T., & Coffman, J. (2016). Risk terrain modeling predicts child maltreatment. *Child Abuse & Neglect, 62,* 29–38.

de Haan, I., & Connolly, M. (2014). Another Pandora's Box? Some pros and cons of predictive risk modeling. *Children and Youth Services Review, 47,* 86–91.

Fraser, M., & Wu, S. (2016). Measures of consumer satisfaction in social welfare and behavioral health: A systematic review. *Research on Social Work Practice, 26*(7), 762–776.

Gillingham, P. (2016). Predictive risk modelling to prevent child maltreatment and other adverse outcomes for service users: Inside the "black box" of machine learning. *British Journal of Social Work, 46*(4), 1044–1058.

Horwitz, S. M., Hurlburt, M. S., Goldhaber-Fiebert, J. D., Palinkas, L. A., Rolls-Reutz, J., Zhang, J., … Landsverk, J. (2014). Exploration and adoption of evidence-based practice by US child welfare agencies. *Children and Youth Services Review, 39,* 147–152.

Kessler, M. L., Gira, E., & Poertner, J. (2005). Moving best practice to evidence-based practice in child welfare. *Families in Society, 86*(2), 244–250.

Logan-Greene, P., & Jones, A. S. (2018). Predicting chronic neglect: Understanding risk and protective factors for CPS-involved families. *Child & Family Social Work, 23*(2), 264–272.

Mendoza, N. S., Rose, R. A., Geiger, J. M., & Cash, S. J. (2016). Risk assessment with actuarial and clinical methods: Measurement and evidence-based practice. *Child Abuse & Neglect, 61,* 1–12.

Oh, D. L., Jerman, P., Boparai, S. K. P., Koita, K., Briner, Bucci, M. … Harris, B. (2018). Review of tools for measuring exposure to adversity in children and adolescents. *Journal of Pediatric Health Care, 32*(6), 564–583.

Peterson, C., Florence, C., & Klevens, J. (2018). The economic burden of child maltreatment in the United States, 2015. *Child Abuse & Neglect, 86,* 178–183.

Royse, D., Thyer, B., & Padgett, D. (2016). *Program evaluation: An introduction to an evidence-based approach* (6th ed.). Belmont, CA: Brooks/Cole.

Russell, J. (2015). Predictive analytics and child protection: Constraints and opportunities. *Child Abuse & Neglect, 46,* 182–189.

Russell, J., & Macgill, S. (2015). Demographics, policy, and foster care rates: A predictive analytics approach. *Children and Youth Services Review, 58,* 118–126.

Schwartz, I. M., York, P., Nowakowski-Sims, E., & Ramos-Hernandez, A. (2017). Predictive and prescriptive analytics, machine learning and child welfare risk assessment: The Broward County experience. *Children and Youth Services Review, 81,* 309–320.

Smithgall, C., Jarpe-Ratner, E., Gnedko-Berry, N., & Mason, S. (2015). Developing and testing a framework for evaluating the quality of comprehensive family assessment in child welfare. *Child Abuse & Neglect, 44,* 194–206.

Stowman, S. A., & Donohue, B. (2005). Assessing child neglect: A review of standardized measures. *Aggression and Violent Behavior, 10*(4), 491–512.

Thurston, H., & Miyamoto, S. (2018). The use of model based recursive partitioning as an analytic tool in child welfare. *Child Abuse & Neglect, 79,* 293–301.

Van der Put, C. E., Assink, M., & Van Solinge, N. F. B. (2017). Predicting child maltreatment: A meta-analysis of the predictive validity of risk assessment instruments. *Child Abuse & Neglect, 73,* 71–88.

Walsh, C. R., & Reutz, J. R. (2015). Selecting an evidence-based practice in child welfare: Challenges and steps to identifying a good fit. *Child Welfare, 94*(2), 107–113.

CHAPTER 8

THE JUVENILE COURT

OVERVIEW

Some children experience abuse and neglect and never come to the attention of child protection workers. Others live in families having major involvement with child welfare agencies, but for any number of reasons, they may not receive the treatment needed for hurtful child maltreatment. In either case, there is ample evidence that untreated childhood trauma contributes to delinquency and juvenile justice system involvement. This chapter specifically focuses on youth who become known to the juvenile justice system and are unofficially or officially recognized as juvenile delinquents. The juvenile court does not exist to punish young people who break the law but aims to rehabilitate—and to keep troubled youth from becoming adult criminals.

Each day approximately 70,000 juvenile offenders are in a residential placement such as a correctional facility, a juvenile detention facility, or a group home. Two thirds or more of the children and adolescents who are arrested each year have some type of mental disorder (Slaughter, 2018). Of particular concern are those with severe antisocial behavior. Intervention ordered by the juvenile court may keep them out of prison when they become adults.

Some readers of this book will very likely find careers working with this largely teenage population. The aim of this chapter is to provide information about the *who*, *what*, and *why* pertaining to this population.

What Is a Juvenile Delinquent?

A juvenile is an immature person. A **juvenile delinquent** is a term often applied to a young person, or minor, under the age of 18 who breaks a law that often would not be an offense if committed by an adult. They may also be known as **status offenders**—if their act comes to the attention of law enforcement or other authority. For instance, drinking alcohol would be a status offense for a 14-year-old but not for a 40-year-old. Other examples of major status offense categories would include running away, truancy from school, breaking a community's curfew ordinance, not responding to parental direction (being undisciplined, ungovernable, incorrigible, beyond the control of one's parents—the legal term may vary depending on the state), and underage liquor law violations. These young people may be noticeably defiant of the authorities in their life (e.g., teachers, school administrators) by fighting with them or more subtly so by doing no schoolwork or ditching school frequently.

Sometimes parents or guardians are in touch with or are known to social service agencies or child protection authorities because the juvenile is so disobedient as to be unmanageable (staying out all night, involvement in gang activities, etc.). These young people may have a path to the juvenile court when their parents or guardians inform a social service agency or child protective services that they cannot manage the youth at home. Ongoing caseworkers may also be aware of delinquency issues because of the family's prior child maltreatment and current involvement with child protection authorities. Teenagers who are not supervised by adults tend to get arrested and come before the juvenile court. There is an overlap in some cases, with CPS and the juvenile court both becoming involved because a child's parents were not exercising their parental roles and responsibilities. To be clear, however, the juvenile court is separate and different from the civil court system where the CPS petitions alleging neglect or abuse and other hearings such as termination of parental rights go.

The term *juvenile delinquent* is applied to young people who commit minor crimes known as **misdemeanors**—like throwing eggs at a teacher's house after dark, stealing candy or cigarettes from a supermarket, etc. However, more serious criminal acts such as joyriding in a stolen a car, stealing purses, property damage, violence against others, drug use or selling drugs, or breaking into homes, as well as simply being an accomplice to other adolescents engaged in these acts, can bring a young person into the juvenile justice system as well. A **felony** refers to the most serious type of crimes (e.g., simple and aggravated assault, arson, selling drugs, vandalism, etc.). States vary in their definitions of felonies and misdemeanors. Sometimes it depends upon the dollar amount of the item stolen or destroyed. For instance, stealing a new cell phone valued at more than $500 would likely constitute a felony but stealing a used cell phone of much less worth could be a misdemeanor. Typically, felonies might be associated with a sentence of at least one year in prison (for adults).

Unlike adult criminal courts, juvenile courts are concerned more with the rehabilitation of youthful offenders than punishment. It is not an adversarial system but one in which the court is empowered by the state to act **in loco parentis** (Latin for "in place of the parent"). Parents of juveniles before the court can feel that the system is adversarial because they might have to hire an attorney to defend a son or daughter or because a judge's orders may seem punitive. However, juvenile court judges have a responsibility to ensure that the process is fair, to protect the juvenile's rights, and to develop a plan to improve the juvenile's behavior or character. Along that line, a judge may order the juvenile to pay for damages to property (e.g., in a case of vandalism or destruction of stolen property)—that is not considered punishment but is called **restitution** and is simply restoring value to the owner or person harmed. It normally would not be considered a punitive order. Restitution holds the youth accountable for his or her actions. Generally speaking, the juvenile court practices restorative justice to rehabilitate young persons and keep them from future criminal behavior as adults. Working with these juveniles to help them find hope and a positive future for themselves is just as important as rescuing a younger child at risk for emotional or physical abuse or neglect.

What Is the Juvenile Court Process?*

After a young person has been charged and/or arrested, what happens next depends on the specific law as it was written in a particular state, whether the juvenile was charged with a crime categorized as a misdemeanor or felony, whether the young person has a history (prior appearances before the juvenile court), the evidence of the juvenile's participation in the crime, whether the young person is unmanageable, and so on.

Juvenile courts generally have an intake department that receives and screens the referrals to the court. The professionals in the intake department attempt to assess how involved the court needs to be. The decision might be to dismiss the case for lack of "legal sufficiency" or to resolve it informally (without going through the juvenile court judge) if the youth and his or her family are best served by an informal action, such as voluntarily agreeing to social services, restitution or payment of a fine, or informal probation. For instance, the youth might agree to begin attending school, abide by a parental curfew, or participate with the family in receiving family therapy.

A written agreement may be developed between juvenile intake and the child and parent(s) stating what is required of the youth and the family. This agreement may be known as **a deferred prosecution agreement** and written for a specific length of time (e.g., to cover the school year). If the requirements of the agreement are met, there would be no other processing of the complaint and no involvement by the juvenile court. However, the prosecuting attorney in that jurisdiction (e.g., the district or county attorney) may not agree with the deferred prosecution agreement and may decide to cancel the agreement and proceed to the juvenile court. This petition then places the case on the court's calendar (or **docket**). A CPS agency can also consult with and assist the juvenile court when a child needs to be placed in residential treatment.

When a petition is filed with the court, a **summons** (an official legal notification) is then delivered to the juvenile's parents or guardian requiring them to appear before the court on a particular date and to bring the young person. The summons also contains information about the right to an attorney. Parents who do not respect the court by failing to appear before it can be held in **contempt of court** (where the judge may impose a fine or even order the parent or caretaker to spend time in jail). When juveniles skip out or refuse to show up at juvenile court, the judge can issue an order placing them in a juvenile detention center temporarily. Detention refers to secure facilities where youths who are thought to be a risk to skip their court appearances or likely to commit another crime may be kept temporarily.

Generally, an adjudicatory hearing is set for a judge in a courtroom to be presented with the evidence specific to the case. The local prosecutor representing the state has the responsibility to try to establish the facts of the case "beyond a reasonable doubt." This means that the judge cannot decide for or against the youth based on a suspicion or hunch but must feel there is no other logical explanation supporting the facts or evidence. In other words, a reasonable person would view the evidence as convincing and have no doubt about the essential facts of the case as presented—clearly involving the youth's role. The youth may choose to admit to the offense(s) or to request an attorney to contest the charge(s). If the evidence of the youth's involvement is established beyond a reasonable doubt, the next step would be a disposition hearing. However, if the youth committed a very serious felony (rape, homicide, armed robbery) and typically is somewhat older (e.g., 16 or 17), the judge may decide **to waive the case** to an adult criminal court. This means the case will be transferred outside of the juvenile court. A case can also be dismissed at this point or continued until sometime in the future. Of all the cases coming to juvenile courts, about half are adjudicated delinquent (Hockenberry & Puzzanchera, 2018). However, the percentage rises with more serious offenses.

---

* This material draws heavily from https://www.nccourts.gov/help-topics/family-and-children/juvenile-delinquency.

Those cases not handled informally, dismissed, or continued in contemplation of dismissal will have a disposition hearing. In this hearing, the judge decides on a plan for the individual juvenile. With input (often letters or records) from professionals in the community—such as school officials, juvenile court counselors, mental health therapists, and CPS or social service workers—a predisposition report may be prepared by workers in the juvenile court or probation department. This report will assist the judge in deciding on a range of options available to the court. Further, the judge may allow victim statements, and recommendations from the juvenile's own attorney as well as the prosecutor. Depending on the seriousness of the offense(s), the judge will decide on community supervision with a probation officer, mental health assessment or evaluation, treatment, community service, restitution, fine, placement in a group home or residential facility, or confinement in a detention center. Probation is the most common sanction imposed by juvenile court judges (Hockenberry & Puzzanchera, 2018). Youths brought before the court as a dependency or unmanageability issue might be placed in the custody of the child protection agency, and there is also a range of options for them, including foster care, group homes, and treatment facilities. Review hearings can be scheduled to examine a juvenile's progress.

What Does the Problem of Juvenile Delinquency Look Like in the United States?

According to a publication of the National Center for Juvenile Justice entitled *Juvenile Court Statistics, 2016* (Hockenberry & Puzzanchera, 2018), there were an estimated 850,000 delinquency cases in 2016 in courts having a jurisdiction over juveniles. Note that these are the cases handled formally by the nation's juvenile courts. Cases handled informally and dismissed are not counted in the juvenile court statistics presented in this chapter. Twenty-nine percent of the cases were offenses against people, 33% were offenses against property, 25% involved a range of offenses against the "public order" (e.g., disorderly conduct), and 13% involved drugs. Table 8.1 provides detail for each of these four broad categories.

TABLE 8.1 **DETAIL OF TYPES OF OFFENSES HANDLED BY JUVENILE COURTS 2016**

Type of Offense	Number of Cases
AGAINST PERSONS	
Criminal homicide	1,000
Rape	7,900
Robbery	20,300
Aggravated assault	26,200
Simple assault	158,700
Other violent sex offenses	7,600
Other person offenses	23,200
Total	244,900

AGAINST PROPERTY	
Burglary	55,300
Larceny-theft	126,800
Motor vehicle theft	15,700
Arson	2,700
Vandalism	41,900
Trespassing	24,500
Stolen property offenses	9,700
Total	283,600
Drug law violations	107,400
PUBLIC ORDER OFFENSES	
Obstruction of justice	109,200
Disorderly conduct	56,100
Weapons offenses	18,300
Liquor law offenses	5,300
Nonviolent sex offenses	11,300
Other public order offenses	14,500
Total	214,700

Source: Sarah Hockenberry and Charles Puzzanchera, "Details of Types of Offenses Handled by Juvenile Courts 2016," Juvenile Court Statistics, 2016, pp. 7. Copyright © 2018 by National Center for Juvenile Justice.

With each type of offense, the young person's case was most often referred to the juvenile court by law enforcement—81% of the time in the most recent annual report available. This occurred in 92% of the drug law violations, 91% of the property offenses, 89% of the offenses against persons, and 56% of the public order offenses. Other major sources of referral were schools, relatives, and other—which includes CPS and social service agencies.

Offenses against persons were most likely to result in the youth's detention (36% of the cases). This was followed by property offenses (28%), public order offenses (27%) and then drug law violations (8%). Percentagewise, fewer White youth are detained for delinquency offenses than are youth of other racial groups.

Reported Characteristics of Juvenile Delinquents (Age, Gender, and Race)

While children of an age that most adults would consider to be very young can become status offenders or even commit offenses such as destroying property and hurting other people that bring them before a juvenile court, most of the cases involve older youths, as shown in Table 8.2. As children reach adolescence, there are more opportunities to get into trouble. There is less adult supervision, and teens can travel farther away from home, either by driving or other means, which can give them greater access to drugs, alcohol, and so forth.

TABLE 8.2 JUVENILE COURT CASES DISPOSED BY AGE (FOR EVERY 1,000 JUVENILES IN THE POPULATION)

Age of child	Percentage of Total
10	1.7
11	3.7
12	8.9
13	18.1
14	30.1
15	42.0
16	53.6
17	60.3*

Note: This percentage would be higher except in 9 states, 17-year-olds are legally adults and are transferred to criminal courts.
Source: Sarah Hockenberry and Charles Puzzanchera, "Juvenile Court Cases by Age," Juvenile Court Statistics, 2016, pp. 10. Copyright © 2018 by National Center for Juvenile Justice.

As might be expected, males come before juvenile courts many times more often than females. In fact, 72% of the estimated cases coming before juvenile courts involved males (Hockenberry & Puzzanchera, 2018). Females, like males before the juvenile court, were involved most often in offenses against persons and property, followed by public order and then drugs.

When the cases before juvenile courts are examined by racial classification and type of offense, we can see in Table 8.3 that the offenses committed by youths of different races or ethnicities are remarkably similar.

TABLE 8.3 OFFENSE CATEGORIES BY RACE

Type of offense	White	Black	Hispanic	Indian*	Asian
Against persons	27%	32%	27%	25%	25%
Against property	33%	35%	30%	38%	37%
Drug law violation	16%	7%	15%	16%	13%
Public order	24%	26%	27%	22%	25%
Total	100%	100%	100%	100%	100%

Note: The American Indian classification includes Alaska Natives.
Source: Sarah Hockenberry and Charles Puzzanchera, "Offense Categories by Race," Juvenile Court Statistics, 2016, pp. 18. Copyright © 2018 by National Center for Juvenile Justice.

Table 8.4, however, suggests that our nation still has not made a great deal of progress with eliminating disparities in education, health, and employment. Historically, persons of color have not had the same opportunities to acquire higher education and thus higher paying jobs. Nor have they had the same access to affordable medical care, which can be provided by employers and which can keep a person on the job and earning a wage. Further, single parents with limited education may live in impoverished neighborhoods where there are more opportunities for encountering those breaking the law and being of interest to law enforcement.

These neighborhoods increase the odds of young people engaging in behaviors that result in a referral to a juvenile court. Also, single parents may have difficulty providing appropriate supervision, especially if they have employment responsibilities.

Unfortunately, Black and Hispanic youth are disproportionately more likely to be held in detention than White, Asian, or American Indian youths. Although Black youth constituted 36% of the cases referred to the juvenile court, 40% of those in detention were Black. Similarly, while Hispanics made up 18% of the cases referred to the juvenile court, they represented 22% of those in detention, while White youth made up 44% of the referred cases but only 35% of those in detention. Estimates of LGBTQ youths in the juvenile justice system are about 15%. This group has a "higher tendency to encounter certain environmental risk factors" (Slaughter, 2018, p. 13) in detention. Note that the statistics in Table 8.4 do not refer to any detention decisions made by law enforcement officials prior to court appearances or while a juvenile is being held after a disposition hearing while awaiting court-ordered placement in another facility.

TABLE 8.4 RACIAL PROFILE COMPARISON: JUVENILE COURT CASES VS. CENSUS REPRESENTATION

Racial group	% of delinquency cases	% of U.S. population
White	44%	55%
Black	36%	14%
Hispanic	18%	23%
American Indian*	2%	2%
Asian	1%	6%
Total	100%	100%

Note: The American Indian classification includes Alaska Natives.
Source: Sarah Hockenberry and Charles Puzzanchera, "Racial Profile Comparison: Juvenile Court Cases Vs. Census Representation," Juvenile Court Statistics, 2016, pp. 18. Copyright © 2018 by National Center for Juvenile Justice.

The Juvenile Justice/Services Worker

As you might imagine, the juvenile court is a busy place—especially in large cities. While the juvenile court judge is certainly in charge, there are a host of other supporting staff. There may be a juvenile court administrator or director to ensure the court functions smoothly. A court clerk keeps the calendar for the court and tracks legal documents coming into and going from the court, such as subpoenas, judicial orders, and so on. When a youth is committed to detention or probated, the agency then responsible for the young person may be known as the Department of Juvenile Justice (although the name will vary by the state). Each youth will be assigned a case manager or Department of Juvenile Justice worker (sometimes known as a DJJ worker). These professionals are involved in assisting with individual treatment plans and case planning conferences for those youth going into out-of-home placement. They may also provide community supervision for youth who return home from detention, residential treatment centers, or out-of-home placement. The DJJ worker is likely to be the first official to know if a youth has violated his or her conditions of placement or probation and would be responsible for communicating this to the juvenile court judge. DJJ workers visit the youth in their homes, schools, or places of employment and talk with parents, teachers, police, and others in the community to ensure the youth's compliance with curfew or other conditions of probation and to assess his or her behavior at home and in the community.

DJJ workers can be involved in the prehearing collection of data needed to understand the juvenile. This may involve looking at other offenses the youth has committed or assessing for substance abuse or mental health issues. This information may be used by the judge in deciding how best to help the youth coming before the juvenile court.

Later, the DJJ worker may interview youth in their out-of-home placements to determine progress they have made toward accomplishing goals and the court's plans for them. DJJ workers can inform the judge about youth who are noncompliant with treatment plans, and this can result in new orders from the court, such as longer periods of supervision. While all of this sounds very punitive, the DJJ worker can also be a strong advocate for youth are really working hard and trying their best to avoid the behaviors or actions that resulted in their involvement with the juvenile court.

DJJ workers engage in assessing, counseling, consulting, and writing reports and sometimes must be a bit of a detective (unofficially, of course) to monitor the youth on their caseloads. The goal is always rehabilitation and, as far as possible, to prevent youth from becoming chronic or more serious offenders. DJJ workers can make recommendations to help strengthen the traumatized teens and their families and in this sense are similar to the ongoing CPS workers discussed in Chapter 5.

What Are the Conditions That Produce Juvenile Delinquents?

You probably have enough information from this text to able to answer this question yourself. If you are not sure, just think about the conditions we have already discussed that create dysfunctional families and the neighborhoods that are nurseries for just about every type of social problem.

The families of youth who become involved in the juvenile justice system often struggle with substance abuse, mental illness, low income, and an absence from the family due to incarceration. These are homes where the parents were

> temperamentally oppositional, uncaring, or avoidant ... may not be able to respond well to their child's temperament. Such parents are likely to role model antisocial, aggressive, addictive, or avoid-ant ways of dealing with people, responsibilities, and stress. Because of strong genetic influences, temperamentally oppositional, uncaring, and avoidant children are particularly likely to have parents with similar temperaments (Lahey et al., 1999). When this occurs, a child's temperament may bring out "the worst" in a parent, and vice versa, leading to a vicious cycle of harsh, neglectful, hostile, defiant, and aggressive behavior on the part of both the child and the parents (Patterson, 1993 as cited in Ford, Chapman, Mack, & Pearson, 2006, p. 16)

In a large study of juveniles who were being processed intake for detention in the Cook County Juvenile Temporary Detention Center (Chicago, Illinois), researchers found that 92.5% had experienced at least one trauma, 84% had experienced more than one, and the average number of traumatic incidents experienced was 14.6 (Abram et al., 2004). Three quarters of the juveniles reported having "seen or heard someone get hurt very badly or be killed;" 60% of males and almost half of the females had been "threatened with a weapon," and about half of the male and female youth had been in a situation in which "you thought someone close to you was going to be hurt very badly or die" (Abram et al., 2004, pp. 405–406). Remember these are teens aged 10 to 18 years—not combat veterans of Iraq or Afghanistan.

Besides violence in their neighborhoods, many of the juveniles lived in domestically violent households and had been neglected or maltreated themselves. Another study drawing on interviews with youth at intake at the same Cook County Juvenile Temporary Detention Center found that two thirds of males had experienced moderate physical abuse (such as being "hit very hard," "hit with an object," or "beaten or kicked"). Female adolescents reported even worse abuse. Three quarters of them had experienced moderate physical abuse, and 35% were victims of severe physical abuse ("hurt by an adult that resulted in bruises, broken bones, or severe injury"). Forty-one percent of the females had experienced some type of sexual abuse. For about a third of the females, their sexual abuse was an assault—an attempt at penetration or intercourse; about 1 in 4 (22%) experienced actual penetration or forced intercourse, and 1 in 5 of the female teens experienced both severe physical abuse *and* sexual abuse (King et al., 2011).

Still another study conducted in a northeastern state of 12- to 16-year-old boys from two juvenile detention centers found that 86% experienced at least one potentially traumatic event and 71% had experienced two traumatic events (Stimmel, Cruise, Ford, & Weiss, 2014).

Note, however, that the teens taken to the Cook County Juvenile Temporary Detention Center were more likely to have been accused of serious types of offenses or at least had a history of prior offenses or detention. That is to say, the youth placed in the facility were not likely to be status offenders who broke a curfew ordinance or were caught drinking alcohol in public. Even if that was the initial offense, there may have been other factors that escalated the situation, such as their defying a police order or resisting arrest, that contributed to a greater likelihood that they would end up at the detention center instead of being returned to their parents. Indeed, King et al. (2011) also reported that of those teens being processed for holding at the detention center, 53% of the females and 44% of the males who did not claim any mistreatment (prior childhood abuse or neglect) were found to have a psychiatric disorder. The rates for psychiatric disorder are exorbitant for teens who experienced maltreatment. See Table 8.5.

TABLE 8.5 **PREVALENCE RATES OF PSYCHIATRIC DISORDERS BY CHILDHOOD MALTREATMENT TYPE**

Gender	No maltreatment	Moderate physical abuse	Severe physical abuse	Sexual abuse	Sexual and severe physical abuse
Males	44%	77%	75%	65%	82%
Females	53%	74%	80%	88%	92%

Source: King, 2011.

The connection between the violence a young person experienced and offending with violence as a juvenile is "particularly troubling in light that juvenile offenders who are victims of violence often continue to demonstrate offending behavior into adulthood" (Stimmel et al., 2014, p. 185).

TEST YOURSELF

What was going on in Cook County, Illinois, that would explain why so many adolescents in detention had seen or heard someone get seriously injured or killed? You might want to think outside the box! Do not read below the dotted line until you are ready to see the answer.

Although it is difficult to accurately count membership in gangs, as early as 1995, Chicago seemed to have more gangs than Los Angeles—the nation's second largest city (Miller, 2001). An FBI report in 2011 estimated that Los Angeles might have the largest number of gang members, and a study by Chicago's Crime Commission in 2012 stated Chicago might be in first place, with the nation's largest city (New York City) being well behind. Why?

One explanation is that New York City created public housing projects that were economically integrated, while Chicago's model was to build housing projects for those on public assistance, disability, or Social Security—housing mostly the poor and nonworking families. You may want to read about other possible explanations mentioned by Moser (2012).

More Contributors to the Development of Juvenile Crime

How is it that poverty and impoverished neighborhoods contribute to juvenile crime? Family life seems to play a large role. Particularly deleterious to the development of young people are families in which there are inconsistent discipline and boundaries; marital conflict; a lack of parental affection, warmth, and emotional connection and involvement with the children; many children in the home; low levels of parental education; poverty; involvement with the child welfare system; incarceration; a single parent; and changing parental figures (Lane, 2018). The following highlights have also been taken from Lane's (2018) reflection on what we have learned about teen crime:

Peers

- "the more time youths spend hanging out in unstructured settings with peers, particularly delinquent ones, the more likely they are to commit crime and use legal substances" (p. 285).
- Some teens join gangs for companionship, but others "are drawn to gangs because of protection, long-term friendships, trouble in school, lack of social skills, defiance, excitement, financial gain and so on" (p. 286).

Living in Poverty

- Children from impoverished families "are less likely to go to preschool, to be read to every day, and to be ready to learn when they enter kindergarten" (p. 287).
- These youths "are more likely to have low achievement, repeat a grade, and drop out, and nearly half of Black and Hispanic youth attend high poverty schools. … Data show that violent crime, fights, gangs, and out-of-school suspensions are more common in high-poverty schools and those with larger minority student populations" (p. 287).

The Juvenile's Response to Trauma

There is considerable evidence that traumatic victimization in a young person's life seems to contribute to behavioral problems, which later can become labeled and processed as juvenile delinquency. This pathway seems to be wider when it is difficult for the young person to manage impulsivity, unspoken anger, and aggressiveness toward others and when the preteen or teen is oppositional and indifferent to the violation of social rules. As we learned previously, victims of trauma may have deficits with regard to their emotion regulation and social information processing.

PRACTICE TIP 8.1 If the neighborhood you grew up in was relatively quiet, one where you felt safe most of the time, and if your family life was reasonably warm with only a few bouts of dysfunctioning, then it might be hard for you to see any redeeming qualities in a "delinquent" young man or woman who has stolen a car, sold drugs on a street corner, or worse—deliberately hurt another person to the extent he or she was hospitalized. The public's tendency may be view them as criminals—not as young people who were themselves traumatized as children.

How do you open up your mind to imagine them as having potential to finish their schooling, to get jobs, to become successful parents? It starts first with reframing how you see them. They are, first of all, individuals whose angry defiance can be viewed as "self-protective assertions of an unwillingness to be further victimized" and a "reaction to feeling alone and powerless," and who are victims of "unavailable, untrustworthy, unloving, or unreliable" parents/caretakers who have betrayed and taught them that "relationships can never be trusted" (Ford et al., 2006). Most, if not all, are victims of circumstances they did not cause within their homes. They are likely to feel devalued, devoid of any importance to society, with low self-esteem and a sense of shame despite any "attitude" or swagger and bluster they may show.

Second, instead of judging them for their fitness for the human race, change your thinking to wonder how they have managed to carry their terrible burdens. Or as Boyle (2010, p. 67) puts it, "stand in awe" at what they have had to carry "rather than in judgment at how they carry it" by their acting out to call attention to their plight.

If you want to work with juvenile delinquents, take the advice of "Danny," a teen runaway interviewed in a residential treatment program who recommended asking the questions, "Why is this kid running away? Why is he acting like this?" (Buffington, Dierkhising, & Marsh, 2010).

Father Greg Boyle, who began working in the 1980s in east Los Angles—an area with the highest rates of gang activity and gang-related homicides in the city—started, along with other members of the Dolores Mission Church, an organization that later became Homeboy Industries. This nonprofit agency is the largest gang intervention, rehabilitation, and reentry program in the world, serving over 10,000 former gang members each year (https://homeboyindustries.org/). Homeboy offers a comprehensive range of services, such as mental health, substance abuse support, legal services, tattoo removal, case management, education, employment training, job-seeker workshops, and job placement.

This is what Father Boyle (2017) has said about the gang members he has worked with in his most recent book: "Every single homie [friend] who walks through our doors brings with him or her a storehouse of unspeakable acts perpetrated against them, from torture, abuse, and violence to abandonment, neglect, and terror" (p. 56).

These young men and women who joined gangs and engaged in many serious criminal activities experienced maltreatment in childhood that is difficult to imagine until you read about or hear the stories they tell. Here is one example Father Boyle uses to introduce a young man ("Sergio") who had been homeless, a heroin addict, and imprisoned.

> I knew patches of his backstory: drinking and sniffing glue at eight, which eventually led to crack, PCP, and finally heroin. He had been first arrested at nine for assault and breaking and entering, jumped into a gang at twelve, and did two and a half years for stabbing his mom's boyfriend who tried to abuse him. ... He began his story ... "I guess you could say my mom and me, well, we didn't get along so good. I think I was six when she looked at me and said, 'Why don't cha just kill yourself? You're such a burden to me.'
>
> "I think I was, like, nine years old ... when she drove me to the deepest part of Baja California, walked me up to the door of this orphanage and said, 'I found this kid.' ... I was there ninety days before my grandmother could get out of my mom where she had dumped me, and my grandmother came and rescued me. ... My mom beat me every single day of my elementary school years, with things you could imagine and a lotta things you couldn't. Every day my back was bloodied and scarred. In fact, I had to wear three T-shirts to school each day. The first one cuz the blood would seep through. The second cuz you could still see it. Finally, with the third T-shirt, you couldn't see no blood." (Boyle, 2017, pp. 53–54)

A second example comes from a young man describing an incident that occurred when he was 7 years of age. Father Boyle (2017) relates:

> His mother and father had been screaming ferociously at each other, and the fight reached a crescendo when the father, with a certain calm and a single punch, decked the mother out cold. As she lay there on the floor, unconscious, his father turned to him and said, "Now, *that's* how you hit a woman." (p. 57)

What is common to a lot of the youth who get into serious trouble with the law is the anger they feel. This anger arises from the abuse or violence in their homes, from not being parented by someone who cares for them, from feeling powerless about their situation. Boyle (2010) identifies the problem as a "lethal absence of hope" (p. 89) that is almost palpable when "Manny," a gang member with tattoos "etched across his face in every imaginable way—diagonally on his cheek, filling the space of his neck, in Roman numerals on his forehead," describes the murder of an older youth walking Manny as a 6-year-old to school: "Suddenly, one of 'em is right by us, standing next to Rafa. … In an instant … my face is splattered with blood and little pieces of Rafa's brain—all over my face" (pp. 64–65).

You can also read about and feel the anger from teens' stories available on the Juvenile Justice Information Exchange (https://jjie.org/?s=stories). One example is shared below.

First, the background: One of DeAngelo Cortijo's earliest memories as a young child is finding his mother unconscious on the kitchen floor surrounded by pill bottles, seeing the ambulance take her away, and feeling that he would never see her again. His ardent desire to reunite with his mother led to his acting out in foster care, numerous fights, and later probation and juvenile detention for stealing cars.

> One of the lowest points in his ordeal, Cortijo said, was visiting day, no matter what youth facility he was in. It seemed like every other kid in the joint would get visits from his mother, or there would be calls, or thoughtful letters at mail call. … He would metabolize that disappointment into unadulterated rage, which would lead to another fight, another spell in solitary, letting the disappointment marinate into something darker. Cortijo would coil with rage and resentment and look for an opportunity to unleash it on somebody. (Khan, 2016)

The Legal Rights of Juveniles

Below is a list of things you will want to remember about the legal rights of minors.

- Children may not understand the words or concepts associated with their **Miranda rights**. They may not understand that they are *not* required to give law enforcement information and that anything they say might be used against them. That is, they have the right to remain silent and not talk to the police without an attorney present. If they cannot afford an attorney, one will be provided for them. What they understand may depend on their age, their level of intelligence, and any cognitive impairments or mental disorders they may have. Research indicates that more juveniles waive their *Miranda* rights than adults—which means they are more likely to incriminate themselves (Feld, 2017).
- There is no definitive age guideline that establishes when a child can be considered competent to stand trial, exercise Miranda rights, or waive counsel (Feld, 2017).
- Parents are usually required to attend all hearings involving their child in juvenile court. Judges more often rely on information coming to them from a juvenile probation officer or defense attorney than

seeking information from parents in court. Saying this a different way, "judges often do not want parents to speak inside the courtroom, even though there is no official court rule that would prevent their participation" (Pennington, 2017, p. 29).

- Unlike a child in a CPS proceeding, who will have an advocate with his or her GAL and perhaps a court-appointed special advocate, there is no national requirement mandating that a juvenile appearing before a juvenile court judge will have a GAL (Robbins, 2008).

- Probation officers, court intake workers, and prosecutors who do preliminary screening of juvenile delinquency cases often do not have or use formal assessment or screening tools, and their decisions are not "subject to judicial or appellate review" (Feld, 2017, p. 502).

- Parents and their children may have conflicting interests (e.g., when a juvenile assaults his or her sibling or the parent/guardian). Also, parents may have to pay for their child's attorney and could pressure the child to confess in order to conserve their funds.

- A historic juvenile delinquency case decided by the Supreme Court you might want to read more about is *In re Gault* 387 U.S. 1 (1967), nicely summarized at http://jaapl.org/content/jaapl/45/2/140.full.pdf. In the case, a 15-year-old boy (Jerry Gault) and his friend allegedly made a prank or obscene phone call to a female neighbor, who called the Gila County (Arizona's) Sheriff's office. Jerry Gault had previously been ordered to serve 6 months' probation earlier for being with another boy who stole a wallet. The sheriff's office decided to hold the boys in detention without notifying Jerry's mother. The complainant didn't show at the initial hearing or at a later one, but the judge sentenced Gault to a juvenile corrections facility until he was 21. He did not have an attorney and was not informed of his right to one. The Supreme Court ruled that Jerry Gault had essentially the same rights to due process in the legal system that is accorded to adults. In particular, this includes

1. timely and specific notice to the youth and his parent/guardian about the charges,
2. notification to the youth and his parent/guardian of the right to an attorney,
3. the privilege against self-incrimination,
4. the opportunity to confront and cross-examine one's accusers, and
5. the right to a recording of trial proceedings if requested (Willis, 2017).

Juvenile courts need social workers who understand child trauma and its effects and want to intervene to help these individuals and their families with counseling and guidance. Juvenile justice workers are employed in private as well as public agencies. While working with judges and law enforcement officers, juvenile justice workers must create plans for each youth that intervene to stop the slide to adult criminal behavior. Unlike child protective services, the focus is not on the actions of the parents but the behaviors of the child/adolescent that bring involvement with the juvenile court. As a CPS professional, you will likely work alongside juvenile justice workers at times, and it will be important to understand that their purpose and view about responsibility and accountability for offenses may be slightly different than yours.

Main Points

- This chapter contains a lot of legal terms, such as misdemeanor (minor offense), felony (major crime), summons (an order to appear before a court), and in loco parentis (the legal right for the court to act as a youth's parent). Status offenses are those that apply only to minors (such as breaking curfew or being truant from school).

- Tabular data is supplied to help you see a profile of juvenile delinquents in terms of their age (they tend to be older teens), gender (males in majority), and race (about 40% White).
- While living in impoverished neighborhoods with high crime rates and peers who are involved in delinquent activities are risk factors, it is important to remember that many of those being seen in juvenile courts have been traumatized by violence, abuse, or neglect and are in need of mental health services.
- Juvenile offenses are broadly categorized as those against persons, against property, drug law, and public order violations.
- Conditions responsible or favorable to the development of juvenile delinquents are those that have been discussed in previous chapters and have been associated with the incidence of child abuse and neglect.
- Juveniles do have legal rights, but their age, bravado, and lack of knowledge about their rights and the legal system may not always work to their advantage.

Questions for Class Discussion

1. Do you think that certain status offenses, such as being truant from school or violating a community's curfew, are unfair to teens? Why or why not?
2. Do you think that ordinances and laws that set up status offenses help identify teens at risk for more serious offenses so that they can get help? Or do they "label" or categorize young people in a way that seems to confirm that they have become delinquents?
3. Does the legal standard of "beyond a reasonable doubt" seem clear and workable? Would you feel comfortable if the standard were applied to an offense you committed?
4. To what extent do poverty and lack of opportunities for persons of color contribute to our nation's juvenile delinquency? What examples have you seen or do you know about that convince you that juvenile crime and poverty are connected?
5. If you were a national politician, what would you advocate for or what new funding or programs would you argue are needed to prevent juvenile delinquency? What would you propose?

Self-Assessment for Personal Consideration

1. How comfortable would you be in working with youth who have been referred to the juvenile court?

1	2	3	4	5	6	7	8	9	10

   Not comfortable   *Very comfortable*

2. How comfortable would you be in working with the parents of gang members?

1	2	3	4	5	6	7	8	9	10

   Not comfortable   *Very comfortable*

3. How comfortable would you be in working for a juvenile court?

1	2	3	4	5	6	7	8	9	10

   Not comfortable   *Very comfortable*

Additional Resources

Decker, S., & Pyrooz, D. (2015). *The handbook of gangs*. Chichester, UK: Wiley-Blackwell.

Fox, K. A. (2013). New developments and implications for understanding the victimization of gang members. *Violence and Victims, 28*(6), 1015–1040.

McShane, M. D., & Cavenaugh, M. (2015). *Understanding juvenile justice and delinquency*. Santa Barbara, CA: Praeger.

Peterson, D., & Panfil, V. R. (2017). Toward a multiracial feminist framework for understanding females' gang involvement. *Journal of Crime & Justice, 40*(3), 337–357.

References

Abram, K. M., Teplin, L. A., Charles, D. R., Longworth, S. L., McClelland, G. M., & Dulcan, M. K. (2004). Posttraumatic stress disorder and trauma in youth in juvenile detention. *Archives of General Psychiatry, 61*, 403–410.

Boyle, G. (2010). *Tattoos on the heart: The power of boundless compassion*. New York, NY: Simon & Schuster.

Boyle, G. (2017). *Barking to the choir: The power of radical kinship*. New York, NY: Simon & Schuster.

Buffington, K., Dierkhising, C. B., & Marsh, S. C. (2010). Ten things every juvenile court judge should know about trauma and delinquency. *Juvenile and Family Court Journal, 61*(2), 13–23.

Feld, B. (2017). Competence and culpability: Delinquents in juvenile courts, youths in criminal courts. *Minnesota Law Review, 102*(2), 474–573.

Ford, J. D., Chapman, J., Mack, M., & Pearson, G. (2006). Pathways for traumatic child victimization to delinquency: Implications for juvenile and permanency court proceedings and decisions. *Juvenile and Family Court Journal, 57*, 13–26.

Hockenberry, S., & Puzzanchera, C. (2018). *Juvenile Court Statistics, 2016*. Pittsburgh, PA: National Center for Juvenile Justice.

Khan, D. (2016). Troubled no more, youths bring stories of their resilience to probation professionals. Juvenile Justice Information Exchange. Retrieved from https://jjie.org/2016/04/26/troubled-no-more-youths-bring-the-story-of-their-resilience-to-probation-professionals

King, D. C., Abram, K. M., Romero, E. G., Washburn, J. J., Welty, L. J., & Teplin, L. A. (2011). Childhood maltreatment and psychiatric disorders among detained youths. *Psychiatric Services, 62*, 1430–1438.

Lahey, B., Waldman, I., & McBurnett, K. (1999). Annotation: The development of antisocial behavior. *Journal of Child Psychology and Psychiatry, 29*, 669–682.

Lane, J. (2018). Addressing juvenile crime. What have we learned, and how should we proceed? *Criminology & Public Policy, 17*, 283–307.

Miller, W. B. (2001). *The growth of youth gang problems in the United States, 1970–98*. Washington, DC: Office of Juvenile Justice and Delinquency Prevention.

Moser, W. (2012, January 27). Why are there so many gang members in Chicago? *Chicago Magazine*. https://www.chicagomag.com/Chicago-Magazine/The-312/January-2012/Why-Are-There-So-Many-Gang-Members-in-Chicago

Patterson, G. R. (1993). Orderly change in a stable world: The antisocial trait as chimera. *Journal of Consulting and Clinical Psychology, 61*, 911–919.

Pennington, L. (2017). Socializing distrust of the justice system through the family in juvenile delinquency court. *Law & Policy, 39*, 27–47.

Robbins, A. R. (2008). Troubled children and children in trouble: Redefining the role of the juvenile court in the lives of children. *Juvenile and Family Court Journal, 59*(1), 3–15.

Slaughter, E. (2018). Juvenile incarceration and justice in the United States. *American Jails, 32*, 8–10, 13–14.

Stimmel, M. A., Cruise, K. R., Ford, J. D., & Weiss, R. A. (2014). Trauma exposure, posttraumatic stress disorder symptomatology, and aggression in male juvenile offenders. *Psychological Trauma Theory: Research, Practice, & Policy, 6*, 184–191.

Willis, C. D. (2017). Right to counsel in juvenile court 50 years after *In re Gault*. *Journal of American Academy of Psychiatry Law, 45*, 40–44.

CHAPTER 9

SPECIAL POPULATIONS

OVERVIEW

The purpose of this chapter is to provide an overview of several special populations that you will likely encounter when working in child protection. While this chapter is not intended to be all-inclusive, it will highlight children with substance abuse issues, those who have mental health concerns, those who are sexual offenders, children with intellectual disabilities, pregnant teens, runaways, gang members, human trafficking victims, and children of immigrants. What makes these groupings special is that the children are doubly burdened. That is, they may have been physically, emotionally, and/or sexually abused or neglected, *plus* they are in an unfamiliar country (as in the case of immigrant children or human trafficking victims); they may be living on the street or in other precarious situations (as in the case of runaways or gang members). They may have little control over their behavior or future without specialized treatment (such as those with mental health or substance abuse issues). Formulating specific plans for intervention, integral to child protection, should be rooted in a clear understanding of their situation or constellation of problems and needs.

Introduction

In 2016 approximately 4.1 million referrals of child abuse or child maltreatment were made to child protective service agencies in the United States (Children's Bureau, 2018). Agencies across the country work diligently to respond to these issues and to design services that will minimize their future reoccurrence. As a practitioner, you will have a number of concurrent cases that will bring different challenges. The purpose of this chapter is to provide a broad overview of some of the situations and special groups you will likely encounter in child protection. We are unable to instruct you about every possible special need or situation that can arise, so we will focus on those that are commonly found.

Recognition of children's special need is key, and moving forward with strategic techniques in practice are helpful in facilitating change. It is important to meet clients where they are and to recognize that sometimes they may have conditions that may not be easily resolved. As suggested in the chapter overview, many of these situations may overlap one another in the same family. Additionally, some of these situations will likely require significant effort and resources to address. The challenges may be very frustrating at times. Nonetheless, you have an opportunity to be a part of a solution to improve the lives of children and families.

Substance Abuse

Jill knew better, as she was not brought up this way. Raised by a middle-class family in the suburbs, her mother was a schoolteacher and her dad was an executive at the local bank. If they had any idea about what she had been up to, there would be hell to pay. But Jill couldn't help herself. She enjoyed spending time with her friends and having fun. Over the course of time, her occasional dabbling in marijuana resulted in a cocaine habit. It was serious and was becoming a problem.

The first time she tried cocaine, she was at a party with her friends and was told it would help numb the pain from her recent breakup with her boyfriend. She had seen her friends use it every once in a while and thought she would try it out. It was only one time, she thought; surely it wouldn't be a big deal.

Like the flip of a switch, she fell in love with the feeling associated with using cocaine. She began to enjoy the lifestyle, planning her week around the expectation of getting high with her friends and strategically planning how they would obtain their fix. Jill became skilled at scheming to concoct a story to tell her family, always ending up at a house with limited supervision and a room full of teenagers who were ready to party.

And then it happened. Driving home on a Sunday morning at about 3:00 a.m., she was pulled over by law enforcement. Arriving at the driver side window, the police found a small bag of cocaine in the console and asked Jill to get out of the vehicle. She was only 16 years old, unable to communicate, and began to break down. Concerned about her safety and ongoing supervision, law enforcement contacted child protective services to assess the situation.

Jill's story is unique, as it involves a child living a privileged life with abundant resources. Jill's case will not reflect most of the families you find yourself working with—yet there are some similarities that must be considered. Specifically, substance use is widespread and prevalent when one works in child protection. Further, children will use substances—this is not only a characteristic of the adults that you will encounter. Similarly, when there is domestic violence in a home, you will often find that substance use will be an additional challenge.

In addition to the variety of individuals who are using substances, the type of substances may vary. While some substances are legally obtained, others may not be. An example of a legally obtained substance could be alcohol or prescribed medication. While intended to be used in an appropriate capacity by an adult, these also create a level of access issue that may present a risk factor for younger individuals in the home. Families periodically engaging in drinking wine or having a cocktail at the dinner table may not be a problem, yet open bottles could heighten the risk of underage substance abuse by providing easy access for children in the home. The same thing goes for medication. If a family member has been prescribed pain medication for an injury, this could produce a risk of access for inappropriate use by an adolescent in the home.

Illegal substances are also important to consider. While legislation has been changing in certain areas related to marijuana, for the most part it is still illegal. And for the purposes of this chapter, we are discussing children using illegal substances which is always illegal. The types of illegal substances that children will use are endless. Unfortunately, you will likely be involved with adolescents who are engaging in the use of cocaine, methamphetamines, morphine, heroin, and other types of strongly addictive substances. It is important to consider the regional trends in your area to understand the preferred drugs being used and recognize that children involved with the child welfare system are at a higher risk of this behavior.

Yarnell, Traube, and Schrager (2016) used data from the National Survey of Child and Adolescent Well-Being (NSCAW I) to examine the use of marijuana, alcohol, and drug use for a sample of adolescents involved with our nation's child welfare system over time. Findings documented polysubstance abuse by children involved with the child welfare system and suggest a primary need for prevention associated with marijuana use—as a presumed "gateway drug."

In addition, the literature has highlighted an increased risk of injection drug use for children involved with the child welfare system. Barker, Kerr, Dong, Wood, and DeBeck (2017) examined a sample of 581 street youth, finding that involvement with a CPS agency significantly predicted the initiation of injection drug use before the age of 18 and that 39% of the sample engaged in this behavior.

Recognizing the risks of substance abuse by children under the supervision of the child welfare system, there are protective factors that should be considered. In a study by Brown and Shillington (2017), data from a sample of 1,054 youth involved in the child welfare system between the ages of 11 and 17 revealed that having a protective adult relationship moderated (worked to lessen) the relationship between adverse childhood experiences and substance abuse.

Pittenger, Moore, Dworkin, Cnisto, and Connell (2018) used a nationally representative sample of child welfare system–involved youth to quantitatively examine potential protective factors (e.g., peer relationships, spirituality, caregiver monitoring, etc.) and their impact on the use of cocaine, alcohol, and marijuana. While these factors had limited predictive value, substance use prior to or at the time of child welfare involvement was determined as a critical risk for later substance use. Implications focused on the need for timely screenings and early referrals to treatment.

There are programs that focus on the reduction of substance use for children involved with the child welfare system. One example is the KEEP SAFE program. According to Kim, Buchanan, and Price (2017), this family-based and skill-focused program significantly reduced substance use for foster youth by improving relationships with caregivers and minimizing associations with deviant peers.

PRACTICE TIP 9.1 Working effectively with children who are using substances involves staying informed and having relationships with community partners. Have a good background knowledge about the most common forms of substances used in your area. The heroin epidemic may be your biggest concern. Or you might work in an area that is becoming a hotbed for ecstasy. Having relationships with community partners (especially law enforcement) will help you stay informed about your drugs or trends. Community partners may also be able to assist in facilitating random drug screens (e.g., urine, hair follicle, etc.) as an important component in ongoing services.

As described in Chapters 4 and 7, make sure to look for signs and symptoms of substance use. Nonverbal communication patterns, changes in behaviors, and open-ended questions can be helpful in assessment. Seek additional training if you need it. The key component of working with children and families who face this challenge is to truly expect this type of behavior to be present, so that its occurrence does not come as a surprise. Some agencies are now considering utilizing a differential response system for specialized involvement with families, which can be adjusted based on the needs of the family (Lalayants & Prince, 2016). For example, referrals for low-risk substance use could be handled differently than those associated with severe physical abuse. This type of response may help motivate families in the change process, allowing the agency to proactively assist in support and eliminate the consequences of the caregiver's name being listed on a formal abuse registry. Develop a list of treatment resources available in your area.

Mental Health Issues

Kyle was a rowdy 12-year-old and didn't have many friends. He was often angry and would lash out at people in class. Kyle would go home each day after school and play video games, the kind where he could destroy things and hurt people. After his father left, things changed for Kyle. One day at school, Kyle had had enough. When asked by his teacher to calm down, Kyle threw his book bag at her and then shoved her against the wall. He screamed as loud as he could and felt like he was going to explode. Kyle was taken to the principal's office—he was finally ready to talk to someone.

Kyle's story is an example of a scenario that could lead to CPS involvement. While the context of the situation will change, children with mental health issues will be encountered frequently. It is clear that adverse childhood experiences and child maltreatment increase the risk of mental health difficulties for children. Research has shown their influence on the future development of psychiatric disorders (Greger, Myhre, Lydersen, & Jozefiak, 2015). As a child protection worker, you will be involved with children who experience mental health issues and need specialized treatment to assist in their long-term health and well-being.

To better understand the extent of the mental disorders among children and adolescents in the child welfare system, Bronsard et al. (2016) conducted a systematic review and meta-analysis. Utilizing eight studies obtained from 3,104 children, it was estimated that nearly half of the children and adolescents involved with the child welfare system met the criteria for a mental health disorder. Prevalence estimates were as follows:

- Disruptive disorder (27%)
- Conduct disorder (20%)
- Anxiety disorder (18%)
- Oppositional defiant disorder (12%)
- Attention-deficit/hyperactivity disorder (11%)
- Depressive disorder (11%)
- Post-traumatic stress disorder (4%)

While it is expected that children involved with the child welfare system will have specific mental health needs, it is important to act as soon as possible. Hoffman, Bunger, Robertson, Cao, and West (2016) conducted focus groups with 50 caseworkers at a public child welfare agency and identified a consensus on the importance of early intervention in addressing mental health problems for children in early childhood. Unfortunately, respondents faced difficulties in identifying these needs and described workplace barriers to integrating services.

Identifying needs for treatment is a key factor; however, a study in the state of Washington revealed that 89% of eligible youth ages 3 to 17 received mental health screenings at the time of entry into out-of-home care (Pullmann et al., 2018). Yet the results did not show that many children with service needs received services. Implications from these studies suggest a need to (a) expand mental health screenings for other children (not just those going into out-of-home care), (b) follow up to ensure that children receive the mental health services, and (c) work to eliminate any in-agency barriers that work against integrating services for children and their parents.

Research has also identified disparities related to the existence and utilization of mental health services. Garcia, Circo, DeNard, and Hernandez (2015) identified micro, mezzo, and macro barriers hindering effective mental health service delivery to youth and families of color served by the child welfare system. Respondents acknowledged individual-level factors like lack of engagement and cultural competency. They mentioned the need for job support, interagency collaboration, and competent training strategies as mezzo-level factors that could help. The appropriation of funding, availability of resources, and development of effective practice strategies were macro-level factors that could assist in addressing this issue. Socioeconomic differences have also been identified as a contributor to the disparities in the use of mental health services for children involved in the child welfare system (Kim, Garcia, Yang, & Jung, 2018).

It is clear that a number of factors influence access and treatment for mental health problems experienced by children involved with child welfare. Jaggers, Richardson, and Hall (2018) affirmed this position when they examined records from 2,110 children and found that a child's gender and age, the effectiveness of the intervention, and the extent of agency involvement were significant predictors of the severity of the child's mental health problems.

PRACTICE TIP 9.2 A robust body of literature has improved the understanding of barriers and challenges associated with the effective screening and facilitation of mental health services for children involved with the child welfare system. As a practitioner, the primary focus needs to be on the needs of the child. Understand the availability of services in your area. Is there a therapist who specializes in working with children who have experienced trauma? Maybe there is a seasoned professional who has vast experience with children with reactive attachment disorder. Having a keen knowledge of these services, or lack thereof, can result in effective avenues for advocacy as well. Collaborate with your community partners and with the school system. Also, as mentioned in Chapter 7 consider using a variety of assessments in the screening process. Rely on seasoned colleagues who may have a better understanding of what to look for or how to design professional services with individuals experiencing specific mental health needs. Facilitating services to assist children who are experiencing mental health issues and integrating trauma-informed and strength-based treatment and service planning are critical factors to good care (Kisiel, Summersett-Ringgold, Weil, & McClelland, 2017).

Sexual Offenders

"We've got a problem, Susan!" Tina had been an eighth-grade school teacher for several years now and had never seen anything like this. She raced to the principal's office and let her know that a distraught family was waiting in the hallway. They had arrived with their daughter's iPod, which contained graphic video footage of a classmate sexually violating their child at an after-school event the week before. It was troublesome and concerning, and Susan did not know what to do. She immediately called child protective services for help.

Children involved with the child welfare system may have a history of perpetrating sexual offenses. Often identified as juvenile sex offenders (JSOs), these are children who have perpetrated a sexual crime on another child victim. While the majority of states take a punitive approach to this situation, the child welfare professional will need to focus on treatment as a priority (Prisco, 2015).

Children who have a history of sexual offense may be formally prosecuted for their behaviors and at some point could be involved with the juvenile justice agency in addition to the child welfare system. This unique population has highly specialized and specific needs. On the one hand, they are working toward reunification with society when they reach the age of majority. On the other hand, there may be extreme consequences of their behaviors and a high risk of long-term consequences. For that reason, it is of critical importance that the child protection worker is explicitly focused on the child's individual needs, the child's well-being, and the facilitation of preventative strategies to minimize the possibility of future reoccurrence of this behavior.

While children with a history of sexual offense may not represent the typical child you will work with in child protection, there are challenges in working with this special population. First, it is difficult to quantify the prevalence of juvenile sexual offenses, as children's records are often protected from the public and sexual offenses are often underreported. Yet Ryan and Otonichar (2016) suggest that about half of all sexual offenses against children are committed by youth under the age of 18. Society has also battled over whether juvenile sexual offenders should face prolonged formal consequences that may follow them for the rest of their life. Specifically, there are conflicting beliefs in society about whether a child under the age of 18 who sexually abuses another child should be registered as a sex offender. Those who believe that children should be listed on an official sex offender registry primarily focus on this avenue as a means for public protection. Those who are against this method primarily focus on the long-standing consequences associated with labeling setting up the child for future failure (i.e., a self-fulfilling prophecy). Keep in mind that while most would believe that human beings should deserve a second chance, we are talking about the sexual abuse of a child, by a child. This is a challenging situation, one that Sterling (2015) identifies as beginning an "impermissible life sentence" (p. 295).

Research has shown that being registered as a sex offender has negative effects on an individual's well-being. In a study that compared 251 boys who were receiving treatment for inappropriate or harmful sexual behavior, compared to those who did not have to register as a sex offender, registered children showed more problems in the areas of peer relationships, safety, victimization, and mental health (Letourneau et al., 2018). Further, those who registered as sexual offenders were significantly more likely to have attempted suicide and had more severe suicidal cognitions.

A fundamental belief in child welfare is that children should have an opportunity to be redeemed and restored. A key factor supporting this belief is understanding that a good portion of children committing sexual offenses may have been victims themselves. With that as a backdrop, specialized services can hopefully assist in breaking this cycle. While it is understood that specialized treatment programs for sexual offenders are often recommended and required, research is inconclusive about the effectiveness of these programs with respect to recidivism.

On the one hand, Prisco (2015) argues that specialized treatment is effective in reducing recidivism with juveniles. On the other hand, a systematic meta-analysis conducted by Kettrey and Lipsey (2018) indicated the absence of rigorous evaluation of these specialized programs. The authors could not provide definitive conclusions about the successes of these programs.

Whether working directly or indirectly with children who have committed sexual offenses against other children, a few important characteristics associated with this population must be kept in mind. As identified by Yoder and Ruch (2015), using strategies to engage the family in building rapport and using a strength-based approach can be helpful. Working with the family through empathy, trust, and feeling safe were identified as key factors in this process. Additionally, valuing the family and utilizing them as an agent of change can help assist in the healing process and make a difference when moving forward. Juvenile sexual offending has serious implications throughout society. Working in child protection will afford you the opportunity to assist in breaking this cycle.

PRACTICE TIP 9.3 Here more than possibly any other area, it is important to seek out community service providers that are specialized in working with juvenile sex offenders. Recognize the availability and options for specialized treatment in your area or geographic region. Also, consider using an assessment tool to benefit your initial involvement and ongoing services with the family. Examples include the Juvenile Sex Offender Assessment Protocol II (J-SOAP II), the Estimate of Risk of Adolescent Sexual Offense Recidivism (ERASOR), and the Violence Risk Appraisal Guide–Revised (VRAG-R). While it is unlikely that you will be utilizing these instruments in a clinical sense, having an awareness of these well-known tools can help you understand how clinical providers in specialized programs evaluate progress and assess future risk for reoffending. As mentioned in the study by Barra, Bessler, Landolt, and Aebi (2018), it is important to consider multiple factors when working with sexually abusive youth, such as the severity of the sexual offending and the offender's own history of aversive childhood experiences.

Intellectual Disabilities

As the elementary school guidance counselor for the past 18 years, Rachel had a significant history of working with children. Since Michael's family had moved in from another state about a year ago, Rachel began to have increased concerns about him. Michael was 7 years old and had difficulty in communicating and understanding social rules in the classroom. It was hard for him to think about the consequences of his actions. Michael's two older siblings did not show any of these same issues at the school. Concerned, Rachel made a phone call to Michael's parents and asked them to arrange an appointment to have a formal assessment with their pediatrician.

Broadly speaking, an **intellectual disability** does not refer to a specific condition but is more of an identification of limitations associated with functioning and cognition. These issues are often related to communication skills, social skills, and learning disabilities but can also refer to autism spectrum, Down's syndrome, and the individual's ability to meet his or her own needs. Causes can be associated with illness, genetics, or issues from pregnancy or birth. Often referred to as cognitive or intellectual disabilities and previously identified as mental retardation, it is likely that you will experience this challenge when working with children in child protection.

According to the Centers for Disease Control and Prevention (2017), 1.14% of children ages 3 to 17 were diagnosed with an intellectual disability in 2016. While this might not seem like a very large group, it is important to recognize that when compared to those without a disability, children with intellectual disabilities are more likely to experience abuse (Aguila-Otero, Gonzalez-Garcia, Bravo, Lazaro-Visa, & del Valle, 2018; Lightfoot & LaLiberte, 2011). Further, children with intellectual disabilities are often overrepresented in the CPS service population and have specific issues that must be acknowledged.

A study by Paquette et al. (2018) utilized data from caseworkers in child protective services to compare the characteristics involved with the maltreatment of children with and without intellectual disabilities. Results indicated that the maltreatment of children with intellectual disabilities was primarily associated with self-destructive behaviors, caregivers with intellectual disabilities, older children, having a physical disability, substantiated neglect, a greater number of past investigations, and caregivers without drug abuse issues. Further, a Canadian study also sought to compare differences between the substantiated maltreatment of children with and without intellectual disabilities. Examining 5,797 cases, children with intellectual disabilities experienced more severe maltreatment and were referred for ongoing services at higher rates (Dion, Paquette, Tremblay, Collin-Vezina, & Chabot, 2018). Also, children with intellectual disabilities have a greater likelihood of having parents with issues such as alcoholism or mental health problems, and greater frequencies of intellectual disability in their mothers (Sainero, del Valle, Lopez, & Bravo, 2013). The presence of intellectual disabilities may also present challenges for family reunification, as foster children with intellectual disabilities have been found less likely to achieve reunification and more likely to experience an adoption disruption (Slayter, 2016).

PRACTICE TIP 9.4 As a practitioner, it is especially important to recognize the vulnerability of children with intellectual disabilities. For example, there are limitations in functioning that may keep some children from living independently. It is important to develop alliances with specialized community partners in an effort to assist these individuals as much as possible and with an eye to preparing for the future. Collaboration with the school system is important, and it is likely that the child will have an Individualized Education Program (IEP) that was developed to design a specially tailored educational plan for their needs. The IEP is a systematic strategy with a teamwork approach, which is periodically reviewed for progress and relevance. You may want to increase your knowledge about the realities associated with intellectual disabilities. A great resource is the American Association on Intellectual and Developmental Disabilities, which contains information on best practices, diagnoses, and systems of support. More information can be found at the association's website (http:www.aaidd.org/).

Pregnant Adolescents

Ramona was raised in a devoutly religious family that did not discuss sexual intercourse or even suggest that it might happen until she married. There was no "birds and bees" discussion with her mother. Ramona hadn't thought about the consequences of her behavior—until the morning she woke up vomiting.

With her mother at work, Ramona called her best friend, who knew that Ramona had been doing some "really serious stuff" with her boyfriend. The two girls took off to the drugstore and purchased a pregnancy test. Ramona was hoping she would not see two pink lines, but she did. She was pregnant. She thought, "How could this happen to me?" and "What should I do now?" A hundred thoughts bombarded her mind, but Ramona knew she could not consider having an abortion, and she knew that her family would be upset. However, she went home knowing she would be having a difficult conversation.

As she expected, her mother became outraged and shouted that she was ashamed of Ramona and that she was "not going to have a 15-year-old mother and baby living in her home."

Calming down slightly, she picked up the telephone and contacted the local child protection agency to see if there was a group home where Ramona could go. Ramona was no longer welcome in her mother's home.

Child protection often involves working with adolescents who have become pregnant. Teenage pregnancy is a national concern, and in 2017 a total of 194,377 babies were born to women ages 15 to 19 (Martin, Hamilton, & Osterman, 2018). Related to specific involvement with the child welfare system, challenges immediately become apparent when trying to navigate the priority of whether the needs of the mother or the fetus become the primary focus (Dalwai & Soans, 2018).

Agencies must consider the needs of the teenage mother and also the needs of the newborn child. Hopefully, having support systems in place will allow the newborn baby to stay with the mother. Yet situations may arise in which child protection workers may have to consider finding a different placement for the infant—especially if the teenage mother is unable to meet the needs of her own child. It may be unrealistic to expect a very young mother to be able to have the support and competency that is necessary to meet not only her own needs but also the needs of a baby.

While there may be a slight decline in recent overall number of teenage pregnancies (Martin et al., 2018), children involved with the child welfare system are at a higher risk of pregnancy and sexually transmitted infections, or STIs (Albertson et al., 2018). A qualitative study identified a number of factors found to influence pregnancy and the risk for STIs for youth involved with the child welfare system, such as difficulties with controlling impulses, communication, emotional regulation, and trust appraisal (Ahrens, Spencer, Bonnar, Coatney, & Hall, 2016).

Children involved with the child welfare system have likely had adverse early life experiences potentially affecting their development and sense of safety. The resulting high risk for teenage pregnancy presents challenges in working with this population, yet programs are beginning to assist in improving the knowledge, attitudes, and behaviors of the sexual health of vulnerable youth.

Boustani, Frazier, and Lesperance (2017) found benefits in these areas when examining the impact of an evidence-based sexual health program (Sisters Informing Healing Living and Empowering) for at-risk youth. Additionally, the evidence-based Power Through Choices (PTC) program has been identified as an effective sexual health education intervention. In a study by Oman, Vesely, Green, Clements-Nolle, and Lu (2018), the PTC program reduced the odds of system-involved youth engaging in sexual intercourse without the use of birth control.

Research has also explored the experiences of teenage mothers who spent time in foster care, identifying their strategies for parenting differently, avoiding the child welfare system, reducing isolation, and enhancing support for their families as key factors to breaking the cycle of child abuse and neglect for their own children (Aparicio, 2017). Despite the recognized risk factors associated with adolescent pregnancy, one study explored youth care workers' ideas about possible benefits of this circumstance for some teens. Three potential benefits to teenage pregnancy were mentioned: youths' effort to prove themselves as an adult, the opportunity to secure their relationship with a partner, and the desire to create an emotional connection with a baby; however, deficiencies in knowledge and having multiple risk factors were identified as problematic (Boustani, Frazier, Hartley, Meinzer, & Hedemann, 2015).

PRACTICE TIP 9.5 It is likely that as a child protection worker you will be involved with adolescents who are pregnant. Helping facilitate access to reproductive health care services and education is a key component in this effort. The local health department should be a good resource. Additionally, educational components can be accessed online. As a practitioner you must not only be concerned with the adolescent mother but also help her prepare for the health and safety of a new life. It is important to focus on proactive services and safety measures (e.g., identifying appropriate child care and arranging the services of a pediatrician) to assure that the newborn baby does not have to be removed from the mother's care and custody. This does happen and is extremely difficult on a number of levels. The mother and her newborn child will benefit from a structured plan that can meet both of their needs long term. Biological fathers should not be overlooked as a system of support and contribution. As mentioned in the Ahrens et al. study (2016), strategies for effective service implementation with this population should be trauma informed and address emotional regulation. Interventions that involve peer mentors may also be especially helpful for working with pregnant teenagers involved with the child welfare system.

Homeless and Runaway Children

Jesse was hungry, and it seemed like she hadn't eaten for days. She had made a nest behind the local convenience store and was keeping it secret that she was sleeping there. It was cold and miserable. Yet she couldn't go home. She'd had a falling-out with her family and left. She was determined not take the physical and verbal abuse any longer.

She had almost no money—her small amount of babysitting savings quickly disappeared. For the third time in two days, she entered the convenience store and asked for a donut or free sandwich. The store clerk could see the desperation in her eyes and the wrinkles in her clothes—the same outfit that she had worn yesterday. He tossed her a ham sandwich, and as she began to devour it, a law enforcement officer walked in. Jesse turned her back to the officer, hoping he wouldn't notice her. The clerk and the officer quietly exchanged a few sentences, then the officer took Jesse a cup of hot chocolate and asked why she wasn't in school. As a result of his questioning, the officer called child protective services to assist.

Inadequate housing and homelessness are formidable social problems faced by the child protection system (Fowler, Brown, Schoeny, & Chung, 2018). According to Woods (2018), approximately 1.7 million "unaccompanied youth" are either living in unstable living conditions or experience homelessness each year. Homelessness refers to individuals or families that are without a stable or permanent residence. Some individuals respond to this circumstance by staying with others for a while, "squatting" in an abandoned residence, or sleeping on the streets or in a shelter. Children who run away from home may become homeless and are highly vulnerable to the many dangers of living on the street.

While homelessness may not be a permanent status, there are some factors that need to be considered when working with individuals experiencing this challenge in child protection. Housing is important in family stability and has been found to directly impact child separation and reunification (Rog, Henderson, Lunn, Greer, & Ellis, 2017). In a study by Putnam-Hornstein, Lery, Hoonhout, and Curry (2017), administrative records of 2,241 young adults ages 17 to 24 receiving services for homelessness were examined. Half of these individuals had been involved with child protection as children. Female youth were significantly more likely to have a CPS history than males.

Forge, Hartinger-Saunders, Wright, and Ruel (2018) found that LGBTQ youth were more likely to become homeless and to be victimized while homeless than their heterosexual counterparts.

In our example, Jesse left her family's home, as she was no longer willing to be abused. Without resources or support, she did not make it far. In the real world, runaway youth face significant challenges that affect their well-being. For example, they may end up involved in gang activity, prostitution, or human trafficking.

TEST YOURSELF

Why might a child think that running away from home was a better option than staying at home?

According to Crosland, Joseph, Slattery, Hodges, and Dunlap (2018), youth generally run "to" something or "from" something. Results from their qualitative analysis indicate that youth may run to positive social supports, peer relationships, preferred activities, or illicit activities. They may also run away from negative social interactions, a restrictive placement, boredom, or a hostile living environment.

PRACTICE TIP 9.6 It is important to focus on addressing past trauma when facilitating services with individuals who have faced housing instability or children who have run away (Putnam-Hornstein et al., 2017; Jackson, 2015). Seek assistance from resources and agencies that specialize in this area. Provide families and children with resources like the National Runaway Safeline (https://www.1800runaway.org/) or the National Youth Crisis Text Line (https://www.crisistextline.org/). Consider programmatic options that may assist your agency in improving housing stability. The Family Unification Program is a federal program that offers housing subsidies for families that are involved with the child welfare system. A recent study by Fowler et al. (2018) identified the integration of this model as cost saving and effective (vs. placement in foster care). Additionally, the Cottage Housing Incorporated's Serna Village Program is a supportive housing program in Sacramento, California, that is working to reduce recidivism rates for children with a history of foster care (Lenz-Rashid, 2017). Treatment models that consider the need for housing stability are also important for family reunification for families with co-occurring substance use and child maltreatment (Murphy, Harper, Griffiths, & Joffrion, 2017). Efforts to address this challenge should be intentional and strategic. While an individual may not remain homeless, the underlying conditions and consequences of this situation are important to consider in practice.

Gang Membership

Life just wasn't easy for Justin. He felt like an outsider. His family had relocated to the city when he was just 12 years old. He had problems at home, and he never knew his biological father. Further, his mother had a history of having serial relationships. She always had another boyfriend in the house, and Justin felt pushed aside.

Justin was bullied at school, and was desperate to fit in. He felt isolated and alone; he wanted to be a part of something. Then he met Hawk, who seemed to be a confident young man who didn't have the same problems as Justin. Hawk offered Justin a chance to be a part of a family that took care of each other. Desperate for acceptance and to not have to defend himself anymore, Justin wanted to be a part of it.

Two weeks later, Justin was caught at the liquor store after pointing a fake firearm at the clerk and attempting to steal a case of Captain Morgan for initiation into his new "family." Because of his age, law enforcement contacted child protective services for assistance.

While it may seem a bit unrealistic now, you may actually find yourself working with children who are involved with gangs as a CPS worker. According to the federal government, the definition of a "gang" includes having an association of three or more people, sharing a collective identity, creating an atmosphere of fear, engaging in violence and intimidation, and potentially having rules for joining and operating within (U.S. Department of Justice, 2015). Although it may be difficult to obtain precise data on the presence of gangs in your service area and the affiliation of their members, the literature provides some general information that is helpful.

When examining the demographic characteristics of gang involvement for youth ages 5 to 17, Pyrooz and Sweeten (2015) found that youth gang members were disproportionately Hispanic, Black, and from single-parent households and a lower socioeconomic status. Further, the study estimated a total of approximately 1,059,000 youth gang members in the United States in 2010, with about 401,000 youth joining gangs each year.

Seeking to explore contextual factors associated with gang involvement, Lenzi et al. (2015) asked questions of a sample of 26,232 students participating in the California Healthy Kids Survey. Results indicated that higher levels of empathy and parental support negatively influenced gang involvement, while the association with deviant peers and not feeling safe in school were positively associated with gang membership. A PRISMA systematic review by Raby and Jones (2016) summarized the literature on risks associated with male street gang affiliation. In what can be considered a developmental model, favorable factors to gang membership arising as early as preschool in the youth's life include familial gang involvement and poverty, low parental supervision, and parental neglect. At the point of school entry, the youth may be rejected by prosocial peers but bond with those who are more antisocial. Because of adverse childhood experiences, they may perform poorly in school and be less committed to it. School suspensions also seem to act as influential factors. Gangs provide security and protection in threatening environments. Regardless of the reason that individuals become affiliated with gangs, it is important to recognize that gang involvement is highly associated with heightened levels of crime and violence.

PRACTICE TIP 9.7 When working in child protection and facilitating services for children who are involved with gangs, it is very important to develop a working relationship with local law enforcement. Law enforcement is likely to have a better knowledge and understanding of the key players associated with these networks, and they may be able to provide information that you should know. For example, you might be able to identify specific gangs by their colors, emblems, tattoos, graffiti symbols, paraphernalia, items of clothing, or other noticeable signs. There may be certain geographic areas in your community where you should be especially careful when visiting. Law enforcement may also be able to assist you in collaboration with other specified agencies, such as the Federal Bureau of Investigation (FBI), the U.S. Immigration and Customs Enforcement (ICE), or the Drug Enforcement Administration (DEA). Additionally, you may need to coordinate with the juvenile court worker or DJJ worker if the minor gang member has been arrested. Explore ways to improve your knowledge about gangs and learn some of their slang or jargon—this can be helpful when you need to ask questions of individuals who are affiliated with gangs. Preventing gang involvement is generally thought to be more effective when efforts are started before the teenage years (Pyrooz & Sweeten, 2015). Lastly, gang activity can have a direct connection with human trafficking, the next challenge we want to consider.

Human Trafficking

Christina's family lived in Ciudad Juárez, just across the American border from El Paso, Texas. They had wanted to come to America for years, in search of a better life. On a warm Sunday afternoon, Christina and her younger sister were picked up by a gentleman who threw the duffel bag full of their belongings into the trunk of his car. Told by her mother that he would find both of them jobs and take care of them, Christina wondered why the man wasn't friendly and when would she see her mother again.

Christina eventually saw her mother about 7 months later, as part of a federal hearing in Texas. Things had been much different than what Christina and her mother had been told.

Specifically, this gentleman was no gentleman at all. He was a smooth-talking criminal—one who engaged in the prostitution of children. His job was to secure unsuspecting children and adolescents and to take them to his contact, who plugged them into cities across the United States. He purposely chose attractive children from poor families and promised they would earn lots of easy money. In fact, most of them were kept locked up in small rooms and allowed no money, identification, or cell phones. They were sex slaves to profiteers who kept a low profile and were almost invisible to most law enforcement officers. Only when several arrests were made and Christina and her sister were discovered to be minors was the child protection agency contacted.

Human trafficking is a modern-day form of slavery, in which individuals are exploited through coercion, force, and the deprivation of liberty. Human trafficking can also be associated with unfair labor practices, whereby the victim may end up in agricultural work, janitorial work, or domestic servitude for a fraction of the minimum wage. Human trafficking is a bit different than human smuggling of individuals across international borders, but it can also be involved in that activity (Child Welfare Information Gateway, 2019). Human trafficking is not just found in major cities, and it is possible that you will come across these situations when working in child protection.

Family members are frequently responsible for the child's pathway into trafficking and commercial sexual exploitation, which can include, besides prostitution, performing in pornography and strip clubs. In a sample of 31 child welfare-involved children referred for behavioral assessment and treatment, all of the cases involved a family member as the trafficker (64.5% the mother, 32.3% the father, and 3.2% another family member). However, in 44% of the cases an acquaintance or paramour assisted the parent. The pursuit of illegal drugs was identified as a key factor in the trafficking of children (82% of the cases), and children living in rural areas experienced more severe sexual abuse. Related to mental health, approximately half of the sample had attempted suicide, and PTSD was the most common diagnosis. Hospital emergency rooms were responsible for identifying the sexual exploitation in about half of the young victims. Eighty-four percent of the sample (58% female, 42% male), with an average age slightly less than 12 years, had excessive absences from school or truancy issues (Sprang & Cole, 2018).

The majority of the literature on child sex trafficking focuses on the female as the victim. A small study of sexually exploited children in Miami, Florida, found female victims were often ages 13 to 18 years old, Caucasian, and from single parent homes and low socioeconomic background (Klimley, Carpinteri, Van Hasselt, & Black, 2018). However, not all child victims of sex trafficking are female; Cole (2018) examined the understudied experience of male sex trafficking victims and their pathways into commercial sex. Her study indicated that pathways into commercial sex exploitation for boys focused on two paths: (a) exploitation by a family member or (b) involvement in these behaviors to support themselves or pay for drugs (i.e. "survival sex").

Individual and contextual factors are also important to consider. Varma, Gillespie, McCracken, and Greenbaum (2015) investigated factors associated with commercial sexual exploitation of children by comparing two separate groups of children in a pediatric health setting. When compared with children who had allegations of child sexual abuse (and no indictors of commercial sexual exploitation), children involved in commercial sexual exploitation were more likely to have had experiences with law enforcement, child protection, violence, and substance abuse. They were also more likely to have run away from home and have a more extensive history of sexual activity. Similarly, O'Brien, White, and Rizo (2017) identified externalizing behaviors (e.g., substance use, runaway behavior) as key factors associated domestic minor sex trafficking in a sample of children involved with the child welfare system.

PRACTICE TIP 9.8 A key element associated with effective practice with families and children who have been involved in human trafficking is the collaboration with local agencies. Similar to gang involvement, agencies like the FBI or ICE may have a better knowledge of immigration issues and policies and be able to provide consultation that can assist. Remain aware of changes in policy and legislation, as efforts are being made to recognize minors as victims instead of perpetrators in crimes associated with domestic minor sex trafficking (Roby & Vincent, 2017). Further, "safe harbor" laws are being considered as a paradigm shift that will redirect victims of child sex trafficking from the criminal justice system and into the child welfare system (Barnert et al., 2016). Consider using assessment tools when working to identify victims of sex trafficking. One example includes six short questions that are beneficial for screening purposes, such as "Has the youth ever had a sexually transmitted infection?" (Greenbaum, Dodd, &

McCracken, 2018). Focus on building a quality relationship with children that you work with. A qualitative study of young people who traded sex and were involved with the child welfare system illustrated the need for practitioners to prioritize relationship building as a key to improving outcomes (Abel & Wahab, 2017). Additionally, a focus on community education (helping the community be alert to possible trafficking in neighborhoods) and providing effective mental health treatment for victims of sex trafficking is an absolute priority (Stewart, 2016).

Look for red flags, including unique *branding* tattoos, bruises, injuries, and sexually transmitted diseases. Also, individuals who are involved in trafficking may have multiple cell phones.

When very young children have been sexualized by adults, they may engage in masturbation or behaviors such as walking around nude or touching other children or adults inappropriately. The worker needs to carefully evaluate the foster home parents and presence of other children in out-of-home placements. Sexualized behavior could result in a placement disruption—or worse, continuing sexual abuse of the victim.

LGBTQ Youth

Tyrone was strong and masculine for his age; he enjoyed playing team sports, and his father was very proud of him. He was a star athlete in his community and there was no shortage of girls wanting to date him.

On the outside everything was fine. On the inside he struggled, as he felt like he could not be himself. One day Tyrone decided to tell his father that he liked boys more than girls. Laughing, his father's initial response was of denial. Yet Tyrone persisted. He informed his father that he was gay and wanted to be honest with himself and his family. Tyrone knew that this was not going to end well.

Tyrone's father erupted and became violent. Tyrone ran outside with the car keys and took the family vehicle. At 16 years old, he drove straight into a stop sign at the end of the street. Tyrone was eventually greeted by law enforcement, who contacted child protective services to assess the situation.

As described by Erney and Weber (2018), not all children involved with the child welfare system are "straight and White." This reality is especially important when considering the intersectionality of race, ethnicity, gender identity, sexual orientation, ability, and immigration status, and how the experiences of LGBTQ youth involved with the child welfare system have "largely been overlooked" (McCormick, Schmidt, & Terrazas, 2017). To become an effective practitioner, one must understand that there is an overrepresentation of LGBTQ youth in child welfare and that there are a variety of concerns that are associated with their experience.

Wilson and Kastanis (2015) indicated that 19% of foster youth in Los Angeles identified as LGBTQ, significantly higher than in the general population. Additionally, when compared with their non-LGBTQ counterparts, LGBTQ foster youth in this study were more likely to experience homelessness and additional placements, had higher levels of emotional distress, and were less satisfied with their experience in the child welfare system. Scannapieco, Painter, and Blau (2018) used national data from the Substance Abuse and Mental Health Services Administration to examine mental health disparities between LGBTQ and non-LGBTQ youth involved with the child welfare system. Findings revealed higher levels of suicide attempts, suicidal ideation, depression, and gender identity-related problems for those identifying as LGBTQ. Robinson (2018) conducted 40 semi-structured interviews with LGBTQ youth who experienced homelessness; he identified gender segregation, isolation, institutionalization, and stigmatization as being linked to their sexuality. Respondents identified that the instability in their experience with the child welfare system contributed to their homelessness, and the diverse sample also discussed the intersectionality with being a person of color. A significant body of literature is beginning to develop, shedding light on the important challenges that these individuals face.

PRACTICE TIP 9.9 Effectively working with LGBTQ youth involves a level of sensitivity and affirmation. Without a doubt, *coming out* is an important step but may bring immediate consequences. The scenario introducing this challenge presented the traditional stereotype associated with masculinity, not being believed, and incurring parental anger as possible implications of *coming out*. When working with LBGTQ youth, it is important to promote well-being and focus on strategies to ensure safety.

Fortunately, society is becoming more accepting of persons who do not identify as heterosexual. Agencies are also showing leadership. An example of an initiative working to build systematic capacity for affirmative practice is called the SOGIE (sexual orientation and/or gender identity and expression) initiative in Alleghany County, Pennsylvania (Washburn et al., 2018). When an assessment of workers reported unaddressed needs, biases, and lack of knowledge, a system-wide SOGIE training was implemented (i.e., Introduction to Sexual Orientation, Gender Identity and Expression) and is being evaluated for sustainability and positive outcomes. Another approach is the RISE (Recognize, Intervene, Support, Empower) model that integrates wraparound services and engagement with LGBTQ-specific education and support strategies. Evaluated in a small study with foster youth identifying as LBGTQ in Los Angeles, results showed improvements in support, sense of identity and belonging, and comfort in disclosing sexuality, as well as a decline in rejection behaviors (Lorthridge, Evans, Heaton, Stevens, & Phillips, 2018).

If you feel that you or your co-workers need more information and resources specific to the LGBTQ population, the Centers for Disease Control and Prevention has a valuable website at www.cdc.gov/lbgth-ealth/youth-resources.htm.

Immigrant Children and Families

Esmina had only been in America for the past 18 months, and she felt like things continued to get worse. She missed her family back home and was having a difficult time managing a newborn baby while her husband tried to make ends meet by working every day in agriculture. She experienced legal barriers to accessing services. Further, she had difficulty speaking English. Living in a rural area, she had no friends or family support.

Her landlord was originally understanding when their rent was late. However, her husband's work was seasonal and affected by the weather. He wasn't paid a weekly salary, and he wasn't sure his employer always gave him the right amount. Consequently, the family struggled to make the rent payment and was often late with it.

Becoming frustrated with the "excuses," the landlord terminated their rental agreement and asked the family to leave. Esmina and her family had nowhere to go. Desperate, she found an office of the local child protection agency next to the coin laundry and walked in to see if something could be done to help in their time of need.

While immigration has been a hallmark of the United States, recent national discussions have been critical of this process. Unlike the other special populations addressed in this chapter, the literature on immigrant families and their experience with child protection in the United States is not well developed. Depending on where you live and work, you may not frequently work with immigrant families; however, you will encounter them when working in child protection.

It is not uncommon to hear the expression that the United States is a country of immigrants, as many of our ancestors traveled here to make a better life for themselves and their families. Although you may encounter recent immigrants from the Congo or Iraq or many other countries, most recently there have been increasing numbers of unaccompanied migrant children entering the United States through its southern border. This is especially important for the child protection agency, as many of these children are fleeing extreme forms of violence in their home countries (Crea, Lopez, Taylor, & Underwood, 2017).

Immigrant children and their families face a number of specific challenges. First and foremost, they may not have the same legal protections as U.S. citizens. For that reason, CPS workers must recognize how this status can affect these families and influence practice. As identified by Slayter and Kriz (2015), the child protection worker must be aware of the "fear factors," such as detention and deportation and separation of children from their families, that may be obstacles to overcome for undocumented immigrant families. They may fear involvement with any government agency, including schools. Their children may not be enrolled in school or may be frequently truant because of parental concerns about potential raids from immigration officials (ICE).

Challenges to delivering services include communication and language difficulties—you may need to work through translators. Maiter, Alaggia, Chan, and Leslie (2017) identified barriers with engaging clients, maintaining confidentiality, and role confusion when seeking to utilize bilingual child welfare workers as a cultural and language "conduit" between service provision and specific cultural groups with limited English proficiency. Implications suggest the need for improved training and working to lessen the impact of power differentials.

When migrant children enter the United States and are unaccompanied, they may end up in foster care. Further, they may have difficulty in maintaining a stable placement and finding permanency. An exploratory study by Crea et al. (2017) found that prior exposure to violence and significant behavioral issues while in foster care were associated with higher odds of placement disruption when examining a sample of unaccompanied migrant children in long-term foster care from 2012 to 2015.

A systematic review by Millett (2016) examined 19 relevant articles and found that immigrants were less likely to be reported to child protective services. However, there were higher rates of physical neglect and insufficient supervision when these cases did come to the attention of child protection authorities. Child protection agencies must find ways to help these families before their problems become severe.

One way to do that would be to put friendly, recognizable faces in the workplace. A study by Lin, Chiang, Lux, and Lin (2018) illustrated the value of this technique by examining the strengths and challenges among Chinese immigrant social workers in New York City. Advantages consisted of emotional connections, being a role model, performing as a mediator, and being open minded to cultural differences. However, challenges emerged. Examples included the unfamiliarity with certain subcultures, power imbalance with clients, and client resistance. All in all, immigrant social workers were likely to be more culturally responsive and to become "cultural brokers" for their colleagues within the system and in the broader community.

PRACTICE TIP 9.10 As a child protection worker, you may discover a broader perspective of how cultures differ—immigrant families may not understand that acceptable practices in their country of origin may be viewed unfavorably in the United States. Further, immigrant children have possibly witnessed or experienced extreme forms of violence and have been traumatized by it—although these details may not always be immediately acknowledged. These children may need trauma-focused counseling and informed practice. Adults also can have been affected in the same way. If encountering these families is not a rare event, you need to develop a list of local resources to support the needs of the families. They may need a skilled, affordable attorney able to navigate the fluid policies and laws associated with immigration. Related to our example, focus on knowledge of concrete services in your local area, like low-income housing and transportation. Be aware of the barriers associated with obtaining these services for individuals who are not from this country. While language and communication barriers will likely remain a consistent challenge, it is likely that your agency will have resources to assist you. In an emergency, you likely will be able to get some translation from an Internet search on your cell phone or laptop. Your agency may have a call center, "on call" translators, or a coworker who is bilingual. Keep in mind that language and communication barriers can compromise the client's capacity to make informed decisions—possibly resulting in long-term negative consequences (Alaggia, Maiter, & Jenney, 2017). Lastly, helping individuals who are new to this country develop strong community relationships may assist in their long-term stability. This is especially true for immigrant children who have been involved with child protection (Crea et al., 2018).

Main Points

While this chapter does not attempt to cover all of the special populations you may encounter, recognize that there will be common elements—whether the child identifies as LGBTQ, has run away, or is a victim of human trafficking.

- Substance use affects children and families in child protection; often, the parents' use is problematic, but children's access and use is also a major concern.
- Whether a cause or an effect, mental health issues are a consistent reality associated with children involved with child protection.
- Juvenile sex offenses are a significant problem—particularly when children have become sexualized and their behavior disrupts foster care placements.
- Children with intellectual disabilities have specific needs (e.g., cognitive, social, etc.), and early intervention is key to effective service implementation.
- Adolescent pregnancy presents challenges requiring a focus on both the young mother and the newborn baby. These individuals need concrete support, help with planning, and education that goes beyond getting a GED or high school diploma.
- Inadequate housing, homelessness, and children who run away present challenges. Understanding the underlying causes of runaway behavior and the need for comprehensive services is critical.
- Gang affiliation inherently increases the participant's involvement with violence and crime. Collaboration with specialized agencies can assist in practice.
- Human trafficking is focused on labor or sexual acts, different than human smuggling. These victims are often severely traumatized.
- LGBTQ youth are overrepresented in the child welfare system. A sensitivity to their orientation may be needed when planning out-of-home placements and developing other services. Programs are being developed to improve CPS workforce training for more affirmative practice.
- Immigrant children are becoming more involved with the child protection system in the United States. Culturally responsive practice and addressing legal and communication barriers is important for the practitioner.

Questions for Class Discussion

1. Consider any additional challenging population that you think you might encounter when working in child welfare. Describe that group.
2. What might be required to work effectively with that group of children or families?
3. Of the special populations discussed in this chapter, which one do you think would be the easiest population to assist with ongoing services? Why?
4. Of the special populations discussed in this chapter, which one do you think would be the most difficult population to assist with ongoing services? Why?
5. Why do you think children involved with CPS have a higher risk of substance use?
6. Of the special populations discussed in this chapter, which do you think would present the biggest challenge to CPS investigators? Why?

Self-Assessment for Personal Consideration

1. How comfortable would you be in reaching out to law enforcement for assistance?

   1   2   3   4   5   6   7   8   9   10

   Not comfortable   *Very comfortable*

2. How comfortable would you be with working with teenagers who are pregnant?

   1   2   3   4   5   6   7   8   9   10

   Not comfortable   *Very comfortable*

3. How comfortable would you be with working with LGBTQ youth?

   1   2   3   4   5   6   7   8   9   10

   Not comfortable   *Very comfortable*

Additional Resources

Aparicio, E., Pecukonis, E. V., & O'Neale, S. (2015). "The love I was missing": Exploring the lived experience of motherhood among teen mothers in foster care. *Children and Youth Services Review, 51,* 44–54.

Franey, K. C. (2005). *Identifying and treating youth who sexually offend. Current approaches, techniques, and research.* New York, NY: Routledge.

Gray, L.-A. (2018). *LGBTQ+ Youth: A guided workbook to support sexual orientation and gender identity.* Eau Claire, WI: PESI.

Notbohm, E., & Zysk, V. (2019). *Ten things every child with autism wishes you knew: Updated and expanded.* Arlington, TX: Future Horizons.

Quest, A. D., Fullerton, A., Geenen, S., Powers, L. & the Research Consortium to Increase the Success of Youth in Foster Care. (2012). Voices of youth in foster care and special education regarding their educational experiences and transition to adulthood. *Children and Youth Services Review, 34,* 1604–1615.

The Centers for Disease Control and Prevention issues periodical reports of drugs being used across the nation by high school students in grades 9 through 12. See the 2016 report from the 1991–2015 High School Youth Risk Behavior Survey, available at http://nccd.cdc.gov/YouthOnline/App/Default.aspx.

References

Abel, G., & Wahab, S. (2017). "Build a friendship with them": The discourse of "at-risk" as a barrier to relationship building between young people who trade sex and social workers. *Child & Family Social Work, 22*(4), 1391–1398.

Aguila-Otero, A., Gonzalez-Garcia, C., Bravo, A., Lazaro-Visa, S., & del Valle, J. F. (2018). Children and young people with intellectual disability in residential childcare: Prevalence of mental health disorders and therapeutic interventions. *International Journal of Social Welfare, 27*(4), 337–347.

Ahrens, K. R., Spencer, R., Bonnar, M., Coatney, A., & Hall, T. (2016). Qualitative evaluation of historical and relational factors influencing pregnancy and sexually transmitted infection risks in foster youth. *Children and Youth Services Review, 61*, 245–252.

Alaggia, R., Maiter, S., & Jenney, A. (2017). In whose words? Struggles and strategies of service providers working with immigrant clients with limited language abilities in the violence against women sector and child protection services. *Child & Family Social Work, 22*(1), 472–481.

Albertson, K., Crouch, J. M., Udell, W., Schimmel-Bristow, A., Serrano, J., & Ahrens, K. R. (2018). Caregiver perceived barriers to preventing unintended pregnancies and sexually transmitted infections among youth in foster care. *Children and Youth Services Review, 94*, 82–87.

Aparicio, E. M. (2017). "I want to be better than you": Lived experiences of intergenerational child maltreatment prevention among teenage mothers in and beyond foster care. *Child & Family Social Work, 22*(2), 607–616.

Barker, B., Kerr, T., Dong, H. R., Wood, E., & DeBeck, K. (2017). History of being in government care associated with younger age at injection initiation among a cohort of street-involved youth. *Drug and Alcohol Review, 36*(5), 639–642.

Barnert, E. S., Abrams, S., Azzi, V. F., Ryan, G., Brook, R., & Chung, P. J. (2016). Identifying best practices for "safe harbor" legislation to protect child sex trafficking victims: Decriminalization alone is not sufficient. *Child Abuse & Neglect, 51*, 249–262.

Barra, S., Bessler, C., Landolt, M. A., & Aebi, M. (2018). Testing the validity of criminal risk assessment tools in sexually abusive youth. *Psychological Assessment, 30*(11), 1430–1443.

Boustani, M. M., Frazier, S. L., Hartley, C., Meinzer, M., & Hedemann, E. (2015). Perceived benefits and proposed solutions for teen pregnancy: Qualitative interviews with youth care workers. *American Journal of Orthopsychiatry, 85*(1), 80–92.

Boustani, M. M., Frazier, S. L., & Lesperance, N. (2017). Sexual health programming for vulnerable youth: Improving knowledge, attitudes, and behaviors. *Children and Youth Services Review, 73*, 375–383.

Bronsard, G., Alessandrini, M., Fond, G., Loundou, A., Auquier, P., Tordjman, S., & Boyer, L. (2016). The prevalence of mental disorders among children and adolescents in the child welfare system: A systematic review and meta-analysis. *Medicine, 95*(7), 1–17.

Brown, S. M., & Shillington, A. M. (2017). Childhood adversity and the risk of substance use and delinquency: The role of protective adult relationships. *Child Abuse & Neglect, 63*, 211–221.

Centers for Disease Control and Prevention. (2016). 1991–2015 High School Youth Risk Behavior Survey data. Retrieved from http://nccd.cdc.gov/YouthOnline/App/Default.aspx

Centers for Disease Control and Prevention. (2017). Estimated prevalence of children with diagnosed developmental disabilities in the United States, 2014–2016. Retrieved from https://www.cdc.gov/nchs/data/databriefs/db291.pdf

Children's Bureau. (2018). *Child maltreatment 2016* (Report, US Department of Health and Human Services, Washington, DC). Retrieved from https://www.acf.hhs.gov/cb/research-data-technology/statistics-research/child-maltreatment

Child Welfare Information Gateway. (2019). *Definitions of human trafficking.* Washington, DC: Children's Bureau.

Cole, J. (2018). Service providers' perspectives on sex trafficking of male minors: Comparing background and trafficking situations of male and female victims. *Child and Adolescent Social Work Journal, 35*(4), 423–433.

Crea, T. M., Lopez, A., Hasson, R. G., Evans, K., Palleschi, C., & Underwood, D. (2018). Unaccompanied immigrant children in long term foster care: Identifying needs and best practices from a child welfare perspective. *Children and Youth Services Review, 92*, 56–64.

Crea, T. M., Lopez, A., Taylor, T., & Underwood, D. (2017). Unaccompanied migrant children in the United States: Predictors of placement stability in long term foster care. *Children and Youth Services Review, 73*, 93–99.

Crosland, K., Joseph, R., Slattery, L., Hodges, S., & Dunlap, G. (2018). Why youth run: Assessing run function to stabilize foster care placement. *Children and Youth Services Review, 85*, 35–42.

Dalwai, S. H., & Soans, S. T. (2018). Defining the best interest of a child: Who comes first-the child or the fetus? *Indian Pediatrics, 55*(10), 853–855.

Dion, J., Paquette, G., Tremblay, K. N., Collin-Vezina, D., & Chabot, M. (2018). Child maltreatment among children with intellectual disability in the Canadian Incidence Study. *American Journal on Intellectual and Developmental Disabilities, 123*(2), 176–188.

Erney, R., & Weber, K. (2018). Not all children are straight and White: Strategies for serving youth of color in out-of-home care who identify as LGBTQ. *Child Welfare, 96*(2), 151–177.

Forge, N., Hartinger-Saunders, R., Wright, E., & Ruel, E. (2018). Out of the system and onto the streets: LGBTQ-identified youth experiencing homelessness with past child welfare system involvement. *Child Welfare, 96*(2), 47–74.

Fowler, P. J., Brown, D. S., Schoeny, M., & Chung, S. (2018). Homelessness in the child welfare system: A randomized controlled trial to assess the impact of housing subsidies on foster care placements and costs. *Child Abuse & Neglect, 83*, 52–61.

Garcia, A. R., Circo, E., DeNard, C., & Hernandez, N. (2015). Barriers and facilitators to delivering effective mental health practice strategies for youth and families served by the child welfare system. *Children and Youth Services Review, 52*, 110–122.

Greenbaum, V. J., Dodd, M., & McCracken, C. (2018). A short screening tool to identify victims of child sex trafficking in the health care setting. *Pediatric Emergency Care, 34*(1), 33–37.

Greger, H. K., Myhre, A. K., Lydersen, S., & Jozefiak, T. (2015). Previous maltreatment and present mental health in a high-risk adolescent population. *Child Abuse & Neglect, 45*, 122–134.

Hoffman, J. A., Bunger, A. C., Robertson, H. A., Cao, Y. W., & West, K. Y. (2016). Child welfare caseworkers' perspectives on the challenges of addressing mental health problems in early childhood. *Children and Youth Services Review, 65*, 148–155.

Jackson, A. (2015). From where to where—running away from care. *Children Australia, 40*(1), 16–19.

Jaggers, J. W., Richardson, E. A., & Hall, J. A. (2018). Effect of mental health treatment, juvenile justice involvement, and child welfare effectiveness on severity of mental health problems. *Child Welfare, 96*(3), 81–102.

Kettrey, H. H., & Lipsey, M. W. (2018). The effects of specialized treatment on the recidivism of juvenile sex offenders: A systematic review and meta-analysis. *Journal of Experimental Criminology, 14*(3), 361–87.

Kim, H. K., Buchanan, R., & Price, J. M. (2017). Pathways to preventing substance use among youth in foster care. *Prevention Science, 18*(5), 567–576.

Kim, M., Garcia, A. R., Yang, S. Y., & Jung, N. (2018). Area-socioeconomic disparities in mental health service use among children involved in the child welfare system. *Child Abuse & Neglect, 82*, 59–71.

Kisiel, C., Summersett-Ringgold, F., Weil, L. E. G., & McClelland, G. (2017). Understanding strengths in relation to complex trauma and mental health symptoms within child welfare. *Journal of Child and Family Studies, 26*(2), 437–451.

Klimley, K. E., Carpinteri, A., Van Hasselt, V. B., & Black, R. A. (2018). Commercial sexual exploitation of children: Victim characteristics. *Journal of Forensic Practice, 20*(4), 217–228.

Lalayants, M., & Prince, J. D. (2016). Child neglect and onset of substance use disorders among child welfare-involved adolescents. *Child Abuse Review, 25*(6), 469–478.

Lenz-Rashid, S. (2017). Supportive housing program for homeless families: Foster care outcomes and best practices. *Children and Youth Services Review, 79*, 558–563.

Lenzi, M., Sharkey, J., Vieno, A., Mayworm, A., Dougherty, D., & Nylund-Gibson, K. (2015). Adolescent gang involvement: The role of individual, family, peer, and school factors in a multilevel perspective. *Aggressive Behavior, 41*(4), 386–397.

Letourneau, E. J., Harris, A. J., Shields, R. T., Walfield, S. M., Ruzicka, A. E., Buckman, C., ... & Nair, R. (2018). Effects of juvenile sex offender registration on adolescent well-being: An empirical examination. *Psychology Public Policy and Law, 24*(1), 105–117.

Lightfoot, E., Hill, K., & LaLiberte, T. (2011). Prevalence of children with disabilities in the child welfare system and out of home placement: An examination of administrative records. *Children and Youth Services Review, 33*(11), 2069–2075.

Lin, C. H., Chiang, P. P., Lux, E. A., & Lin, H. F. (2018). Immigrant social worker practice: An ecological perspective on strengths and challenges. *Children and Youth Services Review, 87*, 103–113.

Lorthridge, J., Evans, M., Heaton, L., Stevens, A., & Phillips, L. (2018). Strengthening family connections and support for youth in foster care who identify as LGBT: Findings from the PII-RISE evaluation. *Child Welfare, 96*(1), 53–78.

Maiter, S., Alaggia, R., Chan, A. S., & Leslie, B. (2017). Trial and error: Attending to language barriers in child welfare service provision from the perspective of frontline workers. *Child & Family Social Work, 22*(1), 165–174.

Martin, J., Hamilton, B., & Osterman, M. (2018). Births in the United States, 2017. *NCHS Data Brief, 318*, 1–8.

McCormick, A., Schmidt, K., & Terrazas, S. (2017). LGBTQ youth in the child welfare system: An overview of research, practice, and policy. *Journal of Public Child Welfare, 11*(1), 27–39.

Millett, L. S. (2016). The healthy immigrant paradox and child maltreatment: A systematic review. *Journal of Immigrant and Minority Health, 18*(5), 1199–1215.

Murphy, A. L., Harper, W., Griffiths, A., & Joffrion, C. (2017). Family reunification: A systematic review of interventions designed to address co-occurring issues of child maltreatment and substance use. *Journal of Public Child Welfare, 11*(4–5), 413–432.

O'Brien, J. E., White, K., & Rizo, C. F. (2017). Domestic minor sex trafficking among child welfare-involved youth: An exploratory study of correlates. *Child Maltreatment, 22*(3), 265–274.

Oman, R. F., Vesely, S. K., Green, J., Clements-Nolle, K., & Lu, M. G. (2018). Adolescent pregnancy prevention among youths living in group care homes: A cluster randomized controlled trial. *American Journal of Public Health, 108*, S38–S44.

Paquette, G., Bouchard, J., Dion, J., Tremblay, K. N., Tourigny, M., Tougas, A. M., & Helie, S. (2018). Factors associated with intellectual disabilities in maltreated children according to caseworkers in child protective services. *Children and Youth Services Review, 90*, 38–45.

Pittenger, S. L., Moore, K. E., Dworkin, E. R., Cnisto, C. A., & Connell, C. M. (2018). Risk and protective factors for alcohol, marijuana, and cocaine use among child welfare-involved youth. *Children and Youth Services Review, 95*, 88–94.

Prisco, R. (2015). Parental involvement in juvenile sex offender treatment: Requiring a role as informed supervisor. *Family Court Review, 53*(3), 487–503.

Pullmann, M. D., Jacobson, J., Parker, E., Cevasco, M., Uomoto, J. A., Putnam, B. J., … & Kerns, S. (2018). Tracing the pathway from mental health screening to services for children and youth in foster care. *Children and Youth Services Review, 89*, 340–354.

Putnam-Hornstein, E., Lery, B., Hoonhout, J., & Curry, S. (2017). A retrospective examination of child protection involvement among young adults accessing homelessness services. *American Journal of Community Psychology, 60*(1–2), 44–54.

Pyrooz, D. C., & Sweeten, G. (2015). Gang membership between ages 5 and 17 years in the United States. *Journal of Adolescent Health, 56*(4), 414–419.

Raby, C., & Jones, F. (2016). Identifying risks for male street gang affiliation: A systematic review and narrative synthesis. *Journal of Forensic Psychiatry & Psychology, 27*(5), 601–644.

Robinson, B. A. (2018). Child welfare systems and LGBTQ youth homelessness: Gender segregation, instability, and intersectionality. *Child Welfare, 96*(2), 29–45.

Roby, J. L., & Vincent, M. (2017). Federal and state responses to domestic minor sex trafficking: The evolution of policy. *Social Work, 62*(3), 201–209.

Rog, D. J., Henderson, K. A., Lunn, L. M., Greer, A. L., & Ellis, M. L. (2017). The Interplay Between Housing Stability and Child Separation: Implications for Practice and Policy. *American Journal of Community Psychology, 60*(1–2), 114–124. doi:10.1002/ajcp.12148

Ryan, E. P., & Otonichar, J. M. (2016). Juvenile sex offenders. *Current Psychiatry Reports, 18*(7).

Sainero, A., del Valle, J. F., Lopez, M., & Bravo, A. (2013). Exploring the specific needs of an understudied group: Children with intellectual disability in residential child care. *Children and Youth Services Review, 35*(9), 1393–1399.

Scannapieco, M., Painter, K. R., & Blau, G. (2018). A comparison of LGBTQ youth and heterosexual youth in the child welfare system: Mental health and substance abuse occurrence and outcomes. *Children and Youth Services Review, 91*, 39–46.

Slayter, E. M. (2016). Foster care outcomes for children with intellectual disability. *Intellectual and Developmental Disabilities, 54*(5), 299–315.

Slayter, E., & Kriz, K. (2015). Fear factors and their effects on child protection practice with undocumented immigrant families: :A lot of my families are scared and won't reach out," *Journal of Public Child Welfare, 9*(3), 299–321.

Sprang, G., & Cole, J. (2018). Familial sex trafficking of minors: Trafficking conditions, clinical presentation, and system involvement. *Journal of Family Violence, 33*(3), 185–195.

Sterling, R. W. (2015). Juvenile sex offender registration: An impermissible life sentence. *University of Chicago Law Review, 82*(1), 295–315.

Stewart, D. E. (2016). Mental health and human trafficking. *Epidemiology and Psychiatric Sciences, 25*(4), 342–344.

US Department of Justice. (2015). *About violent gangs*. Retrieved from https://www.justice.gov/criminal-ocgs/about-violent-gangs

Varma, S., Gillespie, S., McCracken, C., & Greenbaum, V. J. (2015). Characteristics of child commercial sexual exploitation and sex trafficking victims presenting for medical care in the United States. *Child Abuse & Neglect, 44*, 98–105.

Washburn, M., Good, M., Lucadamo, S., Weber, K., Bettencourt, B., & Dettlaff, A. J. (2018). Yes we can Allegheny: Implementing SOGIE inclusive system improvements in child welfare. *Child Welfare, 96*(2), 99–124.

Wilson, B. D. M., & Kastanis, A. A. (2015). Sexual and gender minority disproportionality and disparities in child welfare: A population-based study. *Children and Youth Services Review, 58*, 11–17.

Woods, J. B. (2018). Unaccompanied youth and private-public order failures. *Iowa Law Review, 103*(4), 1639–1709.

Yarnell, L. M., Traube, D. E., & Schrager, S. M. (2016). Brief report: Growth in polysubstance use among youth in the child welfare system. *Journal of Adolescence, 48*, 82–86.

Yoder, J., & Ruch, D. (2015). Youth who have sexually offended: Using strengths and rapport to engage families in treatment. *Journal of Child and Family Studies, 24*(9), 2521–2531.

CHAPTER 10

CHILD AND PARENT PERSPECTIVES ON FOSTER CARE

OVERVIEW

People become foster parents for a surprisingly small number of reasons that tend to fall into a handful of broad patterns: couples who are unable to have children of their own; empty nesters who want to do the whole parenting cycle again; those who want to do good in the world; and people interested in money, free labor, or other things besides the best interests of the children they take in. (Welch, 2018, p. 13)

Moving through the text, we have described various topics such as the presence of child abuse and neglect, the history of child protection in the United States, and risk assessment. We have explored the worker's experience in a number of different professional roles and also looked at the permanency options that guide practice and policy. In this chapter, we will review firsthand accounts from individuals involved in the foster care process, providing an inside look at what it may be like for those involved. We will examine the experience of children who enter foster care, hear about their perceptions, and learn about the kinds of problems they may encounter as they move from home of origin to out-of-home care. Keep in mind that a portion of children in foster care have mental health or behavioral issues that may result in their having multiple placements—we present some information about that, too. Then we will turn our attention to foster parents and who they are, what they experience in fostering a child, and their interactions with child welfare professionals. Lastly, we will offer some guidance to help the child welfare worker understand what the child in foster care may be thinking and feeling.

Children in Foster Care

For all intents and purposes, "foster care" means that the government is now the legal custodian of a child and is responsible for making decisions with regard to his or her care and treatment. The child has been temporarily removed from parental custody by court order and is now on the sometimes bumpy road to permanency. To be clear, this road presents a number of challenges.

Life for children in foster care is hard. They miss their families, their pets, and friends—almost everything familiar is gone. What is "normal" for abused and neglected children likely is very different from the homes that children from healthier families grew up in, and this affects their adjustment to new foster homes. Maltreatment is always damaging, and some children are injured much more than others. Their trauma can affect their behavior and adjustment in foster care and adoptive homes. We have not sugarcoated the issues that may arise but present an honest portrayal of what child welfare workers will likely encounter as they go about their investigations, case planning and management, and placement of these children in out-of-home care.

Government statistics show a slow but continual growth in the number of American children in foster care. The opioid epidemic is certainly a factor, as homes are broken and destroyed by addiction, but too few jobs paying a living wage is also a major contributor to poverty when not enough resources are divided by too many mouths to feed and clothe. No child should ever be chronically hungry. No child should ever be beaten or left alone for many hours or days at a time or disciplined in strange and bizarre ways. Children—especially those under the age of 12—should not have to be the principal caregiver for their siblings or adults in the family. Substance abuse, extreme poverty, mental illness, and physical and intellectual disability can all be associated with child neglect and abuse—leading to investigation, if not intervention, by a child protection agency.

According to the most recent report from the Administration on Children, Youth and Families (2017), 437,465 children were estimated to be in foster care in the United States. About a third were in a relative's home, 5% in a group home, 7% in an institution, 45% in a nonrelative foster home, 1% in supervised independent living, 5% in a trial home visit, 4% in a preadoptive home, and 1% in runaway status.

In terms of sociodemographics, slightly less than 10% were 17 or older, and about a third of all the children were 3 years of age or younger. The median age of those entering foster care in the federal fiscal year 2016 was 6.3 years; males constituted 52% of those in foster care. Less than half of the children (44%) were White, with almost equal percentages of African American (23%) or Hispanic (21%) children making up the next two largest groups.

As you will remember from Chapter 6, the federal government requires children unable to remain at home to be placed in the least restrictive setting that will optimize positive permanency outcomes. The Adoption and Safe Families Act of 1997 (Public Law 105–89) structures child protection agencies' **permanency plans** and sets deadlines. A permanency plan seeks to provide a safe, legally protected permanent home, allowing a stable living situation for children who have been placed in out-of-home care. The ASFA sets five options for permanency: (a) returning the child to his or her parent(s), (b) adoption, (c) referral for legal guardianship, (d) permanent placement (guardianship) with a qualified relative, and (e) other planned living arrangements. The ASFA was enacted to provide better protection of children by hopefully minimizing ambiguous situations where they could get "lost" in the system and to expedite their movement into permanent living situations.

For children who have been placed in foster care by the court, the initial permanency goal is to return the child back to his or her original home (**reunification**) if at all possible. This does not mean next week or immediately, as there are often conditions that have to be corrected first, and the ongoing worker will be involved with the family throughout this important process. Reunification is not always the best outcome for every child, but ASFA guidelines give parents an opportunity to address high-risk behaviors and work to get their child or children back. However, if they ignore the child protection agency's recommendations, don't take them seriously, or refuse to obtain treatment or services needed, then the ultimate consequence could be permanent legal separation of the child though the **termination of parental rights**. As described in Chapter 6, this permanency option is a last resort and only pursued when another least restrictive permanency alternative is unable to be attained (e.g., relative placement, etc.).

Of children exiting foster care nationally, the Children's Bureau (2015) data shows that 51% were reunified with parents or primary caretakers, 23% were adopted, 10% had a guardianship (usually with a kinship caregiver), 7% were approved for living with other relative(s), 2% were transferred to another agency, and 8% were **emancipated** (generally allowed to live independently). Thus, the vast majority of children exiting foster care are situated and supported within a home and are not left on their own.

Why Are Children in Foster Care?

There can be multiple reasons why a child ends up in foster care (see Table 10.1). The largest category associated with removal of children from their homes is neglect, followed by parental drug abuse. These categories should not be thought of as mutually exclusive. Several factors can be involved at the same time. In fact, having two or more co-occurring disorders or diseases is the definition of **comorbidity**. For instance, a caretaking parent can be abusing alcohol or drugs and also have a mental disorder like major depression or generalized anxiety disorder. Sometimes one set of problems will trigger other problems such as loss of one's job due to drug use which could lead to food insecurity and eviction from an apartment because of not paying rent which could lead to homelessness and so forth. A child could be both neglected and physically abused. While the categories in the table attempt to be neat and well-defined, in actuality they may at times overlap.

To take another example, while the data below show that only 8% of children going into foster care were removed because of parent or caretaker's incarceration, that figure probably best applies to a child living in a home with a single parent who is incarcerated. A recent nationally representative study of children ages 0 to 17 found that 40% of children in foster care experienced parental incarceration (Turney & Wildeman, 2017). Let's say that the father of the family goes to prison for selling drugs, but the mother, a user of illegal substances, is left behind to take care of small children. If the mother's problem comes to the attention of child protective services or if the mother is arrested several months later for selling drugs, stealing, or trading sex for drugs, then the children could be removed from the home because of parental incarceration.

All of the categories associated with child removal can be seen in Table 10.1.

Neglect of children is common when the family experiences poverty and there simply aren't enough resources (income, food, shelter, or clothing) to meet general needs. Poverty can follow from months of unemployment or too many mouths to feed on minimum wage employment. When there isn't enough food for children (e.g., the caretaker's inability to find a job), neglect is a possible finding—say, if neighbors have reported a concern that children are going door-to-door looking for something to eat. There is an expectation in our society that if adults don't have enough money for food and other necessities for their children, the adults will reach out to community agencies and do their best to try to obtain these resources. If a family is in severe need and the adult members don't know how or where to obtain help (e.g., parental intellectual disability), children can be deprived of meals—which constitutes neglect, even if the adult caretaker has been looking for a job. Adults with physical disabilities and in poor health may also have conditions that prevent them from cooking, cleaning, and adequately managing the care of children. These issues become compounded when transportation is very limited or unavailable to them (such as living in a rural area with no bus service).

TABLE 10.1 REASONS FOR A CHILD'S REMOVAL/CHILDREN ENTERING FOSTER CARE, FY 2016

Category	Number	Percentage*
Neglect	166,679	61%
Parental drug abuse	92,107	34%
Caretaker inability	37,857	14%
Physical abuse	33,671	12%
Child behavior problem	28,829	11%
Housing	27,871	10%
Parental incarceration	29,939	8%
Parental alcohol abuse	15,143	6%
Abandonment	12,889	5%
Sexual abuse	9,904	4%
Child's drug abuse	6,273	2%
Child's disability	4,554	2%
Relinquishment	2,694	1%
Parental death	2,212	1%
Child's alcohol abuse	1,242	0%

Note: *Percentages will total more than 100% since categories are not mutually exclusive.
Source: U.S. Department of Health and Human Services, "Circumstances Associated With Child's Removal," The AFCARS Report, pp. 2, 2016.

A child protection worker should always keep in mind that "normal" appearing situations, in which parents and families live in "good" neighborhoods and everyone is clean and well dressed, can be deceptive. Just because the parent or parents are "respectable" citizens going off to their jobs every day doesn't mean that they don't have behavior and actions that are harmful to children. Keep in mind that domestic violence occurs in middle-class and upper class homes, too. (Note that domestic violence is not a category listed in Table 10.1). Emotional abuse cannot be identified by bruises on the body. Further, skilled abusers may not leave marks where they would normally show. That is why it is best practice to talk to children first, and separately, as part of the assessment process.

Sometimes parents have adequate resources but don't have good parenting skills—for example, not knowing alternative ways of disciplining children besides harsh physical punishment. Maybe this is the way they were raised and is a learned behavior. Maybe they have an authoritative personality and subscribe to rigid discipline techniques. Unfortunately, these parents may sometimes have children with special needs (e.g., autism spectrum) and lack knowledge of appropriate ways for shaping the child's behavior positively.

Whether or not children have been formally diagnosed or identified as having special needs, many of them have accumulated many adverse childhood experiences (ACEs). They may have been neglected or mistreated by a former partner of their mother or father, a stepparent, or another relative. In other words, children may have been traumatized previously and unrelated to the current abuser living in the family—this situation also complicates assigning a category for the reason for removal of a child. In the Turney & Wildeman (2017) survey, children placed in or adopted from foster care had on average 2.5 ACEs (such as parental divorce or separation, death, incarceration, abuse, violence exposure, mental illness, or substance abuse) compared to 0.6 ACES for children who were not in foster care or adopted from foster care. Statistically, children placed in or adopted from foster care had approximately *4 times* more ACEs than children without foster care experience, even after controlling for the child's age, gender, race/ethnicity, low birth weight, and parent/caregiver relationship to the child.

The combinations of conditions and problems presented by families being investigated are too numerous to list. While some factors may predominate in many cases (e.g., a parent with control and anger management issues), such problems are amplified when there are other family issues, such as living in poverty, and when the child has a special condition or need. Sometimes trying to figure out what is going on in a family seems like trying to figure out a puzzle. Making a too quick decision or snap judgment about the "cause" of the mistreatment could well be the wrong thing to do.

PRACTICE TIP 10.1 Make the best decision you can with the information you have, follow policy and agency procedures, and if you are undecided, it is better to err on the side of keeping a child safe.

What Is Foster Care Like? Personal Accounts

If you were raised in a stable and loving home, some of the experiences and comments made by those who have lived a portion of their life in foster care may surprise if not disturb you. For instance, what do you think would be the most helpful thing about being in foster care? Here are some responses collected by Dunn, Culhane, and Taussig (2010, pp. 1324 and 1328):

- "Getting fed, bathed, not starving."
- "That they love us."
- "[They] make sure we are always clean."
- "I don't have to take care of my brother like I did before. I just have to take care of me."
- "Someone who cares for me."
- "Won't get abused again."
- "Don't have to live on the street [until my parents get out of jail]."
- "I don't have to be around bad things."

Despite the positive comments listed above, the literature on foster youths' overall satisfaction with foster care is not as extensive as we might like. Just over a decade ago, Fox and Berrick (2007) described the number of studies on children's experiences in out-of-home care as "a paucity of literature" (p. 24). Studies that are available, however, provide affirmative results. In face-to-face interviews with 100 children in foster care, Fox, Berrick, & Frasch (2008) reported that about half of the children "indicated their caregiver had talked to them at some time about their current home being a permanent home" (p. 75). In a follow-up question, 77% of the children responded that they would "want it to be their permanent home—the home where you will live until you're grown" (p. 76).

In a large study of 727 children who had been in out-of-home placement for at least 12 months, Chapman, Wall, and Barth (2004) reported that 90% of the foster children "liked" the people they were living with and felt like they were part of their foster family. Only about 11% had tried to leave their current placement. While there were no significant differences between the White and non-White children in terms of the closeness felt to their caregivers, those in kinship care felt that their caregiver cared for them more than children in the other type of placements.

Whiting and Lee (2003) found that most of the children in foster care described good experiences with their foster families. Wald, Carlsmith, and Leiderman (1998) found that a majority of those children living 2 years with foster caregivers described positive relationships. This does not mean, however, that moving from a family of origin to a foster family is without difficulties.

Dr. Jay Miller, the Dean of the College of Social Work at the University of Kentucky, has described his own personal experience of growing up in foster care because of a father with violent mood swings and domestic violence. Miller (2009) writes:

> I vividly recall the helplessness I felt as a child because of these countless incidents and felt that I should have been able to do more; yet, I found myself powerless to stop the abuse perpetrated against my mother. I distinctly remember making plans to harm my father so that he could no longer hurt my mother. (p. 91)
>
> When he was eight years old, Miller's mother died, leaving him with the abusive father who "succumbed to a substance abuse problem" (p. 91).

Shuttled between a number of relatives and family friends, he was interviewed one day at school by a social worker.

> I remember feeling overwhelmed with so much that I wanted to tell her. I wanted to tell her about the times when I sat at home scared and immobilized because I did not know where my father was or when he would return. I wanted to tell her about my father's angry mood swings that often precipitated violent behaviors, mostly directed at me. I wanted to tell her the stories of being shuffled between family members and friends and not knowing where I would stay from night to night. I wanted to tell her of the sacrifices that my grandmother had made in order to care for my sisters and me. I wanted to tell her. But I couldn't. Not because I didn't want to, but because I didn't know how. … I remember most vividly my feelings of hopelessness and helplessness as she walked out the door. I remember thinking that she must not really care. (Miller, 2009, p. 92)

After experiencing "several stints in out-of-home care" (Miller, 2009, p. 92), Miller was eventually adopted by his father's sister and her husband, and he went to live on a U.S. Army base in Germany. Not that he made it easy for them—he was acting out and getting into trouble, and he even got expelled from school during his junior year in high school.

> I was expelled for brandishing a weapon during a fight. To me, this expulsion seemed an opportune time for my "new" parents to send me back to the states. I expected them to give up on me; but they didn't. (Miller, 2009, p. 92)

He attended college on an athletic scholarship and graduated in 3½ years and took a position in child protective services. Having now completed two graduate degrees, he has gone on to become a very accomplished scholar, strong advocate for child welfare, and role model for other young people who didn't have smooth sailing early in life.

There are many other stories about children in foster care and "alums" that continue to inspire. When you get a chance, see the movie *Antoine Fisher*. This movie is based on the real story of a young man with a challenging childhood who spent time in an orphanage and multiple foster homes and was effectively "lost in the system" until joining the U.S. Navy. The movie is based on the autobiographical novel *Finding Fish*.

TEST YOURSELF

1. What is the most frequent reason for the removal of children from their homes?

2. What is the term used when a parent may have the two concerns—say, a mental illness and substance abuse?

Do not read below the dotted line until you are ready to see the answer.

----

1. Table 10.1 shows that the most frequent reason for removal is neglect.

2. The term used is *comorbid*.

What Kind of Problems Do Children and Teens Have in Transitioning into Foster Care?

A quote from a caseworker nicely explains why some, but not all, children can have difficulties transitioning from a not-so-great home to a foster care home:

> They [foster youth] go through a constant state of loss. They lose their families first. Then they often lose one foster family after another for lots of times, things that have nothing to do with them. And they lose their friends. They lose their school. They lose their neighborhood, their sense of who they are and where they belong. And it's just a series of losses until finally, I think a lot of kids just feel empty. (Geenen & Powers, 2007, p. 1093)

To start our thinking about children's experiences in foster care, imagine this situation: In your family of origin, your mother loves you deeply and you love her. Yes, well, she makes some bad decisions that you don't like, and sometimes you have to make sure she doesn't pass out before she takes her medicine. And sometimes you have to make meals for your younger brothers and sisters and get them ready for school. But isn't being loved better than being moved into a stranger's house? Would you worry what would happen with your mother? Would you ever see her again? And your brothers and sisters—where would they go?

About a third of children 9 to 11 years of age in Dunn et al.'s (2010) study indicated that being placed in out-of-home care was "very difficult." Why, you might wonder? Aren't they in a better place? What would improve the transitioning from an unstable family of origin home to a foster home? These children responded, predictably, that they missed their mothers, their families, and things about their old homes. To look closer at the data, children who had been emotionally or sexually abused were significantly more likely to say that their lives would have been worse when asked what their lives would have been like if they had stayed with their families of origin. Children who had been physically abused were significantly less likely to say that their lives would be "the same" in their biological families. Girls were more likely than boys to say that their lives would be worse.

Children who have grown up in chaotic environments may feel (but be unable to express) that at least they know how to survive in that kind of a culture. Not being the "adult" any longer who makes decisions for the household requires a lot of mental adjustment and a new set of rules to learn. And foster homes can have much more restrictive rules than the homes left behind. There can be expectations about making one's bed, helping clean the house, going to bed early, frequent bathing, and attending school—even regulations about what television programs can be watched. And speaking of schools, what student would want to run the gauntlet, so to speak, that might be required by changing schools? Having to make all new friends? Learning new teachers?

To add to the strains and stress of leaving one's home and moving to a new place, here are some other factors that can affect foster children. Mitchell and Kuczynski (2010) have written about foster children experiencing the following thoughts and feelings:

- Having little to no warning that they might be uprooted and placed in a different home. ("Yeah. It's like you're being kidnapped and nobody wants to tell you nottin.")
- Coming home from school and discovering their belongings had already been packed. ("I was like, 'Whoa! .. Who are these people?'")
- Not understanding the reason why they must go into foster care. Not understanding the implications of being "placed into care." ("Even though my parents didn't do right ... it doesn't mean I don't like them. But, like, it kinda feels like prison if you didn't get to see them.")
- Some children blame themselves for being placed in foster care. ("And we were dressed in old clothes. ... [My shirt] was like up to here, so it showed my stomach, and they weren't impressed with that so they took us away") (pp. 440–441).

It is natural for some children to blame themselves for being shuttled abruptly from the homes they know to new surroundings. Young children might expect the worst from foster parents and expect that these adults might also hurt them or their siblings. They also had very basic questions, like "Where will I sleep?" and "When will I go back?"

If they are the only child in the foster home, they will often feel lonely and miss the old home and what passed for the old routines. Mitchell and Kuczynski (2010) discuss the ambiguity that can arise in each child's mind. They say there is the ambiguity that results from not understanding the meaning of foster care, the reason for placement, the context of the new home, the people who live there, their characteristics and motivations, and the duration of the foster care placement.

Children with Multiple Placements in Foster Care

While the goal is always to provide a stable family life for children removed from their homes, it is unfortunate that many children will experience many different foster parents and homes. Even though federal guidelines require state child welfare agencies to count the number of placement moves, there is great variation in how a "move" is counted across agencies and states (Chambers et al., 2018). Specialized services like psychiatric hospitalization or time in juvenile detention may not be counted. Given that each move can mean the loss of important relationships, the number of placement moves that some children experience is concerning.

For instance, in one study, Waid, Kothari, Bank, and McBeath (2016) have reported in their large sample of children in foster care from a northwestern state that the range of prior placements was 0 to 22, with an average of 4. Taking a broader perspective, Bell and Romano (2017) identified 54 studies in examining permanency and safety for children in foster family and kinship care. From the data provided in their tables on a smaller set of studies, which specified the number of placements, an average can be computed of 2.5 placements. The number of placements for those in kinship care, as might be expected, was lower than that for children in foster family care. The Children's Bureau (2015) set a national standard of no more than 4.12 moves per 1,000 days in care.

In a study of children who had three or more family foster homes during an 18-month period, Koh, Rolock, Cross, and Eblen-Manning (2014) looked at 37 placements within the group who had multiple moves. They found that approximately half of the placements (19) were disrupted due to stressor or events in the foster parents' lives (7) but also due to allegations or complaints of mistreatment (12).

Placement instability can also be associated with problems that the traumatized children bring with them. In the Koh et al. (2014) study, almost one third of children in the multiple move group received a new psychiatric diagnosis, compared to 5% of children in the more stable group with fewer moves. And while Chambers et al. (2018) don't specifically identify mental health issues as contributing to the extremely high number of moves their foster care alumni experienced (30% with 2 to 9 moves, 25% with 10 to 16 moves, 27% with 17 to 26 moves, and 18% with 27 to 56 moves), it seems reasonable to suspect some behavioral or psychological difficulties might have contributed. However, the other complication with that study is that the participants in the study were contacted at a local drop-in center and a homeless shelter, and 40% of them had not completed high school, and two thirds were without employment—although all of these foster care alumni were at least 18. Perhaps some combination of prior trauma and frequency of moves created an emotional distance, making it difficult for others to engage and help the former foster child.

Emotionally shutting down can be heard in the excerpt from a young woman who attended different school districts. Amber, a 21-year-old African American with 23 placements, is quoted as saying, "Getting transcripts and just trying to finish high school … it was very difficult. After a while I said, 'f**k it'" (as cited in Chambers et al., 2018, p. 80). It can also be heard in this quote from Samuel, age 21, with African American and Latino heritage and 17 placements:

> Being moved back and forth, the people don't pay attention to what grade you're really in. … It really messed with me to the point where I was just like, "you know what? Screw school." … Because nobody really gave a f**k about me to keep me in a stable place. (as cited in Chambers et al., 2018, p. 80)

Emotionally shutting down may be more common in group homes and residential/treatment homes than in, say, kinship care foster homes.

Foster children who have multiple placements may have more trouble graduating from high school because changes in school districts could result in course credits that don't transfer, school records that get lost, or placement in a lower grade because of testing.

Whether or not they experience multiple placements, foster children face a number of educational challenges. Due to emotional disturbances or learning disabilities, estimates are that 30% to 50% of foster children are placed in special education programs; they are also more likely to repeat grades in school, have lower standardized test scores, have a greater number of disciplinary actions, and are more at risk for teen pregnancy and self-destructive and delinquent behaviors (a series of studies cited by Benbenishty, Siegel, & Astor, 2018). The authors go on to find in their own study that compared to the same-aged peers, teens in foster care reported "more victimization and discrimination-based harassment, weapons-use and gang involvement … feeling less safe at school, lower levels of belongingness, lower participation, and less adult support in school" (Benbenishty et al., 2018, p. 264). They were also more likely to skip school and cut class than their peers.

Foster Parents: Their Characteristics

Foster parents are recruited by both public and private child welfare agencies. Generally, foster parents have raised children or currently have children of their own. While it is not always known how successful they were as parents, many do come forward to be foster parents because they like children or have empathy for young children who have been mistreated. Approved foster parents receive financial subsidies to offset the costs associated with raising a child. These amounts differ by state and sometimes by counties within states. Here is a small sample of the rates paid per child in foster care each month.

Alabama: $460–$500	Illinois: $418–$511
Massachusetts: $674–$803	South Carolina: $322–$425

The actual amount of the subsidy depends on the age of the child (with older children getting more) and more is generally granted if the child has special needs (e.g., is medically frail). Oregon has a nice website that provides a good overview of its foster care rates: https://www.oregon.gov/DHS/CHILDREN/FOSTERPARENT/Pages/rates.aspx. And this website attempts to provide current information on each state's subsidies: https://wehavekids.com/adoption-fostering/What-does-being-a-foster-parent-really-pay. Individuals who are considering becoming a foster parent are advised that the monthly subsidy is not large enough to make a profit or "break even" on the costs of raising a child. If a child has a medical condition or special needs for therapy because of learning disabilities or behavioral issues, there may be a slightly larger stipend. States also differ on the frequency and amounts awarded for clothing allowances. Note also that foster children receive Medicaid, as well as free school meals—although they may not want to be associated with the stigma attached to getting their meals that way.

Almost half (45%) of children going into out-of-home care go into the homes of nonrelated foster parents, and about a third go into the homes of relatives (Children's Bureau, 2015). While family members may feel responsibility for children to whom they are related, who are the adults who open their homes to foster children?

Generally, they are middle-aged adults (mean age = 48) who are married (67%), employed (60%), have not attended college (60%), and already have two children in their homes. Slightly more foster parents are non-White (55%) than White (45%). They have cared for, on average, 6.5 children over slightly more than 5 years. For foster parents who were not married, the median length of foster parenting was 16 years, compared to 7 years for married couples. Similarly, unemployed foster parents provided child care longer (13 years), compared to the 7 years for those who were employed (Ahn, Greeno, Bright, Hartzel, & Reiman, 2017).

HOME STUDY REQUIREMENTS FOR PROSPECTIVE FOSTER PARENTS

What questions might someone interested in becoming a foster parent have? Several are listed below and you can find the answers to these and other questions in the website shown below. The publication answers these questions for each state:

- Who may apply to become a licensed foster care provider?
- What are the training requirements to become a foster parent?
- What are the minimum standards for foster homes?
- What is the approval process?
- What are the grounds for withholding approval?
- What is necessary for kinship adoption?

Source: https://www.childwelfare.gov/pubPDFs/homestudyreqs.pdf

Recruiting and replacing foster parents who exit the system is an ongoing and expensive proposition for child welfare agencies. So why do foster parents quit? Once again, Ahn and colleagues (2017) have provided some information. Fifty-eight percent of the foster parents indicated that their own life situations had changed. In some instances, they adopted a foster child or children (23%), moved, or had another change in their personal lives (30%). About 4% said they needed a break. Twenty-eight percent had problems with the agency: not being given enough support (9%), bad experience with a worker (8%), lack of response (6%), or not feeling appreciated (4.5%). Only 11% had problems with the foster children: bad experience with the child or children (6.5%), and not being given enough or correct information about the needs of the children (4.5%). Finally, about 2.5% of foster care providers indicated that foster parenting was not what they expected. Note that respondents could indicate more than one reason for exiting.

The authors found that foster parents with a college education exited sooner (after 5 years on average), compared to those with less than a college degree (11 years on average). The authors speculated that foster parents with more education might have discontinued because they had more demanding jobs that made foster parenting more of a burden.

Others have discussed the interest in fostering children in terms of intrinsic or extrinsic motivation. **Intrinsic motivations** are generally associated with feelings of empathy, altruism, and wanting to make a difference in a child's life. **Extrinsic motivation** is more often associated with external rewards, such as the reimbursement for foster parenting—which is not large by any means. However, there is an economy of scale such that taking three, four, or five foster children could provide enough of an incentive to attract some individuals. Certainly, not all foster parents are alike—and that is probably a good thing.

In an interesting article that looks at the phenomenon of 20% of foster families providing a disproportionately larger amount of foster caregiving than would be expected, Orme, Cherry, and Brown (2017) have speculated about what makes these caregivers foster more children, longer, and be more willing to take children with a variety of characteristics. They raise the possibility that this group of dedicated and resilient care providers might have somewhat different demographic characteristics (e.g., be composed of more stay-at-home moms, have more experience or knowledge of children, and likely have better social support systems). It is also possible that they are more resourceful in getting help when a child needs it or that they have had a better match with a child or children placed into their home.

While foster parents are involved in the decision as to whether to accept a placement, the children who are presented to them involve both the preferences of the foster parents as well as those of the case managers. However, it may be that the more experienced foster parents are more likely to receive the difficult cases, where children have behavioral and mental health issues, and it is possible that these parents could become burned out faster due to the 24/7 needs of the children.

What is abundantly clear is that the child welfare system needs to identify adults who have a good understanding of child development and parenting, whose own lives can tolerate the sometimes difficult behaviors of children who have been traumatized and lived in unpredictable and unstable chaotic environments. Foster parents must have realistic expectations and a certain level of grit to effectively navigate the ever-present challenges in this important role.

Foster Parents' Experiences

Foster parents will have rewarding experiences as well as nights when they go to bed crying to themselves because of trying situations within the home. Cooley, Thompson & Wojciak (2017) report one foster parent saying, "While it was a very stressful, emotional, and difficult job, it has also been extremely rewarding," and another claiming that it was "life-altering" (p. 38). Foster parents may learn that not every child wants to be adopted—despite the abuse in young lives, some children want nothing more than to return back home to live with their biological parents. These children can be angry and sullen about being removed. Lanigan & Burleson (2017) have also indicated some other things that foster parents will likely learn:

- "With each child it's different. So what worked for one child, didn't work for another."

- [for children with a history of trauma] "They may be four and five, but they're really emotionally two and a half to threeish on some things."
- [the foster home] "It's a lot more restrictive than their background experience they're used to. They aren't running around the neighborhood, hanging out, whatever. That's a change for usually all of them" (pp. 908–909).

Because foster children have often been neglected and left to their own devices, it can be expected that they will test the boundaries set by foster parents. Even children who have not been traumatized will do this to see how serious the foster parents are about the rules. You'll remember Jay Miller's account where he fully expected his adoptive parents to give up on him.

Traumatized children can arrive with **externalizing behaviors**, whereby they are physically violent or easily provoked and respond with violence or destructive behaviors. They can threaten and intimate others and can be viewed as disruptive or defiant (such as running away, underage drinking, drug use, etc.) Again, to cite Miller's (2009) published account, "But by the time I was 12, my delinquent behaviors, coupled with the resentment that I felt for my father, meant that I was far beyond my grandmother's control. I ran away several times during this period" (p. 92).

Other foster children express their problems more inwardly (**internalizing behaviors**) and are depressed, fearful, lonely, or anxious. They may have suicidal thoughts or actions and have other unusual behavioral problems, such as stealing, promiscuous behavior, or wanting to stay up all night and sleep during the daylight hours. If food sufficiency was an issue, hiding food in secret locations around the house may occur. These behaviors may seem odd at times. They have been called "survival skills" because they had practical value to the child in a different situation. When the behaviors are problematic, the foster parent(s) should attempt to understand the function that the behavior is serving (e.g., a need for security) and try to find other developmentally appropriate ways to channel the child's behavior.

Traumatized children can benefit from and may need mental health services. Even having loving foster parents or relatives may not be enough to offset their prior trauma, and that can frustrate caregivers who believed changes would come about more quickly. And imagine the shock to foster parents who agree to take a child only to later learn that the child's behavioral problems (e.g., prolonged temper tantrums, stealing, cutting behavior) were much worse than they expected.

Hosting children with externalizing or internalizing behaviors can certainly affect the lives of all those living within the home. Spouses may have different views about the extent of the disruption within their homes and whether it is "worth it." Arguments can arise about the best way to handle a child's behavior (e.g., refusal to eat, aggressiveness, etc.). Here's another set of foster parents describing their experiences, as reported by Lanigan and Burleson (2017):

- "You feel that when you take in a foster child that you're gonna help save them and that's not the way it's going to be."
- "They showed us what to expect, but they didn't really do any training on how to handle things."
- "Just setting up appointments … I think it just rocks your world, though. I work full time and put that as a priority. I'm calling and getting assessments and getting doctor's visits and most of these kids need counseling so I'm working on getting that started, physical therapy, speech therapies—all of the official therapies" (p. 910).

If the foster family has their own young children in the home, tensions can arise when biological children feel jealous of the time and attention the foster children receive. Understandably, they may not want to share their rooms, space, toys, and so forth with the newcomers. One parent described the negative influence on the foster family this way: "I felt like I had three [foster] kids that were just becoming amazing, they were blossoming … and then my two [biological] kids were just going downhill" (as cited in Lanigan & Burleson, 2017, p. 910).

Another issue that foster parents can have to deal with are the foster child's birth parents. Most of the time, their parental rights haven't been terminated, and they can consciously or unconsciously influence the foster child during visitations with the child or in phone conversations in a way that is not beneficial—such as making promises that are not kept, criticizing the foster family, or making false accusations about the character or motivations of the foster parents in an effort to build or continue loyalty to the birth parent(s). Here's a couple more foster parent expressions from the Lanigan and Burleson (2017) article:

- "You always see a huge step back. They're not leaving or coming home the way they left."
- "I really struggle with how I get questioned about my parenting [by the birth parent] and I have to answer to someone who just lost her kids" (p. 912).

Contrast the above two comments, which suggest frustration and possible conflict with things outside the foster parent's control, with the two excerpts from Welch's (2018) stories on foster care and adoption, which show how much the foster parent loved the children placed in her home:

- "Please don't let them take us back. Abby's voice takes on a childlike pleading and a shaky edge as she quotes the older girl."
- "You don't know heartbreak until you look into innocent blue eyes like that and say, 'I'm sorry; we did everything we could, but we can't keep you.' And they heard everything you said, but they're just babies, and they ask why you don't want them anymore; did they do something wrong?" (p. 17).

Foster parents often do become very attached to the children placed in their homes and think of them as their own children—but of course, they aren't. Here's another set of foster parents' comments from the Cooley et al. (2017) article:

One day we get a phone call and it was "well, I'm getting adopted with my siblings," and that was that. It was the end of our relationship. We weren't prepared for that at all (FP4). Another described an especially tough move: "for about a month I think my husband and I both cried. …" (p. 38)

TEST YOURSELF

Foster children may be depressed, anxious and fearful. Would this be considered internalizing or externalizing behaviors? Don't look below the dotted line until you are ready to see the answer.

Aggression and violence toward peers would be considered externalizing. Depression, anxiety, and fearfulness would be an examples of internalizing behaviors.

Foster Parents' Interactions with Child Welfare Professionals

Although there does not appear to be a great deal of information about the length of time foster parents serve in that capacity, the median length of time has been reported by Gibbs and Wildfire (2007) as being 8 to 14 months. Given the range of problems that can arise within foster care homes from providing out-of-home care, it is extremely important that child welfare case managers do everything in their ability to maintain quality foster care homes. Along this line, what can you do as a child welfare professional? Fortunately, Geiger, Piel and Julien-Chinn (2017) conducted a survey of foster parents that provides some great ideas for improving practice:

- 57% reported receiving return phone calls in a timely manner. *This percentage must be improved!*
- 60% were satisfied with their interactions with their child welfare case manager. *This percentage must be improved!*
- 67% felt that the agency valued their work with the children placed in their homes. *This percentage must be improved!*
- 74% of child welfare case managers communicated the permanency plan for the child. *This percentage can be improved.*
- 79% said they knew who to contact and had accurate contact information for when there was an emergency. *This percentage be can improved.*

Their report also contained these two comments from foster parents:

> My case manager is always on-time, calls me back immediately, gives me court reports, includes me in decision-making, invites me to court and other meetings, and I am aware of the permanency plan at all times. I feel as though it's been a blessing to have my case manager. (Geiger et al., 2017, p. 27)
>
> My current and last placement's involvement has been great. The caseworkers have held a meeting every single month and responded to emails and phone calls in a timely manner. They have been open and shared information about the case. They have been respectful, kind and appreciative toward me. (Geiger et al., 2017, pp. 27–28)

QUESTION FOR REFLECTION Which type of child welfare professional do you want to be? The type in the first set of bullet points who didn't return phone calls, didn't provide emergency contact information, or describe the permanency plan—or the type described in the last two quotes?

What is difficult for some foster parents to understand is that confidentiality limits the information that child welfare professionals can share with them. Sometimes foster parents can't know every detail about the child or the family because of litigation or jurisdiction in or involvement of different authorities across county or state lines. Frustration can arise when foster parents want to advocate for or adopt a child when it seems that nothing is happening with the case. And frustration can occur when the foster parents feel that their training is too superficial or "does not come close to being realistic or covering the experiences that you are going to have" (Cooley et al., 2017, p. 38). To be fair, it is not possible to prepare foster parents for every type of problem (or joy!) that they could experience with a foster child. This is one of the main reasons why foster parents are urged to join support groups or chat rooms, where they can meet and development relationships with other foster parents in order to benefit from their years of experience and wisdom.

Understanding Children in Foster Care

Whether you are a child protection investigator, child therapist, case manager, or adoption worker, keep in mind that children who have been mistreated will be anxious and fearful of saying too much—they will not want to make trouble for themselves. Consequently, they may be shy or hesitant to talk with you. This is not a reflection on you or who you are as a person. It is more a statement about who they are, a survivor of abuse or neglect, and where they are coming from—possibly a home where there was a great deal of physical violence, chaos, lack of organization, and lack of security.

Children might also not communicate well because they are depressed, feel hopeless, and believe there is nothing anyone can do to improve their situation. Trust is a big issue, and they may have learned from the adults in their lives that people cannot be trusted to do what they say. Remember that they have had many losses in their young lives. What they need from you is warmth, concern for their well-being, the patience to listen—no matter how many other clients or children you have scheduled to see that day. Don't pay more attention to your cell phone than to the child. Recognize that placement moves will be stressful. You will be a significant person in the lives of foster children; pay attention to what you are modeling for them.

Foster and adoptive families need support—not just the training they completed. Help them not to have overly idealized expectations about the child. Few children (foster or otherwise) are so well behaved that they never cause a problem. Foster parents need you to be available and especially to return calls when they experience a complication. Sometimes they will need information or a referral for services to address a problem in the home. At other times, they may just need to chat about the best approach to gaining a child's trust. They will need to be supported by their significant others, families, and friends. Encourage them to join support groups for foster parents or adoptive parents—even if it is only online participation.

Foster parents want to be part of the team. Don't overlook asking them for their ideas when making plans for the child. Acknowledge their successes and appreciate their efforts.

Remember to take care of yourself, too!

Main Points

This chapter has several goals. One, it refreshes our knowledge about why children may have been removed from their homes and placed in foster care. It goes into more detail about the reasons for removal. Perhaps more important than that, another goal is to help potential child protection professionals recognize that their perspective might not be shared by the children in foster care about the major problems within the child's former home or the "benefits" of foster care. Foster parents may have both positive and negative experiences with the children brought into their homes. As a CPS worker, you will need to be a good listener and mindful that your expectations about the foster care experience may not be shared by all parties.

- Adverse childhood experiences (ACEs) are powerfully detrimental to developing children and provide a strong rationale for some children being placed in out-of-home care.
- Children in out-of-home care may blame themselves, feel unhappy, or be depressed. They have experienced a series of losses with their parent(s) or caretaker(s), their familiar environment, school, friends, pets, even their beds and favorite places to play. They will not always be happy in a foster home and can be angry or depressed.
- Some children will experience multiple placements because of instability within the foster parent's home or a clash of personality styles. Disruptions can also occur due to their own psychological issues and behavior. These children can make the foster parents' experience unpleasant and result in a disruption.
- Foster parents can have different reasons for wanting to bring someone else's children into their own homes to raise. Some are altruistically motivated, and others may consider taking this responsibility to supplement their incomes.
- It is important for child protection professionals to recognize the stresses and problems that foster parents may have, to be available to them, and to respond quickly when contacted. Maintaining good foster parents is certainly easier than constantly trying to find new ones.

Questions for Class Discussion

1. As you read books, whether fictional (like Conroy's *Prince of Tides*) or biographies or autobiographies, how easy will it be now be to recognize adverse childhood experiences?

2. In terms of a first impression, what would suggest to you that a person might not make a good foster parent?

3. Mariscal, Akin, Lieberman, and Washington (2015, p. 115) have reproduced two great quotes from their study of foster care alumni. Consider the pros and cons of whether foster and adoptive parents need to know the specifics of everything the foster child has experienced. Discuss your opinion based on one of the two quotes below:

   a. "They [adoptive parents] need to have room for the child's baggage."
   b. "Get to know the kid, not the file."

4. Do the excerpts from young people who have spent significant time in foster care give you a good balanced idea of their experiences? If you have read stories or accounts from others who have written about their lives in foster care or adoption, are there similarities or differences with what you have learned in this chapter?

5. Based on your reading of this chapter, what do you think would be red flags for you if you were employed by a child welfare agency to assess prospective foster parents and their homes?

6. What were you surprised to read in this chapter? Why?

Self-Assessment for Personal Consideration

1. How comfortable would you be with evaluating potential *foster parents* based on what you think are important qualities?

   1   2   3   4   5   6   7   8   9   10

   Not comfortable   *Very comfortable*

2. How comfortable would you be in evaluating potential *adoptive parents* based on what you consider to be the important qualities?

   1   2   3   4   5   6   7   8   9   10

   Not comfortable   *Very comfortable*

Additional Resources

Augsberger, A. & Swenson, E. (2015). "My worker was there when it really mattered": Foster care youths' perceptions and experiences of their relationships with child welfare workers. *Families in Society*, 96, (4), 234–240.

Bell, T. & Romano, E. (2017). Permanency and safety among children in foster family and kinship care: A scoping review. *Trauma, Violence, & Abuse*, 18, 268–286.

Beam, C. (2013). *To the end of June: The intimate life of American foster care*. New York, NY: Houghton Mifflin Harcourt.

Harwick, R. M., Lindstrom, L., & Unruh, D. In their own words: Overcoming barriers during the transition to adulthood for youth with disabilities who experienced foster care. *Children and Youth Services Review, 73*, 338–346.

Hebert, C. G. & Kulkin, H. (2018). An investigation of foster parent training needs. *Child & Family Social Work, 23*, 256–263.

Moody, A. (2018). *The children money can buy: Stories from the frontlines of foster care and adoption.* New York, NY: Rowman & Littlefield.

National Foster Youth Institute. (n.d.). Youth blogs. Retrieved from https://www.nfyi.org/category/youth-blogs/

TEDx Talks. (2014, February 27). Rethinking foster care: Molly McGrath Tierney at TedxBaltimore 2014 [YouTube video]. Retrieved from https://www.youtube.com/watch?v=c15hy8dXSps

References

Administration on Children, Youth and Families. (2017). The AFCARS report. Retrieved from https://www.acf.hhs.gov/sites/default/files/cb/afcarsreport24.pdf

Ahn, H., Greeno, E. J., Bright, C. L., Hartzel, S., & Reiman, S. (2017). A survival analysis of the length of foster parenting duration and implications for recruitment and retention of foster parents. *Children and Youth Services Review, 79*, 478–484.

Bell, T. & Romano, E. (2017). Permanency and safety among children in foster family and kinship care: A scoping review. *Trauma, Violence & Abuse, 18* (3), 268–286.

Benbenishty, R., Siegel, A., & Astor, R. A. (2018). School-related experiences of adolescents in foster care: A comparison with their high-school peers. *American Journal of Orthopsychiatry, 88*(3), 261–268.

Chambers, R. M., Crutchfield, R. M., Willis, T. Y., Cuza, H. A., Otero, A., Harper, S. G. G., & Carmichael, H. (2018). "It's just not right to move a kid that many times": A qualitative study of how foster care alumni perceive placement moves. *Children and Youth Services Review, 86*, 76–83.

Chapman, M. V., Wall, A., & Barth, R. P. (2004). Children's voices: The perceptions of children in foster care. *American Journal of Orthopsychiatry, 74*(3), 293–304.

Children's Bureau. (2015). Final notice of statewide data indictors and national standards for Child and Family Services reviews executive summary—Amended May 13, 2015. Retrieved from https://www.acf.hhs.gov/sites/default/files/cb/round3_cfsr_executive_summary.pdf

Cooley, M. E., Thompson, H. M., & Wojciak, A. S. (2017). Risk, resilience, and complexity: Experiences of foster parents. *Children and Youth Services Review, 76*, 35–41.

Dunn, D. M., Culhane, S. E., & Taussig, H. N. (2010). Children's appraisals of their experiences in out-of-home care. *Children and Youth Services Review, 32*, 1324–1330.

Fox, A., & Berrick, J. D. (2007). A response to *no one ever asked us*: A review of children's experiences in out-of-home care. *Child and Adolescent Social Work Journal, 24*(1), 23–51.

Fox, A., Berrick, J. D., & Frasch, K. (2008). Safety, family, permanency, and child well-being: What we can learn from children. *Child Welfare, 87*(1), 63–90.

Geenen, S., & Powers, L. E. (2007). "Tomorrow is another problem": The experiences of youth in foster care during their transition into adulthood. *Children and Youth Services Review, 29*, 1085–1101.

Geiger, J. M., Piel, M. H., & Julien-Chinn, F. J. (2017). Improving relationships in child welfare practice: Perspectives of foster care providers. *Child & Adolescent Social Work Journal, 34*, 23–33.

Gibbs, D., & Wildfire, J. (2007). Length of service for foster parents: Using administrative data to understand retention. *Children and Youth Services Review, 29*, 588–599.

Koh, E., Rolock, N., Cross, T. P., & Eblen-Manning, J. (2014). What explains instability in foster care? Comparison of a matched sample of children with stable and unstable placements. *Children and Youth Services Review, 37*, 36–45.

Lanigan, J. D., & Burleson, E. (2017). Foster parents' perspectives regarding the transition of a new placement into their home: An exploratory study. *Journal of Child and Family Studies, 26*, 905–915.

Mariscal, E. S., Akin, B. A., Lieberman, A. A., & Washington, D. (2015). Exploring the path from foster care to stable and lasting adoption: Perceptions of foster care alumni. *Children and Youth Services Review, 55*, 111–120.

Miller, J. J. (2009). "I was in foster care, too": One social worker's journey from promise to practice. *Reflections: Narratives of Professional Helping, 15*(2), 90–94. Retrieved from https://reflectionsnarrativesofprofessionalhelping.org/index.php/Reflections/article/view/880

Mitchell, M. M., & Kuczynski, L. (2010). Does anyone know what is going on? Examining children's lived experience of the transition into foster care. *Children and Youth Services Review, 32*, 437–444.

Orme, J. G., Cherry, D. J., & Brown, J. D. (2017). Against all odds: Vital Few foster families. *Children and Youth Services Review, 79*, 584–593.

Turney, K., & Wildeman, C. (2017). Adverse childhood experiences among children placed in and adopted from foster care: Evidence from a nationally representative survey. *Child Abuse & Neglect, 64*, 117–129.

Waid, J., Kothari, B. H., Bank, L. & McBeath, B. (2016). Foster care placement change: The role of family dynamics and household composition. *Children and Youth Services Review, 68*, 44–50.

Wald, M. S., Carlsmith, J. M., & Leiderman, P. H. (1998). *Protecting abused and neglected children.* Stanford, CA: Stanford University Press.

Whiting, J. B., & Lee, R. E. III. (2003). Voices from the system: A qualitative study of foster children's stories. *Family Relations, 52*, 288–295.

Welch, W. (2018). *Fall or fly: The strangely hopeful story of foster care and adoption in Appalachia.* Athens: Ohio University Press.

CHAPTER 11

WORKING ON A CHILD PROTECTION TEAM

OVERVIEW

While almost everyone recognizes the importance of protecting children, fewer individuals actually choose it as a profession. It is tough and challenging work. What exactly is it like? The purpose of this chapter is to provide a glimpse into what it might be like to work on the front lines, investigating child abuse and neglect and providing ongoing services to alleviate its reoccurrence. These individuals operate on teams that are nested in communities and subject to a variety of legal mandates, policies, and contextual factors. In the case scenario below, Elizabeth receives a new allegation of maltreatment associated with one of her ongoing cases.

Elizabeth: The Case of Kristen

Monday morning. Elizabeth arrived 15 minutes early to her office, carrying her still warm coffee mug. She greeted the office assistant and waved at two other CPS workers who were also at their stations, then sat down. Placing her travel mug beside her computer, she typed in her password, knowing there would be a backlog of messages. As a specialist in working with families who have experienced child maltreatment, Elizabeth is an ongoing CPS worker. She provides consistent oversight through case management and service delivery to address prevailing high-risk behaviors and proactively minimize their reoccurrence.

Elizabeth was especially tired this morning; she had been up late the night before and involved with one of the families on her caseload. Although the identified concerns did not require immediate action on Sunday night, she knew the first priority on Monday would be to create a stable foundation for the family.

The third message Elizabeth received was a phone call from law enforcement about the Jones family. It was alleged that Kristen's mother's "friend," Shane, came by and began making unwanted advances toward Kristen while her mother, Janet, was in the kitchen. Only 29 years old, Kristen's mother has had a documented history of serial relationships and alcohol abuse, and she informed the officer that Shane was "my high school sweetheart and simply came by to visit." Janet stated that she was cooking dinner for about an hour but didn't hear or see anything inappropriate. After interviewing all parties in the household, Shane was arrested for lewd activity and placed in the county jail.

Elizabeth had been involved with the Jones family for more than 2 years. Initially opened because of the criminal child sexual abuse of 12-year-old Kristen Jones by her biological father, Elizabeth's recent involvement with the family had been focused on assuring stability through treatment and therapy. With Kristen's father serving a 10-year prison sentence, her mother has been compliant with services overall, but Elizabeth still had concerns about the mother's unstable parenting techniques and how it might have contributed to the trauma in Kristen's past.

Elizabeth's left hand clutched her stomach at the jitteriness she felt. This was not how she wanted her Monday morning to start. She leaned back in her chair, thinking what the next steps might be. There were many moving parts, and she was worried about a variety of factors. Decisions had to be made to best assure Kristen's long-term safety and stability. Was Janet truly unaware of Shane's inappropriate behavior? Or worse, did she notice it and allow it to continue? And what exactly was Shane's relationship with Janet? Although Shane was arrested, it would only be a matter of time until he was released. What would happen if he returned again to the house where Kristen and Janet lived? Was Janet capable of protecting Kristen? How safe was Kristen in this household? How would she, Elizabeth, as the ongoing caseworker, manage this home environment? At a minimum, Kristen and Janet would need to develop a written safety plan to remove all contact between Shane and Kristen until things could be sorted out a bit more.

Elizabeth took a deep breath and began to jot down some notes on a piece of scratch paper. What a way to start a week!

Elizabeth is a skilled ongoing child protection worker, an important part of a team designated with addressing and preventing child maltreatment. As an ongoing worker, Elizabeth could be responsible for overseeing cases of physical abuse, neglect, emotional abuse, and sexual abuse. Of course, some cases will involve children who have been subjected to more than one type of maltreatment.

What Is a Child Protection Team?

The child protection team is a diverse collection of individuals working together toward a common goal—preventing children from being harmed and improving families. Each professional brings his or her own educational background and worldview, which must be acknowledged and appreciated. Your colleagues might have an undergraduate degree in education or psychology, but often they will have degrees in social work. As seen in the following sidebar, more often than not, they will be female. They may have come from different geographical areas than you and may have somewhat different perspectives on issues such as how to prevent generational poverty and child abuse or what it takes to be a good parent. They can have different life experiences than you—perhaps military experience—or even have been in foster care themselves. They may know firsthand what it is like to grow up in a home where a parent has substance abuse issues or where there was domestic violence. Your coworkers may have been part of a large, warm, loving family or raised by single parents who struggled to provide their children with all their basic necessities.

MORE INFORMATION ABOUT THOSE WORKING IN CHILD PROTECTION

Barth, Lloyd, Christ, Chapman, and Dickinson (2008) have provided a national profile of the child welfare workforce by using data (n = 1,729) from the National Survey of Child and Adolescent Well-Being (NSCAW). The results of this unique study highlighted limited diversity with regard to gender and race, as the majority of the child welfare professionals involved in the study were female (81.1%) and White (67.0%). Related to education, only 39.5% had a degree in social work (BSW or MSW), and almost half (48.8%) had an undergraduate degree in another discipline. What else might you want to know about those working in CPS?

As a new CPS worker, you usually don't get to pick the individuals on the team that you are assigned to. And by a child welfare team, we are referring to the individuals in your local office who are formally aligned as a group to protect children. While your team members may have a common goal, they will have various personalities, backgrounds, and worldviews. There may be other unique differences based on the region or area where you are working.

Location matters, as child welfare agencies function quite differently across the country. The makeup of your team could be contingent on a variety of administrative structures and policies related to the location. Urban areas can have teams that are highly specialized. That is, one team may conduct child protective services investigations on behalf of allegations related only to sexual abuse. This specialty team would operate far differently than a team in a rural area that takes a generalist approach to child protection—where each individual worker on the team handles an ongoing caseload of families and also conducts investigations of any type of child maltreatment. Further, some rural areas use a generalist approach that combines both child and adult protective services. When you interview for a position with the agency, the agency's operational structure and the nature of your frontline practice should be made clear to you.

Beyond the diversity and individual characteristics found among the members of your particular child welfare team, each team or unit will have its own unique set of strengths. Think about successful athletic teams: Some have talented three-point shooters or quarterbacks who are exceptionally good at finding the open receiver. The same is true when working on a child welfare team. Teams within an agency usually are aware of not only their strengths but also the strengths of other teams. Specific team members may be consulted by other CPS workers or teams for a strategic way to approach a family, a judge, or a parent. Effective teams will use their strengths to help one another. At times, individuals on child protection teams may have spouses who are nurses or law enforcement officers. These individuals might be contacted informally to get a better idea of how to understand a problem. For instance, maybe a coworker has a family member who is involved in the local educational system. This person could be a helpful resource for a client needing to obtain a GED or a child needing testing because of special needs.

As a new worker, you will also benefit from seasoned workers on your team who share their wisdom and priceless practice guidance when there are difficult cases. This resource should be treasured and is key to the development of newly hired workers attempting to understand their positions.

Although each team will be different from every other because of the various individuals and backgrounds they bring, you will all be united in your purpose of attempting to help children and families who need external services to bring about stability and prevent any additional harm from taking place. Your group of child protection professionals will become a team—a small community of similarly focused individuals who will support you when you need help and may become as close as family in some instances. As a reminder, the interpersonal characteristics and competencies discussed in Chapter 5 (e.g., organization, attention to detail, strong communication skills, a positive attitude, a strong work ethic, being collaborative and patient, and being a good listener) are essential components that can help you to be fair and objective and to become and remain strong and effective child protection team member.

Supervision

With so many moving parts associated with the Jones family, Elizabeth felt like she was at a crossroads. The Jones family was her immediate priority, and Elizabeth expected she would have only a few minutes before the family walked into the building. However, she did not feel prepared to move forward with a plan. As an ongoing CPS specialist, Elizabeth was responsible for making decisions that influenced lives. It certainly helped when she understood a case enough to pinpoint exactly what people needed and how to maximize their cooperation—but that didn't always happen. Every decision had to be analyzed in terms of its risk and reward. After thinking for a few minutes, she knew she needed to seek guidance and direction from someone who had been there before. Luckily, she knew just the place to go. She reflected on her notes, grabbed a copy of the ongoing case plan, and walked to her supervisor's office to request time for a case consultation.

Elizabeth had an excellent supervisor named Tara, who had been in her shoes before. Tara was from the area, had an established professional network, and had been an ongoing CPS specialist before obtaining her supervisory position. Tara was a valuable resource, a mentor, and a confidant. After knocking on Tara's door, Elizabeth took a seat and began to discuss the dynamics associated with the Jones family with her supervisor, developing a plan to protect Kristen.

While states often divide their CPS services into different service regions or districts, frontline workers usually have little contact with administrators who oversee a region or direct services from a central location in the state. Generally speaking, local offices have their own supervisors and are detached from administrators in regional or centralized administrative units. **Frontline supervision** refers to an individual placed in the local office who is responsible for a team of child protective service workers. These supervisors oversee employees, provide consultation, assist in decision making, and are a critical component in service delivery. They have many administrative responsibilities, such as approving sick leave and vacation time, travel mileage, interviewing new staff members, and so forth.

It could be said that in many ways frontline supervisors are the linchpin in a CPS team serving to keep all the parts together. The reason for this is that supervisors manage all the workers in the office, while helping with all the key decisions and setting the work environment at the local office. They must ensure that the agency's policies and procedures are followed, monitor each worker's performance, and simultaneously support and undergird the workers. This includes serving as a resource regarding other services in the community that might be beneficial to the client (as well as necessary referral, and eligibility considerations) and being a psychological support when the worker encounters a particularly awful case of domestic violence or trauma to children. This function can include a simple debriefing (hearing the details of the encounter or case), consulting about possible diagnoses or motives, and ensuring that the worker is able to practice some self-care. Additionally, the local office supervisor may advocate for his or her workers when their caseloads are too high by reaching out to officials higher up in the chain of command for needed resources in that particular county or geographical area.

The local supervisor often is viewed both as a mentor and as a boss. The importance of quality supervision has long been found to be associated with job satisfaction and retention of frontline child protection workers. Truly, having a good supervisor is invaluable and makes for an efficient and well-functioning CPS team.

Management of the CPS team is directly influenced by the values and goals of each supervisor, but this is also subordinate to directives from the central administration. For instance, it might be a supervisor's wish to assist workers in offsetting the stresses they encountered by promoting time off for self-care. However, if there are staff vacancies because of budget limitations, it may be impossible to hire new staff, and with too few workers the result could be that it is difficult to get additional vacation time approved.

Or the supervisor might decide to improve team functioning by identifying a weekly schedule whereby one individual takes incoming investigations only on a certain prearranged weekday. An example could be that if you worked in a rural agency with a total of five workers on your team, you would only be responsible for receiving new investigations on Monday. This strategy would allow the members of the team to strategize their other responsibilities and be ready to answer calls, travel, and conduct interviews on this assigned date. Additionally, supervisors may work with their team to create flexible work schedules. For instance, if a colleague had specific responsibilities with child care, he or she could come to work an hour late to accommodate personal responsibilities. Such managerial practices can go a long way toward keeping team morale high. But at the same time, if there is a shortage of workers on the team, the supervisor may find it difficult to allow flex time or other considerations.

Supervisors are a "fount of knowledge." There are layers of laws and policies associated with working in public child welfare that as a new worker you will not know right away, and it will be the supervisor's role to help you learn these. CPS workers realize that it takes new employees a year or longer to learn all the nuances involved in understanding legal provisions, ways to engage and motivate difficult families, and when to require more from a family and when to back off. Seasoned workers will make statements like "it will take you 2 years to actually learn 80% of this job." Statements like these speak to the reality of the complexity of these positions and the need for supervisors.

Frontline supervisors combat the new worker's precarious lack of knowledge by providing consultation. This function is critical whether it is provided ad hoc (e.g., whenever the worker asks for it) or strategically delivered at a weekly scheduled supervision appointment. Either way, workers on the CPS team greatly benefit from this experience.

Imagine you have been assigned a case in which you are responsible for investigating a child fatality. It is expected that this type of tragic event will result in a comprehensive investigation and will take exponentially more time to complete with additional community contacts, consultations, and greater documentation. Consulting with and relying on the practice wisdom and knowledge of a knowledgeable supervisor can reduce your anxiety and aid in writing the final report on the case. While supervisors must be well-versed in agency policies and procedures, they are often able to pull from their vast practice wisdom and draw on their own prior cases. Supervisors almost always have been "in the trenches" themselves and know the problems that their workers face. When working on a child protection team, you will find that every case is a little different, with twists and unusual turns; supervisory consultations are expected, required, and terribly important. Remember the old expression that "two heads are better than one"?

Frontline supervisors on child protection teams truly develop a "culture" within the local office. One way or another, their actions set the tone. Having a personable and receptive supervisor who is supportive and who connects with his or her supervisees and vitally cares about their well-being creates a climate of two-way appreciation. That is, you will appreciate the time you get to spend with your supervisor. You will feel that your development as a child protection professional is growing. Your supervisor will value your dependability, the excellent job you do, and your dedication and will trust you to perform your job with fairness and objectivity.

When this positive office culture is in place, you will feel like your supervisor looks out for you and your best interest, and you will be glad to reciprocate—to help out and maybe take on extra assignments to eliminate a bottleneck in the agency. The saying comes to mind here from the military: "I have your back" is a good description of the ideal relationship between a CPS worker and his or her supervisor.

However, the opposite is also true. Like anyone else, supervisors can be overwhelmed with the stress associated with the responsibilities and liabilities that come with making key decisions and managing the work and health of their supervisees. They can snap at staff or be too curt or judgmental. If any unfairness is present within the office (e.g., some employees get easier cases or more time off, or any other special treatment), an unhealthy and unproductive culture can develop. But for the most part, the supervisors you will encounter will be dedicated, knowledgeable, and hardworking professionals. That does not mean they never make mistakes. Like everyone else, they are human.

Frontline supervisors continue to be an absolutely critical component of an effectively functioning CPS team. If your supervisor's leadership style clashes with your own personality, try to remember the tremendous responsibility on his or her shoulders. However, if you objectively assess your interactions and reactions and conclude that your place on that particular team is not a good fit, then it might make sense for you to inquire about your options and the possibility for transferring.

THE IMPACT OF SUPERVISION

As seen in the work of Barak, Travis, Pyun, and Xie in 2009, quality supervision is a critical component of working on an effective child protection team. Using a meta-analysis to examine the effects of supervision on the outcomes of 10,867 professionals in child welfare, mental health, and social work settings, the researchers examined 27 research articles published from 1990 to 2007. The results of this study showcased the significant benefits of having a responsive and effective supervisor. Supervisors who provide interpersonal interaction and emotional and social support can influence better employee job satisfaction, retention, and commitment. Also, quality supervisors can alleviate negative outcomes, such as burnout and job stress. Robust in the scientific literature, supervision is an intrinsic part of working on a child protection team.

TEST YOURSELF

Frontline supervisors are an essential ingredient in child protection, as their leadership and support are part of the glue that holds the local office together. Recognizing the necessity for this vital position, identify factors that you think might have a great impact on the child protection supervisor's job satisfaction and longevity.

In statewide study of frontline public child welfare supervisors, peer support and sense of accomplishment were identified as the highest ranking sources of job satisfaction on the Child Welfare Employee Feedback Scale. While they were dissatisfied with their salaries, dissatisfaction with administrative support and the negative impact of their workload were both significant predictors of their leaving the agency within the next 12 months. Agencies must seek strategies to support frontline supervisors, as their turnover is especially problematic.

More information can be found here:

Griffiths, A., Murphy, A., Desrosiers, P., Harper, W., & Royse, D. (in press). Factors influencing the turnover of frontline public child welfare supervisors. *Journal of Public Child Welfare*.

Making Referrals

After her supervisory consultation with Tara, Elizabeth realized that she needed to integrate comprehensive services for the Jones family. Although some services were already in place, the family was at a breaking point and had unmet needs. Tara suggested that Elizabeth connect Kristen with trauma-informed treatment options as soon as possible. If Kristen were able to access appropriate therapeutic treatment to address her past trauma, she might be able to live a healthier life later as an adult. However, there was a major barrier to accessing this very specific treatment option. For example, the Jones family lived in a rural area with only one community mental health center. Further, Janet's lack of financial resources and unreliable transportation made it difficult to legitimately consider better options outside the local area. In spite of this, the strategy was clear. Elizabeth was determined to make sure that Kristen's needs were met, and she began to consider avenues for making this a reality.

In this case we are reminded that a referral (the reception of a formal report alleging the maltreatment of a child) can originate from community partners (e.g., law enforcement). This happens when the CPS agency receives an allegation of possible maltreatment, accepts it, and assigns it to the investigator for action. Similarly, here we use the word **referral** to describe the process of the child protection worker directing a client to a specialist in the community for services. A referral can be part of a treatment plan (a strategy for improving a situation for a client or family) as well as an activity or process. Ongoing child protection workers make referrals to obtain specialized support or services for their clients outside of the CPS agency. For example, an ongoing caseworker or supervisor might use language such as "Elizabeth will be making a referral for parenting classes for the Jones family." Evident in this statement is the focus on a *strategy* to align a community resource to fulfill a client's specific unmet need. However, for the Jones family to actually engage in parenting classes, a process (activity) was required to arrange for these services. This section will explain both aspects of making a referral in this section.

Referrals as Part of a Case Plan Strategy

As recognized in the Jones scenario, making a referral is for the purpose of obtaining services to address a problem (often a deficiency). As a professional member of a child protection team, it is your duty to help clients secure meaningful and appropriate services for their needs. Often referred to as **case management**, this integral skill is the backbone of ongoing services (as described in Chapter 5). For instance, some impoverished families may never have applied for food stamps, which is a strategy that could quickly improve the level of nutrition available to children. Depending on where the CPS agency is housed, it could share a facility with support entities such as a food stamp office or other government assistance programs. A knowledge of where to go and who to contact with community resources like this can quickly benefit your clients. You will soon learn whether it is best to accompany your client on these visits or whether it is something the client can do on his or her own. These are considered informal types of referrals.

More "formal" referrals can be made to obtain assistance from specialized resources. In the aforementioned situation, Elizabeth worked to obtain specialized trauma-informed therapeutic services for Kristen. In order to formally refer her to this program, an effective worker would need to have a working knowledge of the accessible resources in the local area, their cost, length, contact information, and exactly what it would take to begin services. The CPS professional might make the appointment in a formal referral or accompany the client to the agency.

> **PRACTICE TIP 11.1** Best practice always involves presenting your client with options and creating a climate of investment, empowerment, and self-determination. However, barriers to access may influence the receipt of these services. Making a formal external referral involves a process, and some referrals are much more labor intensive than others.

Making a Referral as a Process

When seeking external help from an agency for a specific service, the amount of effort associated with this task can best be described as a continuum. On one end of the spectrum is the informal type of referral that requires little of the caseworker's time and energy. This might involve giving a client a phone number and/or providing him or her with directions to an agency. A couple of examples of quick external referrals could be acquainting a family with a local food bank or free clothes closet and providing phone numbers so that a parent who didn't finish high school could acquire information about completing a GED program. Although these referrals are rather simple and may only involve brief paperwork and limited time on behalf of the CPS worker, these could be valuable resources that could begin to improve a family's situation.

Toward the middle of this spectrum would be helping a client begin a treatment program—perhaps anger management or a batterer intervention program. The CPS worker might be asked to provide (with an appropriate release from the client) a copy of the court order and possibly a current copy of the case plan to ensure that appropriate services were provided. This example would include an especially heightened focus on confidentiality for those involved, assuring compliance with legal mandates. For instance, the intervention program may need to know if there are court orders limiting contact between individuals within the same family structure.

On the far end of the spectrum would be highly specialized and comprehensive services that may be limited in quantity or availability. This type of formal referral would possibly include a variety of records, court orders, case plans, and other documentation with proper release. Another complication is that these highly sought-after programs with limited slots for new clients may have wait lists of several months before services can begin. A CPS worker's role might involve advocating in an emergency or extreme case to see if the client could be seen quicker—in a sense, making sure the other agency is aware of the necessity for urgent services.

An example of this type of scenario would involve a family who has had their child in foster care for a period of time. The CPS worker will need to prepare information for the child's permanency review, resulting in the court's decision to either maintain the current permanency goal of reunification or possibly consider seeking the termination of parental rights and adoption. When families are in this position, the court may request professional feedback about the outlook for potential family reunification through a comprehensive assessment of the family's attachment and parent–child bonds. Unfortunately, highly specialized services of this sort are often located in urban areas and are in limited supply and high demand. Their lack of availability for families in rural communities or regions can be a major barrier to the "ideal" set of services needed to best assist families. However, there may be other professionals in the community who can be brought in to consult.

CPS workers might also want to discuss with their supervisors or even seasoned coworkers about the best therapists or physicians to evaluate a parent's recovery from substance abuse or compliance with needed medications.

While the amount of effort required of the child protection worker to complete a referral varies quite a bit, the importance of engaging in this process is not to be minimized. Although it takes a small amount of energy to make a phone call, say, to a food bank, that simple act may can keep children healthy and allow families to begin to stabilize and start a process toward long-term improvement. Addressing other problems—such as completing high school, obtaining better housing, or getting help for medical or psychiatric issues—could also result in needed improvement of a family's well-being and ability to stay together without the reoccurrence of high-risk behaviors.

Collaboration with Community Partners

You should expect that wherever you are employed in child protection, the same social issues are going to present themselves again and again. There will be families with such insufficient income that they don't have enough to eat or their housing is problematic, either because they don't have money to pay utility bills or the conditions are deplorable (e.g., broken windows, lack of indoor plumbing or running water, or features making it unsafe for children to live there). Lack of transportation may be a difficulty. There will be families in which a parent or other family member has a mental illness that presents a threat to the children or other family members, as well as families in which a parent is physically violent and terrorizes or harms others. Families with substance abuse issues will always be a part of the caseload. Some families you will encounter will experience homelessness, sleeping in their cars, "squatting" in homes that are abandoned, or living in makeshift shelters. Alternatively, there will be families that have adequate or good income and live in nice homes but in which there is emotional abuse, domestic violence, or secret sexual abuse.

Knowing that you will encounter these problems makes it important to learn, know, and possibly cultivate community partners to assist your families and address their problems. **Community partners** can refer to psychotherapists, educators, employers, medical providers, rehabilitative professionals, and a variety of additional individuals focused on providing services to ameliorate certain conditions. Community partners can also be agencies that specialize in concrete services (e.g., public transportation, financial assistance, etc.). It is possible that your local office will have a resource guide that identifies the available services in your region. However, information and policies can change frequently. Based on funding, community need, and other prevailing factors, it is important to keep such information updated so that you will be able to respond as rapidly as necessary when engaging with families that are in need of certain services.

PRACTICE TIP 11.2 You may want to keep your own personal file of essential agency information and contacts.

Of critical importance for a referral are the purpose of the agency, their hours of operation, contact information, cost, length of treatment, and provided treatment modalities. Also, it may be helpful to know if this program is approved by the court. Developing a knowledge and understanding of these resources will not only help you become more effective when working with clients but will also assist you in developing relationships with your community partners, who can be your *best friend* when moving cases forward.

You should know if there is an inpatient rehabilitation facility within commuting distance that would be accessible for your clients. Or are there barriers (e.g., eligibility requirements) for obtaining the services? How long would the client be in treatment? And if the single parent needs inpatient rehabilitation, will children have to be placed in foster care during their parent's stay in the facility? How will this influence the goal of family reunification? What is the cost, and who pays for the service? These are examples of questions the CPS professional will surely want to ask in the process of making a referral to a community partner and discussing the case with a supervisor.

The point is, frontline child protection professionals need to know the details about social and rehabilitative services available in their area. The best way to do that is to build legitimate professional relationships with key

Figure 11.1

individuals who are working in these capacities. Engaging in gestures of thankfulness are vital, as it is reasonable to think that community partners (e.g., therapists, law enforcement, court personnel, etc.) may feel unappreciated at times. Gathering your team to bake cookies during the holidays for the especially helpful professionals who have assisted with difficult cases or sending out thank-you notes is a way to cement positive relationships.

Make no mistake about it, building solid relationships with key community partners will make your job much easier as a frontline worker. It's all about saving time and being efficient. With established relationships, it is not difficult to ask for and receive help. If you go the extra mile and have a good working relationship with someone at the community mental health agency, for example, you may be able to bypass some frustrating minutia on a Friday afternoon at closing time. In today's professional world, individuals move from agency to agency, and any effort made to develop a positive working professional relationship with an influential person at the local service agency will surely pay off for years to come as a member of a CPS team.

Working with District and Prosecuting Attorneys

Elizabeth contacted the premier trauma-informed sexual recovery center in the state to try to arrange treatment for Kristen. The facility was known to have a good reputation for positive outcomes with traumatized children but also to be in high demand, so it could be difficult to obtain a placement for Kristen there. It was an ambitious goal—especially since the center was 3 hours away, but Elizabeth knew she had to try before settling for a program with a more mediocre record of success with its clients.

Elizabeth knew that this program was expensive and that Kristen's support system would need to be on board to make this happen. Elizabeth met with Janet Jones to obtain her commitment to this strategy. Given that the case was already involved in the court system, Elizabeth believed the appropriate avenue for obtaining the necessary support would be to make a professional recommendation in court for this specialized treatment.

This required Elizabeth to make a phone call to Kristen's GAL. Assigned by the court, the GAL's function is to represent the best interests of the child. The GAL was in agreement, and Elizabeth worked with the county attorney to have the case put on the docket for review. Because Elizabeth had a good professional relationship with court personnel, the hearing would be expedited. Elizabeth needed to work quickly to complete and disseminate her report with detailed recommendations before the hearing.

GUARDIAN AD LITEM

The United Nations Convention on the Rights of the Child (1989) stated that children should be involved in decisions regarding their welfare. Further, if they are capable, they should have an opportunity to participate in relevant judicial or administrative proceedings. Bridging the gap between this philosophy and its implementation is the guardian ad litem, or GAL. Similar to a public defender, this individual may be appointed by the court but acts as an independent representative for the child. The GAL may be a seasoned attorney who has a passion for serving children. He or she may be fresh out of law school and interested in building professional experience. The GAL will be involved throughout a case and will often work to build a relationship with the child, interview the child's family, and speak with therapists and other members of the community to best represent the interests of the child. The GAL's involvement is the primary vehicle for delivering the voice of the child, and the GAL is free and clear from any obligation to prioritize the interest of any other parties.

As an outsider, the GAL is not subject to following the same policies that you will be as a child protective services worker. This important bit of knowledge can be very valuable in court, and here is why. Imagine a hypothetical family you have been working with and it becomes clear that the court is preparing to consider a placement in foster care. You know that the child has an "uncle" that isn't actually related, but is appropriate, safe, and willing and able to meet the child's needs long term and keep the child from moving into foster care (discussed as fictive kin in Chapter 6). The issue is that the "uncle" isn't actually related to the child, and you have policies at your agency hindering your ability to make this formal recommendation. The child has known this person for many years, and the family is requesting this placement if it gets to that point. Although you cannot violate policy or statue, the GAL can bypass these circumstances and directly recommend this placement if he or she feels it is in the child's best interest. This situation isn't too unusual, as you will learn that children have connections with coaches, church members, and others in the community who could provide an avenue to keep them out of foster care and remain in the comfort of their local area if appropriate. Although a child may need to be placed outside of a community, there are often many reasons for keeping the child closer to his or her home. For further information on the topic, you may wish to read the following:

Donnelly, C. (2010). Reflections of a guardian ad litem on the participation of looked-after children in public law proceedings. *Child Care in Practice, 16*(2), 181–193.

Mabry, C. R. (2013). Guardians ad litem: Should the child's best interests advocate give more credence to the child's best wishes in custody cases? *American Journal of Family Law, 27*(3), 172–188.

Although your job title may be "caseworker," "social services worker," "investigator," "child and family specialist," "case manager," or any number of other descriptors, you will never be able to forget that you are involved in the protection of children. You likely will not be paid commensurate with the importance of your job; however, your position holds a certain amount of authority, and the legal system will respect and honor it. This perception also extends to interaction with other professionals and community partners, but CPS workers often must engage and work with family members who are uncooperative and want nothing to do with the worker or the CPS agency.

Broadly speaking, child protective services are often involuntary. They are directed by state statute and implemented beyond the client's control. As described in Chapter 4, the child protective services investigator has the legal authority to access individuals' information and to take steps to protect vulnerable populations. Technically speaking, a client has the "right" to refuse to comply, but there may be significant consequences associated with this decision (e.g., court involvement). After an investigation and substantiation of child maltreatment, the ongoing work is also influenced by this power difference in the CPS professional's favor.

Going back to Kristen's family, let's say that the court was concerned about Janet's past history of alcohol abuse and ordered her to complete a substance abuse assessment. Janet can either comply with the court order or choose to face the consequences of refusal. While it may seem like not much of a decision, many individuals refuse to go the additional step and seek rehabilitation services on their own—a service that would possibly be mandated for parents with alcohol or substance abuse issues. Requiring involuntary services may seem to go against social work values, but they are often necessary for protecting vulnerable populations. As a CPS worker, you will be working with clients who are troubled by addiction or other difficult problems and have little self-determination. With this type of client or family, the goal will always be focused on long-term safety and stability. The CPS worker must ask himself or herself: Is the family genuinely addressing the high-risk behaviors, or is this dynamic merely creating short-term compliance to rid the agency from their lives? Successfully working in child protection requires the understanding that some families need extra help and possibly involuntary services. Involvement with the local court system is one of the most integral relationships in child protective services to ensure that some families receive needed services.

Different states and regions have different models for court procedures involving the protection of children. As mentioned earlier in this book, in some areas child protective services cases are funneled through a family court model, and in some other areas this interaction will be through a district court or possibly other courts with different names. Hearings such as the termination of parental rights may happen in circuit court. (For a quick refresher, you might want to refer to the Child Welfare Information Gateway—particularly this page: https://www.childwelfare.gov/pubs/factsheets/cwandcourts/.)

It is important for the child protective services practitioner to remain clear that civil court and criminal court are two separate entities. As discussed in previous chapters, there are different levels of "evidence" that are required for each. Keep in mind that not all allegations of child abuse (civil court) address criminal charges, which must be brought to a criminal court. As a reminder from Chapter 4, a *preponderance of evidence* may be all that is needed to meet the state's statute for substantiating an investigation of child neglect, but a criminal finding of child abuse would require evidence that is *beyond a reasonable doubt.* You will need to understand the workings of the court system in your state or municipality. This may feel a little intimidating initially (after all, you didn't decide to be a lawyer), but it will be part of your orientation to your position. It is also good to remember that until you are familiar with the legal procedures, your coworkers and supervisor will be available to help you.

With respect to the operational structure of the court system, the court clerk is a key individual in this process. Often the clerk will assist the CPS worker in filing paperwork to put motions on the docket (to get the case and its recommendations on the court's schedule) or file petitions to be heard by the court. The clerk can help you obtain copies of court orders in a timely fashion that are important when making referrals, placing children in school, receiving medical treatment, or for a variety of other important circumstances. Do anything possible to build and maintain this relationship.

The prosecuting attorney, possibly known as the district or county attorney, will be working with you as you move forward to file court petitions or seek to place a case on the docket for review. Getting to know the local GAL is helpful because this individual can be the biggest advocate for the child in the courtroom. The GAL is paid to serve the child's best interest and is not obligated to comply with the same policies that you are as a CPS worker.

At the local level, judges are elected to their courts. Typically, these are lawyers who are well known in the community because they have been practicing law for a number of years. However, it is difficult to estimate how much any one judge may know about substance abuse, mental illness, intellectual disability, and the dynamics underlying domestic violence and child abuse/neglect. Judges who are new to their positions may be open to learning from CPS about the rationales behind certain recommendations. Other judges may not understand that individuals suffering from drug addiction have very little "free will" or volition and maybe unable to make rational decision as long as they are using harmful substances. Judges, just like others, can have biases and beliefs that affect their decisions. For instance, some judges may believe that a child is almost always better off with the mother than with the father. Or they may be unconsciously class oriented and give more breaks to a parent of substantial means than to a working-class parent. Sometimes you may not agree with the decisions that judges make.

PRACTICE TIP 11.3 To build good relationships with the court system, always be respectful and professional in spite of any challenges from defense attorneys, angry parents, or even skeptical judges. You may encounter the judges and attorneys on other occasions, and it is best to keep in mind that their comments have little to do with liking or disliking you as a person. In trying to understand a particular circumstance or evidence, there can be alternate interpretations. Remember the expression "Every coin has two sides." Defense attorneys will attempt to present their clients' motivations or actions in the best possible light.

Relationships with lawyers and professionals serving in the legal arena may be strained at times—especially if you need to go against the testimony of another professional. For example, a wealthy father accused of physically and emotionally abusing his young son might bring his own witness, perhaps even a physician, as an "expert witness" to testify that the child has *not* been irreparably harmed—that the physical abuse he received was no worse than his playing Pop Warner football. Realizing the client's defensive strategy and not taking biased opinions or criticisms personally is important, as it is to answer all of the judge's questions completely and respectfully—even if he or she questions your conclusions.

Also, make sure to provide all relevant parties with clear and detailed copies of your court reports in a timely fashion. If at all possible, you want to prepare well and anticipate questions that could arise. You do not want to be surprised by questions about the recommendation you are making in a court report. Also, best practice is to give each individual with an active role in helping determine the outcome of the case all of the information needed to make the best decision for the child's best interest. Rightfully so, individuals involved in this process can become frustrated with a CPS professional who does not provide them with all the necessary information in a timely manner. Spell-check and proofread your reports. They need to look like they were prepared by a professional rather than by a teenager preoccupied with social media. Court involvement is at times the only avenue to advocate for vulnerable children and to hold individuals accountable.

Finally, despite hurtful and egregious acts, every person is entitled to a fair trial and to representation in court. Despite your best efforts, a judge may not decide to rule against a parent you strongly feel has harmed a child and may continue to threaten that child's well-being. On such days, you should consider practicing some self-care (see Chapter 12), ventilating with your team members, and debriefing with your supervisor.

Bureaucracy and Red Tape

Elizabeth obtained the necessary external support to obtain a placement for Kristen at the state's premier sexual recovery facility. She worked hard to "sell" the program to Kristen, who slowly warmed to the idea. As Elizabeth began to finalize the plan, a problem arose. She received a phone call from the agency's central administration advising that they could not approve Kristen's services at this facility, as it would violate policy. That is, the agency's contract with this specific treatment program had recently expired. Although the contract would likely be renewed at some point in the future, Kristen could not receive services until the contract was approved at all levels of the state's bureaucratic structure. Elizabeth felt sick to her stomach. She knew that the facility only had one bed available and was only saving it for Kristen for up to 24 hours.

Elizabeth had successfully obtained a specific court order supporting Kristen's placement at this specialized treatment program, and her own agency threw a wrench into the plans. This was not the first time that Elizabeth had experienced this type of drama. Some of her team members called it "hurry up and wait." Unfortunately, this expired contract could possibly result in Kristen losing an opportunity to obtain specialized services from those who best knew how to help her. Attempting to refocus, Elizabeth put the phone down and left her building, taking a 5-minute walk to decompress and consider how she could work around this apparent dilemma.

To revise Gertrude Stein's line, "a system, is a system, is a system." CPS agencies function differently across the country, but there are similarities in all large bureaucracies. Rather than get into the nuances of how states and agencies do things differently, it is important to realize that all child welfare systems involve layers of red tape. These agencies have their own policies that are rooted in state statutory laws designed to protect vulnerable children. Further, involuntary services provide a layer of relevant court orders. Additionally, federal law such as the Adoption and Safe Families Act guides practice and provides timelines related to family reunification. Occasionally, agency policies and procedures can slow up or completely stop the forward progress of a worker's case. However, it is good to remember that these bureaucratic layers function to protect CPS workers, too.

Even in cases such as Kristen's, there are many issues for child protection professionals. For instance, suppose that one of Kristen's siblings did see Shane expose himself to Kristen but didn't reveal that information until after Shane got out of jail. What if Janet Jones actually had a more substantial relationship with Shane and they decided to get married? What if Kristen ran away from home and was later found in a motel with a 54-year-old man who befriended her on Facebook? What happens if Janet's alcohol use led to an overdose of prescription medication and the EMTs arrived barely in time to save her life?

All of this is to say that even if there had been no glitch in getting Kristen into treatment, a CPS professional could still have a great deal more involvement with the Jones family—even with consistent oversight by the CPS worker and the support of everyone associated with the case. There is likely to be another court appointment, new court orders, the need to negotiate a new case plan, and a variety of other actions that take time and effort to make this possible. The good news is that once you develop a knowledge of how this process works, you can become more efficient in assembling all the pieces and effectively facilitating services.

In a bureaucratic environment, it often feels that progress comes very slowly. Often, significant documentation and multiple levels of approval are needed to move a case forward even a little bit. To successfully navigate the system, it is important to have a keen awareness of this context and to learn how things work. There is also a code of conduct, so to speak, that should be understood. Specifically, everyone in a bureaucracy has a supervisor. This hierarchical structure must be respected, and following the chain of command is critical. Going above a supervisor's head (not following the chain of command) even for a simple and well-intended reason could be consequential. For example, if you sent an e-mail to request guidance from your regional specialist about an investigation without following protocol and consulting with your immediate supervisor first, it may give the appearance that you are unwilling to seek local consultation or that your supervisor is not competent to provide that consultation. Perception matters. Breaking the chain of command, without an adequate and defensible reason, could result in poor performance evaluations or even a damaged professional reputation.

On a positive note, bureaucracies often have specialized units for a variety of tasks that CPS workers should utilize. If Kristen were to enter foster care, many agencies have an independent living coordinator (as seen in Chapter 6) who works with foster children of a certain age to teach them life skills to prepare them for their future (e.g., laundry, doing the dishes, balancing a checkbook, etc.). Reaching out to this professional for timely support would be meaningful for the adolescent's development and future independence. Although there are significant frustrations related to the "hurry up and wait" mentality of working in a bureaucracy, stay focused on the positive. Recognize and use support systems that are in place, and learn how to be effective in navigating your cases through the required paperwork.

Public Perception of Child Protection

A final topic of discussion related to working on a child protective services team has to do with the public perception associated with this work. What the public thinks about you and your agency is important, but a few factors must be kept in mind. By its nature, child protective service workers deal with troubling and disturbing human behavior. You will likely have to deal with unsavory individuals at unusual hours and to go places where you would rather not be. You may even be somewhat traumatized by what you learn about a child's experience. But the types of trauma that you may need to respond to—even in the middle of the night—are often kept out of the public's sight. CPS workers are involved with highly confidential and sensitive information that may never become public, and you won't be able to explain or defend your actions or recommendations to anyone outside of those directly involved with the case.

Given this context, the public's perception of child protection really depends on who you ask. Most people in the community may know very little about your role, although they may have heard that you are a "baby snatcher." The media often portrays social workers (and specifically child protective service workers) in a negative light with this stereotype. Just so you are clear, it is the court order from a judge that results in the removal of a child, not the wishes or cavalier decision of an individual CPS worker. What is most difficult is that whenever a child dies from abuse or neglect, the public might conclude that the child protection worker is to blame. The agency and its workers can be lambasted in the media. As a CPS worker, you will need to develop "thick" skin so as to not internalize harsh words and criticism.

On the other hand, the most important perception is that which comes from those who have been assisted—those whose homes have been stabilized and who have had the risks associated with abuse or neglect removed from their family units. Hearing kind words from a child who has benefited from involvement with the local CPS agency will be a much appreciated boost to your work that you will long remember. While you did not get into this line of work seeking affirmation around every bend, periodically receiving a heartfelt thank-you from a single mother, foster child, or a survivor of domestic violence is something that will stick with you.

Child protection workers are not often publicly recognized for the incredible work that they do, and this lack of appreciation may in some way contribute to CPS workers leaving their positions. For instance, in a statewide qualitative study of 369 child welfare professionals in Georgia, workers reported that feeling undervalued by the agency, policy makers, and the general public was contributing to employee turnover (Ellett, Ellis, Westbrook, & Dews, 2007). However, the work that CPS workers do is vitally important. All of us must seek to avoid contributing to any negative public perception of child protection and to actively counter it. Families with problems can become healthier with qualified and competent CPS workers to guide them. Personally thank your fellow CPS coworkers to keep their morale high. Encourage those around you by sharing successes stories when clients have done really well—respecting their confidentiality, of course.

Years later, Elizabeth received word that she had a visitor in the lobby of the CPS office. Kristen, now a high school senior, stopped in just to see Elizabeth and say hello. Now an honors student with multiple college scholarship offers, she was a confident and self-assured young woman. Kristen described how Elizabeth's commitment and advocacy helped her change her life's trajectory. In that moment, Elizabeth realized, once again, that she had made the right choice of a career.

Main Points

- Child protection teams are made up of individuals who have diverse backgrounds, viewpoints, and life experiences. The unique experiences of each individual create a strong and effective team.
- Child protection teams include a supervisor, who plays a critical role in the facilitation of services for families, provides consultation to each worker, and serves as a liaison to the larger agency administration.
- Child protection teams are located in communities, nested alongside community partners that facilitate the delivery of services to clients.
- Establishing good relationships with community partners is critical to success when working in child protection. It is a reciprocal relationship. You will make and receive referrals with these important agencies and organizations.
- One of the most important community partners is that of the court system, and developing strong alliances with prosecuting attorneys and the GAL is especially helpful.
- Child protection agencies are bureaucratic administrative systems, and a knowledge of the procedures and policies is essential.
- The public perception of child protective services can be contingent on who you speak with and their knowledge of the complexities associated with protecting children from harm.

Questions for Class Discussion

1. What positive characteristics would you hope to find with your coworkers on a CPS team? What negative characteristics could concern you?
2. What positive characteristics would you hope to find with your immediate supervisor on a CPS team? What negative characteristics would concern you?
3. If you were to start tomorrow as a child protection worker, what community agencies do you think you would likely be making referrals to? Brainstorm and make a list of these.
4. Discuss your impressions of our courts based on any involvement you have had with our legal system. Did you feel you were treated fairly or unfairly?
5. What is the impression you get of our court system based on television shows and movies? Do you feel it is a balanced, accurate portrayal?
6. What do you feel the public perception is of child protection workers in your community? Did you have the same perception prior to reading this text?
7. Describe some possible barriers that may influence service delivery in your area.

Self-Assessment for Personal Consideration

1. On the scale below, rate how confident you are that being a child protection worker is the right career for you.

1	2	3	4	5	6	7	8	9	10

Not confident   *Very confident*

2. How much do you think that red tape and bureaucracy would bother you as a CPS worker?

1	2	3	4	5	6	7	8	9	10

No bother   *Very bothersome*

3. Assess your ability to work well on a team of coworkers versus working completely independently.

1	2	3	4	5	6	7	8	9	10

Not good team worker   *Good team worker*

4. How well do you do with receiving feedback and supervision?

1	2	3	4	5	6	7	8	9	10

Not well   *Very well*

Additional Resources

Duchschere, J. E., Beck, C. J., & Stahl, R. M. (2017). Guardians ad litem and children's attorneys in Arizona: A qualitative examination of the roles. *Juvenile and Family Court Journal, 68*(2), 33–52.

Greeno, E. J., Bright, C. L., & Rozeff, L. (2013). Lessons from the courtroom: Perspectives from child welfare attorneys and supervisors. *Children and Youth Services Review, 35*(9), 1618–1624.

Grobman, L. M., & Clark, E. J. (2011). *Days in the lives of social workers: 58 professionals tell "real-life" stories from social work practice* (4th ed.). Harrisburg, PA: White Hat Communications.

Hunt, S., Goddard, C., & Cooper, J. (2016). "If I feel like this, how does the child feel?" Child protection workers, supervision, management and organisational responses to parental violence. *Journal of Social Work Practice, 30*(1), 5–24.

Kim, H.-J., & Hopkins, K. M. (2017). The quest for rural child welfare workers: How different are they from their urban counterparts in demographics, organizational climate, and work attitudes? *Children and Youth Services Review, 73*, 291–297.

MPTF. (2016, April 11). A day in the life of a social worker [YouTube video]. Retrieved from https://www.youtube.com/watch?v=_xqSY3nODbg

Phillips, J. D. (2016). A qualitative study of collaboration between guardians ad litem and caseworkers in the child welfare system. *Children and Youth Services Review, 60*, 61–67.

National Child Welfare Workforce Institute: https://ncwwi.org

Child Welfare Information Gateway: https://www.childwelfare.gov

References

Barak, M. E. M., Travis, D. J., Pyun, H., & Xie, B. (2009). The impact of supervision on worker outcomes: A meta-analysis. *Social Service Review, 83*(1), 3–32.

Barth, R. P., Lloyd, E. C., Christ, S. L., Chapman, M. V., & Dickinson, N. S. (2008). Child welfare worker characteristics and job satisfaction: A national study. *Social Work, 53*(3), 199–209.

Donnelly, C. (2010). Reflections of a guardian ad litem on the participation of looked-after children in public law proceedings. *Child Care in Practice, 16*(2), 181–193.

Ellett, A. J., Ellis, J. I., Westbrook, T. M., & Dews, D. (2007). A qualitative study of 369 child welfare professionals' perspectives about factors contributing to employee retention and turnover. *Children and Youth Services Review, 29*(2), 264–281.

Griffiths, A., Murphy, A., Desrosiers, P., Harper, W., & Royse, D. (in press). Factors influencing the turnover of frontline public child welfare supervisors. *Journal of Public Child Welfare*.

Mabry, C. R. (2013). Guardians ad litem: Should the child's best interests advocate give more credence to the child's best wishes in custody cases? *American Journal of Family Law, 27*(3), 172–188.

Figure Credit

■ CHAPTER 12

SELF-CARE, FINDING BALANCE, AND PREVENTING PROBLEMS

OVERVIEW

Self-care is a topic that in the past several years has become very important and received much discussion and research in other professions besides social work (e.g., medicine, nursing, mental health professions, etc.). Already you expect or know that child welfare work can be pretty intense. Vicarious and secondary trauma are real, and we don't discuss them merely to scare you. Rather, our intent is to prepare you for the career you are considering. You need to recognize that in working to improve the conditions of the children and families you will encounter, there can be a "cost of caring." If you are prepared for this, you may be able to fend off discouragement or looking to find another job soon after you're hired. Practicing self-care will allow you to avoid some of the problems that have been associated with too much stress. Wise ol' Ben Franklin is given credit for having written, "By failing to prepare, you are preparing to fail."

Sarah's Story: A Dedicated Child Protection Professional

After finishing her social work degree, Sarah interviewed for several positions but kept thinking about the offer from the public child welfare agency. Since taking her first Child Abuse and Neglect course, she had known she wanted to work in a capacity where she could improve the lives of children and families in her community. Sarah's strong desire to make a difference, her easy-to-know personality, and her internship with the CPS Investigation Unit put her at the top of the list of those the agency wanted to hire, even though she was only 21 years old. First things first, though. Sarah had a wedding to plan.

Even during her honeymoon with Jeff in California, Sarah got two job offers but knew which position she would take upon her return.

Like all new child protection workers, Sarah's first weeks on the job consisted of formal training, during which a deluge of agency policies and procedures had to be learned. Initially told she would not have a full caseload until after her training was complete, she realized that some of her newly hired colleagues were pulled out of training because of cases they had inherited their first day. Sarah's excitement about her new position never faded, even though some of those who started the training with her had resigned within a couple of months.

Although "trained," Sarah realized how much she didn't know. She just hoped that she would have time to learn more before the really tough cases came her way. The training, after all, didn't address every situation she knew she might encounter.

"How could it?" she asked herself when she ran into one of her clients in the supermarket who wanted to talk right there about getting an emergency protective order. On another occasion at a restaurant with her husband, Sarah worried that a male client with mental health issues would follow them to learn where she and Jeff lived. By several months into the job, she had learned to quickly scan rooms and locations for problematic clients or situations, and this strategy usually worked well for her. But 5 months into the job, a wealthy client filed a lawsuit against her and the agency, alleging that she had coerced his child into testifying against him—this was definitely not something she had considered.

Despite the nuisance of that case, Sarah knew she was making a difference. She got satisfaction from providing families with resources, getting positive feedback in home visits, and seeing children and their mothers smile again, as well as from the professional relationships she had developed with community partners.

After she had experience under her belt, Sarah looked for ways to be more effective. Realizing the technological limitations that agency investigative workers had, Sarah drafted a memo pointing out that the agency's laptops did not provide remote access to the server, creating difficulties when she or her colleagues were in the field making notes about home visits. Additionally, the cell phones provided by the agency to help protect the workers' personal information could not always access a signal in one of the rural counties. She made a list with a couple of her colleagues—they also needed new tablets with dictation ability to expedite the mountains of documentation necessary in this line of work. Because of the state's financial situation, however, the agency couldn't afford new laptops or phones across the board right then.

Budget constraints affected other aspects of Sarah's work. A recurring issue was that Sarah's team was never fully staffed, creating high caseloads for the rest of the workers. Although she loved her job, having too many clients made her feel like she was never doing enough—because her sessions were often interrupted by another phone call or crisis. As she would leave her office at night, she often thought, "What have I forgotten? What must I do tomorrow?"

Aware of the strain and stresses associated with this challenge, Sarah and her colleagues would sometimes discuss in staff meetings how important it was to practice self-care. However, the self-care did not occur. There was no time to take leave to exercise or have a personal day. Anyone taking leave would place further burden on colleagues left the office—something a good team member just would not do.

When Sarah's coworker Daniel left his CPS position, the team members each had to add six of his cases to their existing caseload. About two weeks after that, Sarah realized that she had been so tired that she had quit exercising—and she used to love jogging with her husband on the weekends and afternoons when she could get home a little early. Also, she had quit making salads for her lunch and usually ate fast food in her car in-between appointments. The joke in the office was that they were on a "drive-thru diet." Several of her dresses were now too tight.

While the weight gain was a little concerning, more troubling was that Jeff, her new husband, was beginning to complain that she was always too tired for them to do anything together. It was not uncommon for her to go back into the office on Saturdays to "catch up" and to think about what she could have done differently in the case of sexual trauma that she could never forget. Even when some college friends came into town and wanted to get together, Sarah begged off. While she wanted to see her friends again, she felt pressure to complete paperwork she hadn't had time to finish on Friday so that her Monday wouldn't be so stressful.

When she got back home Saturday afternoon, she found a note from her husband of 6 months: "Gone camping. Wish you were here but I think you are married to your job—not me. Jeff"

Self-Care

What is self-care? Let's start by reflecting on Sarah's situation. If we view it objectively, we can see several ways that Sarah was not practicing good self-care. Can you identify them? (a) Not sleeping well, (b) anxiety about unfinished work or cases, (c) fatigue, (d) not exercising, (e) eating too much fast food, (f) minimizing social contacts and social support opportunities, and (g) not maintaining an appropriate work-life balance.

Self-care can be thought of simply as actively managing our lives so that we stay healthy. Being healthy is important to all of us, but so is having the energy to enjoy our friends and family members and to participate in recreation and exercise as a way to take our minds off our work for a while and reduce stress. The ability to sleep through the night can be taken for granted—until you realize you are tossing and turning because you can't sleep. No one wants to be tired all the time or gain so much weight that she or he has to buy new clothes all the time.

Another way to think about self-care is any activity that helps you feel good about yourself (Richards, Campenni, & Muse-Burke (2010). The idea here would be to do the things that help you relax and enjoy life. If you like to hike or kayak, then you should make the time to engage in these activities. If reading a good book once you get home helps you relax and forget about the pressure from work, then you shouldn't feel guilty about spending some time in your favorite activity. Obviously though, one would have to use common sense. For instance, going shopping with friends might be your idea of a good time, but maxing out your credit cards could be a really bad idea, causing a great deal of stress later on. The aim of self-care activities should be stress reduction or prevention—to help the harried professional attain or maintain a sense of well-being.

Why Self-Care Practice Is Important

The very nature of child protective services work is stressful because children are hurt, mistreated, and neglected, and the empathetic professional is exposed vicariously to the trauma that these children experienced. There are several terms that are often used interchangeably to describe the unfortunate effects on practitioners, and we'll describe these more in greater detail a bit later. These terms include *secondary traumatic stress*, *compassion fatigue*, *burnout*, and so on.

What effect does too much job stress tend to have on professionals helping clients with trauma? Emotional exhaustion can lead to withdrawing and disengaging from one's clients and work, becoming more negative and cynical, and having thoughts or intention to leave one's current position—which contributes to high turnover rates and continuity of care problems for clients (Bressi & Vaden, 2017).

What is so stressful about child protection work? To begin with, mistakes in judgment can literally mean that a child or family member living in a dangerous household can be seriously harmed or even killed. Inadequate funding at the local or state level can mean that your agency can't hire as many CPS workers as are needed; this results in larger caseloads. At the same time, there is a greater demand for documentation, which means that workers have to spend time completing paperwork instead of actually being in the field, seeing clients and families. To add to this mix, there can be negative relationships and personality clashes within the office with coworkers or even with one's supervisor. Other organizational risk factors can include lack of control to influence decisions or to gain access to needed resources, not feeling sufficiently recognized or rewarded for accomplishments, lack of support from coworkers, perceived lack of fairness about one's own treatment within the agency, and conflict between one's individual values and organizational values (Maslach & Leiter, 2016).

When such factors are present in a major way, CPS employees can become less satisfied with their jobs and engage in greater absenteeism, and their lower morale could spread to others in the same work environment.

Do Child Protective Service Workers Experience Much Stress?

A study of children's services staff in five different locations in the United Kingdom found that overall their level of stress was above the average for the general population but levels varied significantly from a low of 9% in one location to a high of 36% in another (Antonopoulou, Killian & Forrester, 2017). A study of child protection staff based in Canadian hospitals found that 40% of those who left their positions indicated they were burned out because of job stress (Bennett, Plint, & Clifford, 2005). At the same time, 69% of the current hospital-based CPS staff found their jobs "extremely" or "quite" satisfying even though one-third exhibited burnout.

Back in the United States, child welfare workers in California had higher workloads, more role conflict, and greater depersonalization than social workers employed in other fields (Kim, 2011). Lee, Pang, Lee, and Melby (2017) found that almost two thirds of child welfare workers rated their work-related stress as either high or very high. These are just a few of the studies that establish that child protective services is a demanding profession. This statement is not at all made to discourage you but simply to educate you and help you realize the importance of practicing self-care. The next portion of the chapter will go more in depth into how the tragedy and trauma that CPS workers, therapists, case managers, and others are involved with can affect them personally and their co-workers. Although these concepts are related, they are also somewhat distinct.

Secondary Traumatic Stress

Secondary traumatic stress (STS) can occur in professionals who bear "witness to the intense or horrific experiences" (Figley, 1995, p. 7) of others. To be more specific, child protection workers not only *hear* about the trauma experienced by children and vulnerable adults, they usually *see* the results of harm (e.g., bruises, broken bones, faces and postures full of fear and anxiety), and they must *ask* in interviews to get the details about the injuries, then *tell* these stories to others in person and *write* about them in reports—which causes the original events to be replayed in their own minds in the telling or writing. Secondary trauma can also be referred to as **vicarious trauma** due to the cumulative exposure to the trauma experienced by clients and shared with their workers, therapists, etc.

The symptoms of STS often resemble those of PTSD, and according to the website of the National Child Traumatic Stress Network (https://www.nctsn.org/), up to 50% of child welfare workers are at risk for developing STS or related conditions associated with PTSD. The website lists these symptoms of vicarious trauma and STS:

- Hypervigilance
- Hopelessness
- Anger and cynicism

- Sleeplessness
- Fear
- Chronic exhaustion
- Guilt
- Minimizing
- Inability to listen
- Avoidance of clients

Individuals can react to stress differently, and it is good to remember that there can be a wide variation in the symptoms expressed as well as their intensity. Here's another set of symptoms associated with secondary traumatization of child welfare workers:

- Anxiety or new fears
- Emotional detachment
- Sadness, depression
- Intrusive imagery or thoughts about victims or clients
- Nightmares
- Social withdrawal, disconnection from friends and family
- Changes in worldview (more futility or pessimism)
- Increased physical ailments and illness
- Greater use of alcohol/drugs (Osofsky, Putnam, & Lederman, 2008)

Compassion Fatigue

The concepts of secondary traumatic stress and compassion fatigue are often used interchangeably, but **compassion fatigue** has been described as a broader term reflecting "the chronic use of empathy combined with the day-to-day bureaucratic hurdles that exist for many social workers such as agency stress, billing difficulties, and balancing clinical work with administrative work" (Newell & Nelson-Gardell, 2014, p. 430). It is apparent when one feels drained of empathy. CPS workers want to practice self-care in order to avoid compassion fatigue, which weakens or detracts from the professional's "ability to express or experience empathy towards others. ... The emotional reserve is usually depleted for professionals who suffer from compassion fatigue, leaving little left for the client" (Dattilo, 2015, p. 394). As a result of this depletion, workers have a reduced ability to provide empathy or enjoy their work and may become characterized by their irritability, sense of isolation, reduced ability to make decisions and care for clients, and increased absenteeism from the job. Taking a break from one's work for a time, physically and emotionally, and reconnecting with social support can help the worker enhance work satisfaction and feel renewed (Figley, 2002). Figley (2005) notes, "Those who are selfless and compassionate have an Achilles heel—they don't pay enough attention to themselves."

Burnout

One can experienced **burnout** from too many demands or too much of a job like having a 24/7 caretaking role without relief for weeks at a time. Burnout can occur whenever we become physically or emotionally exhausted—when we feel that we don't have the energy to get up and do or give anymore. It is generally considered a condition associated with chronic job stressors and has three major effects: (a) overwhelming fatigue, exhaustion, and depletion of energy; (b) feelings of detachment from the job (along with cynicism about it); this detachment is sometimes described as depersonalization, where there can be irritability, loss of idealism, and negative attitudes toward clients; and (c) a sense of ineffectiveness, reduced productivity, or lack of accomplishment (Maslach & Leiter, 2016).

Unlike compassion fatigue, burnout leaves one with a sense that one's efforts make no difference and with apathy toward one's work. Burnout can result from increased workload or job stress and exhaustion. *It does not have to be trauma related.* In fact, it is common to many, if not most, of the helping professions. If not addressed, burnout can contribute to a lower quality of provided care, impair a worker's decision-making about child risk, reduce job satisfaction, and increase job absenteeism and staff turnover (multiple studies cited in Salloum, Kondrat, Johnco, & Olson, 2015).

Situations in Which Self-Care Is Especially Important

The risk factor common to developing compassion fatigue or burnout comes from the very nature of helping those with major problems. Helping others can have a downside (the "cost of caring"), which can affect empathic professionals who give, and give, and give of themselves. That's always going to be in the background—something that all of us in this field must recognize. Putting that aside, research indicates that *organizational factors* also contribute to burnout, compassion fatigue, and secondary traumatization. These risk factors include:

- Extremely high caseloads, excessive paperwork
- Lack of professional autonomy (lack of control or influence over agency policies and procedures)
- Unfair treatment within the work environment
- Lack of support from coworkers
- Inadequate supervision
- Insufficient training
- Conflicting roles, expectations, or values
- Inadequate resources to meet demands (or inability to access needed resources)
- Interruptions during demanding or critical tasks (being pulled off a job and later put back on)
- Physical risks or concerns about safety
- Little recognition for contributions or achievements

Too much work (e.g., overload, excessively high caseloads) reduces one's ability to have a satisfactory completion of all the tasks involved, which contributes to job dissatisfaction. Perhaps more important is that more work than one can manage significantly reduces the amount of time that one has to recharge one's batteries by resting, recreating, and having the time for social activities.

PRACTICE TIP 12.1 Be observant of significant changes in your work and life. For instance, receiving too many cases too soon can be very stressful for a new worker. Breaking up with a loved one or death in the family might keep you from focusing and being able to manage your time or cases well. If you are feeling scattered or unfocused, for whatever reason, make an appointment with your supervisor.

When you must work with a child or family in which there has been major trauma, you will need some time to debrief, ventilate, discuss, plan, or just not think about the problems associated with the family. Having to go immediately right back into the field to address another equally problematic situation with horrendous trauma can take its toll. Recognize that you might need more "quality time" with your supervisor or other team members to debrief and discuss the situation or any challenges you are feeling. *You are* the best judge of when a problem is present. Always be honest with yourself and with your supervisor. If you need more time or more help, don't be ashamed to ask for it. Talk with the more experienced workers to see if they have found helpful ways of managing cases or paperwork if that is a problem. Above all else, don't isolate yourself and don't try to be Superwoman or Superman!

Frustration with a job mounts when one can't access needed resources and when there is perceived organizational unfairness or conflicting values. When one is working as hard as possible but getting little support, disengagement from the job and clients can result—perhaps followed by other symptoms of secondary traumatic stress discussed earlier. If you need more support, be assertive and ask for it.

Continuation of Sarah's Story

The note hurt. Sarah felt as if someone had punched her in the stomach. After reading it again and again, trying to understand what provoked Jeff to leave without her on the camping trip, Sarah dropped heavily into the nearest kitchen chair and simply stared at the note. Although she knew she hadn't had the energy to go to movies or simply out to a restaurant recently with Jeff, she wanted to argue that they were married now—they saw each other every day. But part of her really missed the good times they had together. She guiltily recognized that she had also been so focused on her cases and work that she had neglected Jeff. Maybe this job was too much for her to handle. And there was something else she had never told anyone else.

Monday morning Sarah knocked on the door of Beth, her supervisor.

"Have you got a moment?"

"Sure," Beth said, "come on in."

"I'm not really sure where to start," Sarah said, looking down while flicking a ballpoint pen.

"Well," Beth said, "what brings you here? Is it that Roberts case I assigned you last week?"

"No, not that," Sarah said softly. "Jeff says that I never have any downtime, that I'm always working—and he's right." Her voice broke. "I don't want to lose him."

"Okay, go on. Do you need a couple of days off?"

"No, there's something else. I can't quit thinking about the Wilson case. I'm spending about 60% of my time just thinking about how best to handle it."

"I'm not familiar with that one. What's different about it?" Beth leaned forward.

"Becky, the 10-year old, revealed to me last week that her father took her to the basement and waved an X-Acto knife in her face. He said that if she told anyone about 'their games,' he would slice open the bottom of her foot and she wouldn't be able to walk for a month."

"Oh, wow."

Taking a tissue from Beth's desk, Sarah dabbed her eyes and said, "Becky reminds me of me."

Personal Risk Factors

Besides organizational risk factors, you as a CPS worker may have a vulnerability to secondary traumatic stress and burnout. These include the following:

- Younger age
- Fewer years of professional experience
- Personal history of trauma

In this chapter's fictitious case (although it was loosely based on real individual who had a very supportive husband), Sarah had all three personal risk factors. That is, she was young, was inexperienced, and had been a victim of childhood trauma herself. Certainly, there is nothing a fresh college graduate can do about being young and inexperienced, except to learn quickly what one needs to know to do the job well *and* to engage in self-care to prevent some of the problems already described. It is also important to pay attention to any troubling sign or symptoms that one is developing of secondary traumatic stress or burnout. It helps to talk with coworkers and your supervisor and to try to keep the job from intruding into your personal life after hours.

As for any past trauma in your own life, you may have received therapy to process that—or you might wish to consider entering into therapy now if the cases you have as a CPS worker are bringing you flashbacks or triggering symptoms. When hired as a CPS worker, you might want to let your supervisor know about your history (and you shouldn't have to go into great detail) so that he or she can also help watch out for you—especially if you begin to struggle with certain cases. You will need to be especially vigilant of your own emotional responses to cases and begin positive coping efforts when you feel troubled.

TEST YOURSELF

How is compassion fatigue different from secondary traumatic stress? Do not read below the dotted line until you are ready to see the answer.

Secondary traumatic stress involves the experience of seeing, hearing, or being involved with another individual's trauma. Its symptoms can be almost like PTSD (e.g., nightmares, emotional detachment, intrusive images), and it involves a shift in worldview (more negative). Compassion fatigue results from giving a great deal of empathy to clients without time to renew and recharge through time off or self-care practices. While one's emotional energy is depleted, it can be restored again along with an improved attitude about work and clients. Compassion fatigue is thought to be easily treatable.

Self-Care Assessment: Instruments

Several assessment scales are discussed in this section, and two are provided so that you can visualize the issues that they measure. These can be used for self-assessment or on a larger scale in a department or organization.

The Secondary Traumatic Stress Scale (STSS) contains 17 items and was developed from the DSM-IV–TR's criteria for PTSD. Accordingly, its three subscales (Intrusion, Avoidance, and Arousal) align with the B, C, and D criteria for PTSD. Respondents indicate how frequently in the past week they have experienced one of the symptoms. One easy way to interpret the scores is to use 38 as a cutoff—scores above 38 indicate that "steps need to be taken to address secondary traumatic stress" (Bride, Radey, Figley, 2007, p. 160). The STSS can be used as a screening instrument for secondary traumatic stress. It is reliable and has demonstrated construct, convergent, discriminant, and factorial validity. As of May 2018, it had been cited in other studies 110 times.

SECONDARY TRAUMATIC STRESS SCALE

The following is a list of statements made by persons who have been impacted by their work with traumatized clients. Read each statement, then indicate how frequently the statement was true for you in the past 7 days by circling the corresponding number next to the statement.

	Never	Rarely	Occasionally	Often	Very Often
1. I felt emotionally numb.	1	2	3	4	5
2. My heart started pounding when I thought about my work with clients.	1	2	3	4	5
3. It seemed as if I was reliving the trauma(s) experienced by my client(s).	1	2	3	4	5
4. I had trouble sleeping.	1	2	3	4	5
5. I felt discouraged about the future.	1	2	3	4	5
6. Reminders of my work with clients upset me.	1	2	3	4	5
7. I had little interest in being around others.	1	2	3	4	5
8. I felt jumpy.	1	2	3	4	5
9. I was less active than usual.	1	2	3	4	5
10. I thought about my work with clients when I didn't intend to.	1	2	3	4	5
11. I had trouble concentrating.	1	2	3	4	5
12. I avoided people, places, or things that reminded me of my work with clients.	1	2	3	4	5
13. I had disturbing dreams about my work with clients.	1	2	3	4	5
14. I wanted to avoid working with clients.	1	2	3	4	5
15. I was easily annoyed.	1	2	3	4	5
16. I expected something bad to happen.	1	2	3	4	5
17. I noticed gaps in my memory about client sessions.	1	2	3	4	5

Brian E. Bride, et al., Selections from "Development and Validation of the Secondary Traumatic Stress Scale," Research on Social Work Practice, vol. 14, no. 1, pp. 13. Copyright © 2004 by SAGE Publications.
Note: "Client" is used to indicate persons with whom you have been engaged in a helping relationship. You may substitute another noun that better represents your work, such as consumer, patient, recipient, and so forth.
Source: Bride, Robinson, Yegidis, & Figley, 2004.

The **Professional Quality of Life Scale (ProQOL)** is also a short instrument that contains three subscales, measuring (a) compassion satisfaction, (b) burnout, and (c) compassion fatigue/secondary traumatic stress. Respondents on the 30-item self-report scale indicate how often each item was experienced *in the last 30 days.* Scores are summed for each of the three 10-item subscales. There is no overall or total score that combines the three. Several items have to be reverse scored. (See the free ProQOL manual for specific details on computing scores.) Cut scores are based on the 75th quartile. For compassion satisfaction, higher scores reflect high satisfaction related to ability to be effective in your job.

On the burnout subscale, higher scores suggest a high risk for burnout. On the secondary traumatic stress subscale, higher scores are associated with symptoms of secondary traumatic stress. High scores may indicate you need to examine your feelings about your work and work environment and to discuss these with a trusted colleague or your supervisor.

Dr. Beth Hudnall Stamm, creator of the ProQOL, has transferred ownership to the Center for Victims of Torture (http://www.CVT.org). The instrument is distributed free of charge for noncommercial users. It may be used freely without requesting permission as long as it is not sold and the author is credited. See the website http://www.proqol.org/ for a comprehensive bibliography on the instrument (over 600 studies as of January 2016). Multiple translations are available. Check http://www.proqol.org/ for the most recent version and to request permission to use the ProQOL for research purposes.

Drawing on "trauma-informed self-care practices adapted directly from the practice recommendations in the Child Welfare Trauma Training Toolkit (Child Welfare Committee National Child Traumatic Stress Network, 2008)," Salloum et al. (2015, p. 56) have developed a 14-item **Trauma-Informed Self-Care** measure using "I" language—such as "I utilize peer support" (p. 57). Other items address regular supervision, safety training, release time, realistic goals and expectations, practicing stress management activities, and so on.

You might also wish to examine the **Child Welfare Worker Stress Inventory** (Levy & Poertner, 2014) listed in the references. However, the article introducing this scale does not provide any data that would be useful for comparison.

Informal Assessment of Self-Care

Besides the standardized instruments that have been prepared to assess secondary trauma, burnout, and so forth, as a practitioner you can also reflect on the problems or symptoms that you are experiencing that may be suggestive of a need for self-care. Realize, however, that the signs or symptoms you experience from too much job-related stress may be very different from what a co-worker or friend of yours might feel. Each of us is unique and our bodies may respond in dissimilar ways.

For many people, too much stress may produce these signs and symptoms:[1]

Physical Signs of Great Stress

- Headaches, tightness in the neck, back, tense muscles
- Grinding of teeth, clinched jaw, dry mouth
- Stomach (diarrhea, constipation), increased or decreased appetite, nausea, sour stomach, acid reflux
- Heart palpitations, chest pains, panic attacks
- Disordered sleep (insomnia or excessive sleep)
- Nervousness, twitches, tremors
- Sweaty hands

---

1. These signs and symptoms are drawn primarily from two sources: Cox and Steiner (2013) and WebMD. (n.d.).

PROFESSIONAL QUALITY OF LIFE SCALE (PROQOL)
Compassion Satisfaction and Compassion Fatigue (ProQOL) Version 5 (2009)

When you [help] people you have direct contact with their lives. As you may have found, your compassion for those you [help] can affect you in positive and negative ways. Below are some questions about your experiences, both positive and negative, as a [helper]. Consider each of the following questions about you and your current work situation. Select the number that honestly reflects how frequently you experienced these things *in the last 30 days.*

1 = Never   2 = Rarely   3 = Sometimes   4 = Often   5 = Very Often

_____ **1.** I am happy.

_____ **2.** I am preoccupied with more than one person I [help].

_____ **3.** I get satisfaction from being able to [help] people.

_____ **4.** I feel connected to others.

_____ **5.** I jump or am startled by unexpected sounds.

_____ **6.** I feel invigorated after working with those I [help].

_____ **7.** I find it difficult to separate my personal life from my life as a [helper].

_____ **8.** I am not as productive at work because I am losing sleep over traumatic experiences of a person I [help].

_____ **9.** I think that I might have been affected by the traumatic stress of those I [help].

_____ **10.** I feel trapped by my job as a [helper].

_____ **11.** Because of my [helping], I have felt "on edge" about various things.

_____ **12.** I like my work as a [helper].

_____ **13.** I feel depressed because of the traumatic experiences of the people I [help].

_____ **14.** I feel as though I am experiencing the trauma of someone I have [helped].

_____ **15.** I have beliefs that sustain me.

_____ **16.** I am pleased with how I am able to keep up with [helping] techniques and protocols.

_____ **17.** I am the person I always wanted to be.

_____ **18.** My work makes me feel satisfied.

_____ **19.** I feel worn out because of my work as a [helper].

_____ **20.** I have happy thoughts and feelings about those I [help] and how I could help them.

_____ **21.** I feel overwhelmed because my case [work] load seems endless.

_____ **22.** I believe I can make a difference through my work.

_____ **23.** I avoid certain activities or situations because they remind me of frightening experiences of the people I [help].

_____ **24.** I am proud of what I can do to [help].

_____ **25.** As a result of my [helping], I have intrusive, frightening thoughts.

_____ **26.** I feel "bogged down" by the system.

_____ **27.** I have thoughts that I am a "success" as a [helper].

_____ **28.** I can't recall important parts of my work with trauma victims.

_____ **29.** I am a very caring person.

_____ **30.** I am happy that I chose to do this work.

Behavioral Signs of Great Stress

- Feeling overwhelmed, easily triggered crying or anger
- Low energy, neglecting responsibilities
- Social withdrawal
- Inability to concentrate or organize; difficulty making decisions
- Forgetfulness
- Rumination about details, excessive worrying
- Nightmares, irrational fears
- Inability to quiet your mind or relax
- Easily frustrated
- Feeling depressed, hopelessness, worthlessness, sense of failure
- Increased use of alcohol or drugs

What Do I Need for Self-Care Practice as a CPS Professional?

The short answer is that there is not one thing that you need. In fact, to properly address self-care that will prevent problems when you are under stress, you need several sources of support. No one structure or source of support will be sufficient. Lee and Miller (2013) note that there are five different categories of ways we can think about ways to keep ourselves healthy.

1. Physical domain: Exercise, movement, physical activity (e.g., walking, jogging, playing tennis—any form of active recreation); eating healthy meals; getting enough sleep; cutting back on caffeine and alcohol; regular medical checkups
2. Psychological/emotional domain: Practicing mindfulness and stress-management activities (e.g., meditation, deep-breathing exercises, practicing positive thinking); visual imagery; active problem solving (as opposed to rumination)
3. Social domain: Engaging in fun activities with friends; spending time with people who are positive, who listen and care for you; participation in group activities (e.g., volunteering in the community)
4. Leisure: Doing something you enjoy doing like reading, hiking, quilting, playing music, horseback riding, bowling, journaling, sketching, restoring furniture, scrapbooking, photography, solving cross-word puzzles, working jigsaw puzzles, biking, in-line skating, camping outdoors
5. Spiritual: Meditation, prayer, attending worship services, participating in religious practices such as reading the Bible or Koran

In addition to the categories listed above, Lee and Miller (2013) also discuss ways that CPS professionals can engage in self-care by thinking, planning, and managing work tasks.

Workload and time management: It is important to allow oneself to take breaks during the day, to take vacations, and to try to work efficiently so that one does not have to take work home in the evenings or on weekends. Thinking about what is important to accomplish first each day and prioritizing tasks may contribute to accomplishing those items that you might worry about if they didn't get completed. Use your time wisely.

Self-knowledge: Recognize your limitations. When you need consultation, additional expertise, or supervision, then seek it. Don't pretend that you have skills when you don't and need to make a referral.

Attentiveness to personal reaction to work stress: If stress levels are really high and your efforts at self-care are not succeeding, you may need to take this up with your supervisor or do debriefings with sympathetic colleagues after tough cases, and perhaps even consider personal therapy after a horrendous case or experience.

Professional support and self-advocacy: Sometimes the bureaucracy at one's place of employment adds to the stress of simply doing one's job. However, joining with other colleagues after work to discuss and problem solve work-related issues could result in several individuals advocating for solutions to the group's concerns. Even if there is no quick resolution to the issues, at least you will have realized that you are not the only one experiencing the problem. Networking with others certainly brings more clout to the issue and may ultimately result in some abatement of the problem later. Addressing the problem is certainly more professional than getting fed up and quitting.

Professional development: Learning more about a problem can make you a better professional. Attending conferences, getting more training, and reading journal articles might nourish your intellectual side. You can form a book group among your friends and take turns sharing insights, or perhaps a specialized group would want to learn more about an intervention. Even if the group meets once a month for an hour after work, you can learn vicariously from others' experiences and knowledge, which can enrich you as a professional—and it also counts as a social support activity.

Job satisfiers: You might want to keep a file of any positive letters or thank-you notes and drawings you get from children or their families that remind you in a good way why you are engaged in child protective services. Try to create a pleasant work space for yourself—perhaps a photo of a favorite beach or wooded area that you can look at to calm yourself when you are having a stressful day. Try writing poetry, even if you can't find words to rhyme. Express yourself in writing about the rewards of the job. Visually imagine successful clients or families—or what would be a good day on the job. Find a mantra or song that makes you feel confident—and access it often. Realize that it is important to regenerate your energy and passion for the job from time to time. That's why vacations should be taken. Being away will give you more energy when you come back to the job.

Creating a Self-Care Plan for Yourself

Okay. You've read the chapter and have a reasonable knowledge about the importance of self-care. You're probably thinking that it's "no problem," that you'll be able to do this or that whenever you start that new child protection position and run into a little more stress than you expected. You might be right. Or you could guess wrong as you throw yourself into your new job, and then one day that insidious stress sneaks into your life and Boom! On that day you realize you aren't handling stress very well.

To prevent that from happening, it might be a good idea to give some thought now, before you are actually working in a full-time child protection position, to what would help you manage stress if and when you begin to feel caught in its undertow.

At the end of this section, you will see a sample self-care plan that is just an example. You should delete the items that you feel you would never do and also add to the list things that you know you like to do. In other words, make a draft of a customized self-care plan on a blank sheet of paper. Even if you don't actually take a CPS position, it might be good to have a self-care plan no matter where you decide to work after graduation!

MY SELF-CARE PLAN

Recognizing the importance of self-care, I will endeavor to participate in the following activities on a regular basis:

Physical Self-Care

_____ Eat healthily (e.g., bring my lunch)   _____ times a week

_____ Exercise   _____ times a week

_____ Good sleep   _____ hours a night

_____ Engage in an outdoor activity   _____ times a week

_____ Consume caffeine, alcohol in moderation   _____

_____ Take breaks as needed   _____

Psychological/Emotional Self-Care

_____ Spend time reading in a quiet place   _____ times a week

_____ Practice stress management techniques   _____ times a day

_____ Engage in a hobby   _____ times a week

_____ Go to a movie, play, or restaurant   _____ times a month

_____ Seek debriefing or supervisory support whenever I need it   _____

_____ Schedule a day off once in a while   _____

_____ Listen to my body and how it reacts to issues at work   _____

Social/Relational Self-Care

_____ Spend time with my friends (not at work)   _____ times a month

_____ Visit or call family members   _____ times a month

_____ Volunteer in a community project/agency   _____ times a month

_____ Schedule time with someone who cares for me, makes me laugh, or feel good about myself   _____ times a month

_____ Make time for coworkers after work   _____ times a month

Spiritual Self-Care

_____ Meditate   _____ times a day

_____ Pray   _____ times a day

_____ Read something inspirational   _____ times a day

_____ Attend a worship service   _____ times a month

_____ Talk with a person I consider to be spiritual or to have a nonmaterial set of values   _____ times a month

_____ Reflect on my self-talk and place in the universe   _____ times a month

PRACTICE TIP 12.2 No one knows you better than you know yourself. As you begin working as a child care professional, you will develop routines. You may discover, for instance, that you need to get a full 7 or 8 hours of sleep each night. You probably won't be able to get by with 3 or 4 hours or to take naps in the afternoon—if that was your practice in college. You may decide that you need to eat a full breakfast before work or that you need to plan your meals ahead of time so that when you come home tired, you will have food to prepare or ready to eat. In other words, pay attention to your needs.

If you find that you are unable to get to sleep (insomnia), want to do nothing but sleep, feel much more anxious, or binge too often on fast food—whatever is a major change in your normal patterns—then talk to someone you trust about it. While child protection workers tend to be a very selfless and dedicated group of professions, don't "blow off" the need for a personal self-care plan. Everyone needs a little time away from the job, a little respite from the daily grind. Be proactive and take a day off when you recognize your own signs of stress.

Main Points

We may all believe we don't need to practice self-care until we develop some problems that take us to our family physician or a loved one complains about our insomnia, inability to relax, or other manifestations. Child protection is valuable and meaningful work but it can be stressful—and no, you are not immune.

- It is important to recognize the symptoms of secondary traumatic stress. Do you understand the "cost" in the "cost of caring?"
- Compassion fatigue is common in child welfare when we must give and give and give of our own emotional energy. Know the importance of self-care!
- Burnout is job related—generally when you have too much to do, tight timelines, or too big of a caseload. Unlike secondary traumatic stress and compassion fatigue, you can develop burnout even as an administrator with no client contact.
- A poor working environment (e.g., inadequate supervision, low morale, unequal or unfair treatment, lack of job autonomy) can create conditions of stress and unhappiness apart from actually doing the job you were hired to do.
- Two different instruments are provided for your own self-assessment. Additionally, it is possible to informally reflect on your need to practice self-care. Along that line, a template is provided to start your thinking about what you could do to manage any stress associated with your position in child welfare.

Questions for Class Discussion

1. If you were Sarah, what would you have done to prevent receiving the note from Jeff?
2. What would you have done after receiving the note?
3. The chapter identifies several categories of self-care activities (e.g., social, psychological/emotional, spiritual, etc.). Which kind of self-care activities do you think work best for you? Why?
4. Do you think it would be easier to recognize the signs and symptoms of secondary traumatic stress in a coworker or in yourself? Why?

5. What more do you need to know about self-care? What would you like to ask an experienced practitioner about self-care?
6. Will it be difficult for you to develop a self-care plan? Why or why not?

Self-Assessment for Personal Consideration

1. How comfortable are you with asking for help when you need it?

1	2	3	4	5	6	7	8	9	10

Not comfortable   *Very comfortable*

2. How confident are you that you will actually stick to a self-care plan?

1	2	3	4	5	6	7	8	9	10

Not confident   *Very confident*

3. How knowledgeable are you right now about stress management techniques?

1	2	3	4	5	6	7	8	9	10

Not knowledgeable   *Very knowledgeable*

Additional Resources

Cox, K., & Steiner, S. (2013). *Self-care in social work. A guide for practitioners, supervisors, and administrators.* Washington, DC: NASW Press.

Grise-Owens, E., & Miller, J. (2016). *The A-to-Z self-care handbook for social workers and other helping professionals.* Harrisburg, PA: New Social Worker Press.

Handran, J. (2015). Trauma-informed systems of care: The role of organizational culture in the development of burnout, secondary traumatic stress, and compassion satisfaction. *Journal of Social Welfare and Human Rights*, 3 (2), 1–22.

Salloum, A., Choi, M. J., & Stover, C. S. (2018). Development of a trauma-informed self-care measure with child welfare workers. *Children and Youth Services Review*, 93, 108–116.

Smullens, S. (2015). *Burnout and self-care in social work: A guidebook for students and those in mental health and related professions.* Washington, DC: NASW Press.

Wicks, R. J. (2007). *The resilient clinician.* New York, NY: Oxford University Press.

References

Antonopoulou, P., Killian, M. & Forrester, D. (2017). Levels of stress and anxiety in child and family social work: Workers' perceptions of organizational structure, professional support and workplace opportunities in Children's Services in the UK. *Children and Youth Services Review*, 76, 42–50.

Bennett, S., Plint, A., & Clifford, T. (2005). Burnout, psychological morbidity, job satisfaction, and stress: A survey of Canadian hospital-based child protection professionals. *Archives of Disease in Childhood*, 90(11), 1112–1116.

Bressi, S. K., & Vaden, E. R. (2017). Reconsidering self-care. *Clinical Social Work Journal*, 45, 33–38.

Bride, B. E., Radey, M. & Figley, C. R. (2007). Measuring compassion fatigue. *Clinical Social Work Journal*, 35, 155–163.

Bride, B. E., Robinson, M. M., Yegidis, B., & Figley, C. R. (2004). Development and validation of the Secondary Traumatic Stress Scale. *Research on Social Work Practice*, 14(1), 27–35.

Cox, K., & Steiner, S. (2013). *Self-care in social work: A guide for practitioners, supervisors, and administrators.* Washington, DC: National Association of Social Workers.

Dattilio, F. M. (2015). The self-care of psychologists and mental health professionals: A review and practitioner guide. *Australian Psychologist, 50,* 393–399.

Figley, C. R. (1995). *Compassion fatigue: Coping with secondary traumatic stress disorder in those who treat the traumatized.* Levittown, PA: Brunner/Mazel.

Figley, C. R. (2002). Compassion fatigue: Psychotherapists' chronic lack of self-care. *Journal of Clinical Psychology, 58*(11), 1433–1441.

Figley, C. R. (2005, October 17). Compassion fatigue: An expert interview with Charles R. Figley, MS, PhD. *Medscape Psychiatry & Mental Health.* Retrieved from https://www.medscape.com/viewarticle/513615.

Kim, H. (2011). Job conditions, unmet expectations, and burnout in public child welfare workers. How different from other social workers? *Children and Youth Services Review, 33*(2), 358–367.

Lee, J. J. & Miller, S. E. (2013). A self-care framework for social workers: Building a strong foundation for practice. *Families in Society, 94,* 96–103.

Lee, K., Pang, Y. C., Lee, J. A., & Melby, J. N. (2017). A study of adverse childhood experiences, coping strategies, work stress, and self-care in the child welfare profession. *Human Service Organizations: Management, Leadership & Governance, 41*(4), 389–402.

Levy, M., & Poertner, J. (2014). Development of a Child Welfare Worker Stress Inventory. *Journal of Psychological Issues in Organizational Culture, 5*(1), 7–15.

Maslach, C., & Leiter, M. P. (2016). Understanding the burnout experience: Recent research and its implications for psychiatry. *World Psychiatry, 15*(2), 103–111.

National Child Traumatic Stress Network. (n.d.). Secondary traumatic stress: A fact sheet for child-serving professionals. Retrieved from http://www.nctsn.org/resources/secondary-traumatic-stress-fact-sheet-child-serving-professionals

Newell, J. M., & Nelson-Gardell, D. (2014). A competency-based approach to teaching professional self-care. An ethical consideration for social work educators. *Journal of Social Work Education, 50,* 427–439.

Osofsky, J. D., Putnam, F. W., & Lederman, C. S. (2008). How to maintain emotional health when working with trauma. *Juvenile and Family Court Judges, 59*(4), 91–102.

Richards, K. C., Campenni, C. E., & Muse-Burke, J. (2010). Self-care and well-being in mental health professionals: The mediating effects of self-awareness and mindfulness. *Journal of Mental Health Counseling, 32*(3), 247–264.

Salloum, A., Kondrat, D. C., Johnco, C., & Olson, K. R. (2015). The role of self-care on compassion satisfaction, burnout, and secondary trauma among child welfare workers. *Children and Youth Services Review, 49,* 54–61.

Stamm, B. H. 2009. Professional Quality of Life: Compassion Satisfaction and Fatigue Version 5 (ProQOL). Retrieved from http://www.proqol.org/

WebMD. (n.d.). Stress symptoms. Retrieved from https://www.webmd.com/balance/stress-management/stress-symptoms-effects_of-stress-on-the-body#2

CHAPTER 13

CHILD PROTECTION, CHILD WELFARE, AND YOU: FUTURE CONSIDERATIONS

OVERVIEW

This chapter does not assume that you will become a CPS worker although information will be presented on how actual child protection workers in one study enthusiastically viewed their positions. Unlike the micro focus on the child and family in previous chapters, this one backs further out, and its macro focus allows you to consider other possible careers that may be of interest but assumes you will still be concerned about the problem of child maltreatment. Three levels of prevention (primary, secondary, and tertiary) will be discussed, and the chapter will present ideas and efforts you could make to improve conditions for children at risk at the local level (mostly) but also at the state and national level. This potpourri of ideas concludes with some "big ideas" other experts on child welfare have proposed.

The Satisfaction of Working in Child Protection

If you reflect back over all that you have learned about child protection in this text, you may have already made one of three decisions. *One*, you may be excited about the possibility of working in this field as an investigator, as an ongoing worker, or as someone who provides therapy or services to children and adolescents with special challenges. You may want to work with juvenile courts or be a victim advocate for those exposed to domestic violence in their homes. If this is you, we are very happy for that decision. We know that child protection workers are some of the finest, least selfish, and hardest working professionals around. We welcome you to this work!

Or *two*, you may feel some calling or have some interest in working in child welfare but not be sure you want to do child protective investigations or ongoing work. You may have learned quite a bit about the stresses and pressures of working in child protection, and that may concern you. After all, we have tried to prepare you to understand that working in child protection will expose you to the trauma of others. CPS workers see the effects of abuse and neglect on children and hear their stories of mistreatment. They encounter parents who are unreasonable, mentally ill, addicted to illegal substances—adults who come across as cold, inadequate, uninvolved parents. Many of these have been traumatized themselves, but that doesn't make them easier to work with. If encountering such parents and their children on a regular basis seems like more of a challenge than you want, that's okay. You may still want to work with children as a school social worker, in a health care setting, or as a child therapist, for example. You may want to help those with physical and mental disabilities or work in a nonprofit agency like Big Brothers/Big Sisters or other specialized programs for children and teens.

Category *three* will be those students who prefer not to work in child protection or directly with children. And this is okay, too. We need social workers who can assist the elderly; those who want to work with adults and provide mental health counseling, couples counseling, and substance abuse services; and those who want work as administrators, researchers, or providers of assistance to refugees and international relief.

It is those of you in the second and third categories that we mainly wish to address in this part of this chapter. But first, we want to share with you the positive aspects of working in child protection based on *real* data from *real* frontline CPS professionals who describe why they have remained working in the field when they could have moved on to other jobs. These comments come from a survey conducted by the authors of your textbook (Griffiths, 2019). The open-ended question that the child protection professionals were asked was, "Why do you remain in child welfare?" In Table 13.1 and a few sentences after it, we have summarized how the CPS staffers replied to the question when responses were grouped into those that contained aspects of enjoyment and satisfaction with their positions.

TABLE 13.1 FRONTLINE CHILD PROTECTION WORKERS' RESPONSES TO AN ONLINE SURVEY QUESTION: "WHY DO YOU REMAIN EMPLOYED IN CHILD WELFARE?"

- The happiness of children I help.
- I really enjoy helping people better themselves.
- I love this job.
- I truly love feeling needed and doing things to help others.
- I LOVE my job and my co-workers.
- I love what I do.
- I am still "in love" with the position.
- The sense of fulfillment I get when helping others.
- I am completely satisfied with the position that I hold.
- I love being a social worker.
- I love to help families and children.
- I get a sense of accomplishment when a child is no longer in the system.
- I like the idea that I am helping to protect children and helping them have a chance at a good life.
- I left the agency for 8 months and came back because I loved my job and helping families.
- My love and desire to impact the community in a positive way.
- I love working with kids.
- Love what I do.

Source: Griffiths, 2019.

These comments are just a few of the many responses (n = 133) to the survey question. In fact, over one third of the comments in this category or theme used the word *love* in some capacity. You get something of a feel for that by reading the bullet points above. Forty-three percent used the word *enjoy*, as in "I enjoy the work I do," "I do enjoy working with my families," "I do enjoy social work and get satisfaction from knowing that I am helping make a difference in others." Ten percent used some form of the word *satisfied* or *satisfaction*, as in these responses: "I am completely satisfied with the position I hold" and "The satisfaction helping children brings me." Other interesting comments are those such as, "I am passionate about what I do" and "I have a passion to help children achieve permanency." Another individual phrased it this way: "I am passionate about what I do, and I adore my co-workers. When you see your first reunification in court—that is the feeling you always strive for. In my office, my co-workers all share that same goal." In sum, you can see that child protection professionals do enjoy their work despite the challenges that come with it.

Students choose the major of social work and adults change careers at times to become social workers because they want to help others. Child welfare is a field for responsible, committed individuals who greatly desire to help vulnerable children and their families. And if you don't want to work "in the trenches," so to speak, there will still be other ways to make a difference, as we shall see in the remainder of the chapter.

Thinking About Prevention

Let's dream for just a moment. What kind of a world would it be if you and your close friends had the kind of political clout and ability to implement programs, policies, and national funding tightly focused on the prevention of child maltreatment? Where would you start?

Before we can actually begin to think about strategies for preventing or minimizing the problem of child abuse and neglect in this country, we first have to acquire a foundational and conceptual understanding of the three types of prevention. Once we do that, then we can begin to stretch our minds a bit and think more specifically about preventing child maltreatment.

In public health and medicine, a long-established way of thinking about prevention of diseases and social ills has been to conceptualize a three-tiered approach. For instance, **primary prevention** generally involves large-scale, general population or public efforts to intervene ahead of the problem—to stop it from starting, in other words. Familiar examples would include obtaining a vaccination against the flu or measles, banning substances from food or supplements that are known to be carcinogenic or harmful to human beings, and adding fluoride to our water to prevent cavities and tooth decay. Sometimes our government at a local or state level passes legislation limiting harmful practices such as cigarette smoking in restaurants, which can significantly reduce the hazard of secondhand smoke to nonsmokers. Local school boards can establish the vaccinations that they require before students can be registered for school. At times, the federal government can make recommendations rather than legal mandates. An example of this would be the Centers for Disease Control and Prevention's recommendation for children 11 and 12 years of age to receive the human papillomavirus (HPV) vaccination routinely. The soundness of a primary prevention strategy is that it eliminates the hazard or toxic influence before it can produce problems.

Secondary prevention is another level of efforts aimed at avoiding or reducing problems while they are in their earliest stages. The idea at this level is to attempt to stop a problem before it becomes worse or even to reverse it (e.g., snuff out tiny flames or smoking embers before they can become a forest fire). Screening or assessing is often applied at this level—think of blood pressure screening to identify those at risk for heart disease and stroke. Individuals can have high blood pressure and not even know it because there are no symptoms—that's why it is called a "silent killer." At this level, we can think about secondary prevention as allowing for the identification of two large categories—those at risk for the problem (the targets) and those likely not at risk.

Tertiary prevention involves focused intervention only on those individuals and families who have been assessed or diagnosed as having the problem or issue of concern. Think about someone who trips over a throw rug and breaks a leg. At that point, the problem cannot be prevented, since it already exists. Once the broken leg has been repaired (possibly surgically), set, and placed in a cast, time will need to pass for the healing to occur. More importantly, however, is that the person with the broken leg may need a period of rehabilitation or physical therapy in order to walk without a limp. Tertiary prevention now can involve removing any throw rugs in the home that might help to prevent future falls, installing handrails for any steps (e.g., for the front or back doors, etc.).

Tertiary prevention can also be thought of as treating or managing a problem with medication, as with some forms of mental illness and drug addiction. Once someone has become addicted to heroin, tertiary prevention would be those efforts aimed at restoring or rehabilitating the individual to a healthier life without any use of illegal substances and thus minimizing any reoccurrences of the problem.

EFFECTIVE PREVENTION PROGRAMS

Suppose you accept a position where your responsibilities are to try to prevent child maltreatment from occurring. How do you begin to think about addressing such a large problem? Nation and his colleagues (2003) have identified a series of principles of effective prevention programs. They are comprehensiveness of effort, use of varied teaching methods (including skill development and not just providing knowledge), sufficient dosage (adequate number of sessions, length of sessions, duration of the program, and "booster" or follow-up sessions), sociocultural tailoring of the efforts to the target community and norms of participants, use of well-trained staff, promotion of positive relationships, and clear goals and objectives that allow for outcome evaluation.

Where Do We Start to Improve the Safety and Protection of Children in America?

Recent authors have discussed some of the reasons making it so difficult to effect policy or program changes in our country—changes that could immediately begin to reduce the number of children affected by abuse and neglect, lessen the severity or duration of their mistreatment, and keep it from beginning at all:

> child welfare cases almost always include families struggling with mental health and addiction problems, poor access to health care and mental health care, histories of intimate partner violence, and the sequelae of ongoing intergenerational polyvictimization, traumatic, and other adverse experiences. These child maltreatment synergies are pernicious and nontrivial—indeed, they generate "wicked problems" (Wicked Problems Institutes, 2014). (Clark & Yegidis, 2016, p. 512)

What makes improving child welfare and child protection for our nation's children a "wicked problem" is that contributors to the problem are broad and deep, such as institutional racism that keeps families in poverty, a general reluctance to intrude or become involved in the way parents raise their children, parents' lack of knowledge about ways to direct or correct children's behavior without physical or emotional abuse, parents' perception that they know best when they really don't—and worse, their failure to reach out and ask for help when there are obvious indications of problems with a child or within their family. To further complicate matters, there are times when parents are truly at fault because of impaired judgment, but in many other situations the parents are products of very poor role models and are complicit only in parenting in a style that their own parents used. It is hard to blame those who never had the opportunity to go to college, those who never had the resources to move out of dangerous neighborhoods or rural areas with few opportunities for employment and high wages, or those denied advancement in good jobs because of the color of their skin. While it is tempting to blame the parents whenever a horrific case of abuse or neglect comes to our attention, many citizens in this country don't want the government more involved in their lives. Indeed, while most Americans may want abused and neglected children to be helped, where should the line be drawn in terms of what is too much and what is too little governmental interference in the welfare of children and their parents?

Starting with Primary Prevention

So where do we start? Beginning with primary prevention, one idea that has been used for many years in Europe and England has been the use of nurses or other health professionals for home visitation when there is a new birth. After all, we know that poor or bad parenting can result in allegations of child abuse or neglect, so perhaps as a primary prevention effort, providing free educational programs that promote the development of positive parenting strategies could reduce the incidence of child maltreatment. While some form of home visitation is present in every state as well as tribal areas, territories, and the District of Columbia for high-risk families, the U.S. Preventive Services Task Force (2018) recently released a report concluding that "the current evidence is insufficient to assess the balance of benefits and harms of primary care interventions to prevent child maltreatment" (p. 2122).

This is despite Desai, Reece, and Shakespeare-Pellington's (2017) study of systematic reviews, meta-analyses, and comprehensive reviews that examined interventions targeting child maltreatment prevention in postnatal home visiting programs that found the programs to be effective in early childhood years. They report the following studies about existing home visiting programs meeting their criteria:

- Rates of depression, anxiety/stress and self-esteem in program participants were reduced (Alderdice, McNeill, & Lynn, 2013).
- Bilukha et al. (2005) found reduced levels of child maltreatment in homes in 19 of 26 studies.
- Avellar and Supplee (2013) found that 5 of 6 home visiting programs reduced child maltreatment rates. One of these studies (Olds, Sadler, & Kitzman, 2007) found mothers engaged in fewer neglectful behaviors 2 years after intervention, and at 15 years after intervention there were still significantly lower maltreatment rates for the group involved with treatment.
- The meta-analyses of Chen and Chan (2016) and Geeraert, Van Den Noortgate, Grietens, and Onghena (2004) reported that intervention groups reduced child maltreatment and harsh/dysfunctional parenting practices.

Further, another study designed primarily to improve maternal and child health by prenatal home visits found that besides reducing preterm deliveries and low birth weight infants, the recipients of home visitation actually had fewer substantiated reports of child maltreatment (6% vs. 11%) (Williams et al., 2017).

The findings of the U.S. Preventive Services Task Force may strike you as strange, given what appears to be ample evidence countering their conclusions. What's going on? The research that has largely been conducted has been less than perfect for several reasons. In the best of all research designs, the intervention groups and the control groups are randomly selected—that's important. However, intervention group recipients actually get something out of participating in a research study. A pregnant mother might get tips about nutrition and eating right, assistance with meeting basic needs, answers to questions about caring for a baby, parenting skill development, and advice about breast-feeding and bonding with the child. In some studies, the control parents might receive some sort of an incentive (e.g., a small monetary reward) for completing a questionnaire or answering a set of questions, but their engagement and investment in the research would certainly be less than those who have the benefit of a home visitor who is there to help mother and newborn thrive. Later, when it is time to compare this group against those who received the intervention, those in the control group may not keep appointments or contribute data because they have no investment in the study—unless the incentive for participating is sufficiently rewarding.

Another research issue is the problem of what is known as **surveillance bias**. This occurs when researchers and data collectors are in the homes of those receiving the intervention more often than they are in the homes of the control families—giving researchers more opportunities to observe poor parenting. When the data are viewed statistically, those in intervention groups may appear to have more incidents or issues than those in control groups when in fact the control group participants just were not observed (or caught) as many times.

Another problem with conducting this type of research is that there are no standard outcome measures. As we have discussed previously, what constitutes child abuse or neglect can be defined differently in various geographical areas or jurisdictions. There are also low-quality studies due to lack of rigor or measurement issues and small samples sizes. There are few long-term follow-up studies, few studies on whether child maltreatment can be prevented in homes with interpersonal violence, and almost no studies on whether primary prevention programs with parents prevents sexual abuse (Desai et al., 2017).

When it comes to preventing child sexual abuse, the most common prevention approaches are school based. Researchers Walsh, Zwi, Woolfenden, and Shlonsky (2015) report important increases in children's knowledge of sexual abuse topics and protective factors in a meta-analysis of 24 studies. Rudolph and Zimmer-Gembeck (2018) note that child sexual abuse education programs seem to be able to demonstrate an increase in knowledge and protective responses when the children are provided with hypothetical vignettes. The authors add, "However, whether these programs can assist children in the event of an actual threat of molestation remains unknown" (Rudolph & Zimmer-Gembeck, 2018, p. 546).

Evaluation of child sexual abuse prevention programs suffer from the same research-related methodological problems discussed earlier, such as flawed (nonrandom) sampling strategies, loss of research participants during posttests or follow-up measures, lack of fidelity (no way to ensure that the persons providing the prevention programming were following the prescribed model), and lack of control groups—to name a few issues (Rudolph & Zimmer-Gembeck, 2018).

There is no way to know if young children are able to stand up to stronger, more manipulative adults who aren't strangers but family members or friends of the family. Further, there have been some reports of children receiving the sexual abuse prevention programs coming away with negative side effects such as fear of strangers, wariness of any touch, nightmares, anxiety, and school avoidance (Rudolph & Zimmer-Gembeck, 2018). These reactions defeat the benefits of the prevention programming—at least for some children—by creating more problems.

What Can I Do for Primary Prevention of Child Maltreatment?

What can you do to foster primary prevention of child maltreatment? First of all, while it is critically important to have frontline workers in child protection, we also very much need those who have a good understanding of research to lead studies and conduct meta-analyses and systematic literature reviews that lead us to make good decisions about what works and what doesn't in terms of prevention programming. To advance the point from the programming to prevent child sexual abuse a bit more, we need to know if negative side effects of the prevention program affect only 2% of the children or 25% of the children. We need to follow those who have received preventive programming and to interview them 3, 5, and maybe 10 years later to see if they were able to successfully ward off any child sexual abuse by using what they had learned in the programming. These efforts would likely be very expensive and need to be funded by the federal government, but such program evaluation is necessary and vital if we are to identify successful programs from those which are not.

We need practitioners and researchers who can "think outside of the box" and can design new approaches to primary prevention intervention. For instance, with regard to child sexual abuse programming, what approach might you recommend instead of the use of hypothetical vignettes that may create adverse reactions in children?

We need practitioners who learn research methods and acquire the competency to begin research studies to lead others in evaluating programs in their agencies and communities. To assist social workers in having more hands-on practice with conducting research, at least one social work faculty member has gone on record stating that our accrediting body (the Council on Social Work Education) should require that a research thesis be an option for MSW students (Stoesz, (2016).

At the community level, perhaps the local health department or a hospital, clinic, or medical practice would be willing to help with sponsoring a public service announcement on positive parenting or resources when parents feel overwhelmed. Could you can help by working to get this information out to new parents—possibly by creating a pamphlet and making it available at the public health clinic, hospital, and so forth? You may be able to find a civic organization willing to help with the publication costs.

Finally, we need individuals who can dream big dreams about ways to tackle the problems in society like poverty, racism, drug addiction, and lack of educational opportunity that set up conditions for children to be neglected and mistreated. There are no easy answers here about how to proceed. What ideas do you have? What do you think might work?

Focusing on Secondary Prevention

Secondary prevention, you'll recall, has to do with providing interventions or resources to persons or families identified as being *at risk*. Providing parenting classes to pregnant teens in high school would be an example; providing substance abuse counseling, 12-step programs, or rehabilitation services for those parents or soon-to-be parents who have been assessed as possibly at risk and needing additional support when a new child enters their lives would be another example (Scott, Lonne, & Higgins, 2016). As a student or brand-new practitioner, you might assume that since social services in your community seem well established, any service needed by any client would be available. That would not be accurate. In fact, the social service systems in many if not most communities have gaps. Programs may not be available during evening hours or on weekends. In areas with small populations, the services may not exist at all—especially specialized services. Access to certain services can be limited to part of the population. For instance, medical care can be affected if there are too few physicians who accept Medicaid patients. Families may not have transportation (e.g., there is no bus service) in rural areas, or they may need child care if they have to travel for services. If impoverished, families may not have enough money for copays for medicine or even for programs that they are required to complete by the child protection agency. There can also be language barriers. Once gaps in service or barriers are identified, steps can be taken to mobilize resources.

What Can I Do for Secondary Prevention of Child Maltreatment?

What you might be able to do in a small or medium-sized community is talk to service providers of the more prominent agencies (e.g., food pantries, mental health centers, child protection workers, etc.). Ask them what services are missing in the community. Find out which ones have barriers to service utilization (e.g., no evening hours, a location not easily accessible by foot or bus). Volunteer to create a resource directory for the community if there isn't one. Make it available online so that others can find it. Or if there is a good one, add to it with new information you may discover as you conduct your survey of service providers. From your conversations with service providers, create a wish list of the services needed in the community. Become an advocate. Write letters to the local newspaper and inform community members about needed services. Talk to the radio or television station and see if someone there will interview you on what the community needs. Speak to church groups or the United Way office in your community. Become a foster parent yourself.

Some needs (like obtaining a volunteer Spanish translator) for an agency might be easy to meet. Other needs, like the provision of child care in a rural community so that parents can avail themselves of needed services, might require a group of persons to form a child care cooperative, in which mothers volunteer to provide child care in return for receiving child care. Retired individuals might be recruited to provide free taxi services within a 10-mile radius or so. With a large enough pool of drivers, each one might need to be on "duty" only 2 or 3 hours a week. All you need would be an organization or church that is willing to sponsor the beginning effort to get it going—and a catalyst like yourself to start the process. You know people. Recently in a course, juniors in college were asked how many contacts they had in their cell phones. In a class of approximately 40 students, the average number of cell phone contacts was 263, and the median was 197. The point is, each of you has dozens of people you talk to regularly. It doesn't have to be you alone. You have support!

We need more research and more researchers on the secondary prevention side. Rolock, Perez, White, and Fong (2018) state, "Little is known about the lasting and binding nature of families formed through adoption or guardianship" (p. 11). The authors also note, "While there is an intention of enduring parent–child relationships, where children are provided a sense of continuity, life-long connections, and a sense of belonging, recent research has found that these intentions do not always endure" (Rolock et al., 2018, p. 11).

Ideally, children in foster care should not have multiple placements. Ideally, when they leave the child welfare system, they should have strong attachments to family or support systems to aid assist them as they move through life and make decisions about jobs, relationships, and the thousand odd problems that each of us have to resolve as adults. We need to know about their successes and achievements, what made that possible, and their overall well-being. When adolescents and young adults do not have good support systems, they are at risk for "housing insecurity, underemployment, lack of access to mental health services and health care, likely to rely on public assistance, and experience incarceration" (Rolock et al., 2018, p. 14).

We should never accept the notion that we as a society are doing all that is needed or enough in child protection. As internationally recognized child welfare expert Richard J. Gelles (2017) notes, "Aside from expenditures for foster care, the total federal allocation for child welfare was about the same as the cost to build one jet fighter" (p. 49). An infusion of more money would allow CPS agencies to hire more staff and to increase salaries to prevent competent professionals from leaving for positions in which they are better paid. Larger infusions of funds for child protection agencies could allow for increased training, increasing emphasis on self-care, and stipends for students who would commit to working in child protection agencies. Should financial incentives be provided to parents-to-be to attend parenting classes?

What can you do to help? As a private citizen you can vote for progressive politicians who want to adequately support and assist child protection efforts in this country. You might volunteer to work for them and ensure that they are aware of this issue. Vote against politicians who aren't interested in protecting vulnerable children and families. If you can't find candidates you would like to support, consider running for office yourself.

Starting with Tertiary Prevention

Tertiary prevention involves the provision of help and services once abuse or neglect has occurred. The idea here is to prevent any more abuse from occurring. Depending on the seriousness of the incident (imagine a scenario with an official-looking car and perhaps a police car in front of a home), a family can have its problems exposed to the neighbors and possibly to the community. Pushing the scenario a bit further: Mothers injured from domestic violence may have to be transported to the hospital. Fathers or boyfriends may be taken to jail or forced to leave their homes or apartments. Children may have to enter foster or kinship care until their parents "get their acts" together. CPS services offered to such families will be noticed by others. Depending on their communities, there may be a good or average mental health system that can provide services to the children and the mother—and possibly provide anger management for the father, perhaps along with counseling, too. If the children are especially traumatized or sexually abused, specialized therapists could be a 60-minute or longer drive away.

What Can I Do for Tertiary Prevention?

In a situation such as the one describe above, each member of the family needs a friend, a kind, supportive individual who will be there for the person when he or she needs to talk or process what has happened and what might happen next. In some communities, young children may be able to access therapeutic services, perhaps involving play therapy. If they are older, they may have a child therapist. They could be matched or placed on a waiting list for a Big Brother or Big Sister. If organizations don't exist in your community, maybe you can be the catalyst to start one on a small scale. Even if you aren't inclined to start an organization, maybe you could volunteer to be a Scout leader, Camp Fire leader, or Big Brother or Big Sister. If you have the time, you can volunteer at a nonprofit agency serving maltreated children, assist a school social worker or guidance counselor, or contact a children's hospital or pediatric wing of a hospital. Some schools use volunteers to help children with their reading. You can also volunteer with CASA (Court Appointed Special Advocates; http://www.casaforchildren.org/). Within each community we need individuals with their heads up and their eyes and ears open for opportunities to educate the public. For instance, if there is a case of shaken baby syndrome that hits the newspaper or public media, perhaps the community could benefit from a public awareness campaign of the danger of this practice and phone numbers for those who could help when a parent or caregiver is at a breaking point with a crying infant. You might be able to contact a local radio or TV station and ask them to do a small feature on the danger of shaking babies and list some resources to contact when parents or caretakers feel overly stressed.

Society also needs professionals who can examine the data originating in each county and state involving abused and neglected children (provision of services information), as well as the outcomes of interventions with traumatized and mistreated children and their families. Even if you aren't employed in a position to be able to look at this kind of data, perhaps as a student you can request a field education placement to start examining this data, or you can volunteer if you have already graduated and have some time to devote.

If you don't want to get involved with analyzing statistical data, you might still be able to conduct systematic literature reviews on topics that would be valuable to the CPS staff or administration. We need individuals who can prepare such reviews of programming or new programs of interest to support ongoing workers. It's possible from such reviews that recommendations may emerge that would identify better ways of handling certain client problems.

Last but not least, you can decide to be a child protective services professional. You can do investigative work or be an ongoing services worker, an adoption specialist, or a recruiter and trainer for foster parents. Within CPS agencies, we need those administrative types who are able to "see the larger picture" and able to recommend changes in internal policies or procedures that will help child protection workers become even more effective and efficient. We need administrators in CPS agencies who not only understand the importance of self-care for their employees in direct services but who also make it an expectation and cultivate a climate within agencies wherein supervisors insist on self-care and employees are able to practice it.

If you don't want to work directly in child protection, you can be a victim advocate for women who have been in abusive relationships or work in a shelter for them. You can be school social worker in an elementary, middle, or high school. You can work more directly with maltreated children with emotional and behavioral issues in residential treatment programs, outpatient programs, and alternative schools. You can become a clinical practitioner and provide trauma-informed therapy to abused and neglected children. You may want to focus on families and provide family therapy or remedial parenting skills training, anger management, or other focused skills (Scott et al., 2016).

TEST YOURSELF

Can you explain the difference between secondary and tertiary prevention? Do not read below the dotted line until you are ready to see the answer.

Tertiary prevention concentrates on rehabilitating and restoring. Helping someone recover from an addiction and reducing future addictive behaviors would be an example. Another example might involve going to the dentist and discovering several cavities that have to be addressed and then cutting way back on sugary drinks or snacks to prevent additional cavities. Secondary prevention can involve screening to find those at risk or at the earliest stage of developing a problem, when intervention can reverse the problem (e.g., taking blood pressure medicine for hypertension). Another example might be using an assessment instrument to identify teen parents whose attitudes and expectations concerning children might put them at risk.

More Issues and Macro Ideas

Other writers have addressed issues with our current system of child protection in America and suggested different avenues and perspectives. There are many more ideas about ways to improve child welfare practice in America than can be covered in this book. For instance, Myers (2006) presents several notions that Duncan Lindsey proposed in a 2003 book. Lindsey argues that child welfare in America used to mean serving a broad range of disadvantaged children but has been transformed into a system that is designed "primarily to protect children from battering and sexual assault" (as cited in Myers, 2006, p. 176). Lindsey suggests that severe physical abuse and sexual abuse should be investigated and handled by law enforcement—not child protection workers. Myers is personally against the proposal, but without some serious efforts to examine what works and what doesn't in child welfare, we will be locked into repeating what we have been doing in the past. These and other writers have suggested ideas about what might improve child welfare in this country. What ideas might you have?

Should we require every new parent to complete a mandatory course or training on how to parent effectively? Would Lindsey's idea of government-funded children's allowances to combat the poverty associated with abuse and neglect actually work? To dig deeper into some of these issues about the way our public child welfare system was constructed and other efforts we could take, you may want to consult books such as those listed below:

- Gelles, R. J. (2017). *Out of harm's way: Creating an effective child welfare system*. New York, NY: Oxford University Press.
- Lindsey, D. (2003). *The welfare of children*. New York, NY: Oxford University Press.
- Myers, J. E. B. (2006). *Child protection in America: Past, present, future*. New York, NY: Oxford University Press.
- Wulczyn, F., Barth, R. P., Yan, Y-Y. T., Harden, B. J., & Landsverk, J. (2005). *Beyond commonsense: Child welfare, child well-being, and the evidence for policy reform*. Piscataway, NJ: AldineTransaction.

As you read through this book, you might have made some mental notes about things that concern you about child welfare in America. One of these might be the disproportionate percentages of children of color in foster care, going through the juvenile justice system, and so forth. Often linked back to generations of families denied the same opportunities for economic and educational advancement as afforded White people in society, we must figure out ways to reduce poverty, to provide safe neighborhoods in which to live and raise children, and to ensure that everyone with a medical need has sufficient insurance to allow them to access medical care. We must reduce substance abuse, reduce the stigma of receiving mental health services, and open the access to these services in geographic areas now devoid of them. Home visitation programs for new mothers and their infants could provide practical care strategies and tips that reduce frustration with crying infants and help with parent–child bonding. As Richard Gelles (2017) notes:

> Over the last forty years perhaps the most consistent finding in research on child maltreatment is that, with the exception of child sexual abuse, living below the poverty line is highly related to the risk of child maltreatment. For single parents, it is low income, not the stress of raising a child alone, that explains the high rate of child maltreatment in single-parent households (Gelles, 1989). (p. 87)

What can we as a society do about reducing the number of families living in poverty? Is it a question of what we are willing to invest in—so that our nation's children can have a brighter future?

In terms of child welfare workforce issues, society needs to pay all those who work in child protective and child welfare settings strong and adequate salaries to attract the best, brightest, and most committed to serving children. Myers (2006) argues that in many communities social workers are paid less than teachers—and teachers are "notoriously underpaid." Even worse, among the professionals who work in child welfare, "social workers have far and away the most difficult job" (Myers, 2006, p. 189). How do we get more equitable pay? We must advocate for ourselves. We must keep the public informed about the problem of child abuse and neglect in our society.

Unfortunately, politicians and policy makers often give lip service to wanting to tackle problems with a simplistic solution. They propose taking a hard line on criminals but are ignorant of the conditions in society that allow child abuse and neglect to tragically affect young people and lead some into gangs and juvenile delinquency. They may blame refugees for our nation's problems but completely fail to talk about their plans to eliminate racism, poverty, unemployment, and lack of educational opportunity. A good guess is that they unconsciously and privately blame those who struggle in society (the often poor, non-White, and perhaps nonvoting adults) for creating families with problems. Often the product of middle-class and affluent families, these White privileged parents are relieved that *their* children (when they have problems) can access health and mental health services, private schooling, or tutors. Their own ability to provide for their children usually allows them to put the plight of more troubled and traumatized children out of their minds.

Consequently, we must keep children's needs before the public. The American public needs to know, for instance, that children who have been severely neglected and abused are very likely going to have significant challenges perhaps over their lifetimes, which can increase society's costs. Only by tackling the conditions in society that significantly contribute to child maltreatment will we stand any chance of decreasing the number of children harmed. This investment will save taxpayers funds, and we must be able to use this information to show taxpayers in concrete terms how spending money to prevent abuse and delinquency will provide rich dividends to society. Americans are a kind and sympathetic people, but they will not be motivated to fight the problems of child maltreatment as long as they remain ignorant of its breadth and depth.

In his chapter entitled "Improving the Child Protection System," John Myers (2006) notes:

> To spearhead the charge against abuse and neglect, social work must once again produce leaders like Jane Addams, Julia Lathrop, Grace and Edith Abbott, Carl Carstens, Sophinisba Breckenridge, Vincent De Francis, and Florence Kelley. These pioneers ceded nothing in influence and creativity to medicine or law. Where are the leaders for social work in the twenty-first century? (p.186)

Myers goes on to say that what our nation's children need from social work educators is "greater political advocacy and agitation." He wants social workers to "force other professionals, politicians and policymakers to accord them equal status in the arena of ideas, politics" in order to "reclaim the mantle of leadership" (Myers, 2006, p. 187). Are you ready to take the mantle of leadership that is needed in each community across our country? If not, what can you do to support those in the lead?

What will the future be like for children in America? What are *you* willing to do?

Main Points

- You can still do a lot to improve conditions and possibly decrease child maltreatment—even if you decide not to work directly in child protection.
- Despite the stresses and strains of child protection, this chapter has also revealed that many CPS professionals love, enjoy, and are satisfied with their careers.
- Primary prevention aims to stop a problem before it starts. Chapter discussion suggests ideas for how you might engage in the primary prevention of child maltreatment.
- Secondary prevention comes into play when screening can identify those at risk or when a problem is in an early stage, when it can be reversed or kept from progressing. There are some ideas for what you can do in the way of secondary prevention of child abuse and neglect.
- Tertiary prevention is applied once a disease or problem like child abuse has already occurred. The focus then is to restore function, rehabilitate, improve quality of life, and reduce negative impact.

Questions for Class Discussion

1. What approach would you use in designing a child sexual abuse prevention program? Would you target children in early childhood, middle childhood, or adolescence?
2. With regard to protecting children from abuse and neglect, do you think we need more governmental power to intervene in families and homes, or do you believe that currently existing laws are enough?

3. What ideas do you have about "greater political advocacy and agitation" on behalf of child protection?
4. What does it take to become a leader like Jane Addams? Is it even possible in this day and age?
5. At what level (primary, secondary, or tertiary) of prevention do you think you can make the most difference as a citizen concerned about child maltreatment in society?
6. Which of the suggestions given in this chapter for addressing the problems of child maltreatment can you see yourself doing in the future?
7. Should taxpayers take on additional responsibility to ensure that every part of the country has access to a full range of social and human services needed to restore troubled individuals and families?

Self-Assessment for Personal Consideration

1. How comfortable would you be in advocating with community leaders and politicians for greater investment in child protection and related services?

   1   2   3   4   5   6   7   8   9   10

   Not comfortable   *Very comfortable*

2. How comfortable would you be in organizing a public information campaign to inform your community about resources available to parents who are overly stressed or overwhelmed and need help?

   1   2   3   4   5   6   7   8   9   10

   Not comfortable   *Very comfortable*

3. On the scale below, rate how confident you are that being a child protection worker is the right career for you.

   1   2   3   4   5   6   7   8   9   10

   Not confident   *Very confident*

Additional Resources

Jenson, J. M. & Fraser, M. (2016). *Social policy for children and families: A risk and resilience perspective.* Sage Books, Thousand Oaks, CA.

The Child Welfare Information Gateway provides information on programs designed to help parents learn about children's age-appropriate development, ways to involve children in positive play, and positive discipline techniques. These programs are especially valuable for new parents who did not have the best parents as role models and do not have a good notion about how to parent. Here is the website: https://www.childwelfare.gov/topics/preventing/prevention-programs/parented/. There is a link on that same page listing parenting programs found in each state. There is no information about how current that list is, however.

The Child Welfare Information Gateway also provides information on 70 "rigorously evaluated programs" for parents with abuse or neglect in their families and information on early childhood programs, parent support groups, home visiting programs, school-based child maltreatment programs, and more—such as parenting a child who has experienced trauma—for Spanish speakers. That link is: https://www.childwelfare.gov/search/?addsearch=parenting+education+programs.

References

Alderdice, F., McNeill, J., & Lynn, F. (2013). A systematic review of systematic reviews of interventions to improve maternal mental health and well-being. *Midwifery, 29,* 389–399.

Avellar, S. A., & Supplee, L. H. (2013). Effectiveness of home visiting in improving child health and reducing child maltreatment. *Pediatrics, 132*(Supplement), S90–S99.

Bilukha, O., Hahn, R. A., Crosby, A., Fullilove, M. T., Liberman, A., Moscicki, F. ... & Briss, P. A. (2005). The effectiveness of early childhood home visitation in preventing violence. *American Journal of Preventive Medicine, 28,* 11–39.

Chen, M., & Chan, K. L. (2016). Effects of parenting programs on child maltreatment prevention: A meta-analysis. *Trauma, Violence & Abuse, 17,* 88–104.

Clark, J. J., & Yegidis, B. L. (2016). Inconvenient truths: A response to the article by David Stoesz, "The Child Welfare Cartel." *Research on Social Work Practice, 26*(4), 510–514.

Desai, C. C., Reece, J. A., & Shakespeare-Pellington, S. (2017). The prevention of violence in childhood through parenting programmes: A global review. *Psychology, Health, & Medicine, 22,* 166–186.

Geeraert, L., Van Den Noortgate, W., Grietens, H., & Onghena, P. (2004). The effects of early prevention programs for families with young children at risk for physical child abuse and neglect: A meta-analysis. *Child Maltreatment, 9,* 277–291.

Gelles, R. J. (1989). Child abuse and violence in single-parent families: Parent absence and economic deprivation. *American Journal of Orthopsychiatry, 59,* 492–501.

Gelles, R. J. (2017). *Out of harm's way: Creating an effective child welfare system.* New York, NY: Oxford University Press.

Griffiths, A. (2019). Unpublished manuscript.

Lindsey, D. (2003). *The welfare of children.* New York, NY: Oxford University Press.

Myers, J. E. B. (2006). *Child protection in America: Past, present, future.* New York, NY: Oxford University Press.

Nation, M., Crusto, C., Wandersman, A., Kumpfer, K. L., Seybolt, D., Morrissey-Kane, E., & Davino, K. (2003). What works in prevention: Principles of effective prevention programs. *American Psychologist, 58,* 449–456.

Olds, D. L., Sadler, L., & Kitzman, H. (2007). Programs for parents of infants and toddlers: Recent evidence from randomized trials. *Journal of Child Psychology and Psychiatry, 48,* 355–391.

Rolock, N., Perez, A. G., White, K. R., & Fong, R. (2017). From foster care to adoption and guardianship: A twenty-first century challenge. *Child & Adolescent Social Work Journal, 35,* 11–20.

Rudolph, J., & Zimmer-Gembeck, M. J. (2018). Reviewing the focus: A summary and critique of child-focused sexual abuse prevention. *Trauma, Violence, & Abuse, 9,* 543–554.

Scott, D., Lonne, B., & Higgins, D. (2016). Public health models for preventing child maltreatment: Applications from the field of injury prevention. *Trauma, Violence, & Abuse, 17,* 408–419.

Stoesz, D. (2016). The child welfare cartel. *Research on Social Work Practice, 26,* 477–483.

US Preventive Services Task Force. (2018). Interventions to prevent child maltreatment: Recommendation statement. *Journal of the American Medical Association, 320,* 2122–2128.

Walsh, K., Zwi, K., Woolfenden, S., & Shlonsky, A. (2015). School-based education programmes for the prevention of child sexual abuse. *Evidence-Based Child Health: A Cochrane Review Journal, 4.* doi:0.1002/14651858.CD004380.pub3

Williams, C. M., Cprek, S., Assolu, I., English, B., Jewell, T., Smith, K., & Robi, J. (2017). Kentucky health access nurturing development services home visiting program improves maternal and child health. *Maternal and Child Health, 21,* 1166–1174.

INDEX

CPSIA information can be obtained
at www.ICGtesting.com
Printed in the USA
LVHW051401211222
735644LV00004B/19